HAUNTED HERITAGE

Tor Books by Michael Norman and Beth Scott

Haunted America
Historic Haunted America
Haunted Heritage
Haunted Homesteads*

*forthcoming

HAUNTED HERITAGE

MICHAEL NORMAN
AND
BETH SCOTT

A TOM DOHERTY ASSOCIATES BOOK
New York

A Forge Book
Published by Tom Doherty Associates, LLC
175 Fifth Avenue
New York, NY 10010

www.tor.com

Forge® is a registered trademark of Tom Doherty Associates, LLC.

ISBN: 0-765-30173-3

First Edition: October 2002

Printed in the United States of America

0 9 8 7 6 5 4 3 2 1

Michael Norman dedicates this book to his sisters
Nancy Ball and Jane Norman.

Contents

3. THE SOUTH

ENTR'ACTE — THE LUMINARIES

4. THE WEST

All that we see or seem
Is but a dream within a dream.

—Edgar Allan Poe

Introduction

This was a most unexpected book.

An odd statement from an author, you might say, but nevertheless an accurate assessment of the work you hold in your hands. Words elsewhere note this is a continuation of the *Haunted U.S.A.* series created by Beth Scott and myself. The earlier *Historic Haunted America, Haunted America,* and *Haunted Heartland* were collections of American ghost stories published over the past fifteen years. Earlier, we wrote *Haunted Wisconsin,* which, it seems, was the unintended first book in the future series.

Thus, *Haunted Heritage* is really the fifth book in that series, but one that came about in a serendipitous manner.

When Beth died in 1994, leaving me to complete the manuscripts for *Haunted America* and *Historic Haunted America,* both published by Tor Books, I assumed that would end not only our collaboration but my foray into the world of telling stories of the supernatural. I was wrong in the latter assumption. Though Beth is gone, publisher Tom Doherty and editor Brian Thomsen expressed enough enthusiasm for publishing another two volumes of ghost stories to pique my interest in continuing the series, through this volume and another title scheduled for 2004.

As with the earlier books, this is a collection of contemporary and historical ghost stories, all asserted as being true, or as true as any ghost story can be. Many of the ghost tales from earlier eras may correctly be classified as folklore, legends or traditions. Unlike a legendary Paul Bunyan or the fictional schoolmaster Ichabod Crane, however, these stories of supernatural lore seem to have some basis in an historical event. The stories of various campus ghosts are in this category—a young coed or befuddled professor died in an unexpected or dramatic manner in a campus building and from that point forward reports of their continued presences frequently take on almost mythic qualities.

Stories set in the present-day and told by living witnesses are, of course, altogether different. Though they may at some future point in time pass into the lore of a specific region, at the moment they are portrayals of what *real* people say *truly* took place. Do I know *for a fact* that what they say happened really did transpire? In a word, no. I have ambled in after the fact, recorded their takes on the events and pass the stories along to you, the reader. Does this make the story any less interesting or any less credible? I trust it does not. My purpose has never been to "prove" the credibility or lack thereof of the people I've written about. I am telling their stories in what I hope is an interesting way and then assuming the readers will want to make up their own minds about each story. It is for this reason that I don't work with self-described psychics or other folks who probe purportedly haunted houses, armed with supersensitive tape recorders, heat detectors, motion sensors and other equipment supposedly designed to sniff out presences from the beyond, and then issue their finding—which often include descriptions of odd sounds, vaporous substances, and unexplained temperature shifts.

I say to all those ghost hunters, good luck. So far I haven't seen, felt or sensed anything out of the ordinary even after being in countless haunted places. But that's probably just me.

What I like to do is tell stories. And if readers want to believe them, that's fine. If they don't, that's all right, too.

But let me add one caveat.

Many readers—and a good number of Americans, I suspect—will scoff at the notion that something remains of a life once it passes into history. I once held firmly to that notion, and still do in the main, but I have to confess that now I am not as certain as I used to be. I've always thought I am an "open-minded skeptic," as I once described myself to an interviewer. But over the last twenty-five years I've listened to enough people describe their personal experiences with what they took to be supernatural occurrences to know that not everything I've heard can be explained with contemporary human knowledge.

This is not to say that floating figures in white sheets are hovering behind that dead oak tree in the town cemetery. Casper lived through the hands of animators. The swirling miasmas that suddenly shift into demonic beings exist mainly in the imaginations of novelists, screenwriters and talented filmmakers. That is not what many of the folks included in this book say they have seen. Their experiences, for the most part, are far subtler, far less gruesome, yet nonetheless life-changing events for which they are still seeking explanations. Perhaps, like the unexpected hint of our dead father's cologne we detect on his old suit, we leave behind more of ourselves than we suspect. An indiscernible aura suspended in space waiting to touch a passing life.

There are many people who helped bring this book about. Editors Brian Thomsen, Jim Minz and publisher Tom Doherty encouraged its development and they have my gratitude. My agent Mark Lefebvre has been my rock of support for many years. His wife, Marian Lefebvre, is a copy editor without equal and I thank her for the work she did in catching my errors of commission and omission. The University of Wisconsin–River Falls allowed me some released time to work on this book. My family's support is, as always, gratefully acknowledged.

Numerous individuals and organizations provided information. I have endeavored to acknowledge their contributions below, but should I have missed someone I apologize and will include that information in future editions as it is brought to my attention:

Cheryl Ames, Virginia; Sheila B. Anderson, Dover (Delaware) Public Library; M. E. Baker, Hale Homestead, Connecticut; Nick Barracato, Long Island; Roy

Bauer, Ontario; Ellen Berkov, Anne Arundel (Maryland) County Public Library; Victoria Brouillette, Minnesota; Carolyn Brown, Oregon; Michael Brown, Oregon; Greg Champion, New Mexico; Beverly Christ, Wisconsin; City of Eagle River, Wisconsin; City of Lewes, Delaware; City of Mobile, Alabama; City of Pittsfield, Massachusetts; City of Sioux Falls, South Dakota; City of Watersmeet, Michigan; Hattie Clements, Kentucky; Dr. Roger Cognard, Nebraska Wesleyan University; Connecticut Society of the Sons of the American Revolution; Karen Norton Cook, Nebraska; Laurie E. Coughlan, Hampton National Historic Site; Courtland (Alabama) Public Library; Brian Cuthrell, University of South Carolina;

Ric Damon, Ripon College; Delaware State Museum, Lewes; Suzy Driver, Michigan; Edisto Beach, South Carolina; Fiona Fuhrman, Illinois; Douglas Glamann, Wisconsin; Virginia Gregory, Mississippi; Susan Hansen, Library Special Collections, Middle Tennessee State University; Ed Heacock, New Jersey; Dr. Carol Hendrickson, Marlboro College; Nancy Hicks, Florida; Historic Orpheum Theatre, Sioux Falls, South Dakota; Inn at Loretto, Santa Fe; Elizabeth P. Jacox, Idaho State Historical Society; Barton Johnson, Pennsylvania; James R. Jones, Wisconsin;

Kentucky Department of Public Information, Frankfort; Deb Kirchner, Millikin University; William E. Koch Folklore Collection, Kansas State University; Ralph Krugler, New York; Trudy LaFramboise, Rollins College; LaFonda on the Plaza, Santa Fe; La Posada de Santa Fe; Jerry LeBarre; Kristine Lemay, Marlboro College; Little Rock (Arkansas) Public Library; Ray Loftesness, South Dakota; Janet C. Lu, Nebraska Wesleyan University; Felicia Lujan, New Mexico State Records Center and Archives; Marlboro College, Vermont; Gillian McNamara, Long Island; William M. Michael, Illinois; Dr. David Mickey, Nebraska Wesleyan University; Millikin University, Illinois; Lawrence Millman, Massachusetts; Mobile (Alabama) Convention and Visitors Corporation; Moosehead Inn, Saskatchewan; Jack Mortenson, South Dakota; Mount Saint Mary's College, Maryland; Ruth Ann Munden, Pennsylvania;

National Trust Historic Hotels of America; National Park Service, Hampton National Historic Site; James B. Nelson, Wisconsin; Neosho (Missouri) Chamber of Commerce; New Mexico State Records Center and Archives; Jim Nolan, Pennsylvania; Dianna Noyes, Marlboro College; Rev. Daniel Nusbaum, Mount Saint Mary's College, Maryland; Ed Okonowicz, University of Delaware; Dale Orsted, Saskatchewan; Dr. Michael A. Persinger, Ontario; Tom Petersen, Iowa; Sandy Petersen, Iowa; Dr. Don Petzold, Wisconsin; Mardell Plainfeather, Montana; Leslie Plank, Marlboro College; Preservation Society of Newport (Rhode Island) County; Judy Quillin, Wicomico County (Maryland) Free Library; Michael Renegar, North Carolina; Nancy Roberts, North Carolina; Tristan Roberts, Marlboro College; Rollins College, Florida;

Saskatchewan Tourism Department; School of American Research, Albuquerque; Jean Shrier, head of reference, Peoria (Illinois) Public Library; Sioux Falls Community Playhouse; South Carolina Historical Society; Doris Sorber, California; St. James Hotel, New Mexico; Roy Strom; Deborah Tallmann, Wisconsin; Allen Tallmann, Wisconsin; Katherine L. Tatum, Georgia; Tennessee State Library and Archives; Frank Theofan, Saskatchewan; Nancy and Warren Todd; Town of Coventry, Connecticut; Mildred Trevey, Maryland; Dan Turnipseed, Alabama; United States Department of the Interior; Vilas County (Wisconsin) Tourism Department; Winter Park (Florida) Public Library; Susan Woolf, Ohio;

Wyoming State Archives and Historical Department; Ezra Zeitler, Wisconsin; Micah Zeitler, Wisconsin; Zwaanendael Museum, Lewes, Delaware.

Michael Norman
June 2002

THE NORTHEAST

A Revolutionary Haunting

Monuments to America's Revolutionary War heroes adorn the landscape in countless New England villages and counties. From Boston Harbor to Fort William Henry on Maine's rugged seacoast, inland to historic old Fort Ticonderoga and Saratoga, patriot homes, battlefields and birthplaces mark the intense interest Americans have in that bloody fight for independence.

One of the emerging nation's first martyrs, Nathan Hale of Connecticut, is just such a Revolutionary hero, a soldier-spy whose exploits are known to countless schoolchildren. Though his life was short, his valiant efforts on behalf of the patriot cause are still held as a model of unselfish bravery. Several monuments commemorate his life.

A boulder marks Halesite, near Huntington, New York, the place where it is believed the British captured him.

In South Coventry, Connecticut, is the remarkable Hale Homestead, where Nathan was born in 1755, the sixth of twelve children of Deacon Richard and Elizabeth Strong Hale.

The Homestead today is open to the public, administered by the Coventry Historical Society for the Antiquarian and Landmarks Society of Connecticut. The home and grounds are evocative reminders of the colonial era as costumed docents guide visitors through the intricacies of eighteenth-century life. Nathan Hale's Bible and fowling gun are on display.

Tourists may not know, however, that the colonial Hale family must have been fonder of their home than even the family could have anticipated. The Homestead is reputedly haunted by the ghostly visages of Nathan Hale's own family.

The story of the Hale Homestead must begin with the Revolutionary hero himself. Ironically, Nathan Hale could have avoided the great conflict. A graduate of Yale College at the age of eighteen, the calm, pious young man with remarkable athletic skills accepted a teaching job in East Haddam, Connecticut, in 1773. By all accounts, Hale was quite a good teacher during his year in East Haddam. He moved to New London the next year and began what he probably assumed was going to be a life of teaching and scholarship.

It was not to be.

Hale was excited by the ideals embodied in the American Revolution and volunteered to fight in July 1775, one month after his twentieth birthday. He was commissioned a lieutenant by the Connecticut assembly and joined colonial troops in driving the British from Boston.

When His Majesty's forces invaded the New York area, Hale, by now a captain, marched with colonial troops to drive the Redcoats from their new encampment. Captain Hale was a daring and resourceful soldier, commended by his superiors for many acts of bravery. On one occasion, his men captured a British supply ship from under the cannons of a British war vessel.

The ragtag American soldiers, however, were growing dispirited. General Washington's troops were facing disintegration in New York. Soldiers began to desert, slipping away from their posts, headed for home. The commander-in-chief needed information about British troop movements in order to prepare his tactics, and he needed it badly. He turned to an elite fighting force, the Rangers, for help. Washington asked their commander to find a volunteer who would penetrate the British lines to collect intelligence on enemy positions, tactics, and troop strength.

Captain Nathan Hale had been awarded a place in the small Rangers outfit after he captured the British supply ship. On the Rangers commander's second call, Captain Hale stepped forward. He would take the assignment.

Disguised as a Dutch schoolmaster, a role ideally suited to his background, Hale successfully crossed British lines and gathered the vital information. But, as every American knows, the young patriot-spy was captured by British troops on September 21, 1776, as he attempted to make his way back to the American side. A British loyalist cousin may have betrayed him.

Hale was tried as a spy before General William Howe, the British commander, and sentenced to hang on the following day. Calm and courageous even as the noose was dropped over his neck, Captain Hale asked for a Bible and gave the executioner, Major Cunningham, a letter to his family. The British officer denied him the Bible and ripped up Hale's last letter.

So, just three months after his twenty-first birthday, Nathan Hale met his death. His reputed final words have been included in history books for decades: "I regret that I have but one life to lose for my country."

Contrary to generations of history books, however, he probably didn't say that. According to a recently found war diary penned by British Captain Frederick Mackenzie, who witnessed Hale's execution, the young soldier's final words were: "It is the duty of every good officer to obey any orders given him by his commander-in-chief." Mackenzie's record of what Nathan Hale actually said is not as stirring as the oft-quoted passage cited above, but certainly still befitting the man's stoic nature.

In the same year Nathan Hale lost his life, 1776, his father, Deacon Richard Hale faced a daunting challenge: How could he provide room for his own twelve children and a cluster of pretty teenage girls brought into his life by the widow he had married in 1769?

Born at Newbury, Massachusetts, in 1717, Deacon Hale had moved to Coventry in the 1740s. He bought a large farm and married a local girl, Elizabeth Strong, in 1746. To that union were born twelve children, eight boys and four girls. Not surprisingly, Mrs. Hale died in 1767 following the birth of her twelfth child. Little Nathan was twelve.

Two years later, in 1769, Deacon Hale married Abigail Cobb Adams, the widow of Captain Samuel Adams. She brought to the marriage several teenage girls. One of them, Sarah Adams, married John Hale, one of Nathan's older brothers.

The precise date of Deacon Hale's house remodeling isn't known, nor do records indicate if it occurred before or after Captain Nathan Hale's execution. He rebuilt the mansion as a two-family house shared by father and son, and their wives who were also mother and daughter. As the children of this blended family grew to adulthood they moved away, although several members of the family lived at the Homestead over the years.

The haunting of Hale Homestead has been documented since at least 1914. In that year, the great American antiquarian, George Dudley Seymour (1859–1945), purchased the vacant Hale Homestead and spent the rest of his life making it a centerpiece in his quest to immortalize his favorite American hero, Captain Nathan Hale.

He also came to believe the Homestead was haunted.

Indeed, one of the first documented ghost sightings involved Seymour himself. He had completed the acquisition of Hale Homestead in the spring of 1914 and embarked on a journey to visit it. He had gone by train from New Haven to Willimantic where he then rented a buggy to take him and an unnamed friend to South Coventry. Heavy rains had turned the roads to muddy ruts. Both men were tired from the long trip.

Seymour recorded his impressions of the Homestead in his diary:

"Isolated, dilapidated, unpainted, and vacant, the (Hale) house presented a forlorn picture, heightened on the inside by streamers of paper falling from dampened walls. . . . [Seymour's friend] jumped out of the buggy and ran to the window, and what should he see but Deacon Hale's ghost looking out of the [school room] window to see who had arrived. As my friend put his face against the pane, the Deacon stepped back to the inner end of the room and vanished into thin air. My friend was so jarred by the apparition that he did not mention the matter to me for hours. I must say that the Deacon's ghost never appeared again to my knowledge."

A patent attorney by profession, Seymour probably did more than any other single person to make Nathan Hale famous. He not only "collected" houses associated with the Hale family, but also commissioned artist Bela Lyon Pratt to sculpt a new statue of Hale. There were three already in existence, but Seymour disapproved of them all. Pratt's statue is now almost universal, gracing the headquarters of the FBI and CIA, the Chicago *Tribune* building, Phillips Academy in Massachusetts and three Connecticut cities. A miniature version is at the Hale Homestead.

Seymour successfully campaigned for Nathan Hale's portrait on a postage stamp. Bela Pratt's one-and-a-half-cent stamp carried his portrait from 1925 to 1938. Interestingly, there is only a "shadow portrait" of Hale extant, so Pratt's statue and stamp are, to some extent, imaginative likenesses.

But George Dudley Seymour was also keenly aware that not all history is to be found in dusty tomes. He collected all manner of legends and stories connected with Nathan Hale, indeed he seems to have been addicted to writing down nearly everything he thought or heard . . . including accounts of the ghosts at Hale Homestead.

Local residents told Seymour that the ghost of Lydia Carpenter, one of the

Hale family's servants, "was said to be always listening to catch scraps of household gossip." It may also be Lydia who has been seen sweeping the upper hall toward morning and the woman in white who putters around the kitchen at an early hour.

In addition to Deacon Hale, Seymour found that another member of the Hale family had been sighted at the Homestead.

Seymour wrote that the ghost of one of Nathan's brothers, Lieutenant Joseph Hale, "who was confined, it was said, in one of the British prison ships off the Jersey coast . . . came home to die, and his ghost clanked his chains in the great cellar of the house."

However, more recent research casts doubts on Seymour's account of Joseph Hale's war service. He served in the Lexington alarm with several of his brothers (six Hale sons fought for the patriot cause) and was a Knowlton Ranger with the rank of lieutenant and when a musket ball grazed him he was captured at Fort Washington, New York. That was on November 16 or 17, 1776, barely two months after his brother's execution.

Whether Joseph ever was confined to a prison ship is unknown but he certainly didn't "come home to die." Records indicate that he was exchanged for a British prisoner and was serving as a lieutenant in Colonel Ely's regiment by 1777. He met Rebeckah Harris, the daughter of prominent judge Joseph Harris, in New London, and married her on October 21, 1778. They returned to Coventry where they bought a house near his father's farm.

In 1784, he became "low in consumption," a term used in earlier days to describe tuberculosis. He died that same year, leaving his young widow with four small children born during the Revolution.

George Seymour wrote that Joseph "was assigned the northwest chamber of his father's house" during his final days. According to a historian at the Hale Homestead, it is possible that Joseph did "come home to die," in 1784 even though he had a house nearby. His widow and children did live at the Hale Homestead following his death.

So if it is Joseph Hale rattling around in the Homestead cellar, the chains he drags are not those that he wore when he died.

There are two additional candidates for the ghosts at the Homestead—John and Sarah Hale, Nathan's older brother and stepsister who were married, lived and died in the house.

John Hale emulated his father in many ways. Born in 1748, he died shortly after Deacon Hale in 1802. Like his father, John became a deacon of the church and served in various public offices. From 1791 to 1802, he was a delegate to sixteen sessions of the Connecticut General Assembly. He served as justice of the peace, town clerk, and treasurer for many terms between 1786 and his death. Earlier, he was a lieutenant in the Revolution's Knowlton Rangers.

He continued to live at the Homestead after his marriage to his step-sister, Sarah Adams Hale. Their only child was stillborn. Sarah died a year after her husband, in 1803. She was fifty.

Another person who believed the Homestead is haunted, perhaps by the ghosts of John and Sarah Hale, was Mary Elizabeth Campbell Griffith, of Manchester, Connecticut. Her late husband, Harold Griffith, was the Hale Homestead caretaker for George Dudley Seymour.

Mrs. Griffith moved to the Homestead in 1930. She lived in the building's ell for many years. Her two daughters were born there.

In an oral history of the Hale Homestead collected in 1988, Mrs. Griffith recalled one perplexing episode:

"It was early in the morning. Harold (Mr. Griffith) was out milking. Everyone else was in bed. I heard somebody come down the back stairs. I didn't even look. I asked Harold when he came back, and he said, no, he hadn't been in the house at all. . . . Clump, clump, clump. It was so plain. I never could explain that. . . ."

George Seymour believed the house was haunted, Mrs. Griffith said. But she seemed to excuse that eccentricity by adding, "He'd been to England, and liked that sort of thing. . . ."

According to Mary E. Baker, Hale Homestead Administrator, staff members have not seen any ghosts nor found evidence of their presence.

"However, we strongly believe in bringing history to life," she said. "Sometimes that includes bringing the people who lived here back for a few hours for special programs. This is done at Halloween time and on special weekends when the Nathan Hale Fifes and Drums put on colonial encampments and battle reenactments. On such occasions, 'Nathan Hale' himself can sometimes be seen here, trying to recruit men to join the militia, or signing autographs with his feather quill pen for children. Even on ordinary days, it is not uncommon for one of the Hale family members to be on hand."

Visible *and* invisible.

Coventry and South Coventry are located on the Willimantic River in Tolland County in east-central Connecticut. The Homestead, 2299 South Street, is open from mid-May to mid-October for a small admission fee.

Visitors may also want to visit the Nathan Hale Cemetery above Wangumbaug Lake. A 45-foot-tall granite obelisk is dedicated to the memory of the famous patriot.

Patty Cannon

Patty Cannon was evil.

There's not much doubt about that.

A description of her crimes against man and child might begin with the escaped slaves she captured and sold back into captivity, to end with the countless anonymous peddlers and unfortunate travelers who made a final, fatal mistake by taking lodging at her infamous public house in western Delaware.

Even in the raucous, rough 'n' tumble 1820s, she stood several ax handles above most other reprobates.

But history might be as recent as today when it comes to Patty Cannon. Her ghost may roam the old paupers' field where her bones came to rest—at least for a time.

Patty lived on a property that straddled the Mason-Dixon line at Reliance on the Delaware/Maryland border. There she operated an inn where she'd take in wayfaring travelers, feed and entertain them, and then, when they had gotten quite comfortable, murder them.

She'd drag their lifeless bodies to a corner of the basement, rummage through their packs and clothing for whatever she might be able to turn into a profit, and then stack their remains up in the corner until she could safely dispose of them. No sense in calling too much attention to herself, so she'd wait until there was a good load to put in her wagon and then haul them away for a quick burial at some isolated field.

It's not that the authorities didn't suspect Patty was up to something nefarious.

That's why she chose her living accommodations with such care.

When the Maryland constables came looking for her, she'd hotfoot it across the road into Delaware and stay in her barn until they'd given up and gone home. When the Delaware authorities showed up, she'd cross back over the state line and sit on the porch of her Maryland home.

It's not clear why the police from the two states didn't ever figure all this out and show up at the same time.

In any event, Patty's wickedness didn't end with straightforward murder.

Stories were told of her taking crying slave children (Maryland was a slave state in the 1820s) from her servants and killing them in most horrible ways.

She operated a kind of depraved *reverse* Underground Railroad. Slaves who had bought their freedom often went into Delaware and Pennsylvania to find work. Patty's gang of thugs would secretly scout out farm fields in those states, kidnap the black freemen, drag them back to her house, and chain them in the attic or in the cellar, next to the cadavers. Georgia and South Carolina slave traders came up the Nanticoke River near her home and, on an island in the river, they'd attend Patty's appalling auctions of her human goods.

As it happens, Patty Cannon's undoing was directly connected to one of the slave auctions. Patty killed a slave trader and, for some reason, put his body in a blue trunk she owned and then buried it behind her own house. Some time later, she decided to rent out the land. Years passed. One day a tenant's plow horse tumbled into a fissure that had suddenly opened in the ground. After he pulled out his horse from the bottom of the hole, he spied Patty's blue chest. Thinking he'd found Captain Kidd's or Blackbeard's treasure, he pulled it out and forced open the lid. Of course, there was no treasure, only the rotting carcass of the old slave trader, still neatly wrapped in one of Patty Cannon's tablecloths. Even the butcher knife she'd used to kill him with was in the trunk.

Patty had gone too far this time.

There was her trunk. There was the body. There was her tablecloth. And there was the murder weapon.

Perhaps after so many years of cleverly eluding authorities she thought her deeds would forever go unpunished. If so, that was her final, fatal mistake.

Lawmen skillfully lured her into Delaware where members of her gang had already been jailed. They'd turned states' evidence by providing enough testimony about murders and kidnappings to hang their old boss several times over.

Patty Cannon's arrest and jailing made news throughout western Delaware. Criminal trials were often the spectator sport of choice in early America—on the days before her trial was to start the lines of eager onlookers, all hoping to get good seats, already stretched around the block.

The she-monster of Delaware had other plans.

On the night before the trial, perhaps after waving to the crowds gathered outside her jail window, she slit open the hem of her dress and took out a vial of arsenic. It was a means of disposal with which she was already familiar—two of her husbands had been dispatched with just this sort of poison. She drank it down, thus no doubt disappointing several hundreds of Delawareans.

They buried Patty in a Georgetown paupers' field. Everyone thought they'd seen the last of the most notorious female criminal in Delaware history.

Think again.

Her body lay undisturbed for decades until the time came when county officials decided to enlarge the Sussex County courthouse and jail and concluded that the paupers' field had to give up its graves for the expansion. According to one legend, a young man helping to dig up and move the interred discovered he was working on Patty Cannon's remains. He picked up her skull, tucked it inside his jacket and took it home as a "gift," for his father, it is said.

Patty Cannon has not gone gently into eternity.

In 1960, a man walked into the Dover, Delaware, Public Library carrying a hatbox and some documents. He wanted to know if they'd like a permanent addition to their collection of artifacts and opened the box.

Inside was the skull of Patty Cannon. Apparently, the documents somehow proved her identity.

She's still there, in the library, in Dover.

"Her skull is in a red zippered skull bag. At the moment it is being stored in a staff workroom," says Sheila B. Anderson, the Dover library director. "We take it out when people ask, and occasionally, in conjunction with programs."

She hastens to add, however:

"The Dover Public Library is not haunted; Patty did not die here, and somehow we managed to inherit her skull."

According to famed Delaware storyteller Ed Okonowicz, a favorite time to display Patty's skull is at Halloween.

"They pull out the skull, put it on a table and tell ghost stories," Ed says. "*Life Magazine* and *Reader's Digest* have taken pictures of it. It's probably the only public library in the United States that has a skull in a hatbox."

Does Patty Cannon's ghost haunt her old environs? If anything dead might want to harass the living, it would certainly seem to be a mass murderer like Patty, whose torso and head have remained unattached for more than a century.

Ed Okonowicz has studied Patty's more unearthly legacy.

"That is a very secluded area near Reliance. It's a single-lane, rural area that even now at night . . . well, it's eerie around there. Reports continued for years of her ghost roaming the paupers' field area," he says. "Some of the librarians at the old Dover library would say the reason paintings kept falling off one particular wall was because Patty's skull doesn't have its jaw. They claim that Patty's jaw somehow got into the wall (during remodeling) and was in some way causing the paintings to fall down."

The old Patty Cannon house is a private residence, but it still stands. Although an historical marker has been positioned nearby, it says nothing about the at least forty murders she was said to have committed. The inscription only notes that she was made famous in a book by a local author, Ed says with a chuckle.

"There are many respectable Cannons in the area today. They get a little edgy when we start talking about Patty and always make sure to point out that they're not related to her. Of course, at this point no one at all is related to her!"

He laughs again at the irony.

"The final touch to her story is that there's a ferry very close to where her home is, a little state-run ferry," Ed says. "Close to it there's a housing development with very nice, bold, ornate lettering on a black background that reads *Patty Cannon Estates*. It's like naming something after Charles Manson."

It could be that Delaware is one of the more haunted states on the East Coast, at least that's what Okonowicz has set out to establish in his numerous book-length collections of ghost stories and nighttime tours of haunted places. He thinks some of that spirited history might be attributable to the state's location on the Delmarva Peninsula, a roughly 180-mile-long swath of land that separates Delaware Bay and the Atlantic Ocean on the east from the Chesapeake Bay on the west. It's named after all or portions of the three states it includes: Delaware, eastern Maryland and eastern Virginia.

"We've . . . gone through everything from the American Revolution to the War of 1812 to the Civil War so that adds to the folklore, history and ghost stories," he says. "In fact, Delaware's only battle in the Revolutionary War took place literally a mile and a half from the (University of Delaware) campus." Okonowicz is a former public information specialist for the university and a part-time writing instructor.

Not surprisingly, he discloses, that particular battle is the source for another Delaware ghost story.

Welsh Track Road lies about a mile south of the University of Delaware stadium on Route 896. Welsh Track Church is close by the intersection of those two thoroughfares.

In 1777, British troops left New York in an effort to capture Philadelphia. They traveled around the Delmarva Peninsula, past Cape Charles, Virginia, and then up to the north Chesapeake Bay. The 16,000 troops landed on the Elk River, near the top of the bay, and from there marched toward Philadelphia.

As the British drove through Delaware, Patriot forces moved to stop the advance in what came to be known as the Battle of Cooch's Bridge in August 1777. Historians term it a skirmish, but in Delaware, it's called a battle, Okonowicz says. Earlier that same year, Betsy Ross had made the new flag and the legend is that the Battle of Cooch's Bridge was the first land battle in which the Stars and Stripes was carried.

The skirmish, or battle, took place when several dozen Patriot volunteers hid in the graveyard at Welsh Track Church, concealed behind stone walls and tombstones. They were discovered by His Majesty's troops who lobbed cannonballs into the area, trying to clear a path on their way to Newark, Delaware, and then, they hoped, on to Philadelphia. The church still shows signs of the artillery having hit its west side.

One of the youngest Patriot soldiers was a fifteen-year-old named Charlie Miller who, according to legend, sat astride his white horse rather than hide as the other American forces did. That turned out to be a fatal mistake. A British cannoneer took aim and blew off his head.

Reports were that young Charlie's white charger with his headless corpse still in the saddle galloped off in the direction of what is now the median strip of Interstate 95.

The British, with their superior force of 16,000 troops, won the Battle of Cooch's Bridge. Commanding officer General Charles Cornwallis stayed in the Cooch house, which is still occupied, before leading his forces at the Battle of Brandywine, which took place in September 1777.

The ghost of Charlie Miller was there, too.

During the Battle of Brandywine, Patriot soldiers claimed to have seen him lopping off the heads of British artillerymen in revenge against those who had so ungraciously separated his own cranium from the rest of him the month before.

The story is also told that this headless swordsman saved General George Washington's life on the night before the battle. Two British snipers had set up to kill the American commander but Charlie's apparition showed up at their hiding place. The Redcoats' plans, and their lives, were ended on the blade of his sword.

History is still very close by in Delaware. The Cooches remain a prominent Delaware family, counting among family members numerous lawyers, politicians, and merchants. One ancestor was a colonel in the Delaware regiment during the Revolution. Despite their Patriot ancestry, however, they are not ashamed that General Cornwallis actually stayed in the Cooch house, according to Okonowicz.

It isn't known if Charlie Miller's descendants—if there are any—are pleased with his career as Delaware's most famous headless swordsman.

Cape Henlopen, Delaware, with Rehoboth Bay to the south, the Atlantic to its southeast, and Delaware Bay to its north, offers a bountiful supply of resident ghosts and ghost stories, most centering on the peninsula's seafaring history. From its discovery by Henry Hudson in August 1609 to today, the Cape's eerie legends of ghost ships, haunted lighthouses, and lost treasure have formed an entertaining chapter in the region's history.

Following Hudson's discovery, it wasn't until 1631 that the Dutch West India Company established a twenty-eight man whaling station they called Swaanendael near the present-day Lewes-Rehoboth canal. The colony lasted a mere three years before Lenni Lenape Indians massacred the small group of settlers over a Dutch coat of arms the settlers erected on their settlement's stockade fortification. The Dutch resettled in 1658, but William Penn took possession of what is now present-day Delaware in 1664 on behalf of the English Crown, and a short time later the old Dutch settlement was renamed Lewes for a town in Sussex, England.

While whaling and fishing have played dominant roles in the Cape's maritime history, it has also seen its share of bloodshed, turmoil, and colorful characters.

The British bombarded Lewes during the War of 1812—at least one building proudly carries a cannonball in its wall. Most of the older Lewes homes have intriguing legends connected to them. At a home on Second Street, a tenant was said to have concealed a load of gold coins in a secret panel. She drew a crude map to show its location, but the drawing was so poorly rendered that after the old woman passed, her relatives could not follow its directions. The gold coins have never been found, although it was speculated that she herself retrieved the coins before she died and put them in a bank.

Captain Kidd and his brigands stomped through Lewes's streets as late as 1700. An interesting legend centers on a passenger that the Captain let off near Lewes. His name was James Gillam, a reformed pirate from the West Indies. He was said to have put ashore with a trunk suspected of containing treasure. What he did with the riches, if indeed that is what he carried, isn't known.

But most of the Cape's supernatural tales are seaborne.

Many coastal towns have legends of phantom ships, and Lewes is no different. The four-masted spectral schooner of Lewes was supposed to have appeared each month in Lewes Creek. The moon and weather had to be right—the quarter phase of the moon and the more fog the better—to see the old ship soaring down the creek under full sail. Which ship was it? Captain Kidd's, it was said, coming back to find the gold he buried in the Cape's numerous sand dunes.

The most famous Cape Henlopen story, however, involves a phantom lighthouse, and the famed sunken ship, the H. M. S. *DeBraak*, which went down off the coast during a squall on May 25, 1798. In fact, many efforts over two centuries to raise the *DeBraak* were unsuccessful due, according to storytellers, to another Cape goblin, the notorious "Bad Weather Witch." Not only did she cause wrecks, but she also forestalled all efforts to raise the British sloop-of-war and its reputed treasure.

All good curses must come to an end, for the *DeBraak* was salvaged in the late twentieth century. Nevertheless, the stories of the phantom lighthouse and the *DeBraak* are remarkable ones.

The shoals around Cape Henlopen are among the most dangerous in all the Delaware Bay. Old sailors claim they are made more so by the intermittent sputters of light that have deceived mariners for centuries into thinking they come from a lighthouse—a lighthouse that's never existed at that place.

A legend that's grown taller with the passing years traces the light back to the time of the Delaware Indians. The Cape was used as a sacred marriage site for the natives. In the Colonial era, the people had gathered for such a ceremony, one that would unite the offspring of two powerful tribal leaders. As the ceremony got under way, a platoon of British Redcoats surprised the party and slaughtered most of the men. A few got away, including the prospective groom. The tribe's women were carried away by the troops. Their bodies were discovered over the coming weeks strewn beside the pathways and along the coastline. As he mourned the loss of his bride, the young brave exacted his revenge by placing a curse on future generations that tribal fires burning on the Cape headlands would lure mariners to their watery graves.

Captain Faulkner of the packet *Devonshireman* probably agreed the curse worked.

He was bound for Philadelphia with a boatload of Quakers, followers of William Penn. He'd made a dozen trips before, so he was well aware of the dangerous Delaware Bay, particularly the narrow passage between Cape May, New Jersey, and Cape Henlopen.

On this night in 1655, his lookout had spotted a light off to the starboard. Although it came on in erratic flashes rather than as a single, burning beam of light, Captain Faulkner figured it for the New Jersey Landing Cape Light. His passengers sighted it as well. They were overjoyed at seeing this first hint of land after so many weeks of being tossed about by the Atlantic Ocean.

So the captain ordered his helmsman to keep to port. The New Jersey coastal shoals were treacherous, as he well knew. Suddenly the ship's wooden hull scraped with a sickening squeal that could only mean he had run ashore. Pounding surf rose on all sides of the ship. The hull planking ripped apart. Within minutes, the *Devonshireman* had gone under. Nearly ten score passengers and crew lost their lives. A few survivors made it to shore, the captain not among them.

The few who lived discovered that no lighthouse had ever existed where Captain Faulkner, his crew, and his passengers had seen the glow.

A century and a half later, the Barstead family of Laurel, Maryland, made preparations for the marriage of their daughter, Louisa Barstead, to Frederick Starr, of the Maryland Starrs. In the days before the marriage, the families rented a picnic barge and set off from Rehoboth with plans to round Cape Henlopen.

As they rounded what is now the tip of Cape Henlopen State Park, a sudden and vicious wind sprang up. As the families clung to the barge in the roiling waters, one of the passengers glimpsed a solitary figure on the headland—a tall man, naked but for a breechcloth, a blanket around his shoulders, and a crown of eagle feathers in his hair. He raised his arms and issued such an anguished scream that the revelers could hear him through the pounding waters. At that moment, the barge was lifted in the air by a tremendous wave and thrown against the rocks. Nearly everyone was drowned, including Louisa.

Her ghost haunts that spit of land.

With her bonnet shading her pale face, and still wearing her pretty pink party dress, she cries unremittingly as she searches for her husband-to-be. It is doubtful that she will ever find him. He was one of the few survivors, reportedly returning to Maryland where he eventually married, raised a family and prospered.

The legacy of the *H. M. S. DeBraak* is equal parts history, myth, and archeology. If anyone knows of it today it is as one of the best-known shipwrecks in any of the North American waters.

From 1803 to 1815, a series of wars initiated by or against France came to be known as the Napoleonic Wars, after Napoleon Bonaparte I. France and its primary adversaries Great Britain and Spain struggled for world trade supremacy. Control of the high seas was essential to each nation. Their navies engaged one another in all parts of the world with the twin goals of destroying their adversaries' trading markets while keeping open or establishing their own.

All three countries valued the newly independent United States as a vital market for manufactured goods. Great Britain in particular wanted to maintain commercial ties despite having lost the Colonies in the American Revolution. To do this, the British assigned Royal Navy ships to escort commercial vessels on transatlantic voyages.

The H. M. S. *DeBraak* was one of those vessels.

Originally a Dutch ship captured by the English in 1795, she was commissioned by the Royal Navy in June 1797 with a crew of eighty-five officers, marines, boys and sailors under the command of one Captain James Drew. At some 340 tons, she was termed a brig or brig-sloop outfitted with two masts and armed with sixteen cannons.

The *DeBraak* was assigned to the fleet "off the Western Islands." She also patrolled the English Channel before being ordered to protect a convoy of merchantmen headed for North America.

Here is where history collides with legend.

According to some accounts, the *DeBraak* became separated from the unarmed trading fleet. While trying to rejoin the convoy, however, Captain Drew sighted an unfamiliar sail not far off the New England coast and took off after it. It was a Spanish treasure ship that the *DeBraak* captured, plundered, and sank. The tons of gold, copper, silver, and cocoa kept the English ship low in the water. Scores of Spanish prisoners were held on deck.

Captain Drew figured his best landfall would be at Lewes. But before he could set anchor, a squall suddenly hit Delaware Bay. The *DeBraak* sank in about thirteen fathoms of water. Captain Drew drowned along with half of his crew and most of the Spanish prisoners. The captain's body washed ashore several days later and was buried at old St. Peter's Church in Lewes.

Another, more prosaic, account of the *DeBraak's* demise makes no mention of hunting down a Spanish vessel. Rather, the ship became separated from its fleet and in trying to navigate its way back was hit by a squall and sunk off Cape Henlopen.

Whichever account one believes, the sinking took place on May 25, 1798, less than a year after the brig first set sail under the Union Jack.

For nearly two hundred years, scores of men and ships scoured the dark waters of the Delaware Bay looking for the wreck of the *DeBraak*. All without success, and most with results that seemed to confirm the existence of the "Bad Weather Witch," or at least an exceedingly bad run of luck. What led them all to risk their lives and fortunes were the golden rumors of the king's ransom of treasure supposedly lost aboard the ship.

Numerous trips were undertaken in the nineteenth and early twentieth centuries to find the *DeBraak*, but the exact location of the ship continued to elude the searchers. It was not for want of trying, or of doing everything possible to dispel the curses of the Cape.

One of the most interesting attempts to exorcise the "Bad Weather Witch" came about during the 1935 Colstad Expedition, according to a history of Lewes.

The group had spent fruitless weeks aboard the salvage ship *Liberty* searching for the *DeBraak*. The skipper was veteran Gloucester seaman Captain Clayton Morrissey. If the boredom of the search weren't enough, countless mishaps injured expedition members and damaged their salvage gear.

Finally, Captain Morrissey had had enough. He called his men on deck. He'd built a grotesque effigy of the "Bad Weather Witch" out of cardboard and rags. An old mop for hair hung in scraggly strands across a face of horribly misshapen features.

The witch was tried and convicted; her punishment was immediate execution at the hands of the sailors. First, they fired rifle shots into the mannequin. When she was sufficiently ventilated, the men pummeled her with volleys of whatever objects lay at hand. At last, the dummy was set ablaze and the remains thrown into the sea.

One would have thought that sufficient to harness the forces of even the most intractable sea witch.

Not so.

The next morning, the helmsman turned the *Liberty* "against the sun" when leaving port. As that is a seafarer's worst of bad omens, he was obligated to circle around, head back to port and set out once again, this time being certain to "dispel the awful omen."

But even that wasn't enough. Severe storms continually interrupted the Colstad team's search efforts. The expedition was forced to abandon its efforts in the fall of 1935.

The world had to wait nearly another fifty years until the wreck of the *DeBraak* was discovered.

A Nevada salvage firm worked from 1984 to 1986 to excavate the site. Sophisticated marine technology led to the ship's discovery and exhumation, but it continued to be the treasure legends that fueled searchers' imaginations. Finally, on August 11, 1986, the remains of the hull were raised. So-called "clam shelling" of the ocean site by powerful machinery brought up over 20,000 artifacts.

But no royal treasure.

According to former state of Delaware official David V. Beard, who monitored the salvage operations for the government, "no substantial treasure was recovered from the ship." Further, he bemoaned the damage to the hull and to the artifacts in the salvage endeavor and points to the outrage it caused in the scientific community and elsewhere as a reason for the passage by the United States Congress of the Abandoned Shipwreck Act of 1988. That act gives states the power to regulate the excavation of shipwrecks within thirty miles of their coastlines.

As Beard later wrote in an academic paper about the recovery operations, while there was no golden treasure waiting to be discovered, there was a wealth of archeological data to uncover from the thousands of relics found on the ocean floor.

Many of those artifacts and the *DeBraak*'s articulated hull are now on display at the Delaware State Museum, Zwaanendael in Lewes. The museum was built in 1931 on the three hundredth anniversary of the first European settlement in Delaware. The building is an adaptation of the town hall of Hoorn, Holland.

This ghost ship has finally reached port.

Nana Rose

As one reviews the triumphs and misfortunes of a life, is it an inevitable next step to seek proof of an existence after death? What would *your* reaction be if you had not one or two, but three personal encounters with loved ones . . . after their passing? For many, that might be evidence enough that some part of our being lingers on through eternity.

Consider the case of Cheryl Ames, late of Massachusetts and now a Virginian. A steady woman in her 50s, Cheryl speaks candidly about the times when her beloved aunt and her own mother unexpectedly revealed themselves in ways most would think impossible because both of them had passed. The events were separated by nearly thirty years, but for her they all might as well have been yesterday, so clearly are they etched in her memory.

Cheryl grew up in Pittsfield, in far western Massachusetts, today a small city of some 46,000 people in the heart of the Berkshires. With a history dating back nearly three centuries to its founding by Solomon Deming, Pittsfield and the nearby countryside are richly blessed in monuments commemorating the pivotal role the region has played in American history and culture. The city gave the American Revolution men like Thomas Allen, the "Fighting Parson" and Colonel James Easton, who rounded up volunteers and marched to fight with Colonel Ethan Allen and his Green Mountain Boys. The women of Pittsfield organized spinning matches and clothing bees for General Washington's ragtag Continental Army.

When Henry Wadsworth Longfellow married Frances Elizabeth Appleton, they made their wedding journey to Pittsfield. Later, the city was home to Herman Melville and Oliver Wendell Holmes. Arrowhead, Melville's residence at 780 Holmes Road, is open to the public. It was here that he finished *Moby Dick*. The farm once owned by Dr. Holmes is also preserved.

The Hancock Shaker Village, on 1200 acres near Pittsfield, is an outdoor museum recalling the religious movement that established this particular community in 1790, one of nineteen that were founded throughout New England. Originally called the United Society of Believers in Christ's Second Coming, the Shakers were given that appellation because of their frenzied movements during worship services. The group was well ahead of its time in their beliefs in sexual equality, pacifism, spiritual contemplation, a strong sense of community, and a personal relationship with God. Unfortunately, the religion withered and died because of what they did *not* believe in—sexual relations between men and women.

Today, the Pittsfield visitor can also find the renowned Berkshire Museum, the Berkshire Opera, the Minor League Pittsfield Mets, and the Albany Berkshire Ballet, among many other attractions. Each Fourth of July, the city hosts one of the most historic parades in America, dating all the way back to 1824 when Revolutionary War survivors, patriots, politicians, and horse-drawn carriages filed through the city streets.

But this setting, as if from Thornton Wilder, was of negligible importance to Cheryl Ames as she came of age in the 1950s. Pittsfield was then a city half its current population and very much a company town dependent on its biggest employer, the General Electric Corporation. The company eventually moved away and, as with many other industrial centers, the city took many years to recover from the loss of its primary benefactor.

Cheryl's home was in what used to be described around there as the "country," actually a neighborhood known as West Pittsfield. In the early 1950s, it was very much on the edge of the small city. Her father owned his own business but came to a sad end when his partner was discovered to have been stealing from him. He declared bankruptcy but never fully recovered. He had to sell his house and move his wife and his children—Cheryl, her twin brother, and her older sister—into a smaller place closer to the city proper. But she remembers with great fondness her first home in West Pittsfield.

"I really enjoyed growing up there," Cheryl says of her childhood home. "The house is still there although it's been extensively remodeled. We used to have two big evergreens in front and in the backyard, there was a garden. My mother was a wonderful gardener. I think she had about every plant possible in the back-yard."

Her warm recollections are not in the least bit tempered by the fact that in this house occurred the first two of what Cheryl believes were paranormal experiences. They both involved her dearly loved Aunt Rose Wilber, whom she called Nana Rose.

"She and my Uncle Bob came over to the house for Sunday dinners," Cheryl says. "All I can remember about Aunt Rose is her pure white hair and her favorite purple dress. Every Sunday she came over, she had on that purple dress. I've got a picture of her in that dress. She was buried in it. Even though she wasn't too much of a 'kid' person, she used to babysit for us every now and then."

Nana Rose died when Cheryl was still a youngster. But it wasn't long before her aunt presented herself in a quite unexpected manner.

Cheryl explains:

"We used to go to bed early, or at least we thought it was early. My brother and I were sharing a bedroom then and we'd gotten our nightclothes on. We were coming out of the bedroom while my mother shut off the light. As we turned the corner into the living room, we saw Nana Rose standing at the other end of the living room rubbing the sewing machine like she was dusting it off. We yelled out 'Nana Rose!' both of us, simultaneously. We ran to hug her, but that's when she vanished. We turned around to my mother. I can still see the look on her face. She was shocked because she saw her, too."

The old Singer pedal-driven sewing machine had belonged to Nana Rose. Her husband gave it to Cheryl's mother after she died. Sitting on top of the Singer was a Tiffany lamp, which had also belonged to Nana Rose. The lamp was turned on at the time the three saw Nana Rose.

"My mother put that lamp on a doily my aunt had made. She did that because Aunt Rose loved that sewing machine. Apparently, she sewed a lot. Then I had the sewing machine after my mother died," Cheryl adds.

What struck Cheryl about her aunt's sudden manifestation was that she did and yet *did not* give the impression of being a living person.

Although it was clear to the three that Nana Rose was wearing her favorite purple dress, there was something about her that seemed different—other than the obvious conclusion that she had been deceased for some time. There was a three-dimensional quality about her. To Cheryl's young eyes, her aunt did give the impression of being alive. Right up to the moment when she abruptly departed.

"My mother then just got us ready for bed," Cheryl says of her mother's subsequent reaction. "She told us that Nana Rose wasn't here with us anymore, that she was dead. But we insisted it had been her and she just said, 'Okay.' She was trying to help us so we wouldn't get scared. But we weren't scared at all."

That appearance may have been a "mistake," Cheryl now believes. "For all I know, maybe she didn't want us to see her to begin with. But she figured that maybe she was safe there (with us). And that sewing machine was her pride and joy."

There was no attempt at communication between the ghost and the family members. That silence did not last long, however.

About six months later, little Cheryl was in the backyard with her mother when they happened to see a neighbor, Ann Barnett.

"I overheard my mother complaining to Mrs. Barnett that she kept hearing someone in the house calling her name and that the voice sounded just like Nana Rose. She said she would turn around to see who was calling her and there would be no one there. But out of the corner of her eye she would see a shadow scurrying away," Cheryl says.

Mrs. Barnett offered a solution.

"The next time you hear that voice," she told Cheryl's mother, "you need to say, 'In God's name what do you want?' but don't turn around to look for her. Rose wanted to tell you something before she died but she didn't get the chance. She's trying to tell you now."

Cheryl didn't know what to think. She hadn't heard any voice, yet she could see how upset her mother was during her conversation with Mrs. Barnett. And Cheryl clearly remembered seeing Nana Rose lovingly stroke the sewing machine. A few days later, the little girl understood her mother's anxieties.

"My mother was giving me a bath in the tub and she was on her knees. The bathroom light was on. All of a sudden, we heard 'Alma!' my mother's name, repeated three times. I look at my mother and then she repeated what the neighbor had told her to," Cheryl says.

"In God's name what do you want?" her mother said forcefully, not daring to turn toward the voice. She continued to stare directly at her daughter.

"The moment she said that I saw a shadow go by right behind her and float through the bathroom sink and into the wall. It scared me to death, let me tell you!" she recalls of that incident. The formless passing shade made no sound nor did it appear to be human in any way.

That was the last time Cheryl's mother heard from Nana Rose and for that she was grateful. Cheryl believes her mother was "tormented" by the persistent calling of her name. She never found out what it was Nana Rose wanted to say.

Cheryl Ames's third strange encounter was another instance of a voice from the grave. The year was 1969. Her mother had passed away two years earlier. Cheryl was twenty-two and had gone through a divorce. She was living with her boyfriend "Jimmy" and her young daughter in Pittsfield.

Then came the night her mother called out to her.

"We were sound asleep. My daughter was in the next bedroom. I had never told Jimmy about my experiences when I was young. It was about 3 A.M. when I heard someone say 'Sissy!' three times. It just woke me right up," she says.

Sissy is the nickname by which Cheryl was known to her family. Jimmy did not know that.

"Who was that?" Jimmy asked, sitting up in bed.

"You heard it?" Cheryl asked.

"Sure I did," he replied, "just like it was somebody in this room. But who's Sissy?"

"Well, that's what my mother used to call me. And that's her voice."

Jimmy sat bolt upright and switched on the bedside lamp.

"You're kidding, right?" he asked.

"No. You're telling me you really did hear that voice?" Cheryl again confirmed.

When Jimmy nodded, she thought back to Ann Barnett's admonition.

"In God's name what do you want?" Cheryl cried out. There was no answer that night, nor any future night. Her mother's voice was stilled.

"I think it happened because the day she died we had made plans to go shopping. She was supposed to call me, but she never did. Her voice sounded just like she was calling me to come in, like when I was a little kid."

Cheryl told Jimmy about her experiences years before with Nana Rose. "All of that certainly made a believer out of him," she adds. "I look back now and I think maybe she needed to tell me something. But if it was going to be like the torment she apparently experienced with Nana Rose then, no, I'm glad I did it. I don't think I could have put up with hearing my name called all the time."

Curious Homes

Sometimes the most innocent-looking dwellings harbor visitors from the other side if the testimony of these New Jersey homeowners is to be believed. And why shouldn't it be? Certainly these are perfectly ordinary people who got caught up in some extraordinary experiences—and dealt with the consequences in a variety of ways.

The Interloper

What would *you* do if the marriage you thought would last until "death us do part" was instead falling apart and suddenly an unseen presence in your home made it clear that he didn't approve of some of the things you were doing?

That was precisely the dilemma Alison Albright* faced some years ago at her New Jersey home. Her first marriage was dying "an unpleasantly slow death," in her words, with the concomitant amounts of stress and tension produced in those types of situations. Complicating matters were Alison's self-described "extra-curricular" activities that she knew to be wrong and probably led to the ghostly visitor.

"It was as if this presence also knew what was going on and was showing his disapproval in a calm series of warnings and reminders. But he was never harmful and I was never scared," Alison said.

When she thinks about that time she says that the events changed her attitude about the supernatural. Alison was always the quickest to say there were no such things as ghosts, although she did and does believe in life after death. "Just not in white-sheeted figures leaping around in cemeteries," she emphasized. She is undeterred in her assessment that "someone" was sharing the house with her, her children, and her soon-to-be ex-husband. The unannounced visitor's appearances were infrequent and always quite unexpected.

Alison's temporary haunting—for the ghost disappeared when she made the

*Name has been changed.

final decision to take her children and terminate her marriage—remained unidentified, although she has a pretty good idea as to who it was.

"We found out that the grandfather of the man from whom we bought the house had lived and died there. He was a very straight-laced Polish family man. Every one in his family was blond except for him; he was very dark and also shorter than average," Alison said, implying that the elderly man's Old World morality would have made it difficult for him to silently watch the goings-on as he sat invisibly in a corner somewhere. When she made what she terms the "agonizing decision" to terminate the marriage, the being which she saw, sensed, and heard, vanished for good.

"I first saw him as I came into our bedroom after being out," Alison remembered. "I asked why I hadn't been told we had company. But I looked again, to welcome whomever this was, and all I saw was space, nobody there. Later the girl who lived in the second-floor apartment of our house came down to tell me there had been a man watching her brush her teeth. She described to me exactly the man I had seen."

As with many a house haunting, Alison's visitor did not keep regular hours nor did he cause her to run in fear for her life. And yet the undeniably strange experience of living with a ghost gave her a sudden shock now and then, as on that late night when she had been unable to fall asleep.

"I was ironing at 2:00 A.M. when I was suddenly aware of not being alone," she recalled. "There was nothing visible at all—except a few goose bumps on me. There was just a clear feeling of having a friend with me. I was neither drunk nor drugged, but quite conscious and wide awake. I was warmly comforted by the presence. When I finished the ironing I was able to sleep soundly."

Although she had seen the old man late that one night, this was the first time she sensed his actual company.

"Several times after that I heard unexplainable noises in the house. Occasionally some clear footsteps walked across the apartment rooms upstairs when no one else was at home," Alison said.

Word about the ghost in the house spread among her friends. Some took it seriously while others did not.

"One of our friends was a former army soldier. He asked if he could sleep in the basement one night to prove there was nothing. In the early morning he was pale and shaken. He said 'something' had brushed his skin in the night and pulled at his blanket. He never stayed overnight again," Alison said.

Another friend laughed and told her that she was in need of a psychiatrist, but that was before he and his wife visited Alison and her family.

"He was a big man," she said. "He and his wife were sitting with me while our children played on the floor. We all clearly heard the footsteps walking across the room above us. Nobody was home upstairs. I offered to take my 'big friend' up there but he wouldn't budge from his chair. He just asked kind of shakily for a whiskey. He never laughed about the ghost again."

Alison was never in fear of her or her children's well-being, but there were two occasions when the haunting was not quite so benign.

"We had some friends over playing with a Ouija Board," she said of one night in particular. "We'd been getting some hair-raising answers. I didn't feel comfortable so we put away the board. I cleaned up later that night but as I walked past my china cupboard on the way to the bedroom there was a horrible crash. Most of the glasses on one shelf had fallen over in one direction. Nothing else in the cupboard was out of place and no glass was cracked or broken. And I hadn't touched the cupboard in any way."

The second bit of harassment almost landed Alison's husband in the hospital emergency room with a wound to the head.

"We'd had an extensive argument about smoking," she said. "I'd been pleading with my then-husband to quit because I hated the habit. I had a large German beer stein with a heavy lid on a window shelf. It had always been there. Well, it fell off, but not straight down as you'd expect. It flew in an outward curve as if it had been thrown. It only missed his head by inches and landed right in the full ashtray scattering cigarette butts and ashes everywhere. There had been absolutely nothing to cause that stein to fall. No door slamming, no strong wind. Nothing."

Nothing, that is, except an old Polish gentleman ghost who clearly sided with Alison's anti-smoking sentiments.

Bodo Otto and Other Odd Gloucesterians

Lying as it does directly south of Philadelphia, Gloucester County, in southwest New Jersey, shares in the centuries-old history of this region of the United States. From the banks of the Delaware River through such communities as Swedesboro, Mickleton, Mullica Hill, and Glassboro, this region of the state is rich in history . . . and rich in tales of the supernatural, including more strange events in work-aday homes.

There is, for example, the 250-year-old Bodo Otto, Jr. house on Kings Highway in Mickleton. Otto was one of George Washington's surgeons. Some reports have it that Otto . . . or someone . . . occasionally disrupts the routine of families who have lived there. Stories about the house first surfaced around 1970 when it was vacant. Police had received reports of "prowlers" one summer night. The police chief and a patrolman searched the house but the results were anything but what they expected. The men's new flashlights died at the same moment while they were in different rooms. Later, the police chief said some strange sounds had come from the room his patrol officer was searching at the moment when their lights flickered and died.

A family that moved into the Otto house in the late 1970s told a reporter that passersby might have mistaken a large cat that was living in the house at the time they moved in for a person. The cat, it seems, liked to look out a third floor window.

A later homeowner, however, said she thought some odd things did indeed take place in the house. As with hairbrushes. Her brush *levitated* one evening! Later explorations with a Ouija Board found that the ghost was of a man murdered in the Otto house sometime in the eighteenth century.

It was "Uncle Charlie" who paid a call on an Episcopal priest and his family at St. Stephen's Church in Mullica Hill. The fellow was quite well-mannered, even if he was visible only from the knees up!

The priest and his family thought at first that a prankster or burglar was some-how getting into the house. Shortly after they moved in, they'd return home to find their possessions rearranged—the couch was disturbed, as if someone had taken a short nap on it, and it looked like someone had been sitting at the dining room table writing letters. The smell of fresh-brewed coffee and fried bacon was a common occurrence. However, no one had been using the kitchen when they smelled bacon and the family drank only instant coffee.

The identity of the "prankster" became apparent one day when the priest and his wife were suddenly confronted with the image of a young man in his late 20s. He was only visible—from the knees up—for a brief few seconds before vanishing. Perhaps he was assuring them of his benign intentions in using their home as his own.

Just who the ghost had been in life remained a mystery.

Other odors haunted the 1784 home of former Gov. Charles Creighton Stratton in Swedesboro. An attorney and her husband lived in the old house for some time. She said they often smelled pipe smoke and perfume, which neither of them ever used!

Imagine hosting an evening of bridge when one of your guests arrives with a question for you: just who is that looking out your kitchen window with such an odd costume on? No one, you reply. And what do you mean by an "odd costume"? It certainly seems peculiar. Not many folks wandered twentieth-century homes in a waistcoat, riding pants, and heavy boots.

No, they don't, unless it's the ghost in another Mickleton-area home. The anonymous homeowner lived there for about ten years, but the haunting was limited to the first four years he and his family lived there—which would probably be more than enough for most people.

He remembered late one night when he was awakened by a cold draft that seemed to be coming up the staircase and into the bedroom where he and his wife were sleeping. A winter blizzard raged outside. He found his way down the stairs where he discovered both the front and back doors standing wide open. The deadbolts in both doors were still in a locked position.

The couple used to hear what sounded like a music box but despite their best efforts failed to discover its mysterious source.

The figure in the kitchen window might have been connected to another incident when the homeowner was working in his third floor study. "I thought I heard my wife come home, but the cats went bananas—the fur on their backs went straight up in the air," he later confided to a reporter. But the tread he heard was definitely not that of his wife. This was the heavy footfall of boots on old wood floors. He got up from his desk and followed the sound until it ended in a front bedroom.

A former Rowan University professor lived for some years in a house off Main Street in Glassboro with the legendary ghost of "Jennifer," a sad little girl who died after falling down the stairs.

At about one o'clock one morning, he heard a child's laughter. The professor was quite surprised since there were no children in or around his home.

Inn of the Seventeen Ghosts

On Monday nights the 284-year-old General Wayne Inn in Merion, Pennsylvania, was usually closed. But this was a special occasion at the stone and timbered restaurant near Philadelphia. Jean and Bill Quinn and four other psychics were seated at the polished mahogany table in a private dining room on the second floor. Joining the circle were Barton Johnson, his wife and two of his sons. Flickering candles provided the only illumination. Tape recorders with sensitive microphones whirred quietly in the center of the table.

Jean Quinn anticipated a long session. She asked people to put on jackets against the anticipated cold, loosen their shoelaces and belts, and visit the washroom.

Barton Johnson rose to close the doors. A penetrating chill descended upon the room as if the windows had been thrown open. No sooner had Johnson seated himself once again than both doors flew open. There were no drafts and no one stood in the dimly-lighted hallway. At least no one they could see.

Johnson was impressed.

Jean lowered her head and immediately went into a trance. Within a very few moments, the small group was astonished as the voices of a procession of entities introduced themselves. Using Jean and the other mediums as their voices, each took a turn speaking. First came Wilhelm, one of the German Hessian soldiers hired by the British to fight in the American Revolutionary War. He seemed to be the leader. Others followed. Two maids, Sara and Sadie . . . a sad little boy . . . an American Indian . . . a black man . . . and eight more Hessians. By the time the séance concluded that night, a veritable battalion of ghosts—seventeen in all— had made their presence known!

Even without its ghosts, the General Wayne Inn has had a colorful history. Built on land purchased from William Penn, the inn was apparently this nation's oldest hostelry in continuous operation until it closed and was put up for sale in 2001.

Robert Jones, a Quaker, opened what he called the Wayside Inn in 1704 to provide accommodations for travelers on the nearby Old Lancaster Road from Philadelphia to Radnor. It became the General Wayne Inn in 1795 to honor local resident and celebrated war hero General "Mad Anthony" Wayne.

The handsome three-story building was designed to resemble an English coaching inn. Large, open fireplaces grace each end of the first floor. Small sleeping rooms were provided upstairs near an overhanging porch on which weary guests could visit in comfortable rocking chairs.

Although some alterations have been made, and it no longer provides for overnight guests, the inn looks as it must have in the decades before the founding of the nation. Its unique characteristics have made it a registered National Historic Landmark.

Barton Johnson, a history buff and officer of the Lower Merion Historical Society, bought the General Wayne in 1970. As a child in Merion, he grew up listening to tales of the haunted inn.

He was, however, far more interested in the mortal past of the inn. That was well documented. There were its many uses over the centuries—as an inn and restaurant, of course, but also as a post office (Ben Franklin sorted the mail there), a general store, and a social center for newly arrived Welsh immigrants.

Johnson knew that many Revolutionary War battles had been waged around Merion. Indeed, the inn had been occupied variously by American Patriots, British Redcoats, and the Hessian hirelings.

Johnson had been told that General George Washington and the Marquis de Lafayette had dined on the inn's famous squirrel ragout and pigeon stew.

During the 1800s, wealthy Philadelphians vacationed in the area. Many took meals at the inn, including Edgar Allan Poe. He is said to have written several stanzas of "The Raven" while seated at his favorite table. Until the 1930s a windowpane inscribed with the initials EAP could be found there, etched by the poet himself.

All of this Johnson knew, but it in no way prepared him for what was to come. Ironically, he had mixed feelings about his immortal tenants. "I don't believe in ghosts," he said, "but I know they're here. Figure that one out."

Johnson's curiosity was permanently aroused in 1971 when he met Jean and Bill Quinn. The famous New Jersey psychics contacted him to seek permission to study the inn. The couple had heard that the inn was haunted and wanted to make their own investigation. Johnson said they were welcome at any time.

The Quinns took him at his word and arrived unexpectedly a few weeks later on an extremely busy Friday night. Remembering his promise, Johnson asked what they would like to see. The basement, they said.

Johnson escorted the couple down the worn wooden staircase to the cellar and watched in vague interest as Jean ran her hands along the ancient stone walls. She quietly stated that she was looking for cold spots. Johnson shrugged his shoulders and left to attend to his customers.

Two hours later, the Quinns reported back. The restaurant was haunted by many entities, Jean told her startled host. Indeed, she had "spoken" to one spirit. He was a "very nice guy" named Wilhelm, she said. Although he took an immediate liking to the Quinns, Johnson didn't think much of her discovery.

Another year passed before the Quinns returned for the séance at which all the ghosts were identified.

Wilhelm, the self-proclaimed spokesghost, told Johnson, the Quinns, and the others that he had been killed during battle. He was unhappy because the Patriot commander saw that he wore a fine uniform and a new pair of boots that could be used by another soldier. They stripped his body and buried him in his skivvies.

Wilhelm said he was still searching for his clothes in order to have a proper burial.

His ethereal companions were generally satisfied with their afterlife at the inn, but a few things didn't sit well with them, Wilhelm said through Jean. They loved the dinner music, but couldn't abide the crash of the drummer's cymbals. And the gin and beer didn't taste quite right; nor did the wine. The only thing they really liked was the tea that, he said, they drank constantly!

All of the spirits seemed to have problems important enough to keep them from resting in peace.

The little boy had lost his mother. He couldn't stop crying long enough for the psychics to learn his name or anything more about him.

Sara and Sadie were saucy revenants from about 1850. They had both worked at the inn and died with a most distressing problem on their minds. A peddler had arrived with a wagonload of Persian rugs. To own such fine carpets at that time was considered the epitome of luxury. He told the women that he was expecting a buyer to meet him at the inn. Several days passed and the prospect still hadn't showed. The peddler asked Sara and Sadie to look after the rugs while he searched for the buyer. They agreed.

Days lengthened into weeks and weeks into months and the peddler never returned. The women feared that they would be accused of having stolen the rugs. At the séance, both women said they were still afraid of being accused of theft. It was difficult to get their story because, as Johnson recalled, "they were reluctant talkers and treated us (at the séance) as intruders." They didn't say how or why they died so young.

Johnson was certain the black man was a twentieth-century ghost, the spirit of one Chase, a long-time employee who worked at the inn when he bought it. Chase's job was to open the clams and oysters and help with the salads and desserts.

Two weeks after Johnson bought the inn, Chase confided in his boss that he had talked to Mr. McClain on the previous night. Johnson remembered the conversation clearly.

"No, Chase," Johnson replied. "You couldn't have spoken to him. Mr. McClain is dead." Richard McClain had been a previous owner of the inn.

"I know that," Chase insisted. "And I spoke to him."

"Well," Johnson said, not wishing to offend him, "if you ever see Mr. McClain again, tell him I said hello."

A few weeks passed and Chase again came up to Johnson. "I saw Mr. McClain again last night and gave him your regards. He said to say hello to you."

"Thanks" was all Johnson could say.

Days later Chase was dead.

There was one ghost Jean Quinn and her group did not meet that night in 1972. He would appear several years later and is, or rather was, another Hessian soldier named Ludwig. He was, perhaps, one of Wilhelm's comrades. His story is a strange one.

It begins in 1976 when Johnson was away on vacation. A part-time contractor and psychic named Mike Benio from Olyphant, Pennsylvania, arrived at the General Wayne with a peculiar request. Every morning at two o'clock, a ghost had been coming into his bedroom explaining that he had been killed in a Revolutionary War battle and was buried in the basement of "an old inn" near Philadelphia . . . in a place called Merion! The ghost wanted Benio to dig up his body and bury it in a cemetery.

When Johnson returned and heard the story from employees, he telephoned Benio with permission to dig on the condition that he didn't endanger the foundation and that he would repair any damage.

Benio spent two days in the basement. He discovered a small room extending under the parking lot at the front of the building. Some broken pottery and what appeared to be bones were scattered on the earthen floor. Were they human remains? Neither Johnson or Benio were able to find out.

Ludwig must have appreciated Benio's efforts, however, as he never again made an appearance.

The Hessians left quite an impression on the inn. There are several other accounts of encounters with old soldiers who never die.

A picture of one of the German soldiers hangs on a wall of the charming main dining room. His severe posture seems quite out of place in the elegant warmth and gentility of this room with its aged ceiling beams and plank walls. Gleaming brass chandeliers throw gentle light on tables set with snow-white linen.

Yet several employees say they have seen someone who matches the man in the painting. A maitre d' had so many run-ins with the ghost in the basement that he finally refused to go downstairs. A luncheon hostess met several soldiers striding through the dining room, sitting in the bar after hours and upstairs in the private dining rooms.

But most frightened of all may have been Nathan, an elderly porter who cleaned the floors at closing time.

The inn opened for dinner at four o'clock on Sundays, but Barton Johnson usually went in at two to inspect the place. One Sunday he found an irregular line of trash strewn across the middle of the dining room floor. He called out for Nathan, but there was no answer. On a hunch, he telephoned the porter's home. Nathan answered.

Why hadn't he finished his work? Johnson asked.

"Well, Mr. Johnson," Nathan stammered. "I was sweeping that dining room when a fellow just like that picture you have came over and walked right through me. I left."

If the ghosts are sometimes frightening, they are also playful. It is not uncommon, for instance, for young women sitting on the barstools to feel someone blowing on their necks. There were men standing nearby, but they all denied culpability. Johnson blamed his ghosts and said that "game" was played for over a year.

Despite Wilhelm's assertions that his spectral friends didn't like modern alcohol, the ghosts do frequent the bar late at night. When Johnson told Jean Quinn of the after-hours tippling, she loaned him a tape recorder. She directed him to load it with a fresh tape, place it on the fireplace mantel near the bar counter and turn it on when he left for the night. He followed her advice soon thereafter.

Johnson played the tape the following morning. He heard nothing for a long time, but then came the familiar noise of swiveling bar stools, a noise unmistakable to the veteran innkeeper.

Then, someone, or something, in the perfectly empty building turned on the water faucet and held a glass under it.

The revelry had begun about a half hour after Johnson closed for the evening.

A ghost may also have been in the bar on another occasion. An elderly woman and frequent customer had been out to dinner and a movie with her nephew. She asked him to stop by the General Wayne for a nightcap. Johnson recalls that she loved to sit on the bar stool, listen to the musical combo playing in the lounge and sip nothing stronger than ginger ale.

On this night, her nephew reminded her that it was Monday and the inn was always closed on that day, but to placate her, he drove past. There were no cars. She insisted that someone appeared to be inside. Her nephew pulled into the parking lot and waited while she looked. In the dim light filtering through a window, she saw a man sitting on a bar stool slumped over the counter. He wore a peculiar-looking soldier's uniform. As he turned toward her, she fled back to the car.

The ghosts at the General Wayne Inn were sometimes malicious.

Johnson unlocked the inn one morning to find the cash register drawer partly open and each compartment filled with water. He glanced toward the ceiling expecting to see stains where the roof had leaked. He saw none. Instead his gaze settled on a row of carafes sitting on a shelf. They were used to serve wine. But on this day each was filled with water.

He emptied the carafes, dumped the water out of the cash register and tried to work it; the machine shorted out.

An insurance adjuster inspected the roof for leaks and found none. He asked Johnson what had happened. "I don't really know," Johnson replied. Although he has no absolute proof of how the water mysteriously appeared, he believes the inn's ghosts were somehow responsible. To him, it is the only "reasonable" explanation.

As word spread of the haunting of the General Wayne Inn, area media ran a number of feature stories, usually around Halloween. A television station got wind of the ghosts and sent a crew to interview Johnson and perhaps capture one of the spirits on film. They stayed all day, but nothing out of the ordinary happened . . . until later. The story was scheduled for several days later during the news at 11:20 in the evening.

The bar was full of patrons when Johnson turned on the television set above the bar. He told the customers about the feature. The first half of the program went fine. But then the ghosts got into the act.

Johnson described what happened next.

"When our segment came on the whole picture started going around—a perfect picture with no flop over and no snow, but it just kept going around the whole time until our segment was over. It's never done that before and it's never done that since. All of my customers were watching in disbelief," he said, shaking his head.

He checked with neighbors to see if they had trouble with their sets that night. None of them had.

The ghosts seem to be particularly active in the winter months. Johnson recalled one incident that, once again, left him puzzled.

A late-winter blizzard struck early one afternoon. A few hours later snow drifts lay high against the front door and Johnson decided to close early. He had served only two lunches and knew there would be little, if any, dinner business.

Johnson locked the doors and went into the kitchen to tell the chef, who had been cleaning the refrigerators and washing a huge mixer with many attachments.

"Let's go right now," Johnson told the chef. "It's getting worse by the minute."

He waited for the chef to put away the mixer's attachments and noticed for the first time a pile of clean hand towels folded into neat squares on the butcher block table. He decided to leave them there until the next morning. The men left together.

By morning the storm had abated and the inn opened for business. A few minutes after the staff arrived, the chef stopped Johnson.

"Who was in here last night?" he asked.

"No one," Johnson replied.

The chef waved him into the kitchen where mixer attachments were scattered across the floor and the clean towels thrown into disarray.

Johnson wasn't particularly surprised; peculiar things like that were happening all the time. On several occasions, the housekeeper found both front doors unlocked when Johnson or one of his sons had securely bolted them the night before.

The ghosts also harassed Mrs. Johnson.

The business office is on the third floor. After a busy day, Mrs. Johnson helps the bookkeeper with the paperwork. Charge cards, in particular, require several forms to be filled out.

In the beginning, Mrs. Johnson would add a column of figures on the small adding machine and decide the total didn't look right. It might be fifty or a hundred dollars off. Then she would "test" the machine. Two plus two equals . . . five? It gave the wrong answer. She would add columns of simple numbers and get erroneous results every time.

Then she had an idea. Was it possible the ghosts hovered nearby and tinkered with the adding machine? On an impulse she ordered the "guys" out of the room. She had work to do, she scolded. The adding machine worked perfectly from then on.

The late co-author of this book, Beth Scott, had a firsthand look at one of the ghosts when she visited the inn to interview Johnson.

Mrs. Scott and Johnson sat at a table conversing near the bar when a distinct figure of a woman in a long, billowing white skirt and long-sleeved blouse hurried past the dark paneled wall. Mrs. Scott saw that her hands and feet were invisible. As the ghost turned, it appeared to be wearing a Dutch-style cap with upswept points at either side. Could the figure have been Sara or Sadie awaiting the return of their peddler, the Dutch cap mistaken for a bonnet? It seemed quite possible, Mrs. Scott thought at the time.

Johnson was remarkably calm about the ghosts wandering the premises of his inn. He seemed to understand that the place belonged to them as much as it does to him. He did not capitalize on their antics and had no idea whether they have helped or hurt business.

He also realized that "his" ghosts were not the horrifying specters of legend or of fiction.

"They are certainly not earth-shattering stories," he explained. "But they are what has happened. And they are unexplainable."

The more recent history of the General Wayne Inn has not been a happy one. In December 1996, co-owner 31-year-old James Webb was fatally shot in the head and his body found in the inn's office. His partner, gourmet chef Guy Sileo was convicted of the murder in August 2001 and sentenced to life in prison.

Prosecutors said Sileo's motive was to cash in on a $650,000 insurance policy he had taken out on Webb's life. Sileo and Webb bought the inn in 1995 and had been facing financial problems since that time.

Following the murder, the inn closed for two years. The Lower Merion Conservancy and the local historical society provided upkeep until the inn was sold in 1999 to local developers. However, the new owners were not able to stay in business and as of mid-2001 the General Wayne Inn was again for sale. One observer said the inn and its property would probably fetch about $1 million.

Ghosts included.

Peleg Walker

The Rhode Island haunt hunter can be excused if he comes away from his historical research more confused about the state of ghosts in this state than in any other North American locale. Consider the following statement from a prominent Providence journalist:

> "The last self-respecting ghost in Rhode Island apparently has packed his chains and headed west. Time was when this little state abounded in haunted houses. Perhaps the competition with ghosts on improperly-working TV sets has proved too much. At any rate, no one has reported seeing an apparition hereabouts in almost 20 years as far as this department of eerie sights can discover."
>
> George Popkin, *Providence Journal*, Dec. 6, 1953

All right, reporter Popkin apparently stalked the supernatural for some time and his observation about the condition of spectral disturbances in Rhode Island during the middle of the last century seems a fair enough conclusion.

But then what are we to make of the following postulation from a story reported in the pages of the same newspaper in the very next year?

> "Rhode Island, the smallest state, has the largest spectral population in the country. The ha'nts include Indians, pirates, slaves, colonial belles weeping over blighted romances, peddlers, counterfeiters, ghosts bent on getting even for ancient wrongs and ghosts just haunting for the fun of the thing."
>
> Robert L. Wheeler, *Providence Journal*, Oct. 31, 1954

Despite Mr. Wheeler's self-assuredness, either we have Little Rhody with nary a ghost in sight, or we have so many of them traipsing about the countryside that they could very well compete in population density with the state's earthly tenants—Rhode Island is second in the nation in persons per square mile, behind only its neighbor farther down the Atlantic coast, New Jersey. But as far as can be determined, no one has asked the Census Bureau to count New Jersey's unnatural populace.

Robert Wheeler did not have the final word in this ink-stained disagreement. Mr. Popkin seems to have continued with his search for some years, but with as little success as he had in 1953. Here is what he wrote some years later:

> "Once upon a time Rhode Island could field as respectable a team in the spectral big leagues as anyone. There were plenty of haunted houses for performing ghosts, then, production costs (mostly sheets) were negligible, and an imaginative audience was willing and able to trumpet their glory. But alas, just as much of the textile industry moved south, our ghosts apparently headed west. We simply couldn't compete with the lower resistance to old wives' tales elsewhere. . . . All in all, you might say Rhode Islanders once husbanded the squeak of every loose board and made the most of it. Now the squeaks are ignored—and the ghosts as well."
>
> George Popkin, *Providence Journal*, Jan., 21, 1962

And so the battle was joined. One would suspect that the good Mr. Popkin would have been mightily pleased if his Olympian pronouncement had taken hold and not another word had ever been written or uttered in Providence, or anywhere else in the state for that matter, about supernatural goings-on. But in the four decades since Popkin declared the state haunt-free, there has accumulated enough evidence to suggest that Rhode Island has enough ghost stories to keep even the most indefatigable seeker of haunted places engaged for many moonless nights.

Is Foster, R.I., Ghost Central?

The town of Foster has been called Rhode Island's Sleepy Hollow, so numerous are the ghost stories in that region. But that's not the only foible about this minute crossroads community. Three miles to the *northeast* of Foster is *South* Foster. If the geographic confusion is plainly apparent on any map, there is no such misunderstanding about the many supernatural tales in that section of Providence County.

Witches seem to be especially popular. Witch Field, near Tucker Hollow, was the home of an old woman in the mid-1800s. She was a virtual recluse in her decrepit house. She dared not show her face and hid away for years. Neighbors claimed that she practiced witchcraft. On her deathbed, she cursed the community, saying that as long as her home stood she would haunt all who made her life such a living hell. Her ghost was regularly sighted until the night a group of men tore down and carted away the last vestiges of her house.

At 812 feet, Jerimoth Hill is the highest point in Rhode Island. There are also witches there, according to old-timers. But the mini-mount is actually four miles northwest of Foster, or one mile southwest of North Foster. Perhaps that's confusing for the witches as well for they haven't been seen in several years.

The most famous historical ghost in the Foster region, however, is Peleg Walker, who lived in the small settlement of Ramtail Village, which, it is said, was abandoned because of his haunting.

Ramtail was a prosperous milling town on the banks of the Ponaganset River, a few miles from Foster. Today there are but faint traces of its old roads, stone fences, and a few sturdy foundations. Nature has reclaimed the rest.

Peleg Walker himself is something of a cipher. He may have been a native of the region, though that is not certain. During his life nearly a century and a half ago, he left no written account of himself and, because of his death at an early age, there were no descendants to carry on his name or personal legacy. What is known about him is that he and several partners owned a mill in Ramtail Village. A disagreement broke out among them and Peleg ended up the odd man out. What the subject matter might have been has been lost, but whatever the reason, the story is that he was bereft. He cursed his partners, swearing that he would not continue his life under the circumstances—one morning, he vowed, they would have to pry his mill keys from a dead man's grip. They and all those in Ramtail Village would regret the day he was banished from the mill. A few days later, Peleg's body was found in the mill hanging from the bell rope that extended up to the belfry. He held the key to the main door tightly in his cold, ashen hand.

It seems that Peleg kept his promise to hold onto the mill key even in death, and even lingered a while in spirit.

A few days after he was interred at the settlement's cemetery, townspeople were brusquely awakened a few hours after dark by the tolling of the mill bell. Normally, it summoned workers in the morning or signaled the end of the work-day. Peleg's partners scurried through the dark streets to find out what the trouble was. They found the bell unattended, but pealing nevertheless. Although it abruptly stopped a few minutes later, the bell on successive nights continued its inexplicable noisemaking. The men finally took it down and all was peaceful once again. They convinced the naïve locals that some pranksters had tinkered with the bell.

That excuse didn't hold up for very long.

The mill in Ramtail Village one night produced a full load between dusk and dawn. No apparent problem, except the mill was unoccupied at the time. On another occasion, several observers swore they saw the impossible—the mill's giant water wheel turning backward, *against* the river current.

No argument by the mill owners could convince townspeople that tomfoolery was responsible for all of this. Settlers streamed from Ramtail Village by wagon, horse, and foot. Within a year, it was abandoned. The rough roads became quickly overgrown and the few buildings—including the mill itself—fell into decay so that by the twentieth century there was virtually nothing left of this thriving little community deserted because of a ghost.

Sarah Hough* didn't have to be reminded of all the ghost stories circulating through the Foster region. The teenager and her family lived one of them in her very own home.

Her father, Richard Hough,* had plans to remodel the nearly two-century-old colonial home on Danielson Pike. Over the next couple of years, he replaced the plumbing, secured the sagging walls, and repaired the roof. It was during the remodeling that the family discovered "Frank," a sometimes ornery poltergeist who once showed up as an apparition.

*The names in this story have been changed.

"I was sleeping in a huge old bed that was given to my parents," Sarah told a reporter several years ago. "It probably weighs 300 pounds. I had gone to bed and was just starting to doze off. I felt some pressure on the side of the bed, and thought the cat had come upstairs. I turned on the light, and nothing was there. I figured it must be the ghost. I turned off the light and felt the pressure again. By now, I'm in a panic. I'm screaming and crying. The sheets on the bed lifted up, and then the whole bed slid across the floor."

For several months after that, Sarah slept downstairs on the living room sofa.

Even before the nighttime intruder, Sarah knew full well her family had one more family member than planned when she herself saw Frank. It happened while she was combing her hair at her bedroom dresser. Her door was open, as was the door to her brothers' bedroom directly across the hall. As she swept the brush through her hair, she caught a glance in the mirror of someone standing in the other bedroom. "It was a tall, black figure standing in the boys' bedroom," she said at the time. "I couldn't see his face real clear, but it was like chalk-white. Then it moved. I ran into the room and turned on the light and there was no one there."

The ghost was named Frank for no particular reason, her father, Richard, said. Neither did he have any idea about his true name, age, or description. Sarah's sighting was too vague to attach many specifics to.

Frank may not have been alone in the house, however. The second youngest child, Richard Jr., awoke crying in the night shortly after he learned to talk. "Lady touch me! Lady touch me!" he whimpered to his parents.

Frank, or his lady companion, were responsible for various other activities frequently associated with a haunting—footsteps, moving objects, and chilling touches by some *thing*.

When Richard and his wife moved into their house, they slept downstairs for some time while they remodeled the second-floor bedrooms. "We woke up when we heard noises in the bedroom upstairs. Heavy walking," Richard said. "This was when we were still sleeping in the parlor. The footsteps came out into the hallway. This was two or three o'clock in the morning. We heard him approach our door, stand there at the doorway. We listened. I thought maybe it was one of the kids, sleepwalking—which they never do. I was just about to say, 'James,* are you all right?' when every single slat in that bed came out, one by one—bing, bing, bing! We ended up on the floor. That was that. We moved upstairs that night."

Despite Sarah's rather ghastly description of the figure she saw in the mirror, and the occasional houseguest who woke up choking, as if someone was throttling them, the ghosts seemed benign, although they did have their moments of playfulness.

"My wife was at the stove one night . . . she had just turned away," Richard said, "when the saltshaker—it was a big one, too—flew off the stove. The kids saw it rise up—it flew six, ten feet across the room. Just missed her."

That selfsame saltshaker was the weapon-of-choice for the resident ghosts when a visiting friend doubted their existence. The woman's name was Marian,* a strong, churchgoing soul, who didn't countenance beliefs in household goblins. She and her husband stayed many nights with the Houghs, all incident-free. But that ended on one particular evening when the Houghs, Marian and her husband were gathered in the kitchen. She indicated in direct language that folks who believed in ghosts were "crazy." Just then, Richard said, the saltshaker rose from the stove and whizzed across the room before smacking Marian in the back of her head. She and her husband packed up and never returned.

Richard also saw his wife's long hair moving as if someone was whiffing their fingers through it.

The Houghs learned a few things about their aged home that helped them understand *why* the haunting took place even if the *who* behind it remained elusive. It had been built around 1800 and the members of one family lived in it for almost a hundred years. However, in the twenty years before the Houghs bought it, the house went through ten different families. Some old-timers said the house had been used in the winter as a funeral home in the old days, with the deceased's body laid out in what came to be the Houghs' front parlor. That would coincide with two observations made by Richard Hough—the haunting focused on the parlor and the supernatural activity increased during the colder months of the year.

Perhaps all this happened in the Hough house simply because of where it was situated—smack dab in the middle of a landscape that would make Ichabod Crane feel right to home. Haunted places in Foster are hardly news. The Houghs knew that. "A lot of townspeople, they've had similar experiences. They understand this," Richard said.

It's always nice not to have to explain to neighbors about that fleeting figure in black floating across your lawn.

Belcourt Castle

If the Providence *Journal's* George Popkin failed to notice the ghosts in Foster, he likewise ignored Newport, renowned for its wealth, eccentricity, and haunted homes, many of which are open to the public.

The compassionate monk of Belcourt Castle is among the most prominent Newport ghosts. He's been known to help the owners fend off potential calamities, such as the time part of him showed up but failed in his attempted warning.

"His hand and arm came through the staircase and pointed at the painting," the home's owner reported. "If we'd known what he was doing, we would have investigated. The next morning the small brass cable broke and the painting—a very valuable madonna—fell. . . ."

He is particularly easy to identify. "He looks just like a monk with a cowl when we see him, and he's seen mostly in the main house near the grand stair," the owner said. "He only comes when we're here alone and it's quiet."

The nameless monk is such a frequent visitor that he's long past his ability to terrify anyone. "We're happy to have him here. It's very real and fun to know there are these things that don't hurt anybody, that stay here and don't want to leave this plane. Who am I to question it? There are many things in the world we don't understand."

Belcourt Castle, just off Bellevue Avenue, close by Easton Bay, is open to the public. Visitors can also see a chair where many who sit claim to sense a ghostly presence.

According to some Newportites, it is something of a status symbol to have ghosts in your house.

Tanya Rhinelander wasn't trying to achieve social standing several years ago when Governor John Collins dropped in at her house for a visit—two hundred years after he died!

"I opened my eyes and blinked and blinked and there at the end of the bed stood a man in a tricorn hat and a colonial-type uniform," Rhinelander said, adding that she screamed and dived under the covers. The late governor—he served from 1786 to 1790—is buried in the old Collins family cemetery in Rhinelander's front lawn.

Mrs. Rhinelander's son was also visited, albeit briefly, by the governor. "It was too weird to be explainable. I was awake and in bed and a figure came into my room. He didn't say a word, just appeared, and then left. It was very strange."

Across town at Prescott Farm, owned by the Newport Restoration Foundation, a remarkably pretty young woman specter is seen on occasion. She may have been the subject of British General Prescott's amorous adventures during the Revolutionary War. He had commandeered the farm and quartered his troops there. Patriot forces grabbed General Prescott at Prescott Farm on the evening of July 9, 1777, as he was in the middle of an intimate tête-à-tête with the woman.

The ghost sightings at the farm go back many decades. One of the first occurred when the father of owner Kittymouse Cook was adding electricity and plumbing to the main house in the late 1920s. "He came back from lunch and told me, 'There's the prettiest girl in your house, over in the corner near the closet by the backstairs.'"

The next year, Mrs. Cook saw the ghost herself. "She was in the prettiest water-silk taffeta dress with a small, tight bodice and little velvet buttons. She had black hair, parted in the middle. Gradually she just faded away."

There is some slim evidence that the general himself may be hanging around as well. Mrs. Cook and her husband, Benjamin, heard a heavy boot drop on the upstairs floor as they were reading in the library.

"Ben Cook looked at me over his newspaper and said, 'Who's upstairs?'"

Mrs. Cook allowed that no one was. Her husband sighed and said, "Oh, Kittymouse, you and your ghost!" He went upstairs to look around but could find nothing. He sat back down to finish the newspaper. Just then pounding footsteps raced down the staircase and out the front door.

At least one exorcism has been attempted in Newport, but it was unsuccessful.

That was at the home of Mrs. Pierrepoint Johnson. She had a superstitious maid. To allay her fears of ghosts in the house, Mrs. Johnson asked the Rev. Henry Turnbull, rector of St. John's Episcopal Church, to come and exorcise the spirits. He showed up wearing full ecclesiastical garb and bearing incense. He went through the entire house.

"It did no good, the ghosts kept on," Mrs. Johnson said. There was no report as to whether the maid was satisfied with the procedure.

ENTR'ACTE—
HAUNTS OF IVY

Haunts of Ivy

Strange Interlude

On a bright October morning at a few minutes before nine o'clock, Colleen Buterbaugh, a secretary to the dean at Nebraska Wesleyan University, rose from her desk in Old Main clutching a fistful of telephone messages she'd accumulated since the previous day for a popular professor. As was her daily routine, she was to deliver the notes from students asking for appointments, or campus and community groups seeking a dynamic guest speaker, to Dr. Thomas McCourt, an engaging Scottish music educator who was spending fall semester on the Lincoln campus.

Classes were changing as Colleen left her first-floor office, made her way out the wide doors of Old Main, down the steps, and then turned north along the sidewalk. She was headed for C. C. White Memorial Hall, the fine arts building and home of the school's music department. Once in the building's door, she went up the half-flight of steps to the main floor that held the music office. As with many old college buildings constructed at the turn of the century, White's first floor was actually several feet above ground level. Another half-flight of steps led to a lower level. The wide staircase itself wound the entire height of the three-story building.

Colleen shouldered her way through the throngs of noisy students as she headed down the hall toward the music office, a two-room complex in the northeast corner of the main level, where music faculty had mailboxes in the outer office. Dr. McCourt had been assigned a desk in the inner area, which was also used as a workroom and held a small library of music books and compositions. Along the hall she listened to the pleasant and familiar hubbub—a percussionist beat out a simple melody on a marimba, several piano students practiced various exercises, and some vocal students worked on their scales. She smiled at the happy sounds, all typical of a weekday morning in the music wing of the fine arts building.

A woman in her forties who has been described by those who knew her as petite and peppy, Colleen really didn't expect to find Dr. McCourt at his desk.

He was rarely there, she had learned from her many previous visits, preferring instead to linger in the classroom counseling his music students or to meet elsewhere with those who wanted a portion of his time. By all accounts, Dr. McCourt was a born entertainer in great demand for his knowledgeable lectures on a variety of musical subjects. So busy was he that the campus telephone operator directed those trying to find him to Colleen's supervisor, Dr. Sam Dahl, whose title was dean of the college, a position roughly equivalent to that of a provost or vice-chancellor. During her regular morning outings to C. C. White, Colleen either put Dr. McCourt's messages in his mailbox or dropped them on his desk and returned to her office.

So it was that at a few minutes before nine, she pushed open the door leading into the music office.

She very nearly fainted.

A pungent, musky odor swept up her nostrils, one that she instantly recognized as coming from something very, very old. She shivered, too, at the suddenly cooled air, hitting her as suddenly as if it had been a blast from an open window on a winter's day.

And there was silence. Absolute and total quiet. It was as if she had been struck deaf.

Gone were the noisy students chattering away on the other side of the door.

Gone, too, was the distinctive marimba and the piano playing she had been listening to as she opened the door. No more young singers' voices.

Stillness so disorienting in its completeness that every reminder of the world a few steps away had been somehow obliterated.

Within seconds, everything had changed for Colleen Buterbaugh.

What then transpired is considered one of the most intriguing cases of psychic phenomena ever reported on a college campus.

On October 3, 1963 . . . the Nebraska secretary who had lived an entirely uneventful life stepped back in time.

In a span that she later estimated was less than a minute in length, Colleen saw the campus as it had looked decades before, and watched as a music professor—*dead for over two decades*—rummaged through a music cabinet.

It was an event which, according to one person who spoke with her immediately following the events, transformed Colleen Buterbaugh from that petite and peppy, lively and outgoing mother and wife into a much more somber person, one who never fully recovered from the ordeal of her experience.

Trying to piece together the sequence of events from that long-past morning is difficult at best. The C. C. White Building was demolished years ago. Colleen herself left Lincoln some time later and her whereabouts are unknown, if she is even still alive. However, based upon interviews with college faculty members and a former college official, all of who have a thorough knowledge of her experience, including two people who spoke with her on that October day, it is possible to reconstruct the scenario of what may have happened to her nearly forty years ago.

Battling against the sharp odor and rattling cold, Colleen struggled to keep her balance and reached out to steady herself on the wooden counter directly inside the door, wondering how this daily routine, this simple errand of taking messages to the music office was now turning into something . . . well, into something very,

very peculiar. The furnishings were all familiar, but the atmosphere was unlike anything she had encountered.

As she glanced around, her attention was drawn through a connecting doorway and into the inner office. At the back of the room, a tall, dark haired woman of indeterminate age was reaching up onto a shelf appearing to be rifling through what looked at that distance like music compositions or some other printed material. She hadn't turned at Colleen's entrance, nor acknowledged in any way her presence, but rather assiduously continued her search for whatever it was that she was looking for.

The woman's back was to the door, and thus Colleen could not see her face. However, she wore a white shirtwaist blouse with lace at the collars and cuffs. A dark brown skirt reached nearly to the floor. Her heavy head of dark hair was done up in a large, tight bun in back and smaller buns over each ear.

Colleen thought the fashion oddly out of place; further, she did not remember ever seeing the woman before anywhere on campus.

In those same few seconds that she stared at the odd woman, Colleen also sensed another being there in the outer office, someone, a man perhaps, sitting at the desk to her left. There was no one in the chair but as her gaze swept across the large window on the east wall, she saw that the outside world was all wrong; the scene before her did not depict the campus that she had walked across only minutes earlier. Nor was it a campus she recognized from any period during her years as a departmental secretary.

The main campus artery of Madison Street was there as it had been since the school's founding in 1887 . . . but Colleen was looking at an avenue of packed earth and not the pavement that had been put down in the early twentieth century. The newly built Willard sorority house was not in view, as it should have been. She should also have glimpsed a corner of the Lucas Library—constructed from 1921 to '23—but it wasn't there either.

The tall, graceful trees were barely visible through the window, looking instead as if they were young saplings recently planted.

Strangest of all, although it was warm enough for an October morning in early fall, Colleen had the feeling that what she saw outside the windows was from a midsummer day on which a visitor would find the peaceful slumber of a small college campus before the beginning of a busy school year.

And then it was gone. As suddenly as this scene out of time descended when she stepped through the door, within an instant it had ended.

The mysterious woman vanished; the view out the window returned to normal; and the dank smell of something old was swept away. The room temperature moderated.

The muffled chattering of students rushing to class returned, filling the hallway with happy sounds; piano playing and marimba music filtered through the closed doors. The aspiring vocalists continued with their practice sessions.

She rushed from the room and back into the familiar hallway. It was as if *no time at all had passed.*

Bewildered. Confused. Frightened.

Colleen was all of these as she quickly retraced her steps to Dean Dahl's office in Old Main. That's when Karen Norton Cook, the director of the alumni office, saw her returning to the building. The two women were well acquainted with one another. Colleen Buterbaugh and her husband even attended Cook's wedding in 1962.

But the alumni director thought something was wrong as soon as she saw her friend.

"I had to go down to either the business office or the registrar's office, I can't recall which now. Both were on the south end of the building. As I stepped out of our office suite into the hallway, I heard the squeak of a door as it opened. That was the north door of Old Main's first-floor hallway. I turned to my right and looked down the hall. Well, here came Colleen lost in her thoughts. I wondered to myself what was wrong with her because she was as white as a sheet. She looked like she'd seen a ghost. I went on down the hall, took care of the business that I had to finish, and then went back to my office."

Karen Cook didn't say anything to Colleen when she met her in the hallway, nor did she realize at the time how perceptive she had been in speculating about the cause of her friend's troubled expression.

Within minutes, Colleen was back at her desk in Dean Dahl's office, shuffling paper and trying to type, all the while attempting to figure out what she should do.

According to Karen Cook, Colleen didn't take long in telling Dr. Dahl what had happened to her.

"Colleen went down the hall to her office and sat down. She tried to type but was so shaken she couldn't work. Dr. Dahl was in his office just south of her desk. He wanted to know what was wrong. She said she'd tell him if he wouldn't laugh. He said he wouldn't, so she told him," Cook remembers.

In a voice the dean later described as agitated, Colleen recounted her experience minutes before. The sympathetic administrator listened closely to his troubled secretary.

"Sam Dahl was a nice, gentlemanly, kind person, and not given to flights of fancy," says Dr. Roger Cognard, a professor of English at Nebraska Wesleyan, who knew the late dean and has made a careful study of the Colleen Buterbaugh incident. "He supported her story since he knew her to be a woman of calmness and reason. He had no particular reason to doubt her."

Dr. Dahl and his secretary returned to the music office to see if they could unravel the mystery. However, about halfway down the hallway in Old Main they passed Dr. E. Glen Callen, a 1919 graduate of Nebraska Wesleyan and who at that time in the early 1960s was nearing the end of his career as a professor of political science and sociology. Tragically, he was killed in an automobile accident only months later. Dr. Dahl and Colleen Buterbaugh told him the story. He didn't flinch. He said that the secretary's description of the apparition appeared to be that of Clara Urania Mills, a professor of choral music who was on the faculty from about 1912 until her untimely death thirty-one years later.

The circumstances of Professor Mills's death reflect a dedication to teaching not atypical on smaller college campuses.

On April 12, 1943, the music professor had struggled to campus from her apartment a few blocks away as a late winter blizzard buffeted Lincoln. Later historians speculated that she was somewhat behind schedule and didn't want to be late for her students in a class in music composition. She went to her office in C. C. White, sat down in a chair, took off her hat and her scarf, and then suffered a fatal heart attack. She still had her coat on when colleagues found her crumpled on the floor a few minutes later.

A single woman in her sixties, Professor Mills had taught on campus for over thirty years. Her office was across and one door down from the rooms in which Colleen Buterbaugh saw the mystery woman some twenty years and six months later.

Following the chance encounter with Dr. Callen, and a possible identification of the woman she saw, Colleen went to the alumni office and told her story to Karen Cook. "Colleen wanted to know who Clara Urania Mills was," says Cook.

Despite the improbability of the tale she told, Cook instinctively knew to believe what she heard. "She was very active, almost hyper sometimes," Cook notes. "She just loved people, always smiling and having a good time. I don't know if I would have believed her story, though, except that I saw her when she came back into the building and something had happened to her. After she came in my office and told me what happened, I said let's try to look Clara Mills up in the yearbook."

Cook had old yearbooks lined up on the bookcase against the wall. Along the top of the bookshelf were arranged several old campus photographs including some of former campus faculty members.

"As she got up from the chair and I got up from my desk, we kind of made a 'V' line to the bookcase. Her eyes got huge, her right hand came up, and she pointed to this picture of faculty in about 1914 and to one particular woman in the back row. She said that's who she had seen. So we got out the 1914 yearbook and paged through it until we found the picture that matched the woman in the picture on the shelf."

Clara Urania Mills.

"I have never doubted that Mrs. Buterbaugh saw what she thought she saw. There was no doubt in her mind that she had some sort of (psychic) experience," says Dr. David Mickey, an emeritus professor of history at Nebraska Wesleyan, and author of a three-volume history of the school. He was a faculty member in 1963 and spoke with Colleen about the incident shortly after it took place.

"I was curious because I graduated from this school in 1939 and Clara Mills died the following spring. I had known her when I was a student. She was a tall woman. Not pretty, but she wasn't homely either, a handsome woman. She was large-framed. When I knew her, of course, her hair was bobbed, but it was a heavy head of hair. She was highly regarded and well thought of."

In addition to having personally known the principals of the case, Dr. Mickey is another who has made a careful study of the Buterbaugh episode.

"There were some who felt this incident had something to do with a desire to get some attention," he says. "But I don't think Sam Dahl sensed any of this. I never heard anything like that from him. It's my understanding that it wasn't an unusual assignment for her to (go) over there to put the messages on McCourt's desk where he would find them later on. But this was the only day that she had anything like this happen."

According to the campus historian, the Scottish music professor himself didn't blink at the notion that his campus office harbored a ghost.

"He laughingly said, well, there were people who didn't want to go into the building anymore," Dr. Dickey recalls. "He said the Scottish people have those experiences all the time. He didn't know why anyone would assume they should have them all. So he went right back into his office and didn't think anything more about it."

The English professor Roger Cognard is just as perplexed in finding any sort of rational explanation for what he describes as Colleen Buterbaugh's "time warp" experience.

"Although I didn't know Buterbaugh personally, I know people who did. Our division secretary knew her as an acquaintance and some of my former colleagues who have now retired from the English department knew her pretty well. They tell me she was a reasonable, normal person, not given to this kind of thing either before or since it happened. I did know Sam Dahl. He was a straight-up guy, a kind of hardheaded Nebraskan, so I guess I would say that something did indeed happen to her. I think she saw something. I don't know what it was, but I suppose it could range all the way from a hallucination to a visitation by Clara Mills. I don't discount the possibility, although by nature I am a skeptic."

Cognard is particularly intrigued that the apparition appeared during such an ordinary errand . . . and in the middle of the morning on a busy school day. He agrees with Dr. Mickey that the secretary's time travel occurred in the course of her normal daily schedule.

"That's what makes the story so bizarre. She was in the middle of doing something very routine, not giving it much thought, and bingo—she's hit with the musty odor, the quiet, the vision and then it all goes away. From what I know about her, I'm sure she thought Dean Dahl would think she was nuts. He didn't, and so the story took on a kind of credence," Dr. Cognard reasons.

In the months and years that followed, Buterbaugh was the subject of numerous interviews by the campus and area newspapers, including the Lincoln (Nebraska) *Journal Star*. The Associated Press and United Press International picked up her story, which brought fame to the small Nebraska college, although not of the sort which may have been preferred by campus administrators.

One of the most intriguing analyses of the incident came when representatives from the famed Menninger Institute in Topeka, Kansas, interviewed Buterbaugh on several occasions.

"She had some psychiatric exams and they wrote a journal article about her," notes Professor Cognard. "I understand the bottom line was that she was pronounced normal with no history of hallucinations or anything of that sort."

Adds Karen Cook: "The Menninger people even took the yearbooks and the pictures. They had her down there. I think it was twice. Apparently, they decided that she did see something, that something happened to her over there. I thought well, I knew that because I saw her when she came back into the building."

Through the years, skeptics have suggested that Colleen Buterbaugh invented the story, or was going through a personal emotional crisis that led her to imagine the entire episode. Some of this doubt is bolstered by the slightly varying versions of the events she seems to have later told interviewers and colleagues. However, as Buterbaugh admitted herself, the entire episode lasted for a few brief moments, perhaps no longer than thirty seconds. It would be difficult for even the most astute witness to process all the information from an incident shorter than a typical television commercial.

The matter of possible marital discord in her life has been suggested as a reason she may have had emotional issues with which she was dealing at the time.

Karen Cook, however, thinks the incident and its aftermath may have actually been the cause of Buterbaugh's difficulties.

"I think this experience really ruined Colleen's life," Cook says. "I'm sure Colleen and her husband were having marital difficulties, but whether the divorce had actually been filed, I don't remember. But the whole incident seemed to have affected her. Before that, at least when I was around her, she seemed one-hundred-percent happy and peppy. I really think it must have been an awful thing to happen to her. It changed her life and not in a good way. With things happening at home, that probably just added to it. I don't think she made it up though, I really don't."

The late Dr. Mary Smith, who taught English at Nebraska Wesleyan for decades and was an authority on the Buterbaugh episode, tended to discount the authenticity of the event, citing her pending divorce, according to Dr. Cognard.

"Mary Smith said Colleen was probably emotionally upset and perhaps had hallucinated it," Cognard says, adding that he doesn't know the factual basis for his late colleague's pronouncement.

However, Professor Cognard says that in most accounts he's read, Buterbaugh seems to have been happily married with several children. "They did family things together—there was no hint of marital discord, as far as I can find. So I don't know what to say about Mary's disclaimer."

History professor David Mickey agrees with Mary Smith about Buterbaugh's personal difficulties, but doesn't think that necessarily played a role in what happened to her.

"I remember at the time Mrs. Buterbaugh may have begun divorce proceedings. There was some reason for her being somewhat perturbed. Some people found her a little flighty and excitable, I think. There was some thought that out of her distress she was trying to find some way of getting attention. But I never sensed that at all when I spoke to her."

Meanwhile, Cook says Buterbaugh did eventually divorce and move out of state, possibly to Colorado. She believes the former secretary eventually remarried, but lost track of her many years ago.

Regardless of the "reality" of what Colleen Buterbaugh did or did not see on that October morning four-plus decades ago, everyone familiar with the case agrees it had an extraordinary and long-lasting effect at Nebraska Wesleyan University.

Karen Norton Cook kept up an interest in the case until her retirement in 1990, and is still considered one of the most knowledgeable sources about the event. She collected newspaper clippings, letters, requests for information, and other material related to the case. Strangely, the neatly catalogued file disappeared about a year before her retirement. Also missing, Cook says, is the bound volume of the campus newspaper that originally reported the incident in late 1963.

The question most often asked is, has the ghost of Clara Urania Mills been seen since 1963?

Although the C. C. White Building was razed years ago, replaced by the Curtis administrative building, there are stories that Clara Mills . . . or someone . . . continues to haunt the campus.

Professor Cognard says campus lore has it that when the White building was demolished, the ghost of Clara Mills migrated to Old Main. "That's where I work and that's where Dean Dahl's office was," Cognard says. "Some students since then have said they see strange lights up in the third floor of Old Main. One or two Pinkerton guards have said they've heard odd noises, gone to investigate, but no one was there."

The professor also said tales are told that the ghost of Clara Mills has been seen walking outside her old apartment building, about two blocks from campus.

Even after four decades, Karen Norton Cook has little reservation in supporting the contention that her friend saw the ghost of Clara Mills and did, indeed, step back in time. But at the same time, she wonders why it was her friend and colleague who was the one to be visited by the ghostly music professor.

"When I was a student there, from 1952 to 1956, I used to spend a lot of time in that building because that's where the yearbook and the newspaper offices were. I worked on the yearbook staff so I was there a lot. And I had some musical background, so I thought that if that ghost were going to appear to anybody, it would have haunted me when I was there late at night, but nothing like that ever happened. But then I began to think, thank goodness it didn't, because who believes you? It just preys on your mind; it does things to your mind. I think it's too bad it happened to Colleen, but there is no doubt in my mind that she didn't create this incident in any way."

Persistent Mary

Ralph Krugler thought the evening study session with two classmates sounded like a good way to make sure one of his first college tests ended successfully. As a freshman early in his first semester at Eastern Illinois University, Ralph had only a vague idea about what professors expected from students or how to prepare for college exams. The offer by two junior women to help him study for the first test in a general education course in which they were all enrolled came as something of a relief to the young Chicago native.

"They said come on over and we'll show you what you need to study," Ralph remembers about that 1988 night on the Charleston, Illinois, campus. "It was late summer with no breeze blowing, about 85 degrees. Sweltering hot." Ralph walked over to their dormitory shortly after dinner.

The coeds lived on the third floor of Pemberton Hall, an all-female residence hall where male guests had to be escorted to and from the rooms. Ralph had met the women earlier in the semester when all three waited in line to be issued textbooks. Once they discovered they shared a class, they devised a plan to organize an informal study group.

"We were in their room," Ralph recalls. "The girls were at their desks and I was sitting on the bed closest to the door. The girl across the hall was staying in and studying, too, so we asked her if she could open her door so we could get a cross breeze from the fans. They weren't working too well. One of ours wasn't running and I think hers wasn't working either."

The trio got to work. After about an hour and a half a lull developed in their conversation.

"We were talking, throwing ideas back and forth when for some reason we all just stopped talking as you'll do sometimes when you're studying together. We were just into whatever it was we were reading, the textbooks or our notes. And then I don't know how to describe it but I wasn't concentrating on what I was reading anymore. It was a weird sensation, like I knew what I was supposed to be doing but something else was happening."

A coldness fell over the room. From somewhere above him, from somewhere on the fourth floor, he heard faint piano music. So, too, did his study mates. "They had a panicked look on their faces. I could see some of their hair standing on end. They let out a scream and ran out. I was completely perplexed. I wondered what in the hell was going on."

What in hell indeed.

Ralph Krugler believes he had his first—but not his last—encounter with the ghost of Pemberton Hall.

Eastern Illinois University's Pemberton Hall is the state's oldest public college residence hall exclusively for women, completed in 1909 under the stewardship of university president Livingston C. Lord. The hall sits within the campus' North Quad.

But "Pem Hall," as it is known, has another, far more unusual, distinction: It's the alleged abode of one of the best-known college ghosts in the Midwest.

The ghost is known simply as Mary. She was a student who was there sometime in the early 1920s. The story is told that on a spring night eight decades ago, a crazed, ax-wielding custodian bludgeoned her to death as she practiced the piano in the hall's fourth-floor music room. The killer was never apprehended. Mary has not left Pem Hall, preferring instead to glide silently through the rooms, locking and unlocking doors, turning stereos and television sets on or off, and generally busying herself with myriad mundane tasks—an ethereal housemother watching over the 225 women who live in "her" hall.

Ralph discovered another of Mary's endearing traits—that now and then she still practices on her piano on the now-locked and deserted fourth floor, in that former music room where she was murdered so many years ago. Stunned residents sometimes hear her lilting notes.

Ralph Krugler graduated from EIU in 1992 as a physical education major with an emphasis in athletic training. He is now the head trainer for the Syracuse (N.Y.) Crunch Hockey Club, an affiliate of the Vancouver Canucks NHL franchise. Despite the passage of over twenty years, he still wonders about that steamy September night when he seemed to be drawn into the world of the supernatural.

Ralph's sister was a senior when he was a freshman and had filled him in on some of the stories about Pem Hall. He acknowledges that he had been thinking about the well-known campus legend of Mary when first he visited the hall to study for that test.

"I knew about it before I ever got to campus. You have those stories in your head, but when something actually happens to you you're not thinking about that," he says, adding that he looked to some physical explanation to account for the odd sensations he went through. He thought the heat and heavy humidity, coupled with the building's lack of air-conditioning, had something to do with it.

"Maybe my mind was playing tricks on me. Maybe I was dehydrated, or had a heat illness. I knew where I was but I didn't understand everything that was going on around me."

Among the bizarre events of that night, he says, is that one of the small fans in the coeds' room stopped working ... and the broken fan started whirring! That's when he believed his mind was definitely playing tricks on him.

Ralph tried to keep on reading but the girls dashed out of the room. At first, he didn't connect his own near-delirium and the distant piano playing with his classmates' strange behavior.

"Everything was very still around me. The piano-playing was brief, maybe less than a minute, and then that stopped. The chill that had come over the room at some point and went away came back, only this time it was twice as cold as it was before. And then all of a sudden that went away, too. When it did I shook my head like I was coming to."

He looked out into the hallway. Some of the doors that he had seen shut earlier that night because the residents were out for the evening were now standing open, but he couldn't see anyone around—the floor seemed deserted.

"I walked downstairs and luckily didn't get busted because you were supposed to be escorted by one of the residents. When I got to the lobby, I came across my two friends who were with their neighbors. They were still scared, but calm. I asked what had happened up there. They asked if I hadn't heard the piano playing. I said yes, but so what? It didn't seem like a big deal because nothing bad took place. Well, they didn't want to go back up there, but one of the girls I was studying with did because she was really interested in what had happened."

The group did return to the third floor. Every door on the floor was open, Ralph says, except for the room across the hall from his friends' room. "That door was closed and locked. The girl who lived there went back down to the front desk for a room key. When we opened her door, the chairs were sitting on top of the desks. That really 'freaked' her out for the rest of the night. We didn't know if it was someone playing a prank or . . ."

Or . . . Mary letting it be known that she was around?

Several of the third-floor residents joined Ralph in going up a flight of steps to the door leading to the fourth floor . . . just in case. They found the door bolted tight, as it normally was.

While Ralph doesn't necessarily rule out a prankster being responsible for some of the strange activity—playing a tape recording of piano tunes, for instance—he does not understand his sudden confusion or why the broken fan started working. "The fan I had seen working was not even plugged in at the time," he says perplexedly, "and the outlet was at eye level. I really didn't hear the other fans working when I was in that haze. They had made a lot of sound. And the chill . . . there just wasn't any explanation for that."

He later found out that a girl living in Pem Hall, and who had been there the previous year as well, frequently found her own chair on top of her desk, or her papers and personal possessions shifted around on her desk, especially on the weekends when her roommate was out of town and the room door solidly locked. Several of her friends claimed they had found their own room doors standing open in the morning after they'd locked up the night before. But none of them had ever heard the haunting piano music.

What Ralph did not know at the time is that within a year he would have another strange encounter involving Pem Hall.

Despite the experiences of Ralph Krugler and others, the ghost of Pemberton Hall is by no means an accepted case in the annals of the paranormal. Skeptics point to two real women who lived in the early twentieth century as possible sources for the origin of stories about a haunted residence hall. However, those doubters say there is nothing in the lives or deaths of either woman to indicate that one or the other is lingering about the hall.

Mary, the ghost, may have her origin in one Mary Hawkins, a hall counselor from 1910 to 1917. A plaque in the hall's lobby honors her service to the university. However, she was not murdered, but rather died of apparently natural causes, albeit at an early age, in a Charleston city hospital.

Doris Enochs, a Pem Hall counselor in the 1970s, believes the late Miss Hawkins was the genesis for the stories. She doubts that the ghostly tales of Mary are true, "but the upperclassmen keep it as a tradition to pass on to incoming freshmen. Everyone who tells it adds more and more to it." Although she said she did not herself believe in ghosts, she admitted "some weird things happen" at Pemberton Hall.

Stella (Craft) Temple was a 1921 resident of Pem Hall. She had a different perspective on the ghostly tales.

"Those myths have no origin in dead dorm counselors or murdered coeds either," she told an EIU campus newspaper reporter several years ago. She contended that the ghost legend originated in the peculiar behavior of a thirty-year-old student and Pem Hall resident with the singular name of Eutere Sharp, a psychology major very interested in hypnotism.

According to Mrs. Temple, Eutere used to hide in the janitor's closet next to a hallway bathroom and jump out at the resident girls as they walked by, apparently to study their responses. In time, the nervous women only walked the halls in groups of three or four.

Eutere Sharp wasn't strange, Mrs. Temple said, but "she had different interests than the rest of us. Her eyes were crazy." And it was her frightening late-night prowls through Pem Hall that gave rise to the legend of a ghost, Mrs. Temple claimed.

Notwithstanding disavowals by Doris Enochs and Stella Temple, others have an equally keen belief that Mary—or *someone*—haunts the nearly century-old building.

Patty O'Neill is one who vouched for Mary. Patty believes the ghost visited her in the spring of 1981.

Midterm exams were at hand as O'Neill studied into the early morning hours. Her roommate was asleep. Before turning off the lights, O'Neill tried to lock the door, but a recent rainy spell had swollen the wood to such an extent that she couldn't shut it all the way. She decided against slamming the door shut, which would undoubtedly awaken her roommate. The women of Pem Hall were trustworthy, she reasoned. They looked after one another and respected a person's privacy. Doors were routinely left unlocked, at least during the day. So she left the door unlocked and went to bed. She turned over to doze off. Her back was to the door.

"I was in a very light sleep when I got an awful feeling that someone was watching me," she recounts. "As I turned over to look, I glanced at the lighted numbers on my clock. It was 2:15 A.M. I saw a figure standing by the side of my bed dressed in something like a long nightgown or a robe. She stood there for several seconds, then turned away. . . . She opened the door and started to leave when she turned around with one hand on the door and looked back at me for several more seconds. She left, closing the door behind her. . . ."

In the morning, O'Neill checked with other residents and learned that in two nearby rooms *locked* doors had mysteriously opened several times the previous night although no students claimed to be up and about.

O'Neill had been living in Pem Hall for three years. She did not recognize the woman she saw, nor did she ever again have a similar experience. She does not believe she was dreaming.

Is it possible that a resident, perhaps from another floor had, indeed, entered her room, either by mistake or for some more nefarious mission? The door was unlocked, after all.

The intruder, mortal or otherwise, was never identified.

Although only a very few students have admitted to seeing Mary over the years, far more have reported peculiar experiences they couldn't easily explain away.

Lucy O'Brien and several companions found all the shower curtains closed in a communal bathroom one day, yet a short time later discovered them open again. A lounge chair in the bathroom had also been moved. There was no indication water had been running in the showers and they'd neither seen nor heard anyone enter or leave the bathroom.

No one pays much attention to voices echoing from stereos, television sets, or radios playing in a residence hall—but words from some source unseen is another matter. Pattie Hockspiel and her roommate Deanne Radermacher had one such unsettling experience. Both were awakened from a deep sleep by a hoarse whisper saying either "hi" or "die," they weren't quite sure which. And they couldn't figure out where the voice came from.

Mary's exploits are so well known that some of the coeds think other spirits have now joined her from a world beyond our own. A "shadowy figure" sometimes exits through hallway doors and into a stairwell, only to vanish before an observer's eyes. Is it Mary, or one of the other two ghosts some students claim live on the abandoned fourth floor?

One is said to be a saucy "pin lady" in a long white gown. She taps on doors at night, begging for safety pins. One night several girls followed her to the fourth-floor landing where she promptly disappeared.

A "lounge ghost" overturns furniture in a recreation room every few years. In 1976, sophomore Nancy Vax recalled that a resident director found all the lounge furniture tipped over and the room in total disarray. The director ran to get help to clean up the mess. When she returned the room had been restored to perfect order.

Shirley Von Bokel, a Pem Hall resident in the early 1990s, says she had reservations about "the ghost business," yet her door swung open when no one was there. "Everybody talks about Mary," she says, "but I'm not sure if it's her spirit that's around my room because people are always coming and going" through the day and into the night.

Journalist William M. Michael decided to investigate the haunting of Pem Hall as part of a Halloween feature for his newspaper, the *Decatur Herald and Review*. He had heard the rumors about Mary and the haunted fourth floor and so determined to spend the night up there.

On a brisk mid-fall afternoon, he climbed the stairs to the top floor. He carried his sleeping bag under one arm. Fifteen curious Pem Hall residents trailed after him.

"You're not *really* going to sleep up there?" one asked incredulously.

Yes, indeed, he replied—and all night, too! It was perfect for a ghost hunt.

"The wind whooshed around the gables, rain rattled against the roof, huge leafless trees shook. The air felt heavy and musty," Michael later wrote of his experience.

"I found the music room where I would spend the night. A light in the closet was burning. Who had left it on? How long ago? Mary? Are you here? My courage began to falter, but then I remembered that Mary is a 'good' ghost—prankish, but the non-hurting type," he wrote.

Michael noted the furnishings were quite dingy; an antique piano with dust-encrusted keys looked as if it hadn't been touched in years. He spread out his sleeping bag on an old cushionless couch and settled down to await the spectral visitor.

He had just dozed off when voices awoke him.

Ah-ha! Ghosts arriving at last?

No such luck.

These voices sounded much too mortal, he thought. He hid behind the door. When it opened, he jumped out.

A group of coeds screamed and then asked him if they could all go with him on a tour to see the rest of the floor. Thus, Michael's short career as a Pem Hall tour guide was launched. Several more groups of residents made their way up the dark stairs that night. All were disappointed to find vast, unfinished rooms and a less-than-attractive music room whose floor was covered by a dirty green rug.

But to assuage their disappointment in not finding Mary, and to add to the ambiance of this pre-Halloween ghost-hunting expedition, Michael spun ghost stories until the wee hours.

Alone at last, he slept fitfully.

At a quarter past three in the morning, he was jarred awake by a pungent smell. The odor of the old couch on which he'd been sleeping had awakened him; oddly, he hadn't been aware of it earlier.

At dawn, the bleary-eyed newsman packed up to leave. As he made his way out of the hall, students crowded around to ask if he'd seen Mary.

"No," he shook his head. "I didn't see Mary, but I sure saw a lot of non-ghosts." He smiled back at his questioners. He added that he was disappointed to have missed Mary.

"Deep down, I didn't think I had . . . a ghost of a chance of meeting her anyway," he admitted, tongue only slightly in cheek.

Although no ghost showed up, there is another interesting sidelight to his overnight vigil, one that involves the late actor and folksinger Burl Ives. Michael says that he and Ives may be the only two *men* to have been publicly identified as having spent an entire night in Pem Hall. Ives attended EIU from 1927 to 1930. A campus story holds that he was seen crawling out of a first-floor Pem Hall window after a late night assignation with a comely coed. His transgression must have been forgiven. In 1986, he received an honorary doctor of humane letters degree for his many years of personal and financial support of the university. An art department building was named for him in 1990.

Ralph Krugler has a postscript to his experience that night in Pem Hall, an encounter every bit as puzzling as his first in 1988.

It came over Thanksgiving of 1989, his second year on the Charleston campus. As part of his academic instruction in athletic training, Ralph was assigned to work with the men's basketball team as an assistant trainer.

"The coach said we were going to have practice, so we had Thanksgiving Day off with a twenty-four-hour period when we could go home. We had to get back for practice Friday afternoon," he says.

He spent Thanksgiving night with his parents in Chicago and then "hustled" back to Charleston for the 2 P.M. Friday practice. Although, as a sophomore, he was still required to live in a campus dormitory, the university didn't extend that policy to vacations and wouldn't allow him to stay in the hall during that time, even though he was working with the basketball team. Instead, he arranged to stay at a friend's cousin's apartment off-campus on Friday and Saturday nights.

"The school shuts down for the holidays and most everyone takes off. It really is a deserted area," he notes.

He didn't know his friend's cousin very well, so after Friday practice he passed the remainder of the day cleaning the team's training room before heading out to find something to eat. He estimates that he left the campus at about 8 P.M. "I went to the other side of town to get some food. I then thought I'd just drive around for a while because I didn't want to hang around the apartment. I drove around Charleston and then on the way back to the apartment I decided to turn on Fourth Street, and then head up through campus and on to his apartment. I came to the intersection of Lincoln and Fourth Streets. Pemberton Hall was on my left. There was a stoplight there and I waited for it to turn green. I hadn't seen another car for the past fifteen or twenty minutes, and maybe one person out walking. I remember the clock on my radio read 10:29, so I thought, perfect, I can go back and go to bed. The light turned green. I turned left so that I was on Fourth Street."

As he rounded the corner, Ralph glanced up at the old residence hall.

A *light shone through a dusty window of the fourth floor—the level that was vacant . . . and locked.*

The rest of the building was dark.

He was stunned. There wasn't any reason for a light to be on up there. He slowed to a stop in the middle of the street, never taking his eyes from the lighted window.

"I thought, at first, maybe it was a maintenance man. The window I saw is where the fourth-floor lobby would be because it sticks out a little bit further than the other rooms. It has its own small arched roof overhead. That was the only light on so that's what made me think it was a maintenance person working up there," he says.

Ralph had the car windows rolled up against the November chill. He couldn't help but wonder why that single light was on in Pem Hall. His own experience the previous year, coupled with the stories of the hall's ghost, made him all the more curious.

"I thought that since I didn't have much else to do, I'd wait and see if anything would happen," he says. He really didn't know *what* to expect.

"Typically there isn't anyone driving around (at that time during vacations), but if there was I decided to turn off my radio and roll down the window so I could hear a car coming because after a few minutes of looking up at that light, I really didn't want to look away. I put the car in park, rolled down the window and kind of leaned myself against the door so my arms were folded on the open window."

The minutes ticked by as he leaned out his car window gazing intently at the window. The light did not dim. The notion that it was a custodian seemed hard to accept because he saw no shadows being cast, as they would have if someone had been moving about inside.

A few dozen yards down the street was a T intersection with stop signs at each corner. Ralph was parked heading east in what would be the top of the T. He hadn't pulled over to the curb so his car was in the middle of the street.

Suddenly, from within his peripheral vision and off to the right, bright headlights came from some distance down the street and in the direction his car was facing.

"I thought oh, great, here comes a car," he remembers. "For some reason it didn't seem to be coming at me nor was it turning left at the intersection. It seemed to be sitting there. I wondered what was going on with this guy. I didn't want to look away because I thought if I did, whoever was up there (in Pem Hall) would turn off the light. I kept looking at the building. Then it seemed that the car was coming at me again because the light was starting to get brighter."

There was no car noise, yet the light swelled in intensity. And it seemed to be only a single light, which Ralph thought was very odd.

"It's not that long a stretch of road. I didn't take my eyes off the fourth floor so I wasn't looking down the road to see what was coming at me. I didn't know if it was a motorcycle, a truck or what, all I knew was that the light was getting brighter and brighter. I have blue eyes so my eyes are sensitive to light anyway. My eyes were starting to hurt, but I still didn't hear any car noise. I wondered what in the hell was coming at me. I even put my hand up to shield my eyes from what it was, but even that didn't work too well. It was driving me nuts. My car was filled with light."

Frustrated and more than a little angry at the mystery driver bearing down on him, Ralph turned to look down the road.

In that split second, his sense of reality and normalcy took another hit.

"There was nothing there. The light was gone," he says. "I quickly looked back up at Pem Hall. That light was gone, too."

What in the hell is this! he thought. But more shock was to come. He looked at the clock. It read 11:06 P.M."It had been thirty-seven minutes that I'd been sitting there. It couldn't possibly have been that long—maybe ten minutes. But over a half hour? . . ." his voice trails off.

He pulled away and drove around the block where he knew there was a time and temperature sign outside a local bank. The bank time coincided with the car clock.

Ralph Krugler still cannot explain what it was that he saw coming down the street at him, nor why there was a light on in Pem Hall that night. But he steadfastly denies that it was his imagination or the result of overtiredness.

He remains sanguine and forthright about the experiences he had at EIU:

"My imagination is not that good to come up with something like that. I've always been leery about telling anybody these stories because I thought they'd think I was a crackpot. But nothing bad happened in either one of them. If people believe me that's fine; if they don't that's okay, too. I can only say that this is exactly what happened to me. It's hard not to believe in the supernatural (after this). There probably is something out there. And that does make the world a much more interesting place in which to live."

Prowling Duncan

The fraternity houses of Kansas State University in Manhattan, Kansas, have sheltered thousands of young men through the years. Here, friendships are formed that last a lifetime. Good times, replete with joy and laughter and the warmth of camaraderie, brighten the weekend hours.

But the Greek life on many campuses possesses its dark side, too. In the history of many fraternities, there lurks the story of the student who died under mysterious circumstances, either accidentally or by his own hand. Supposedly, the events took place "many years ago" and details are usually sketchy. But one day, in this or that particular fraternity house, lights will go on and off and doors will open and close on their own. The witnesses to these unexplained pranks soon begin to speculate that the disturbances are somehow associated with the earlier tragedy—the late student's ghost has returned to haunt his old fraternity.

Interestingly enough, there are fewer of these stories associated with sororities. Whether this is an issue of gender or of fewer unexplained deaths in sororities is open to speculation.

At any rate, stories of haunted fraternities have been told at Kansas State for many years. Here are the legends associated with three haunted fraternity houses at that university.

On a crisp October evening in the mid-1970s, Don Clancy hunched over his desk at Phi Gamma Delta house. It was late and most of his brothers were in bed. Clancy wished he were, too, but he hadn't finished studying. He stood up to stretch and his teeth chattered. The room had suddenly chilled. Funny, he thought. He hadn't detected it growing colder. He got up to check the thermostat.

But before he got to the wall, and from beyond the closed window, he heard footsteps crackle through the drifts of leaves on the outside flight of steps. Every fall, the large elm tree in the backyard spilled its leaves onto these steps, making it easy to hear people coming and going. But who was leaving the house at this hour? Or coming in? Clancy's clock read half past one in the morning.

He opened his door and checked the hall. No one in sight. Then he went downstairs, out the front door and around to the outside stairway near his room. It was washed in moonlight. Someone was coming down those stairs . . . he heard boots crunching the leaves on every step but he saw no one.

The young man ran back to his own room and slammed the door. He was shivering again, but it wasn't the cold at fault this time. Either his Phi Gamma Delta brothers were playing a bizarre trick on him or a ghostly walker was stalking the house.

A moment later, Clancy cracked open the door and squinted into the hall. He sensed, rather than saw, some *thing* sweeping down the corridor. But he did see quite clearly and distinctly enough that the knob of every door was being turned as the unseen walker made its way down the hall.

Don Clancy was being introduced to Duncan, the live-in ghost. He was not the only one to encounter this particular specter.

The legendary Duncan was a former student who had died in the house some years before, when the Theta Xi fraternity occupied it. Apparently, his death occurred during an initiation ceremony, but the details are, of course, sketchy.

One story holds that the pledges were bending over to be paddled, and when Duncan's turn came, he suddenly turned around and was struck in the head so hard he died. A second story attributed Duncan's death to a heart ailment. The fraternity brothers didn't know about it. During initiation rites, he suffered a fatal heart attack when he was placed in a coffin and the cover snapped shut. A third account explains that Duncan died after he fell, or was pushed, down the stairs.

"You have to take these stories with a grain of salt," noted former fraternity president Dave Dawdy. "But . . . it's pretty unnerving to stay by yourself in this house."

The first indication of Duncan's presence came shortly after Phi Gamma Delta bought the house in 1965. The room in which Theta Xi stored its pledge paddles was to be converted into a library. Two paddles had been left hanging on the wall. One of them had Duncan's name inscribed on it.

"We threw the paddles away," noted former fraternity member Rick Lawrence, "but when we started painting the wall the image of Duncan's paddle kept reappearing. We finally had to panel the wall."

Some of the brothers held a séance in the library. After they asked for a sign of Duncan's presence, one fellow started screaming. His fingernails had turned a luminous green. The men, all of whom claimed to have witnessed the phenomenon, believed that their brother was possessed by the dead man's spirit.

But of all the fraternity members, Rod Smith may have had the most chilling encounter with Duncan's ghost. Smith occupied a basement room in the house, and one night he heard a noise outside the door. He flung it open. Standing before him was a lifeless figure whose ghastly face stared vacantly at him.

Duncan is not the only fraternity house ghost to have excited young men at Kansas State.

When the Delta Sigma Phi fraternity moved into the old St. Mary's Hospital building at 1100 Fremont Street, they inherited more than bricks and mortar. Two resident ghosts came with the building—the poltergeist of a former patient and the taciturn countenance of a night nurse.

The patient was elderly George Segal. He was thought to have been the last person to die at the hospital. His death was caused by a tragic sequence of events that may have more than a little to do with his haunting.

While aged patients were being moved into a new hospital building, George rolled off his bed and became trapped between the bed frame and the wall. An attendant checking his third-floor room found it empty and assumed he had already been moved to the new facility. George died where he had fallen.

Although the Delta Sigma brothers never saw George, they heard him, even loudly at times. They credit him—or blame him, as the case may be—with turning lights on and off, opening locked doors and locked windows, and using the third-floor hallway as his own private bowling alley. But for all his irksome pranks, George has been especially helpful on other occasions, once repairing broken clocks that he had found lying around the premises.

George was apparently an ardent fan of the original *Star Trek* television series. Scott Cummins, a fraternity member in that era, explained how they came up with that unique theory:

"There was an ice storm. The electricity was off all along our street, but every day at four in the afternoon the electricity would come back on in our house and stay on until *Star Trek* was over. No other house around us had electricity. We figured that George wanted to watch the show."

What of the ghostly night nurse? She was seen but never heard.

She walked the first-floor halls of the old hospital late at night, carrying her medicine tray in one hand, a candle in the other, a faceless Florence Nightingale making her appointed rounds. She eventually learned that the new owners were not in the business of providing health care and left the building forever.

At Kansas State's Kappa Sigma fraternity house, a hanging led to the building's haunting. Or so it is believed.

Former house brother Mike Dahl recalled that years ago one of their pledges supposedly hanged himself in the file room. Since then the residents have heard all sorts of odd sounds, particularly those that sound like someone is jumping off the roof.

One night a Kappa Sigma member heard the sounds and went to his window. He crawled out onto the roof to see who it was. He found no one, nor any cause for the noises he said he heard.

On another night, several fraternity members were playing cards in the house-mother's room that was situated to one side of the front door, adjacent to a stairway that led to the second floor. Suddenly, the men heard a noise upstairs. Since it was a vacation period and the house was nearly empty, they threw down their cards and raced up the staircase to see what the commotion was. At the top of the stairs, Tom Vera said he saw a white haze that he presumed was a ghost. His companions saw nothing.

The Maid

A fraternity house at the University of Kansas at Lawrence has a ghost dating back to the era when it was home to a former Kansas governor.

Or perhaps it is only a legend created by imaginative fraternity members.

The time was a late evening in April 1911. Earlier, Governor Walter Stubbs had been called back to the statehouse in Topeka. He had arrived back at his Lawrence home after a grueling thirty-mile drive on rough roads. He rang the doorbell expecting Virginia, his maid, to answer and let him in. She didn't. He fished around in his briefcase for his own key, found it, and let himself in.

Everything was in order: Lights were burning in anticipation of his return home, even the mahogany tables glistened with a fresh coat of polish. Odd, he thought. Virginia was a conscientious worker; he found it highly unusual for her not to wait up for his arrival home from the capital.

On the way to his bedroom, he passed Virginia's room. Her door was wide open, the bed still made.

He called out, but got no answer.

He was worried now. He quickly searched the first two floors without any success. He ran up to the third-floor ballroom.

That's where he found Virginia. She was dead, hanging from a rafter.

Murder? Suicide? The house showed no signs of having been broken into and, so far as Governor Stubbs knew, she had no enemies. Her cheerful disposition certainly seemed to rule out for him that she could possibly have taken her own life. She apparently left no note as might be expected in a suicide.

An autopsy and inquest failed to resolve the circumstances of the maid's death.

The governor's family sold the house to the university's Sigma Nu fraternity in 1922.

The legend of Virginia's haunting began.

The fraternity members, of course, had heard the story of Virginia and believed her remains were entombed in the massive stone fireplace, above which hung a cryptic plaque, not unlike that found on a headstone: *The world of strife shut out, the world of love shut in.* The tablet had a blank, recessed area at the bottom where birth and death dates are commonly engraved. Funeral directors have said that such a plaque is rarely used in a home.

The hearth was dark and brooding, hardly the cheerful or inviting centerpiece found in most homes. Originally used for cooking, it opened into both an entryway and the former dining room. That side of the fireplace was walled up before the Sigma Nus bought the house.

For years after they bought it, the fraternity members reported strange goings-on in the house—two sets of distinctive footsteps running down the staircase and glimpses of a ghostly form. Stories told by the men from earlier years were remarkably similar to later tales. Most of the ghostly activity took place in April, near the anniversary of poor Virginia's death.

Some of the students, of course, ignored the noises and scoffed at the story. The huge old house was just naturally spooky, they contended, with its dark nooks and crannies and its creaking floors and stairwells.

But Dave Randall, a former resident of the Sigma Nu house, knew something not of this world might have been in that house. He, too, laughed at the stories until one particular April night. He and a friend were studying well past midnight when suddenly the silence was ruptured by the sounds of footsteps racing up and down the front and back staircases—up to the former ballroom (later converted to fraternity members' bedrooms), then down to the fireplace, making a circle through the house.

Just like a person searching for something. Or someone.

Few men were home that weekend, but Randall and his friend figured that the guys were just having a little fun running through the house, and then hiding. Annoyed, the two men figured to wait at the foot of a staircase to catch the culprits. The footsteps stopped directly in front of them.

The pair raced upstairs to the rooms of the few men there and found them all asleep. The last bedroom was in the general vicinity of where Virginia's body had been found. The room was vacant. Then the room began to rattle. The night was not windy; the windows were all shut and bolted.

Randall told a local newspaper reporter that as they left the room and walked down the hall, the bedroom light went out and the noise ceased. Going back to check, they heard the door rattling again.

"The closer we got to the door," Randall claimed, "the more violently it would shake. I have to admit, we were really terrified at that point."

His friend still thought it was their brothers perpetrating some sort of elaborate hoax and that they would find them hiding behind the rattling door. He kicked it open, but found nothing inside.

The two returned to their studies, but could not concentrate. Something impelled them to go back upstairs to the area of the old ballroom. This time they did not turn on the light as they opened the last bedroom door. A vague figure materialized, a misty form moving rhythmically against the surrounding darkness. There was a slight swishing as if tree branches brushed against the window—except there were no nearby trees.

"I was overpowered by a sense of extreme dread and terror that seemed to come from the *outside*," Randall said.

In that same year, while Randall and others were frightened nearly witless by what they thought were supernatural activities, Keith Sevidge, a fraternity member, took on the story of Virginia as a journalism class project. His extensive research seemed to indicate that the story had absolutely no basis in fact. Someone had indeed died in the house in 1911, but the young researcher could not learn the person's identity. Virginia supposedly died in April 1911, but publicly-filed death certificates were not required in the state of Kansas until later that same year. Before that time, only relatives of the deceased with an interest in the estate could obtain a copy of the death certificate.

Sevidge concluded that Virginia is a legendary figure created by earlier fraternity men to add a measure of notoriety to the old Stubbs mansion. But even he didn't sound all that convinced of his own findings when the local newspaper reported them.

"One summer, when there were only two of us in the house, we would both just get the creeps," Sevidge told a reporter.

Then there's that mysterious plaque above the fireplace. To whom or to what does it refer? It casts long shadows.

"It's a major heebie-jeebies," Sevidge agreed.

Perhaps the stories of haunted fraternity houses are merely a part of collegiate folklore, making the rounds of many campuses with only minor changes to suit the time, place, and circumstance. It is true that the macabre legend of the "fatal fraternity initiation" occurs in various forms across the country. And the other tales bear striking similarities to those told elsewhere.

Father Daniel's Poltergeist

"You may find some strange things in that room."

The priest thought the comment, aimed at him, were odd words of warning in the days before he moved into the small apartment at Bruté Hall, on the campus of Maryland's Mount Saint Mary's College.

Father Daniel Nusbaum quickly discovered the words spoken by a fellow priest and faculty colleague were all too prophetic.

"That's as much as he ever said," Father Daniel recalls. He is an historian at this oldest independent Catholic college in America. "Now that may have caused me to expect something to happen."

What did happen he retells in the calm, reassuring, and yet compelling tones that befit an academic who has spent many of his thirty-three years at the Mount collecting and retelling the ghost stories found on the Emmitsburg campus. Add to this the "strange things" he actually encountered in that room, 252 Bruté Hall, and you will discover a professor who has successfully balanced his intellectual pursuits with a more than passing curiosity in ghost stories, which include his own baffling experiences. He has documented numerous other tales from students and campus staff members.

"I really don't have an explanation for ghosts," he emphasizes. "My mindset is that they're nice stories and if this (a ghost) is what's happening, that's fine, but

I really don't feel any need to find an explanation for them. They're delightful stories but beyond that . . . well, I'm not a serious ghost chaser or ghost buster or anything like that. I can't even imagine getting involved in that sort of thing. I'm not an exorcist; I'm not trying to figure out how to make the ghosts appear or disappear or anything like that. I love to tell stories and I'm a pretty good storyteller."

Situated in the Blue Ridge Mountains of northern Maryland a handful of miles from the Appalachian Trail, Mount Saint Mary's College traces its origins to the late 1700s when French-born priest John DuBois established a church and boarding school in the wilderness north of Frederick. The formal history of Saint Mary's College and Seminary commenced in 1808 when the Society of St. Sulpice closed their preparatory seminary in Pennsylvania and transferred the students to Father DuBois' school.

The nationally ranked liberal arts college became coeducational in 1973 and is now administered by an independent board of trustees. Its nearly two thousand students enroll in one of forty-some undergraduate majors or graduate programs in business and education. A separate seminary continues to educate men for the Catholic priesthood.

But despite its sterling academic and religious reputation, the college seems to have something else that engenders more than its share of tales of mystery.

"The college, of course, is very old. And it's a small college in the mountains, in a very rural setting," Father Daniel says. "The old campus has buildings that date from the 1820s. They're wonderful old stone buildings that lend themselves to these kinds of ghost stories. Over my years here there have been about a dozen occasions when students have told me accounts that don't seem to have any logical explanation, and the students seem well-balanced."

For the most part, Father Daniel notes, the stories are gentle tales in which a spectral appearance does not bring the expected dread, such as the following episode he discovered:

"Sister Innocent had been a Mother Superior when we had a community of nuns on campus back in the 1930s. Well, of course, in time Sister Innocent died. Years later, the older nuns would hear her walking in the convent. And anytime that happened they decided that she needed to have some prayers said for her. They were never afraid of her. They offered up special prayers—nothing like an exorcism, of course, but just said a few prayers for Sister Innocent. I've talked to three different nuns who had this experience. They were very levelheaded, sensible people, and not at all frightened. They just thought, 'Well, there you have it.' "

Another anecdote told with some frequency at Mount Saint Mary's has to do with one of the priest-founders of the college.

"He was a gentle and kind character," Father Daniel says. "He's still referred to as 'the guardian angel of the Mount.' The legend around here is that he appears to distressed students to comfort them. It's very strange, but not scary at all."

The story that is most personal to Father Daniel is his own nighttime encounters with what he believes may have been a poltergeist at work in Bruté Hall. He lived in the residence hall at a time when priest/professors who made up most of the faculty lived on campus among the students.

Father Daniel had a suite with a bedroom, bathroom, and combination office/living room for about three years. His description of the anomalous events he witnessed closely parallels that of a classic poltergeist, or noisy ghost, at work.

"Regularly things would move around in the rooms," he remembers. "Especially at night when I was sleeping, objects would have been moved around (by the next morning). And these all were not events where I wondered if that's where I had put (the objects) the night before. It was obvious that they had been moved. There was a mantelpiece in the bedroom that I had a clock on. It moved from one end of the mantel to the other with great regularity. For some periods of time, it would happen nightly; at other periods, only weekly. The clock wouldn't always move the same way, it would just move, sometimes from one end of the mantel to the other; sometimes . . . it would end up in the middle. It never fell off, but other objects did. I heard it happen, but I never saw anything actually fall off. And, of course, I saw the evidence."

Amazingly enough, Father Daniel eventually accommodated himself to the peripatetic furnishings.

It wasn't just the clock that struck out on its own. His own bed was scooted about the room. Doors within the suite of rooms opened and closed of their own volition.

He was hard pressed at the time to find a logical explanation. It is no easier today, although he tries to do so.

Bruté Hall is very old, he says, so some of the movement might be attributed to the infirmities of building age. The campus itself sits on a mountainside, but earth tremors do not naturally occur there. Neither are there underground mines or mapped caves, according to the knowledgeable professor.

"What might have happened—and in my mind maybe this would explain it— Bruté is on the oceanside of a mountain slope, very nearly at the bottom. The slope has been terraced over the years as buildings were put up at the college. The configuration of the land is not natural. So, as a result, things could have been moving and settling (because of) the earth being moved and walls built."

However, there is another quandary that cannot be settled by geological speculation—Father Daniel said that as far as he knew there were no other similar problems in any other room at Bruté Hall.

Only his room, 252 . . .

Oh, yes. There is also the question of who exactly was using the apartment's bathroom in the middle of the night.

"In the little hallway off the sitting room of this apartment there was a closet on one side and the bathroom on the other side," he says about the layout of his old apartment. "I'd wake up at night because the bathroom door squeaked. It would open and the light would go on and then the door would close. I always thought that was especially weird, because why would a ghost ever need a bathroom? Or the need to turn on the light?"

Father Daniel never saw anyone or any *thing* when that happened. He'd climb out of bed, open the bathroom door and look around, switch the light off, close the door and then go back to bed. It happened infrequently enough, perhaps every few months, but the "little scenario," as he terms it, played out in the same manner each time. He asked other people living in the hall if they'd had similar experiences in their bathrooms. None had.

"After I moved out it was turned into a student's room. That's back when the priests began moving off-campus. Interestingly, students would come up to me and ask if I hadn't lived in 252 Bruté Hall. I'd say yes, and then they'd ask me if anything strange had happened to me while I was there. It turns out the same experiences were had by three or four students who spoke to me in the years following. There was some kind of force there, but again, nobody was ever frightened by it. It just seemed to be odd that things moved around by themselves or fell off shelves. After six or eight years, that was the end of it. Nobody ever reported it again, but I didn't make a point of asking."

While he thinks there could have been a natural explanation for the mystery of Bruté Hall, such as faults in an electrical wiring system that probably dated back to the 1920s, the priest says something more obvious or logical was never forthcoming.

Bruté Hall has been remodeled and repainted, but the priest's former apartment remains fundamentally unchanged. Father Daniel waits and wonders to see if there'll be any more enigmatic goings-on in 252.

Emily's Story

She was an Emily, not a Juliet. Her anonymous paramour was in all likelihood a Samuel or an Isaac and not a fellow called Romeo. But the liaison a century ago between young Emily Mather and her mysterious lover ended as badly as it had for young Montague and Miss Capulet. Yet, Emily has had a continued existence not even claimed for that daughter of fair Verona—her ghost lingers on in the very air at southeast Vermont's distinctive Marlboro College, an enclave of independently minded scholars in the foothills of the Green Mountains.

The caveat proffered by all who have heard about Emily Mather—and that includes nearly all of the small campus's 370 students, faculty, and staff—is that the story may be as thin as the air atop nearby Mount Snow. But substantial or not, Emily's tale is embedded in the culture of this small liberal arts college where "word gets around fast when unusual things happen," as one college official said. And word of what some believe is Emily's spirit has reverberated across the 300-acre campus of white clapboard buildings, woods, and fields for nearly six decades.

In the years since its founding immediately following World War Two, Marlboro College has gone through substantial remodeling to transform what was at one time a dairy farm into the closely-knit college community of today. The admissions building began its existence as a milking parlor; a main academic building was originally a cow barn. The campus takes pride in the collegial atmosphere between students and faculty. Together with staff they helped to build the campus center in 1981. Dormitories are designed to look like ski lodges and the science building includes an outdoor aviary for endangered Asian birds. Students work with faculty advisers to create their own learning plan based upon an individual's unique interests and abilities. The largest classes on campus number anywhere from ten to twenty students. The campus governance system is among the most unusual systems anywhere: A town meeting every few weeks decides college policies—from budget proposals to academic standards—with each student, professor, and staff member having an equal vote. The arts are enhanced every summer when the famed Marlboro Music Festival takes up residence.

If indeed the ghost of Emily Mather walks the halls of some Marlboro College buildings, she will find a welcoming atmosphere.

Little is actually known about young Emily, although her family is known to have lived on the farmstead that forms the center of campus life. The *story* told to all who wish to listen is that sometime in the late nineteenth century, back when the college was a working farm, Emily fell in love with a traveling salesman who called on families in small Vermont villages and on remote homesteads. When her strict parents forbade the relationship and ordered the man away, the despondent salesman threw himself into a stream and drowned. Emily found his body. Distraught over her lover's death, she sneaked into the attic of her family's home and there it was that she hanged herself. The old home where Emily is said to have died is now known as Mather House, the college's main administration building. The stream in which the nameless salesman died still flows through campus.

Suicide was such a shameful act a century ago that Emily's parents buried her in an unmarked grave below their barn, much later remodeled into Dalrymple Hall, a classroom building. There she rested until the 1950s when bulldozers slashed into the earth—and into her anonymous grave—to build Howland House, a student dormitory.

And it is in Howland House where sometimes confusing and uncomfortable events have led some to believe that Emily's razed grave forced her spirit to move among the living.

"The story is that it was my room," says recent Marlboro College graduate Kristine Lemay, who lived in Howland House as an undergraduate, including a year in the room where some believe Emily may be most active. Lemay herself expresses reservations about the veracity of Emily's ghost coming back to haunt.

Some thirty young men and women live in single, double, and triple occupancy rooms in the one-story dormitory built on a raised-ranch concept. Lemay's room was one of the three rooms on the western-side ground level of Howland. Three other rooms of similar design are on the other side.

Lemay was a History and Children's Literature major. She first heard the details about Emily Mather's ghost from a friend, Leslie Plank, who was conducting research into the legend.

"Leslie came to my room . . . and asked why the room was so freezing. Vermont weather is weird but it's not that crazy. My room was cold all the time. I even bought a space heater and had it on most of the day just so I could stay in there," Lemay says. "There were all sorts of banging noises that I chalked up to the people around me. But the problem with that is that only one wall of my room was shared with another person. The other two were outside walls and the fourth was along the hallway. I was always hearing those noises going along one of the outside walls.

Lemay admits that she didn't pay much attention to the odd sounds. She thought her neighbor might be "just having fun" although he denied responsibility. If she ran next door when the noises recommenced, she said she'd usually find him asleep or not in his room.

Lemay says Leslie was less surprised by the noises. "She asked me whether I knew that all the things I'd been complaining about were the things that Emily Mather supposedly does to people. I thought well, okay, if that's what it is . . ." she says, her voice trailing off.

Noises she tried to dismiss, but of particular annoyance to Lemay was the frequency with which items in her room would temporarily disappear. She chalked some of that up to her absentmindedness, but she said there were too many occasions for them all to be mere forgetfulness.

"It really bugged me for a while. All of my stuff was just disappearing. I'd leave something on a completely empty bookshelf and there'd be nothing there when I'd come back. I'd move absolutely everything looking for it. It was mostly minor stuff. I'd go searching for my car keys every time I wanted to leave campus. After a while I got kind of bitter about it."

The lost possessions eventually showed up, usually back in the place where she'd left them in the first place.

One of Lemay's best friends was also affected by the strangeness of the dorm room. "If she stopped by my room and I wasn't there, she would get completely 'weirded out,' " Lemay says. "She always felt like she was being watched, or she was always hearing things. It was driving her absolutely crazy. But that only happened to her in my room."

Kristine and the ghost of Emily Mather, if that's what caused the difficulties, made their peace during fall semester in a most unusual manner.

"There was a pottery auction on campus in November," Lemay remembers. "I bought an earthenware bowl a friend of mine made. I went back to my room, sat it down and put some honey and chocolate in it. I told Emily that it was for her because this was my room and she had to be nice. Most all of the problems stopped after that. I still lost things once in a while, but nowhere near when I'd have empty shelves and then suddenly things were there. Even the room warmed up. If things started getting wacky again, I'd just buy more chocolate and more honey. I guess I was paying attention to her. That's what she wanted."

With many college campus ghost stories, the reality of the haunting, both as to any factual origins of the legend and the ghost's interaction with the living, is often in dispute. And that's the case with Emily Mather at Marlboro.

"The story is probably more of an institutional legend than anything else," says one current Marlboro official. But even with that stipulation, the official added that her own experiences as a student made Emily seem more than just legend and lore: "My friend lived in a room that she was convinced was haunted, and when Kristine (Lemay) and I compared notes it turned out that it was the same room. My classmate lived in that room a good twenty-plus years before Kristine did, and the stories about it being haunted had preceded our time here by many years."

The Marlboro official said her friend often spent the night elsewhere because she could not sleep with the inexplicable thumping in her room. Other Howland residents have reported seeing the figure of a woman with long, dark hair, always with her back to witnesses, gliding down the hallways.

"I wonder if the link is the farm since the ghost story dates back to that time," asks Professor Carol Hendrickson, an anthropologist at Marlboro College. She was the instructor who supervised Leslie Plank in researching the ghost of Emily Mather. One of her interests is how legends and stories relate to particular *places*, such as college campuses.

"To live in a dormitory is to live in a place where there are recycled spirits in a sense. You change rooms every year and if you have any sense of prior bodies moving through space you've got literally hundreds of them in a dorm room. But it doesn't seem that students think about them or worry about them too much. It's just when something horrible happens—like death—that something sticks at a site, or it might become activated, or troubling, or interesting, or story-worthy."

Hendrickson believes that stories passed down orally through many generations can change shape and content. Since Marlboro is dealing with "far renditions" of Emily Mather's death—that is the actual event took place a very, very long time ago—it is difficult for contemporary researchers to know what might or might not have happened between the young woman and the salesman, if indeed the affair occurred in the first place. Nevertheless, Hendrickson sees some parallels between

Emily's story and the college-age recipients of her supposed visits.

"I fall back on the notion of events sticking somehow to a particular site. And then that is crossed with a certain interest in, or revulsion by, or scare tactics associated with death that in this case is a violent kind of death. Emily was a young woman, much like a college student, who maybe hung herself. This wasn't an old lady dying of a bad cough. College students go through very traumatic shifts in their own personal and academic lives. Here they have a story of one person who likewise went through something horrible and had a kind-of answer. The story even has some overtones of *Romeo and Juliet*."

Hendrickson says that from childhood on, people sometimes have a sense that part of their lives remain with material possessions.

"Why do I have such a hard time throwing out my own used clothing?" she asks by way of example. "Because I think some essence of myself is attached to it? I wonder—is that a ghost? Is that not a ghost? People do imbue the things they use and the places they pass through. I back off using the word 'ghost,' but I, personally, see all sorts of ways that lives that have touched objects or places imbue those places or objects with their resonance. Whether you label them ghosts or not, it's up to you."

From whatever sources the reverberations in Kristine Lemay's room derived, she accepted the events calmly and with good humor.

"Emily and I made our peace pretty quickly," she says.

Honey and chocolate might become the ghost-laying tool of choice in future Marlboro College ghostly disturbances.

Incident at Scott Hall

Until recently, the undergraduates at Ripon College never lacked for a setting in which to tell their own ghost stories—the campus once sponsored an informal, annual ghost-storytelling get-together, usually around Halloween. It was the one event that was never hard to fill. Students asked early each school year if it had yet been scheduled, a former residence hall director noted.

Writer Beverly Christ documented many of Ripon's ghost legends. She began her investigation as part of a research paper during her senior year there.

"Upper-class students often enjoy filling in new students about Ripon College ghost lore," Christ says. Returning alums reminisce with undergraduates about the stories they heard back when they were students. Sometimes stories are passed down from parent to child. One coed knew of a purportedly haunted local cemetery and a ghost in a campus building from her parents who had attended Ripon in the 1970s. A recent graduate said that his great-aunt had seen a campus apparition back in 1917!

But the ghosts here are not all historical revenants—most are as recent as today on this picturesque campus in Ripon, the small Wisconsin city famed as the birthplace of the Republican Party.

"Some of the most compelling stories for me were the ones I heard directly from the person experiencing the event," Christ says. "For them, ghost stories are not just 'fun and games,' and they may not be all that anxious to talk about their experiences. In some cases, they seem to be sorting through what happened and I could sense their discomfort as they told me the story. Their reputation is (also) on the line . . . knowing that other people may not believe it's true."

The story she found most credible, the tale "I most often remember as I lay awake at 2 A.M.," she says, concerns a former student and his unsettling experience in Scott Hall, a campus dormitory.

"Bill's* story certainly kept my attention," Christ says of the former varsity football player at Ripon, whom she first heard about a few weeks after his peculiar experience in the fall of 1993. He asked that his identity not be revealed. "He had been very skeptical of anything like ghost stories. His initial reluctance to talk made his story all the more convincing to me—that, and the way he told the story: voice a little shaky at first, nervously cracking his knuckles, catching his breath. One of the first things Bill made clear was that he had told very few people about his experience. He didn't like to talk about it to others."

Bill told Christ that the incident "really spooked him. He was really messed up for a couple of days."

What took place in Ripon College's Scott Hall?

It was an October night during Bill's freshman year at Ripon. He had just returned to classes following his grandfather's funeral in another city. He and Ken,* his roommate, shared ground-level quarters in the hall, which was scheduled to undergo renovation at the time. The two young men had grown up together. Bill said he would trust his friend "with my life."

"It takes somebody with a hammer to wake me up," Bill said jokingly of his sleep habits. But Ken, he said, was different. "My roommate is really a light sleeper. He wakes up when somebody sneezes three doors down. That's what surprised me throughout this whole thing."

The "whole thing" Bill refers to began when he woke up because someone was calling his name.

"There was something standing in the door," he remembered. The person was gray and very tall, but only the top half of the figure was visible. What startled Bill the most is that it was wearing his high school varsity letter jacket!

As a football player at Ripon, Bill was entitled to wear a college letter jacket but hadn't received his yet. Instead, he wore his high school jacket. Each day he followed the same routine when he got back to his room. "I always did the same thing right before I went to bed," he says, which was closing the closet door and hanging the jacket on the doorknob. He had done exactly that on this evening.

He figured the voice and the figure were products of a long day spent studying and went back to sleep.

The voice came again, loudly and insistently—"Bill"—"enough to shake me awake," he says.

He blinked his eyes open. The towering gray figure now was looming over him next to the bed, its face indistinct, its arms so long that the jacket cuffs came just partway down the two pale forearms.

"But all I could focus on was the jacket," he says. He could see his own name stitched on the jacket. As he rubbed his eyes "trying to shake the cobwebs out," the dorm door swung shut. Odd, because it had been locked when they went to bed. The mysterious visitor had vanished.

Bill got up to check the hallway. He thought that a friend was playing a nasty trick on him. As he looked out, the bathroom door farther down the hall closed.

*Name has been changed.

"Come on Pete, what are you doing?" Bill yelled as he treaded down the hall and into the bathroom.

His letter jacket was hanging from a stall door.

He grabbed the jacket and headed for the door. He heard the voice again, softly this time, as if coming from a great distance.

"That just froze me. Somebody was talking to me, 'Stop destroying my house. Stop messing with my house. You're ruining it.' I said aloud, 'Ruining what?' But (the voice) was gone."

Bill got back to his room. Ken snapped awake as soon as he walked through the door. "Now, what I can't figure out is how come he didn't wake up when I left? Like I said, he wakes up on anything."

Bill filled him in on what had just occurred. Ken wondered in particular why his good friend was carrying his old letter jacket.

The following day, Bill related the story to the hall's resident assistant who advised him to speak with a university employee about the matter, a woman with some knowledge of the supernatural.

"I didn't really believe in stuff like that. Ghosts are just something that you see in movies, and people tell (ghost stories) around the campfire," he said. But the counselor had other ideas. She told him that his generous nature and helpfulness were partially responsible for his encounter with the ghost in Scott Hall, that and his grandfather's recent death. He subconsciously wanted to contact the "other side," she told him. The ghost would probably return that night, she added.

Oh, boy! Bill thought.

He needn't have worried. Although something *did* indeed occur that night, Bill didn't remember it at all—he was sleep*walking* and sleep*talking* through the entire incident. His roommate Ken was the sole witness.

Sometime in the middle of the night, Ken suddenly woke up when he heard Bill jump out of bed, thrashing around as if trying to grab someone. Suddenly he was against the door, pushing on it, as if struggling to hold it closed against some outside force.

At the same time, Bill started talking out loud about what it was he was fighting against, just as if he were wide-awake and lecturing Ken on some event they were both witnessing. There was a malevolent spirit present, he intoned. It was someone who had lived on Ken's side of the room sometime in the past. It wanted him out of the building. The struggle to keep the spirit out of the room by holding fast against the door lasted about fifteen minutes, Bill later learned, before he relaxed and went back to bed.

"It's all right now," Bill told his dumbfounded friend, and then fell promptly sound asleep.

"I don't remember saying a word," Bill said. "I don't remember any of this. My roommate—I grew up with him—I can never imagine him making something up like this."

Two more pieces of evidence make Bill believe Ken's account of the nighttime struggle.

When he woke up on the morning after the alleged struggle, he noticed that one arm was bruised and especially sore. "I don't bruise easily," he claims.

There's also the matter of the soundness of his sleep. "I can't understand how it woke me up because usually people have to shake me."

The two roommates stayed together the rest of the year . . . and nothing more happened.

When Bill told his story to writer Bev Christ, he emphasized that he tried mightily to find a sensible, logical explanation for the events. He could not.

"I thought for sure it was my buddies trying to play jokes on me," he said. "It could have been somebody just playing with me, but I don't know how they did it."

What he couldn't figure out is how someone could have gotten into his room, taken his letter jacket, and then put it into the bathroom without him seeing the culprit. Further, he didn't know why his roommate would fabricate such a yarn and then never reveal its falsity.

"I saw it—I saw something I can't explain. At first I thought it was just my imagination, but when my roommate got involved . . ."

Bill and Ken's experiences at Ripon are not isolated incidents. During her research, Beverly Christ discovered that the college's ghostly tradition stretches back decades and involves a number of campus locales.

Former students believe a ghost in Bartlett Hall was once quite active, especially during the 1970s. But it may no longer be in residence. Odd noises came from the attic of this former residence hall, now used for college offices. Footsteps and the grating of furniture being dragged across the floorboards commonly drifted down from the unoccupied top level. Whenever students went up to investigate, however, a thick layer of dust provided evidence that nothing *physical* had been there for a very long time. Ever since an extensive remodeling, the unexplained noises have ceased.

No one seems to know the name of the history professor who "died unexpectedly" yet continued to keep office hours. Students saw the lights burning in his locked office late at night for several days in a row. The students knew the professor habitually worked well past the time when most of his colleagues had stopped for the day. After friends cleaned out his office, the lights were never seen again.

College Days is Ripon's student newspaper. As is the situation with most college newspapers, student reporters and editors work well past midnight on those days preceding a deadline. But it's not every newspaper staffer who hears her name whispered aloud . . . when she is quite definitely alone in the office.

That's what happened to one student editor at Ripon. Someone called her name in a loud whisper "like someone would sound if they were trying to scare you," she recounted. The building was empty save for her in the newspaper office.

Some other newspaper staff members have said footsteps echoing down the empty hallways are not uncommon, as is the distinct scraping of furniture across the marble floors of locked and empty rooms. One time the door to the newspaper office slammed shut "for no explicable reason."

The young woman who heard her name called out thought it might have been a "trick of the mind," but she hasn't stayed late since the incident.

Perhaps it was the former ghost of Bartlett Hall who moved to the college newspaper office and took up journalism.

The newspaper also played a central role in publicizing another Ripon College ghost legend and, even though it was featured in an April Fool's issue of the weekly, there may be more truth to this story than editors had at first suspected.

Tri-Dorms is a student residence hall on campus that, according to Christ, is "a hotbed of current supernatural activity." Whether the doings are real or the product of some overactive imagination is open to debate, but one hall manager told Christ, "we have had some strange occurrences, or rumors of strange occurrences."

One odd presence has been dubbed the "basketball dribbler."

Students on the second floor have heard someone on the level above bouncing what sounded like a basketball. But whenever someone went upstairs to complain either no one was around or students on that floor were gathered elsewhere for a group meeting. However, some students maintain that what is being heard is not something from beyond the grave—it is the old heating system.

Another student said she and her roommate returned from a fall break to find their irons in the middle of their suite's floor and their wall mirrors cracked. The room had been locked. The hall director didn't know the girls well enough to play such a joke on them.

A former resident director told Bev Christ a particularly chilling story about this dormitory:

Once, after the hall closed for vacation, the director made his usual round of room inspections. He had an established methodology of going down one side of a hall checking room by room. The vacated students left the doors open. After he inspected each room, he would close the door. But time after time—especially on the top floor—he stepped out of the last room on one side of the hall, looked back and saw each and every door standing wide open. Doors that he had shut tightly minutes before. He had the only remaining keys. He eventually left and came back later with a colleague to finish the job.

Bovay residence hall has a three-decade-long reputation for being haunted. The reason appears to be the unfortunate death in an automobile accident of a young fraternity member who once lived there. Students who later moved into his room had problems with unexplained tapping at the door several times each night. On one occasion, the student living in the room was convinced someone was trying to play a practical joke. He waited quietly just inside the door until the tapping resumed. He flung open the door ready to pounce on the culprit. The hallway was empty. As he thought about the incident later on, he realized he hadn't seen a shadow cast by the hall light in the crack below the door as he normally would when someone called upon him.

The fraternity member's death was memorialized in a plaque that hung in a Bovay Hall lounge. For several years after his death, students claimed it would take wing and fly off the wall, or objects on a lounge shelf fell off without explanation. Both events ceased at about the time the student would have graduated.

The stories from Bovay Hall were so widely accepted that a top administrator at the college was "absolutely convinced . . . there was no question in his mind" that the student's ghost was causing the problems, according to writer Christ.

Ripon's striking Rodman Center for the Arts includes an art gallery, sculpture garden, theatre and a recital hall. A $1.1 million addition created a singular home for the fine arts on the Ripon campus. But that doesn't preclude it from being included on the informal college ghost tour. In addition to Raphael, the theatre's ghost, detailed elsewhere in this chapter, several students insist there is a "ghostly presence swirling through the recital hall," although details are sketchy.

The college's "archives ghost" presented itself just once, and that was to a young woman as she worked unaccompanied in the archives office. She heard the rustling of paper and then saw an iridescent figure on the far side of the storage room. She was standing near the only entrance. And exit.

An archives staff member thought the ghost might have been that of Sam Pedrick, a Ripon alumnus and later a college trustee. He developed a sizable collection of city and campus historical records. The city section of the collection had recently been sent to the local historical society. The spirit probably became agitated by the move, speculated Bev Christ, and so he made his presence known. Staff members decided it was a friendly ghost. They talked of him as "Sam" or "Mr. Pedrick" from then on. They're still waiting for the collector to make a return visit.

For her part, and despite spending countless hours interviewing Ripon students, faculty, and staff about campus hauntings, Bev Christ is neither more nor less skeptical than she was before her ghostly investigation.

"I've not had any dramatic experiences myself, but I do think there is more to the world than what we know with our five senses. I think there might be a kind of dimension or life force even after a person dies. I was somewhat skeptical going in, yet more or less open (to the idea that a haunting is possible)," Christ says today. "If I ever did see something myself, that would really shake me up."

Ghosts in the Footlights

Lavender Annie

Theatre folk are a notoriously superstitious lot. No actor wants to be wished "good luck" on opening night. That innocent greeting will surely spell disaster. Instead, one proposes to a nervous player that he "break a leg" or "be brilliant" in performance.

Whistling anywhere in the theatre is bad luck.

The production history of William Shakespeare's *Macbeth* is noted for being ill-fated. Most stage veterans refer to it as simply "the Scottish play" or "*that* play*."

Playwright Noel Coward was asked if he had any superstitions. Yes, he is said to have replied, it is unlucky to sleep thirteen to a bed.

Perhaps the strangest superstition of all has been attributed to a Viennese actress of the nineteenth century: She never stepped on stage without a white mouse tucked inside her bodice. Fellow actors swear they saw the tiny rodent nightly peering contentedly from its remarkable lair.

The Annie Russell Theatre at Rollins College in Winter Park, Florida, has a theatrical superstition all its own. It is said that the theatre's actress namesake— now dead these nearly seventy years—will show herself between midnight and 1 A.M. on the Wednesday before a play opens—*if* the show is to be a success. Should Annie absent herself from the proceedings, ill fortune befalls actors and production alike.

The English-born Annie Russell rose to prominence in the late nineteenth century following her New York stage debut in the 1870s while still a teenager. A contemporary of Lillian Russell, although no relation, Annie starred in over sixty professional productions during her lifetime. Among her most notable achievements was originating the title role in George Bernard Shaw's premiere 1905 Court Theatre production of *Major Barbara*.

She also served as the real-life inspiration for Dan Beard's illustration of the character "Sandy" in Mark Twain's *A Connecticut Yankee*, published in 1889.

Annie retired to Winter Park in 1928, but the theatre continued to draw her love and devotion . . .

Mrs. Mary Curtis Bok Zimbalist, a daughter of publisher Cyrus Curtis and a noted patron of the arts in her own right, decided to build a theatre at Rollins College so that her dear friend Annie Russell would have a stage upon which to perform during her waning years. Annie was sixty-seven years old at the time. The Mediterranean-style theatre was dedicated on May 29, 1932, with a production of Robert Browning's *A Balcony*. Of course, it featured Annie Russell. Until her death four years later, she managed the theatre, directed, and starred in plays. During that time she also founded two performing groups at Rollins: the Annie Russell Company, with local citizens, faculty, and students in the plays; and the Student Company, comprised solely of Rollins College undergraduates.

The year 2002 marks the seventieth anniversary of the Annie Russell Theatre, and during most of those decades, stories of the *haunting* of the theatre have been told and retold by alumni, faculty, and undergraduates. Most seem to believe that the ghost is that of Annie Russell continuing to hold center stage in her theatre, although a distinguished-looking Edwardian gentleman makes an occasional appearance. He may have been one of her admirers in those long-ago days when Annie was the toast of Broadway and London's West End.

Tradition ascribes Annie's ghost as being clad in a lavender, floor-length Victorian-era gown with ample lace and modest décolleté. Although contemporaneous photographs picture her unsmilingly—with rather stern, almost schoolmarm features—her ghost is quite friendly, given to playing games and mothering "her" young actors as they learn the art and craft of acting—a passion to which she was devoted.

In the late 1990s, a young actress fell asleep late one night on the sofa in the green room, the place where actors try to relax as they wait for their call to go onstage. When she awoke early the next morning, the coed found that a blanket had been carefully placed over her. A chair was pulled up next to the sofa, a chair that had been on the other side of the room the night before. Although the student asked around, no one had been in the room after she went to sleep. With a knowing nod, those to whom she told the story thought that it had to be Annie there to look after her.

While the uninitiated suspect that sudden indications of a ghostly presence warrant a hasty retreat, all of those who speak of an experience with Annie Russell say hers is a soothing presence. It might be a quick pat on the back for a nice performance—though the hand is unseen—a distant thud to let the stage crew know that Annie's keeping watch as they put the finishing touches on a set as the new day's sun breaks the horizon, or even a rocking chair swaying in the corner of a dressing room. Whatever the method, Annie is never far away.

Such kindheartedness should warrant special treatment, and Annie receives that by making it known she has her favorite seats from which to watch her young charges perform. She likes to keep those available for her exclusive use.

However, there is some disagreement about which seat is her favorite.

Some think the seats are in the balcony, third row up on the aisle as you look from the stage. Others say it is a seat in the second row, the third one in. Theatre professor Jim Fulton told a campus newspaper reporter that he thought she sits in the balcony because his dog always ran to that chair, sat on its haunches and stared. The seat has, on occasion, flipped down and stayed in that position, as if somebody was sitting on it.

Whichever seat she occupies, the signs are everywhere that Annie is a benevolent spirit. Despite the occasional startled reaction from students or faculty, her legendary exploits befit a doyenne of the classical theatre.

A theatre major sighted Annie's ghost on a spring night in 1978. The young woman was in the corridor outside the main theatre when an elderly woman walked by her. Thinking that here was a campus visitor in need of some help, the actress tried unsuccessfully to engage the older woman in conversation; a "weird stare" was her only reply. But even for a theatre major accustomed to interesting fashion statements, the actress could hardly be blasé about the strange visitor's floor-length mauve dress. Later, she learned that while a friend finished painting a stage set, she had seen the same woman looking down at her from the balcony. Neither person ever saw the old woman after that.

A stagehand was high atop a ladder adjusting some lights when someone tugged at his trousers. He shook off the hand and climbed higher. The tugging continued until his hand touched a live wire and the shock knocked him from the ladder. His colleagues rushed to call an ambulance, but were told one was already on the way. Someone had apparently telephoned. Emergency workers were there within a few minutes. The injured man recovered completely. Most suspect Annie was upset that he ignored her warnings and made the call.

Annie is not shy about appraising the performances and plays at her theatre. Two student actors were rehearsing a scene from Cole Porter's musical *Anything Goes*, "just goofing around," one of them later said, when the sound of a single person clapping came from somewhere in the darkened house. They leaped off the stage to see who was watching but found they were still very much alone.

When the college staged Agatha Christie's *Ten Little Indians*, a table centerpiece of the little Indians was stage center. The idea was that one of the small figurines was broken as each stage murder is committed. For three nights in a row after the curtain fell, all the figures on a new centerpiece put in place for the next night's performance were later found smashed. On that first night, the technical director had left about 2 A.M. When he returned later that morning, each Indian on the centerpiece was broken. The same thing happened the next night. Finally, on the third night, he left about 2 A.M., after having replaced the Indians. He hurriedly returned about half an hour later. All but one of the Indians was broken. For the remaining performances, the Indian figures were replaced just before the curtain was raised.

Steve Neilson was a theatre professor at Rollins before he became a campus administrator. He told the student newspaper of two incidents that made him believe "there is a presence in the theatre." High on a backstage wall, some fifteen feet above the stage floor, is a doorway, a "door to nowhere" in Professor Nielson's words. During a performance of *Oliver!*, he was helping crew members turn a revolving stage platform when he heard the distinct strains of a xylophone coming through that doorway high on the wall.

Another professor thinks that is the doorway Annie Russell uses to make her occasional entrances and exits. The legend holds that the door is open during a performance if she is present. That same professor said he thought Annie liked to play games. In his office was a high window. When he came to work early in the morning, he'd hear a tap-tap-tapping at the window. Finally, he figured out what the problem was: he was not being deferential enough to Annie Russell. It ceased when he bid her a daily "Good Morning!"

The second Rollins College ghost, a gentleman revenant, has not been identified any further than that.

He may move between the Annie Russell Theatre and another college facility, the Fred Stone Theatre in a converted Baptist church. One student says that he was backstage at The Fred during a performance when he looked above the stage. A work light is usually kept on up there.

"At first I just saw a shadow pass over the passageway to the attic. I looked up there again," he told a reporter. "It sounds kind of corny, but there was a little gray patch standing there out of place. I could see through it. I could feel it looking down at me. It gave me goosebumps."

Back at the Annie Russell, student Tiffany Scott told a reporter she was trying to locate some objects when she was run out of the traps area under the stage by a gruff male voice.

"Hey, come here!" someone growled at her as she quickly turned around and bravely set off to find out who was trying to scare her. Her quick search proved futile.

"Come here!" again cried someone in the same hoarse whisper, only it was louder and much closer by now.

Tiffany hurriedly flipped off the last light as she headed toward the door.

"Hey! Hey! Come back here!" came the trailing voice.

Tiffany didn't look around.

If there is indeed more than one ghost in this theatre, pray that the one you meet is affable Annie Russell. Her male counterpart seems something less than welcoming.

Elmo's Ire

The silly laughter floated down a hallway in the old theatre building. The two students working late on the next production stopped what they were doing and stared off toward the sound of the sniggering laughter. Their glances at each other wordlessly said what both of them knew to be true—they were the only ones in Mitchell Hall that night. One of them hefted a length of steel pipe and they both crept down the hall toward the storeroom from which the incongruous laughing seemed to be coming. Together they pushed open the single door. The laughter suddenly stopped.

Mirth and joviality are fully expected on college theatre stages across the nation. But at Mitchell Hall on the University of Delaware campus, at least some of those gleeful outbursts may come from the resident ghost, a chap nicknamed Elmo whose legendary appearances on the Newark campus date back several decades.

Built in 1924, Mitchell Hall is an impressive brick edifice that fronts the university's long mall. A wide set of stone steps sweeps up to the three main entrance doors, arrayed grandly beneath an elaborate cornice.

"The story is that a workman by the name of Elmo was working under the dome at the top of the building when the scaffolding he was on collapsed and the poor fellow fell about forty feet to his death across the chairs in the hall," says Ed Okonowicz, a former university official and a collector of Delaware ghost tales. "His ghost is believed to haunt the theatre. There have been the 'usual' occurrences—the footsteps, lights turning on and off. And for some strange reason two small children sometimes appear in the balcony of the theatre. Who knows what they have to do with Elmo?"

Elmo seems to be one of the harmless genuses of phantasms. However, the sudden suggestion of his imminent attendance is alarming to those unacquainted with his mischief.

Such as that 3 A.M. hour some years ago when a student technician was putting the final changes on one of his stagecraft assignments. As he wrapped up, he jumped nearly out of his skin when he heard a saw spring to life in a scene shop on the floor above. He raced up to the room and flipped on the light. As he did so, the shop's saber saw stopped whirring. No one else had been in the building for several hours.

Whatever prowls Mitchell Hall also seems to leave a trail of chilled air. One student claims that after he programmed the lighting board computer, the temperature inside the light booth dropped "about twenty degrees for a second and then returned to normal." The small booth has no ventilation ducts and the door was closed.

Elsewhere, a Mitchell Hall classroom, where footsteps have been heard scraping between the rows of chairs, has a full-time cold spot for which no one can give an explanation.

Elmo has a voice, too, at least that's what one young Delaware theatre major thought when she heard her name whispered backstage during a play rehearsal. "I said, 'What?' but no one answered. Then I heard my name spoken again," she said of the incident. "This time I went to the door to ask the people who were rehearsing if they had called me. Just as I did, the eighteen-foot lead pipe that was leaning against the wall fell where I had been working on the set."

The identities of the children—and perhaps others—that haunt the balcony of the vintage theatre have never been established. But they're there, former theatre students attest.

"The director was talking with us about the show when I heard this heavy asthmatic-like breathing coming from the balcony," says Elena,* a theatre major in the late 1970s. Several students looked around for the source but couldn't find anything to explain it.

An actress in 1984 is said to have actually seen the two small children in the theatre balcony. She was rehearsing on stage when something made her glance toward the upper reaches of the house. A little boy and a little girl holding hands and dressed in pajamas stared down at her. And just as quickly as they appeared they vanished.

Former theatre department chairman Peter Vagenas told the campus newspaper that although he thought at least some of the incidents with lights being left on could be attributed to forgetful undergraduates, he had personally experienced

*Name has been changed.

"lights inexplicably left on . . . strange voices in the theatre, but nothing frightening" to him personally.

Perhaps one campus staff member had the most appropriate reason for believing Elmo and his spectral cohorts most certainly do linger there: "Theatre is filled with so much creativity and imagination that ghosts and ghost stories are inevitable."

They certainly are at the University of Delaware.

Raphael of Ripon

In the classic American comedy *Harvey*, the title character is an eight-foot-tall rabbit invisible to everyone except his friend Elwood P. Dowd. Stage productions of Mary Chase's delightful play rarely, if ever, include an actor portraying Harvey; he remains unseen even to the audience. However, Ripon College may hold a unique distinction when it comes to that play. According to the official history of Ripon, a production of *Harvey* in the speech and drama department's former home at an old Lutheran Church featured a ghost in the role of Harvey!

Raphael is the theater ghost at the Wisconsin college, and he's been around since at least 1964, according to researcher Bev Christ, who also describes him as the most well-known ghost on campus. "People still talk about him," she says.

The old church was razed when the drama department moved into Benstead Theatre. The college's history notes that "unfortunately, the . . . razing dispossessed Raphael, the ghost who had turned lights on and off, locked students out in the cold and rung bells in the . . . church." Just how or why theatregoers thought Raphael decided to take the usually nonexistent role of Harvey himself is not clear.

The theatre ghost apparently made his first appearance when the school's Red Barn Theater burned in 1964, Christ said. A former theater professor told her that Raphael was even blamed for the fire "since no other explanation was ever found." That's when the theatre moved into the former church.

No one seems to know why the ghost is named Raphael, although it may be as simple as a student pulling the name out of thin air when some odd activities occurred in the church. Former students claimed there were "spooky" sounds late at night, especially from the basement or spire. A Ripon professor who also attended the school as an undergraduate said late night theater students heard frequent footsteps.

The Ripon theatre is now in Rodman Center. Did Raphael move along into the new quarters? Apparently so, researcher Christ discovered.

Students say electric plugs left in wall sockets are found lying about on the floor. Locked doors have been found ajar with the room lights on.

One student said she had actually *seen* Raphael. She was sitting in the theatre house between classes when she had a sort of prickly sensation that someone was watching her. She looked up and saw an iridescent glow in a doorframe leading into the theatre. After a moment the glow disappeared without a sound. She hasn't seen it since.

The case may still be open for a haunting at Ripon College's theater, but there is a firm belief in Raphael's presence. Alumni, students, and faculty who know of him are quite possessive. "He is 'our' theatre ghost," Christ said.

What's in a Name?

Millikin University in Decatur, Illinois, and Kansas's Emporia State University hundreds of miles to the west would seem to have little in common.

The Illinois school is one of the first private comprehensive liberal arts universities in the nation, founded in 1901 by the Presbyterian Church. From its beginnings Millikin, about thirty-five miles east of Springfield, in central Illinois, has sought to combine the purely academic pursuit of knowledge with innovative approaches to practical and vocational educational opportunities.

Emporia State, on the other hand, started life as the Kansas State Normal School when President Lyman B. Kellogg opened its doors in 1865. The school had but a single book—a dictionary. Today the campus in east central Kansas, midway between Kansas City and Wichita, enrolls nearly six thousand students in a variety of undergraduate and graduate programs.

But for those in pursuit of American college ghost yarns, the two universities have an odd relationship—both have theatres named for one Albert Reynolds Taylor, a faculty member and administrator at both campuses, albeit at different times in his life. Both theatres are haunted.

During the earlier years of his academic career, Dr. Taylor was a faculty member, and later president, of Emporia State. In 1901, however, he left Kansas to become the first president at Millikin University, founded in that year by James Millikin, a Decatur businessman and entrepreneur.

Dr. Taylor may also be unique in that he served Millikin as president three times in his life—first from 1901 to 1913, then again during two difficult periods for the university, from 1915 to 1919 and in May 1924. He died in 1929 at age 82. His funeral was held at Millikin's Schilling Hall, the central campus building, inside at what was then Assembly Hall, later renamed Albert Taylor Hall in his honor. His interment was in Emporia.

Which campus can lay claim to having the *first* haunted Albert Taylor Hall is imprecise. Both legends have been around for years. However, the ghost stories associated with Emporia's Taylor Hall go back at least four decades, while Millikin's appear to be of a somewhat more recent vintage. The other unique aspect of the Kansas school is that the ghost of Dr. Taylor himself was thought to haunt his namesake, although the veracity of those accounts is doubtful.

At Emporia, Albert Taylor Hall is one of four theatre facilities used for performances. The 1,200-seat auditorium is most commonly the site of large-scale musicals, such as *The Sound of Music*, staged there in 2001. According to campus legend, Taylor Hall is thought to be the repository of several ghosts: Dr. Taylor it is alleged; the spirit of Franklin L. Gilson, founder of the Gilson Players and considered a "father" of theatre at Emporia; and a mystery couple who linger on the iron catwalks above the stage.

With Dr. Taylor's suspected ghostly tenure at Emporia, there is first, the *legend*, passed on to countless theatre students over the decades, and then there are the known *facts*. The two are not always complementary.

The legend: During his years at Emporia Dr. Taylor took a leading role in a theatre production. The name of the play is not known. One evening, fearing he'd be late to go onstage, he dressed in his stage costume at home—a glittering white suit with a cape and a colored neckerchief. He jumped into his fliver, one of the first in the region, and sped toward campus. He crashed head-on into another car. Both Taylor and the other driver were killed instantly. At curtain time, the *ghost* of Albert Taylor appeared onstage, wearing the glittering costume . . . stained with blood. The performance was immediately canceled. But Dr. Taylor continues to appear in and out of costume on an infrequent basis.

The facts: There appears to be little, if any, truth to this story.

Of course, Dr. Taylor did not die in an Emporia car crash—it's doubtful that he even owned an early automobile in those years before 1901 when the horse and buggy was still the preferred mode of transportation. As is well known, he resigned from his longtime position at Emporia at the close of the 1900–1901 school year to become the president at Millikin. He was fifty-four years of age and would remain in Decatur until his death in 1929.

Perhaps a better candidate for who haunts Albert Taylor Hall is Franklin L. Gilson, a former theatre professor and the founder in 1916 of the Gilson Players, a touring group of actors from Emporia State who took stage plays to hundreds of small towns in fifteen states. Dr. Gilson himself often played the lead in many productions, and members of his family held supporting roles in a number of casts. Legend says that Gilson died onstage while directing a production, but again the facts conflict with the legend. Gilson actually died at St. Mary's Hospital in January 1946. He was seventy years old and had been ill with a heart ailment for several weeks.

The ghost in Emporia State's Taylor Hall, whoever or whatever it is, is a prank-pulling character who wanders through the theatre, from basement to stage, unwittingly frightening those who cross his path.

The basement of the Hall contains many small dark, dank rooms. One day a woman employee was sent down there on an errand. When she had finished, she snapped off the lights and headed for the stairs.

Something cold brushed against her shoulder.

"It sure is dark in here!" a voice whispered.

She raced for the light up the stairway.

In the mid 1960s, a scene shop employee was rummaging through the basement for stage props during a production of Bram Stoker's *Dracula*. After turning off the lights at the bottom of the steps, he pulled a cigarette from his pocket.

"Do you need a light?" someone asked.

The cigarette fell from the man's lips as he sprang up the stairs two at a time.

Pranks had been common during the run of *Dracula* but the shop worker didn't think this was one of them.

Several disturbing incidents have been reported on the catwalk in the flies high above the stage.

Once when a student technician worked on the stage lights, several students rehearsing below heard him cry out in terror. They looked up to see him leaning over a railing along the catwalk with his shirt pulled out in front of him, as if some invisible force was tugging at him. The actors scrambled up the ladder to aid their colleague, but whatever had been wrenching at his shirt quickly let go.

In another escapade, theatre students were working on an opera in which a character dies on stage. During a rehearsal, that actor lay on the floor gazing up at the catwalk. He told his fellow actors that he saw an elderly couple dressed in black peering down at him from over the railing. The woman wore a dark veil. No one knows who they might have been—in life.

A production of the musical *My Fair Lady* drew some unanticipated intrusions from the resident spirits.

During the opening night performance, an actress sensed that someone was watching her as she applied makeup in the green room. She swung around on her stool. A man wearing a black cape was looking at her from the doorway. He quickly withdrew when she heard several other actors coming down the hall. They'd passed no one on the way, they told her. Some cast members said they also saw a man in a cape watching from the overhead catwalk.

Perhaps the most frightening incident at Emporia's Taylor Hall occurred during a rehearsal for that same Lerner and Lowe musical. Since the backstage plumbing was loud and could be heard by audience members, the cast often used the quieter restroom facilities in an outer hallway during actual performances. However, there was no light switch in that room because the light controls were on a main panel elsewhere. Two girls went into the restroom with a third girl holding the door open so light could spill in from the hallway. An actress opened a stall door. The caped man was standing on the toilet. She screamed as the other women rushed to her aid. Though she swore he was there, her companions found no sign of an intruder, caped or otherwise.

Professor Gilson does seem to be a good candidate for what haunts Taylor Hall. Although he died in St. Mary's Hospital, the *Emporia Gazette* on January 29, 1946, reported that the funeral services for Gilson were held in Albert Taylor Hall. Perhaps the flamboyant actor/professor is still to make his final *exeunt*.

Assembly Hall at Millikin University was renamed Albert Taylor Hall during ceremonies on October 28, 1939. Earlier, at its founding at the turn of the twentieth century, Millikin had used the auditorium as the site of speeches and presentations by faculty, students, and visiting dignitaries. Renovations in the 1950s modernized the space and removed the reserved seating boxes on both sides of the stage.

Unlike Emporia State, Millikin's ghost was never thought to be old Dr. Taylor but rather it's Rail Girl, a sad little urchin who begs for attention. Her most notable attribute is a craving for sweets so intense that unless student actors leave pieces of candy scattered about before performances something surely will go awry on stage. University spokeswoman Deb Kirchner says the sweet tradition continues at each theatrical event in Taylor Theatre.

The anonymous girl usually plays the role of trickster, although at least once she tried to prove to a doubter that she indeed existed. A young actress told anyone who would listen that she didn't believe the theatre was haunted and snickered at the candy-laying ritual.

That is she laughed and ridiculed until one particular performance night after she got into her costume and headed off to make her entrance.

She had to descend a flight of steps to reach the stage. About halfway down, a pair of hands suddenly gripped her ankles so tightly that she lost her balance and fell headlong down the steps. Her head and shoulders slammed into the concrete floor and she lost consciousness. Although she came around in less than a minute, she missed that night's performance—and the bruise from her fall lasted for weeks.

It was not a prank or an accident she told the theatre staff. Indeed, the staircase was of a solid construction so no one could have taken hold of her from beneath. Although she wasn't willing to state flatly that a ghost was responsible for her mishap, she told one writer that she didn't take any chances afterwards. From then on out, she brought enough candy to share with the woeful Rail Girl.

Furtive appearances by college theatre ghosts are not terribly uncommon. Millikin's little ghost girl has made her own occasional sudden visits in Taylor Theatre.

A novice actress who saw her came away thinking there was more substance than she might have anticipated to the allegations of this ghost child's occasionally crabby behavior.

The coed was rehearsing on stage when a door at the back of the house opened wide. As it did, she says, a cute girl of about seven appeared in the opening. The brown-haired child wore a proper white dress. A pink ribbon around her waist was tied up in a pink bow. She quickly retreated—perhaps at seeing the actress still in the theatre—and the door closed.

The actress darted up the aisle and out the door. The hallway was empty and silent.

Thus, another Millikin student became a believer in the ghost that haunts *this* Albert Taylor Hall.

Puckish Nick

When it comes to theatre ghosts, Kansas State University will not be outdone. In fact, some students there think they know who haunts their Purple Masque Theatre—and it's not an aged actor or diabolical director, but a fellow called Nick, a mischievous former football player.

Speech and drama professor Carl Hinrichs was working in the theatre, ironically enough also on a production of Lerner and Loewe's *My Fair Lady*. The play was well into rehearsals. Hinrichs was the scene designer, and had much work left to do. He was alone at about two o'clock one morning as he poured paint from a five-gallon can into a smaller bucket that he planned to carry back to the main stage where he was working. But before he could finish, a tremendous crash came from the stage.

"Who's there?" the professor cried out as he ran toward the stage. No one answered, nor did he find anything out of place following a brief search.

Hinrichs made his way back to the scene shop. The large bucket of paint was turned upside down in the middle of the floor . . . and some ten feet from where he had left it moments earlier.

Hinrichs had his first encounter with Nick.

The Purple Masque Theatre occupies a portion of the main floor of East Stadium, a cafeteria during the 1950s. The building also served as an athletic dormitory at that time, with the men billeted on the second floor. The story goes that a football player—Nick—was injured in a game, carried into the cafeteria, and placed on a table. He died there. His spirit now returns as a poltergeist, heard and felt but never seen.

Nick's most active period was in the late 1960s. He supposedly talked on tape recorders, clomped through hallways and up and down staircases and played various other tricks, all to gain attention and perhaps some sympathy for his lonely existence. He tried to become one of the crowd and loved sharing the stage with students and faculty. But Nick often ran the show *his* way, sometimes frustrating cast and crew alike.

After a rehearsal for the play *American Yard*, for instance, the theatre doors and the building were locked. In the morning, a stagehand found all the chairs from the set piled in the hallway. The theatre doors were still locked. The worker put the chairs back on stage.

After that evening's rehearsal, and after the house lights had dimmed, the actors found their entrance blocked by the same chairs. No logical explanation was ever found or offered.

At that same rehearsal, when the stage manager ordered the stage lights brought up, the student operating the light board could not comply. "I can't," he blurted out. "I gave them power. I can hear them, but they're not coming on."

Seconds later, the lights came up slowly. The student technician was amazed. He said he had nothing to do with it. Others agreed. Nick, they said, up to more of his practical jokes.

Kay Coles was a theatre major at Kansas State. She told a newspaper reporter that a crew once unloaded chairs in the Purple Masque to be set up later. The men went outside, but rushed back in when they heard a commotion from the theatre. All the chairs were set up and programs were neatly placed on each seat.

"There was nobody around," Coles recalled. "It happened in five minutes, and it usually takes at least half an hour to do the job."

Coles had another baffling experience at the Purple Masque. She and another student had just finished working with the sound system; they turned off the equipment and locked up.

"Suddenly, music started play," Coles said. Her companion unlocked the theatre and found the audiotape of performance music. He turned off the tape machine and again locked the theatre.

The music started again.

"It (the tape machine) came on four more times," Coles said. "We looked for someone playing a joke, but there wasn't a soul around" except for Coles and her companion.

Hers was not an isolated incident. David Laughland was alone in the Masque taping sound cues late one night. In playing back the tape, he heard a voice call out on the tape, "Hi, Dave!"

Laughland rewound the tape and played it again. This time there was no voice.

Nick's pranks always startled, and sometimes frightened, younger actors. One night an actress made a quick costume change and was alone in a dressing room waiting to go on stage. The room held a desk and several wooden storage cubes. Suddenly, one of the cubes rose up, turned over and set itself gently down on the floor in front of her.

"Not nice, Nick!" the girl yelled.

She got up to leave and glanced back over her shoulder. The cube was in its original position.

During the next night's performance, the same actress took a cigarette lighter into the same dressing room, but it would not stay lit, although it did elsewhere in the building.

When Nick was not taking part in productions or harassing actresses, he could usually be encountered clomping through the theatre.

Mark Grimes was a president of the K-State Players group. Once when he was in the theatre's hallway, he heard footsteps. He and a friend later tried an experiment. They stood at opposite ends of the same hallway and both heard footsteps tread the entire length of the corridor between them. The pressure of invisible feet caused a number of the floorboards to creak.

One fall evening during a snack break on stage, three other students all heard footsteps from the floor above. It was "like a two-hundred-pound person walking," according to one of them. The doors to the second floor were locked. Although they had keys to the upstairs quarters, no one dared to go up and check. Next, the heating pipes started to clang, as they always did when the boilers were fired up at the heating plant. The heat came on and the theatre became pleasantly warm. But . . . the students learned later that the campus boilers had not been turned on for the season until three weeks *after* that incident.

Students are not the only believers in the ghost of the Purple Masque. A woman visitor, touring the campus, told her guide that she felt a presence in the theatre. She knew nothing of the supernatural history of the place. Her guide simply smiled and nodded assent.

When her tour group entered the room where stage platforms were stored, the same woman stopped dead in her tracks, then turned and fled screaming. After she calmed down a bit, she stammered out that she sensed a dangerous element in that room. No one should ever enter there alone, she warned.

One student who did go into the room alone said she always felt presences around her that made her uneasy. A few others felt icy hands on their shoulders. No one could quite figure out what the dangerous element might have been— Nick created mischief, but was never known to harm or unduly frighten anyone.

The question remains, however, whether there was ever a Kansas State football player named Nick in the era when the Purple Masque was a cafeteria and football residence.

Eventually, during a séance, a medium is said to have made contact with Nick's spirit. When she asked him what they should do to put his soul at rest and relieve him of his need to occupy the temporal world, he reportedly told them to have a Dalmatian dog run through the theatre at midnight!

The Purple Masque's Nick seems to be the best-documented ghost in Manhattan. The late Dr. William E. Koch, a noted Kansas State professor of English and folklore, says Nick's story is one of the "classics" in Kansas's campus ghost lore.

And likely to remain so for years to come.

THE MIDWEST

The Hill

Back in 1902, the folks in the hamlet of Bartonville, Illinois, just outside Peoria, simply called the rambling set of brick buildings "The Hill." That was never its official name, of course. Most people knew it as the Peoria State Hospital for the Insane. But even that may not have been its original name. One former employee says the place had been called *The House of the Incurably Insane*, though it was certainly not a *house* in any understood meaning of the term and arguably many of its residents were far from "incurably insane"—perhaps only severely physically handicapped or elderly and destitute.

The hospital opened in 1902 with six patients and had 4,000 at its maximum capacity around 1927. By the time it closed in 1973, the hospital had fewer than 2,800 patients.

There are just four buildings remaining from the original hospital—a stone administration building, the hospital's former dining hall, a four-story brick powerhouse, and another vacant building. The grounds are now part of a Bartonville industrial park complex. The buildings are either being remodeled for uses by businesses or may be torn down.

Some visitors since that time have suggested that a few of the 55,000 men and women who passed through its iron gates have lingered well past death either in the decrepit Potter's Field, the institution's own sprawling, oak-shaded cemetery, or in the dark rooms and dank basements of one of the hospital's few remaining buildings.

Local newspaper reporter Valerie Lilley spent several nighttime hours exploring the old hospital with a photographer and two other men, including a psychic, a few years ago. Lilley reported that on her first visit she saw a mysterious orb of light in the old administration building. ". . . at the end outside the room where (Rob) Conover said he heard them (the ghosts), there was a light greenish glow the size of a marble. I blinked my eyes. My pulse quickened. Were my eyes playing tricks? Had I been looking into nothingness too long?" she told her readers.

Later, Lilley returned to the Hospital with another newspaper reporter. This time she ran into two inexplicable encounters:

"Paul (the other reporter) and I continued our exploration and that's when we both walked into the colder tube of air. We were walking on the first floor just about directly below our third-floor campout point when we felt a wall of colder air. We checked back to where we'd come. It was warmer less than ten feet back. We walked into the cold section of the hall again. The wind was no stronger there than behind us. Again, we couldn't come up with a rational explanation.

"Once we were back up on the third floor, Paul stayed at the stairwell and stared at the landing leading up to the attic. I stopped and spotted a faint, white glow. He said he saw it, too.

"I shined my flashlight onto the landing where this thing sat. Gone. Nothing. I turned it off, and then we could see it. . . . It was a white transparent glow on the corner of the landing. Then it faded away. I looked away and back. It was gone. Total darkness. Paul and I went up on the landing and looked for any way an outside light could reflect into the black stairwell. We found nothing."

But the haunting of the old State Hospital has been a regular occurrence over the past century.

A former hospital aide, James R. Jones, had some firsthand experiences with what may have been supernatural phenomena at the hospital, encounters that he cannot explain even today. Jones worked at Peoria State Hospital from 1964 until it closed nine years later.

But even Jones wasn't the first person to encounter a ghost at the old State Hospital. For that, one has to go back to 1910, only a few years after the hospital opened. And it didn't begin as a ghost story at all although it has become the most well-known legend about the former mental asylum.

The old man didn't know where he was going. He would never know. But he heard the rumbling of the wagon wheels beneath him and the voice of the kindly young driver who sat beside him on the seat. The horses stopped in front of a large gray building and the young man helped his passenger down.

Inside the building a uniformed guard, seated at a desk, glanced up. "What is your name, sir?"

The driver placed an arm gently around the old man's stooped shoulders, and said, "He doesn't speak. No one at the poorhouse ever learned his name. The only thing we know is that once he worked as a bookbinder. He has no relatives."

And that is how A. Bookbinder came to live at Peoria State Hospital and where he would die alone, but mourned by more people than he ever could have imagined. He was an odd and tragic figure, but perhaps no more so than many of the inmates of the asylum.

The governor had appointed Dr. George Zeller as superintendent. His choice was a wise one. No longer were the mentally disturbed subjected to ice-water enemas, wrapped in rubber sheets, or kept chained to walls. Dr. Zeller recognized the dignity of each patient and insisted upon their humane treatment by his staff.

The problems of the living were great, but the problems of the dying threatened to become overwhelming. Like A. Bookbinder, many of the 2,000 inmates were elderly and indigent, with no relative to assume the responsibilities of burial. The hospital desperately needed its own cemetery and Dr. Zeller ordered a plot of ground set aside for that purpose. At Potter's Field, the graves would bear numbers, not names. Funeral services were simple, yet dignified, and often attended by persons from the community who had no personal attachment to the deceased.

Six strong male patients, supervised by a male attendant, dug the graves and filled them in with dirt after the caskets had been lowered. Between burials, the gravediggers kept busy placing markers, and weeding around the graves. Bookbinder watched the men for hours from the window of the tiny room that gave a view of the cemetery. At night he dreamed that he was with them, setting the markers just right and clipping the soft green grass. Then his dreams came true. Dr. Zeller himself noted the old man's interest and desire to work outdoors and assigned him to the gravediggers' crew.

At first the supervisor was hesitant to accept such an old man, but he would soon learn that Old Book, as the inmates affectionately called him, was not as feeble as he appeared. His arms were lean and strong with muscles rippling beneath the ever-present blue denim shirt, and his hands, blue-veined and gnarled, were equally strong. His agility was remarkable, the more so because he had spent a lifetime working indoors. He wore his visored cap tilted rakishly over one eye and whenever the supervisor asked him to do something, Old Book leaped to his feet, straightened his cap, and saluted. Once shown how to do a task, he never forgot.

And no one in the institution would ever forget Old Book's reaction at his first funeral. Ordinarily, when the casket was being lowered, the shovelers stood back, silently awaiting the end of the ceremonies. Then, after the mourners had left, they would complete the interment. But at the critical moment at his first funeral, Old Book removed his cap and wept nearly uncontrollably. His workmates were startled, not the least because Old Book didn't even know the name of the deceased.

Old Book seemed possessed of a passion that manifested itself in uncontrollable grief. Perhaps he had experienced an overwhelming sorrow at some time that robbed him of his reason and he found solace for this great sadness in tears. He wept long and copiously during each funeral he attended and many times tears stood in the eyes of the mourners.

Old Book developed an unwavering routine in his mourning. Standing with spade in hand, he would raise his left arm, then his right, to wipe away a tear. As the casket was lowered, he would walk over to the spreading elm tree that sheltered many of the graves. There he would embrace the ancient tree, burying his face in its rough bark while sobs convulsed his body.

In time, Old Book became too feeble to work in the cemetery, and so his nurse kept him apprised of every funeral and usually accompanied him to the services. It was his only interest and his only exercise. No matter how brutal the weather, Old Book assumed his place among the mourners. At the given moment, he would shuffle off to the elm tree to mourn in his own way.

When A. Bookbinder died, the news spread quickly. Because everyone had loved the strange old man, Dr. Zeller decided that all of the patients and the staff should attend the funeral. At high noon on a beautiful June day, patients, accompanied by their nurses, gathered at the gravesite. Other nurses lined the hillside, looking like a great bank of lilies in their starched white uniforms. Even some townspeople came, some of them weeping unabashedly even before the service began. Dr. Zeller later said over 400 persons attended the funeral of Old Book.

The coffin rested upon two crossbeams over the grave with four men standing by to work the ropes by which it would be lowered. A small choir sang the traditional "Rock of Ages." During the last stanza, the men grasped the ropes and leaned forward to raise the coffin so that the supports could be removed and the coffin lowered into the grave.

At that moment the coffin bounded into the air, throwing the men to the ground. Mourners screamed and ran in all directions, some rushing to the grave for a closer look, others rushing out of the cemetery. A contingent of nurses panicked and scampered inside the building. For some it would be the last funeral they ever attended.

Dr. Zeller, who was officiating at the service, helped the four men to their feet and called for silence. But before the commotion died, a wailing that seemed distinctly human came from the direction of the old elm. Every man and woman stood transfixed, for there stood Old Book hugging the tree and sobbing. There was no mistaking him in his old cap, set at the same jaunty angle as he'd done in life. The nurses who'd been at his bedside when he died, the undertaker and the pallbearers all saw the old man, standing as he always had in the dappled sunshine beneath the old tree.

Dr. Zeller ordered the coffin lid pried open. There lay the old man wrapped in his shroud with his hands crossed upon his breast. The apparition vanished and the service continued.

"It was awful, but it was real," the superintendent wrote in *The Institute Quarterly* of 1916. "I saw it, one hundred nurses saw it—three hundred spectators saw and heard it. I am not over-credulous. Long residence among the primitive people of our island possessions has schooled me against the acceptance of many popular beliefs, but this vision I can never dismiss from my mind."

Several weeks after Old Book's funeral the sexton appeared at the superintendent's office. "Doctor, I don't know quite how to say it, but our majestic elm is dying."

Dr. Zeller looked up from the papers spread before him on his desk.

The sexton's eyes filled. "It started at the top of the tree. The leaves all curled up and died. Then the lower ones went, too. I had my men pour hundreds of buckets of water around the roots, but it did no good."

"Better call in a tree expert," said the superintendent. "He'll know what to do. It's probably some sort of disease."

Experts came and went but none could diagnose the problem.

By fall the tree was denuded, every leaf littering the ground beneath it and crackling underfoot. The gaunt branches reached skyward, resembling a human being in supplication. The tree struck dread in all who saw it, and many of the inmates feared to approach it.

At last it was decided to cut down the old elm. One of the workmen sharpened his ax and struck the trunk, once. He cried out, dropped his ax and fled. When he was able to speak he said that as the ax struck the trunk a cry of pain arose from the heart of the tree and it began swaying like a sapling in the wind.

Sometime later Dr. Zeller ordered the tree burned. It was a menace in its present decayed condition. Firemen ignited a pile of dry brush at the base of the tree, but as the flames roared upward the men backed away. They said they heard Old Book's familiar sobbing. One fireman swore that he saw the dead man emerging from the clouds of smoke. They then turned their hoses on the flames and quickly doused the fire.

The graveyard elm still stood.

Periodic efforts have been made to clean up the old graveyard and identify those buried on the old hospital grounds. One expert has estimated that over 4,000 people are buried there. Most of the crumbling grave markers have only a number. Minimal information such as names and dates are only found on the recent burials.

A half-century would roll by before James Robert Jones, a young mental health aide working for the State of Illinois, had his personal "few strange experiences" inside the State Hospital. He worked at Peoria and later Galesburg State Hospital until resigning in 1984. Today he works for a security agency in southeastern Wisconsin.

The story he tells took place primarily in the Talcot Building, an old, sprawling, two-story brick building constructed during the hospital's first years, with four separate wings wrapped around a lobby area. Each wing held infirm patients, most of whom were bedridden and unable to perform even the most basic human functions without assistance. While a few patients were simply elderly with nowhere else to live, Jones said most were also severely mentally or physically impaired.

Jones was on the first floor of the east wing when he heard the elevator bell ring.

"I was still in training and working the second shift at Talcot," Jones said of that time, December 1964. "I didn't pay attention to the bell, but then all of the other employees on the ward came running to me saying that nobody was ringing the bell. It had rung four times," Jones remembered.

He described the elevator as very old-fashioned, with a separate inner, metal lattice-work gate and a solid outer door. Jones was the only male aide in the building at the time.

"A woman came running out scared to death," he said. "We all knew that none of us had been ringing that elevator bell. But I was thinking it must have been something of flesh and blood—probably somebody had broken in. The other employees wanted to investigate so we went down into the basement to check things out."

What they found was about what they'd expected—nothing. The only sounds were normal building noises and air going through the pipes of the steam heating system. But then, as they were leaving to go back up the stairs, Jones, the last person on the staircase, and several others heard something that seemed quite out of place—the clicking of a door lock over and over again.

"The doors in Talcot had loud locks; they made a distinct click when a key was turned," Jones said, "and that's what we were hearing."

Jones and his companions found the sound seemed to be coming from the door to a storage room.

"I asked the ward charge nurse for the key and unlocked it," Jones remembered. "I started to get a little scared. I thought something was on the other side."

Jones opened it but saw only a dark room filled with supplies, wheelchairs, crutches, and canes. A separate door in the room led to the outside, but it was locked from the inside. A transom window that opened for airflow was too small for anyone to squeeze through.

"What made those noises, I don't know. I have no idea to this day what we were experiencing," Jones maintains, "but I worked at that facility for nine years and worked most of the wards there. None of the other buildings and wards had a reputation like Talcot. It was considered haunted by employees."

That storeroom Jones investigated may have had more than a little to do with the building's reputation—it had once been the hospital's mortuary.

Even with his odd, possibly supernatural, experiences, Jones thoroughly enjoyed his work at the Peoria hospital. "The grounds were beautiful and a pleasure to walk through. I always felt quite safe walking around the hospital no matter what time of the day or night it was," he noted.

The strange incidents in Talcot continued until the day the hospital closed in 1973. Jones said a veteran supervisor told him of hearing lonely footsteps moving down the center of the wings' floors. Overnight nurses said the ghostly footfalls also came from unoccupied ward rooms, lights flitted about on outside fire escapes and the elevator, always the elevator, moved up and down on its solitary journey among the floors, perhaps delivering phantom corpses to the mortuary below.

Within a few years most vestiges of the Peoria State Hospital for the Insane— save, perhaps, the burial grounds—will most likely have disappeared with the few remaining buildings demolished or remodeled beyond recognition as the village of Bartonville continues to develop the industrial park. In late 2000, officials spent over $50,000 to pour hundreds of yards of concrete into the abandoned underground steam tunnels formerly used to deliver heat and utilities to the buildings. The village was worried about the tunnels collapsing under heavy truck traffic on the industrial park's newly built roadways, and by the liability they could face if area teenagers were injured during their periodic forays into the damp, creepy warrens. Police regularly arrested trespassers in the boarded-up buildings and in the tunnels, especially around Halloween.

Even city elders, however, understand the power of the abandoned asylum to power the imagination. Several Bartonville village trustees and others were guided through the steam tunnels before the concrete was poured to fill them in. Most of the visitors were "creeped" out, according to one account.

"There are some eerie things," one official said. It remains to be seen whether all those eerie things will vanish as well.

Evil in the Air

Southeastern Iowa is a quintessentially American landscape. Serene country roads stretch straight on until, like the verdant fields of rich black earth through which the asphalt slices, they are at last swallowed by the horizon. Quiet country towns struggle to retain their dignity—and smatterings of essential services—in the face of twenty-first–century competition from mega-malls and discount superstore entrepreneurs. Neatly framed by U.S. Interstates 35 to the west and 80 to the north, the Mississippi River on the east, and the Missouri state line at the southern edge, the two dozen counties of the region face a plethora of modern woes, to be sure, but the issues are generally of a temporal nature.

In towns like Guernsey or Garden Grove, East Pleasant Plain or Mount Pleasant, Keosauqua or What Cheer, nothing much out of the ordinary ever happens. There is certainly the occasional murder and mayhem, but the crimes are usually quickly solved so that the communities return in time to their natural somnolence.

An experience from outside the expected routine of daily life—especially incidents that are clearly *not* of worldly origin—can be shocking to one unaccustomed in handling challenges to our intimations of reality.

That was clearly the case with the Sterling* family on their 350-acre Iowa farmstead. For daughter Linda, her mother Blanche, and two of her nine brothers and sisters, several disturbing events caused them to question whether or not their own placid lives were coming undone through no fault of their own.

Thirteen children had been born to Blanche Sterling and her husband Clarence. A set of twins died young. A son, Brad, was killed at the age of fourteen in a dreadful motorcycle accident within sight of his own front yard. Father Clarence Sterling died in 1999. Ten children survive, as does their mother, who still lives in the sprawling 1950s ranch-style farmhouse her husband built for his growing family.

It is Linda Sterling who's had a couple of brushes with the "other side" and despite the passage of some years she still has a hard time understanding *what* and, perhaps more importantly, *why* they all took place. Although her experiences

*Name has been changed.

may seem of only small consequence to those expecting visits from the supernatural to be accompanied by howling winds and yowling cadavers, they remain defining moments in her life.

"I've told a couple of people what happened to me and they say it can't be true. I'd probably say it wasn't true either if I heard that it had happened to somebody else. But it did happen to me and I have no explanation for it, and no reason for it, really. But even though it sounds crazy, that's what took place," Linda says, with a certain resignation in her voice that she expects to go through life leaving doubters and cynics in her wake.

The motorcycle accident that claimed the life of young Brad Sterling had a profound and lasting effect on his family, as one would certainly expect. So attached was Clarence Sterling to his son, according to Linda, that the old man never fully got over the cruel way in which his boy was snatched from him.

"We never talked about the accident because my dad was so upset," Linda acknowledges. "It was just like Brad had never existed because none of us could say anything. Dad was just a basket case. He never did recover."

Linda was only five when her big brother was killed, so she was too young to remember how her father had been before the accident, but as she grew up, she saw that her father didn't do all the things a typical farm dad might do.

"I know he built swing sets for the older kids (when they were small), but I don't think he ever did that again after Brad was killed. It was very hard on all of us. Dad told my brother Mark that he'd have to take Brad's place. That bothered Mark so much. He realized later that dad was saying he'd never be as good as Brad, that he'd have to become more like him. I understand that even at fourteen Brad had been very much a man's man type of guy. Mark is a doctor now, a very smart man, but he just never got over that."

The circumstances of young Brad Sterling's sudden death are so ordinary as to make his passing even the more agonizing. He was doing what typical Iowa farm kids have done for generations—riding his small motorcycle around the family farmstead. He rode it to the end of the driveway, in and out of the ditch and then back up the driveway.

"It had been a very dusty, dry year," Linda says of that time. "Either he didn't see the car coming, or another vehicle came by and kicked up the dust."

At the end of one swing down the long driveway, Brad rode his cycle onto the gravel country road, directly into the path of an oncoming car. A neighbor woman was driving it. Brad was thrown onto the road, his head crushed under the wheels of the car. He may not have even seen the car coming, assuming, mistakenly and tragically, that the gravel dust had been thrown up by a previous automobile.

"I understand he was very popular in school. He was quite a good baseball player, too," Linda says. "But he could be ornery, I understand. Every morning he'd go around the table and 'cuff' everybody on the head before he sat down."

Her memory of him, of course, is faint. He was nine years older, and there were a lot of kids running around the Sterling household.

But it may be that Brad Sterling is responsible for a brief, but very upsetting, episode during which the boy's ghost might have tried to communicate with Linda and her mother.

"That would have been in 1992," Linda says. Brad had been killed some nineteen years earlier, in the summer of 1973. "I woke up about two-thirty or so in the morning. I felt this weird presence in the room, just like someone else was in there. I wasn't truly scared, so I just lay in bed. Then my mom came in and asked me if I was okay."

Not wanting to upset her mother, Linda assured her that though she was awake, she was fine.

Blanche Sterling had awakened because she thought something was wrong with one of her children. Moms—and dads, too—have an almost sixth sense when it comes to knowing when a child is in distress. Blanche wanted to check on her own brood one by one and started with Linda, who was in her early twenties at the time.

Linda's bedroom had been Brad's.

As Blanche turned to leave, mother and daughter were stopped cold by the voice of a young boy.

"Mom!"

A single word, but enough to make both women stare at one another. It seemed to come from a corner of the room.

"I just heard it once," Linda says. Her mother said later she heard it two or three times. It made her feel very uneasy.

Blanche quickly left the bedroom to check on another son, Jeff. Perhaps he was playing some sort of mean-spirited prank. He was asleep, as was another brother, James. No one else was up at that hour.

A religious woman, Blanche went to the living room and prayed. Linda fell back to sleep. Neither one heard the boy's voice again.

"My mother doesn't believe in ghosts," Linda says. Interestingly, her mother later told Linda that she did not think Brad was the source of the disembodied voice. "She thought it was some sort of demonic activity. She heard the voice, but she didn't know why there would be demons, but that's how she resolved it in her own mind. I've thought for many years that it must have been my brother. Who else would it have been?"

The aftermath of young Brad's death also touched Mark Sterling. He's said that years after his brother's death, he felt a distinctive "pull" toward the place where Brad had been killed. The sensation, he told some of his siblings, was sinister and terrifying.

Is it possible that the spirit of a boy who died too young can return with an attitude and behavior uncharacteristic of him during his few brief years on earth?

That may well be another question to ask since Linda Sterling faced far more than an utterance by something unseen in an early morning hour. For a period of about three weeks in 1990, the young woman was terrified by a sensation of evil so keen that she was barely able to stay in her family's home.

It all began on an early evening near dusk at the end of a routine drive home with her sister. That harmless trip was punctuated by a most disturbing incident.

"I was on my way home when I saw what appeared to me to be someone staggering farther down the road. He would have been just past our house. My sister was with me. I turned to ask her who that was, but when I looked back down the road he was gone. It was so real that I got out and looked along the ditch to see if someone had fallen down and maybe gotten seriously hurt. But there was absolutely nobody there."

The man she saw on the road was in shadow so she couldn't distinguish his age or what he might have been wearing. "I thought it was my younger brother, Jeff. That was my first thought, that he had wrecked his four-wheeler and was hurt and was trying to get back up to the house. I know Brad had been tall and lanky like Jeff was. I suppose it could have been Brad I saw."

But sometime later Linda learned that a neighboring farmer had been killed near there when his tractor rolled over on top of him.

Once she and her sister got home, however, Linda discovered there was what she described as an "evil presence" permeating the house and its surroundings.

"That was so real that I had to leave. It stayed for weeks, but I was the only one who could tell it was there. I was just petrified. I'd get to within about a half mile of the house and I got scared to death. When I first felt it, I was in the house that night and I was sure somebody was in there with me, somebody who was going to hurt me. I had to get out. It was and is frightening to feel that way in my own house. I still try not to think about it too much. I have no explanation for what that evil might have been. But nothing bad ever did happen. . . ."

Did it have something to do with Brad's death? Linda just doesn't know. She doesn't directly connect the vanishing man on the road and the malevolent atmosphere in the house, and certainly cannot understand why a brother who's been gone for three decades would return to cast such a dreadful pall on one of his surviving siblings.

She compares the sensation to what she felt on the night she heard the voice, the idea that someone was around you couldn't see, someone in the shadowy corners of a familiar room.

Although the dread soon passed, she still harbors some reluctance to return to the farm. "I do go back occasionally, but not often, though. I don't really like going there. You'd think I would since that's where I grew up."

Now in her mid-thirties, Linda Sterling is married and leads a comfortable life in a small southern Iowa town. She does not like to dwell on the disquieting incidents from those years past, but neither are any of them ever very far from her consciousness. Beneath the pastoral serenity of even the most isolated hamlet, there can be a suggestion of events so remarkable that they will remain forever unsolved.

The Haunted Trailer

It happened again last night. Tom refused to return to bed. Again, he says "someone" is back there. I know eight-year-olds have active imaginations, and I know the divorce was hard on him, too, and I know an old trailer is a big adjustment from a (large) house, but enough is enough. Tonight "someone" pulled his pillow from under his head. Last night "someone's" breathing frightened him. The night before "someone" kept tugging the covers off his bed. From footsteps down the hallway when I'm asleep to sounds of "someone" moving his toys around in his room, I've heard 'em all. If "someone" were really here, why would he only want to scare Tom?

A mother's words from the pages of a diary she has kept for over twenty years, a record of events that she believes amount to nothing less than a persistent, yet so far unexplainable haunting in the small Michigan town in which she lives.

Her name is Suzy Driver, a middle-aged computer paraprofessional who has held the same position for nearly thirty years. Her home is on the "thumb" of the lower peninsula of Michigan, northwest of Port Huron.

Along with her elementary-school-age son, Tom, Driver moved into the mobile home following a divorce in the late 1970s. She and her former husband had bought the place and used it as a rental property. A separation and subsequent divorce is a distressing experience for any family member, of course, and particularly so for the children involved. That's why she thought her son's complaints were simply products of his difficulties at the breakup of the home he'd known all of his young life.

"Things happened immediately with my son," Driver recalls, "and continued to take place for a couple of years. I'm almost embarrassed now when I look back at some of that. I didn't believe it. I thought it was all because of the trauma of the divorce."

But it wasn't long until she learned that it wasn't only her son who saw things that really shouldn't have been there.

Tom and I pulled into our drive to find the yard filled with neighbor kids. They know this yard is off-limits when we're away. Getting out of my car, I was about to do some serious scolding when, to my surprise, my neighbor walked out my trailer door. I listened in disbelief as he explained how his kids and other neighbors had rushed in to awaken him (he worked the midnight shift as a deputy at the county sheriff's department) to tell him of someone looking out my hall window at them, not once, but several times, only to disappear from view when they noticed him watching. Knowing Tom and I had gone for the day . . . Bill went inside, looked for someone, but no one was found. As Tom listened, his eyes grew big. I can still feel his frantic tugging on my arm. "See mom," he whispered. "I told you."

The suggestion that one's home is not the normal, placid island of contentment one expects is difficult to take in. And this is particularly the case if the odd things that happen are disparate, are separated by days or weeks, and occur over a period of years.

So it was with Suzy Driver.

She first laid her son's irritability and complaints about what he thought was happening at night to the strict rules she set down for his behavior.

"He was a 'little pistol,' " she says of her now-grown son. "I wonder now if some of the worst things he experienced were possibly when he gave me the most grief, when he threw the most tantrums."

There are turning points in one's belief that not all things can be explained away in a logical and rational manner, just as there are other turning points in one's life. For Suzy Driver, the realization came in the form of several seemingly unrelated events that in retrospect told her that not all of her son's problems stemmed from the divorce, her strict rules, or maybe an overly active and vivid imagination. That there was some *one* teasing or some *thing* unseen that had insinuated itself into her otherwise orderly life. And that it would soon make itself known to her as well.

His scream was bloodcurdling. Not again. I rushed from my bedroom (I hadn't even had a chance to crawl under the covers) and raced down the hallway to Tom's tiny bedroom. I remember trying to get his door open but feeling . . . like someone was leaning against it from the other side. I remember shoving it open hard, and switching on his light. I remember loudly telling him, "Wake up Tom, it's only a dream!" And I remember his terrified eyes staring at the bottom of the doorway. And I remember the fear that rippled through me as I followed his gaze and saw the cream-colored afghan bedspread that had been on my bed now tightly rolled into a bedroll which had then been wedged under his bedroom door from the inside. Reassuring him, I gently told him that he must have walked in his sleep, removed the afghan from my bed, and wedged it under his door himself. But I knew even if he did walk in his sleep, which he didn't, that he never could have done so without me hearing or seeing him in this small old trailer. Never. I quit laughing at his stories.

"That was the time I knew something was not right," she says. "I had been in the living room watching television before I'd gone to bed. I can see all the way back to my bedroom and his. Had he opened the door I would have heard it. There's no way he would have done that. My explanation to him that he walked in his sleep was all that I could think of. But I knew better. Right then I thought there was something bizarre going on."

All during her son's early years, Driver said he didn't like to sleep in his small bedroom at the back of the mobile home and particularly disliked being in there at night. Because of that, she says, he spent more time at his father's home, not far from where he and his mother lived.

But the puzzling incidents were piling up as well—the neighborhood children seeing that stranger's face in the window, a bed comforter stuffed under her son's door, someone pulling on blankets and making noises—so that she understood in time that all this didn't seem to be of mother and son's making. She also thought that as her son grew older calmness would return, as it often does in a classic poltergeist situation when children are the targets or unwitting agents of household turmoil.

That didn't happen . . . even when Driver had had enough of Tom's complaints about his bedroom.

We had long since switched bedrooms, my reasoning being that since he was growing taller than I, Tom needed the extra length my double bed offered. The reality was that I was trying my damndest to discourage his conviction that someone was in that room. But footsteps, breathing noises, and shadows simply followed him from one room to another. He hated being in the trailer at night. He seemed to be resentful I didn't believe him. I had stopped laughing. I now slept in his old bedroom and it wasn't long before, when lying on my stomach in his small twin bed, that I began to feel strange sensations, feather-light fingertips moving swiftly across my back. In the beginning I would nervously jump from bed, switch on the light, and wildly turn the light foam mattress over, repeatedly, as if to ward off anything that was on the bed. Nothing ever surfaced, but it soon became such a frequent occurrence that I eventually learned to brush my right arm across my back whenever the sensation would occur, and, deciding against telling Tom, I would soon drift back to sleep. But this was only the beginning.

Mother and son also knew better than to discuss their difficulties with friends and relatives. With the exception of one of Driver's sisters, they hadn't shared their experiences with anyone. She is very careful to stress a desire to remain credible; to make it clear that what she has sought more than anything else are answers and some vindication that all of this hasn't been dreamed up. And though she stopped laughing at her son's worries about someone in his room, and though she had numerous, sometimes unnerving confrontations herself, a full understanding didn't come about until several of those friends and relatives had their own experiences at her home on Main Street.

After Tom left for college, the inexplicable activity in the Driver home seemed to increase and pulled in others.

I was unprepared for the sudden void his entry into college would present. For the first time ever I was really alone. On New Year's Day, a friend who attended the University of Michigan dropped by and made me an authentic Chinese dinner. Our visit was shortened not long after as I'd accepted a prior engagement, but I offered him the use of my trailer to . . . stay and watch the big game on TV. When I got home that evening I (found) a note on the kitchen table asking that I call him. I got a little nervous when he asked me . . . if I had a phone in my bedroom. I answered no. He went on to say that immediately after I'd left, and although the living room phone was silent, a telephone started ringing in the rear of the trailer toward the bedroom. He walked toward the ringing but as he neared the bedroom, it stopped. He'd no sooner sat down again to watch the game when the ringing began again. This time he walked back and peeked into the bedroom but he saw no phone. Again the ringing had stopped. When the ringing began for the third time, he left. He said he was too "uneasy" to stay. Nervously I put the receiver back on the hook. As before, no one had been told of Tom's convictions but (my sister).

Driver has had numerous problems with the telephones in her mobile home over the years. A telephone repairman and his boss were confounded when Driver and her sister complained that their connections could not be made without the aid of a long distance operator. At other times, they'd get "weird background noises," in their words, and odd music would provide the backdrop when they were trying to talk with one another. Driver also told the men that she heard what she could only describe as an old-fashioned screen door opening and closing and footsteps across creaky floorboards.

Unfortunately, Driver didn't get the answers she was looking for. She was told that what she described just wasn't possible with the telephone equipment she had.

Many of the turning points Driver describes have involved confrontations between her or her family and friends and that *something*. The most upsetting incident, she says, involved her sister, Penny.

Penny had driven up from Columbus, Ohio, to visit her sister. She was skeptical of the stories Driver told and joked more often than not that "the ghost did it" whenever a question was raised. On the third day of her visit, Penny and Driver's other sister, Cindy, decided to play a joke on their sister. They hid her car keys. "Why the *ghost* must have taken them," the sisters told Driver.

"I had taken three days of teasing and it was wearing thin on me," Driver remembers of that day.

She needn't have worried that her sister wouldn't understand what was taking place in the Driver home, as she detailed in her diary:

We retired late, Penny to my bedroom, I in Tom's old room. Several times I awoke to find Penny's night-light on, and assuming she was reading, I went back to sleep. At about four A.M., when the light was still on, I went back to her room to ask if something was wrong. There Penny sat, the covers clutched tightly to her chin, her eyes staring straight ahead . . . she started screaming unintelligible things, "the chair!" "the light!," "the bed!" I quickly pulled her from the bed and dragged her to the front of the trailer trying desperately to calm her. "I tried to tell you the bed shakes, Penny," I yelled. "Goddamnit, Suzy, the bed doesn't shake, the mattress vibrates!" Then I knew she had experienced it. She was right, the bed doesn't shake, and the mattress vibrates in different places in different ways.

Penny packed her suitcases the next morning and left with Driver to visit Cindy, who lived nearby. Driver also had a skeptical friend talk with Penny. Her friend admitted that it sounded like Penny had had a "terrible fright."

"She didn't believe in ghosts, she didn't believe in anything. She made fun of everything that went on here," Driver remembers of those several days. But she says her sister's comments about the mattress vibrating, strange, moving lights, and a chair that didn't stay in one place convinced her that her sister had a genuinely frightening experience.

Penny was also worried that Suzy was in danger. Driver assured her that she would be fine; that whatever was in the mobile home didn't really intend to harm her. That didn't seem to allay Penny's fears.

"The most fear I felt was after Penny left," Driver recalls. "When she was driven out. We spent the day at my sister's house, went to Port Huron and did this and that, trying to get Penny's mind off everything. She got very quiet, very subdued. She didn't want to talk."

Despite her sister's fears, Driver stayed, and continues to stay, in her mobile home.

"I live here, this is my home. Whatever this thing is it's never been harmful to me."

Despite her assurances to Penny, Driver really did not like being alone in the room Penny had stayed in, which also served as the TV room. She thought some-one was watching her. There was something about the bed—it was bought new, a box springs, mattress, and frame. She'd feel forceful "vibrations," she says, and had to yell, "Stop it!" before it would settle down.

There was no regularity about the nerve-racking vibrations. Sometimes weeks would go by without any activity.

I'm scared that one of these nights I'll take a knife to the mattress while it's shaking to see if anything happens then. But I know it isn't the bed. It would happen to any bed I moved in. I know it.

Her son, a close friend or two, her sisters. Those are the only people Driver con-fided in. So when a friend called her with the news that the village police chief had received a complaint from a woman about "ghosts in her backyard," and that "the male ghost was holding a rifle," and that this woman lived only a few houses away, Driver couldn't help but be curious. Her friend asked if she could give Driver's name to the police chief. She agreed.

"The policeman hadn't really taken the time to listen to (this woman's) story, thinking it too ridiculous to waste his time on."

Driver said that the lawman was amazed at the events she related about her own life in the mobile home. He wanted her to speak with the complaining woman, but Driver declined. The bizarre events in her own life had been kept quiet for years and she wasn't about to start revealing them to a woman she didn't even know.

Driver did eventually confide in her neighbors, Jack and Vanessa* her concerns following the upsetting events during Penny's visit. If she had been worried that they might laugh at her, she need not have been.

"They remembered that their son, who was a companion of my son Tom, saying that whenever Tom brought his beagle Sooner inside the trailer, (the dog) became agitated and would run and bark . . . toward the rear of the trailer."

*Names have been changed.

Driver was invited back by the couple, but Jack asked her to "make sure 'some-one' isn't with you."

But that visit by her neighbors did lead to the Michigan woman's first—and last—experience with an Ouija board in her home.

It began with a knock at her door late one evening.

I found the neighbor's twenty-something-year-old daughter Gloria* and her cousin Jonathan,* who attended Western Michigan University. They were hold-ing a Ouija board. "Oh, no," I said, "you're not bringing that in here. I saw one of those work at a party years ago and it was eerie." They begged and pleaded to come in and use it. . . . Finally, reluctantly, I gave in. Gloria and Jonathan sat cross-legged on my bed with the Ouija board between them. I sat on the floor beside the bed with pen and paper.

Question: Who is this in Suzy's trailer—tell us your name.
Answer: G–U–Y
Question: Is that your name, Guy?
Answer: G–U–Y
Question: Is your name Guy, or are you a guy?
Answer: U–S–H–U–T–U–P

Tearfully looking up at me, Gloria said, "I'm stopping this right now—it just told me to shut up!" Just then the telephone rang so loudly in the living room that it startled Jonathan, who still sat cross-legged on the bed. He flipped over backward and fell on the floor. Stepping over him, Gloria and I ran down the hallway to the living room, Jonathan following behind. When I answered the telephone, there was no one on the other end.

Another neighbor had an interesting role in Driver's story. His name was Robert* and he and his family lived near her. He was eighteen at the time.

"This is a very rural area," Driver says. "Even though I live in town, there are deep woods behind me. There's my mobile home, a tri-level house beside me to the north, and to the south are three empty lots. Charlie saw the ghosts in the empty lots right next to my mobile home, in the ditch of those empty lots."

Two ghosts, in fact. Two ghosts in three different "scenarios," he told her, on some fourteen to sixteen different occasions.

The two figures were a man and a woman wearing hospital-type gowns, Driver says he told her.

"I think they definitely had been in some sort of trauma," she says. "He saw them first in the middle of the night. He could see some sort of peculiar glow coming from the ditch across from his mailbox. He stepped outside to his front porch to get a better view. He still wasn't clear on what he was seeing, so he began walking down the long driveway. He was getting nervous at what possibly was causing the glow."

Robert stopped walking because he could see what was causing the radiance. A man was standing in the ditch above the prone figure of a woman. Both emitted a "glow," Driver says. Neither figure moved. The man's hair was long and Robert could see that the night breeze moved it a bit.

Frightened, Robert turned and ran back in his house.

Over the course of the next year, Robert would see the same two figures over a dozen times in three different poses, including the one he saw on that first

*Names have been changed.

night. In another, they are standing side by side, both unmoving but for a wind gently riffling their clothing. In yet a third, the man held the woman's body horizontally in his arms as though in mourning. In each "scene," they were always dressed in blue, calf-length hospital gowns. The woman's hair was long and flowed freely down her back.

Driver also remembers that Robert told her the glowing apparitions had been most frightening on a night when the power went off in town. He said that when a car passed by the couple faded away, but then quickly reappeared. "Like they were meant only for me," he told her.

Robert is married now and attending college.

The events that Suzy Driver details have amassed over the years:

- Ghostly voices calling through open windows from outside;
- Mysterious sounds of breaking glass or of someone knocking on the glass patio door;
- Dirty shoe prints found in the kitchen even though no one had been there;
- A wooden ball rolling around on the bedroom floor—but no one sees the ball, only hears it;
- Fleeting dark shadows and sudden flashes of light, usually in one of the bedrooms;
- Her dog "Kafka" growling and whining in the direction of the nearby woods although Driver couldn't see anything amiss.

There is nothing unusual about the location of Driver's mobile home, at least as far as she has been able to determine. She found that an 1892 plat map indicated there was a mill about where her home is now, but another map drawn a few years later omits any reference to the mill. The property was identified as belonging to a J. D. Hickley, but Driver can't find any information about the mill or its apparent demise over a century ago.

A former schoolteacher in town brought the mobile home itself to the site in the 1960s. After he left, the place was rented out until Driver and her former husband bought it as an investment property. She has lived there since her divorce over twenty years ago.

An obvious question, and one that Suzy Driver has been asked many times, is why she doesn't just move out.

Her answer is straightforward.

"There's no harm that's ever come to me. But if I ever felt a threat, if I was walking down the hall and had a shove from behind and it knocked me down, then I'd be gone in a minute. But I just don't feel any threat whatsoever. Besides, and I know it sounds bizarre, it's an exciting place to live."

Driver cites two instances in which she thinks her invisible "protector" actually saved her from harm. In the first, insulating tape wrapped around outside pipes somehow melted from intense heat yet did not cause any damage. In another, reflected sun from a makeup mirror on the kitchen table actually burned a hole in her wall, yet again, no harm was done to her and the damage was repairable.

"It's benign. It doesn't mean me any harm," she maintains.

When it comes to trying to explain her theory about what "it" is, she is equally candid.

"It's an energy," she says. "There's no question about that. There's some sort of energy form here, but I don't have any ideas about what causes it. It's almost like whatever it is wants to get through, to make its presence known. But it also seems to know that should it materialize in some physical form, I would absolutely freak out. I truly believe I would. I think whatever it is has intelligence so it knows that. It's chosen to manifest itself in these other ways."

This happens to be the highest point in Sanilac County, maybe that has something to do with things. But I want more than that. I want answers.

But thankfully, and until she finds those answers, Suzy Driver is grateful that *it* also knows when to back off.

The Hayloft

Picture if you will that time a century ago when raising a family on a North Dakota farmstead meant living in rural isolation for most of the year, unable to spend any but the occasional few hours in a town of several hundred people, which itself might be many rutted miles away by farm wagon. That settlement might have been Mott or Grassy Butte, Drake or Dickinson, or even the grandly named Havana, hard by the South Dakota border.

For Miriam Grinstead, her four sisters, two brothers, and parents, the village closest to their isolated farm was Penn, in Norway Township, a half-dozen miles southeast of Churchs Ferry on the road to Devils Lake. But little Penn with its handful of residents and even fewer amenities could not offer the kind of educational opportunities Miriam's father wanted for the older children. In the summer of 1912 he moved the family another fourteen miles into Devils Lake, a thriving "city" of 6,000 people, where the children could attend school. The family of nine found a grand old Second Street house that had been a hotel in the state's territorial days; the two-story stable once used for guests' horses was still in the back. The family's riding pony had it all to himself until Miriam's father bought a Maxwell automobile and then part of it was turned into a garage.

The hayloft was especially inviting for the seven children. Piles of hay on the solid wood floor were great for jumping on, and there was still plenty of room left for horsing around and playing games on those dark Dakota winter days.

But that benign loft playroom hid a terrifying secret. And eight-year-old Miriam Grinstead would uncover the mystery in a manner so unnerving that she would remember the experience for the rest of her life.

It all began innocently enough, Miriam remembered in a chronicle of the events written some forty years later, with a kindness by her oldest brother, John, who was one of the children who attended a secondary school in Devils Lake. But when he wasn't in school, he helped out his mother by looking after his younger siblings. On those days when the weather conspired against outdoor play, he helped organize games in the hayloft. One day he spotted an oversize hook that had been secured to the ceiling, perhaps used in the old days by looping a cable through it to haul up hay bales or other supplies through a doorway-like opening at one end of the loft. John's ingenuity quickly found another use for the hook. He'd attach a second hook next to it and make a swing for the younger children.

"I remembered with what anticipation we watched him cut the grooves into the piece of wood that was to be the seat in this wonderful swing," Miriam said.

The children loved John's swing. They'd take turns swooshing back and forth above the loft floor even on sunny days when they ought to have been playing outdoors.

Early one morning, Miriam decided it would be great fun to have the swing all to herself, at least for a while. She quickly finished breakfast and made off for the barn, still clutching a final piece of toast. The large barn door swung open easily as she headed for the wooden ladder that led straight up to the loft. She stuffed the rest of the toast in her mouth, gripped the ladder rungs, and climbed hand over hand and up through the floor opening.

As her eyes adjusted to the gloomy loft, she saw that the familiar surroundings of that cheerful children's room were gone. In its place was a scene of riveting horror.

"Dangling from the original hook in the ceiling was a man," Miriam said. "His face was horribly contorted, black, with eyes protruding. There was no sign of our . . . swing, only the rope that was stretched taut with the weight of his body. He was swaying and whirling slowly. He was certainly dead."

She tore her eyes away from the gruesome sight and edged back down the ladder, her hands gripping the sides in deathly fear that if she let go she would collapse on the floor below. Her mouth worked into a scream that rose to a hysterical pitch and volume that brought her sister Agnes running from the house. Miriam collapsed into her arms weeping uncontrollably.

When the child was able at last to stammer out her story, Agnes listened wide-eyed but then, as the oldest girl, she put on a courageous face, glanced upward and headed up to the loft to see for herself. Miriam watched in dismay as her sister peeked through the hole in the floor. She was certain Agnes would come screaming and skidding back down any second.

Agnes did come back down, but not with a reaction anything close to what Miriam had expected.

"What kind of a trick do you think you're playing?" Agnes yelled, shaking her finger at her little sister. "Of all the naughty things you've ever done, this is the worst. You'll have to go into the house and tell mama that you told a lie!"

Miriam meekly followed her sister into the house, all the while insisting that she had seen a dead man dangling from a rope. Their mother was a patient woman. She listened carefully, if not disbelievingly at Miriam's tale. It seemed such impossibility. And she was confused because the two girls' stories were so dissimilar. As the oldest girl, Agnes was considered by her parents to be the most truthful child. It was simply not in her nature to tell lies. Miriam, on the other hand, was just as adamant in describing the scene that had sent her into hysterics.

Mother decided to settle the matter once and for all. She took the girls by the hands and marched with them back to the stable. Miriam could hardly force herself to go back inside, but up the ladder they all went, one by one. She could not believe what she saw—all was now as it should be, even John's homemade swing looked inviting. Agnes had a rather smug, "I told you so" look on her face.

Rather than scolding her youngest daughter for making up tall tales, Miriam's mother was worried that the child was coming down with some strange disease.

"She felt my forehead and took my pulse, then and there, thinking that I must be sick and feverish. I, meantime, kept insisting that there had been a dead man hanging from our swing hook when I first entered the loft. I would not retract my statement. It had been too real and horrifying," Miriam recalled. The hardest part of all, she added, was being suspected of telling a lie in a family that placed enormous importance on truth telling.

To avoid any more unpleasant scenes, the children were forbidden from playing in the hayloft. And it was poor Miriam who was blamed by her brothers and sisters for causing their favorite indoor playground to be put off limits.

The days and weeks that followed were no better for her. That nightmarish scene would not go away. She shared a bedroom with her ten-year-old sister Marie. At night, Miriam often awoke in a sweat, screaming about the man in the hayloft who continued to stalk her dreams. Her appetite weakened. She grew thin and pale. Her nerves were so on edge that she jumped at the slightest noise.

In the end, however, Miriam was vindicated in a dramatic and unexpected manner.

Sister Agnes had returned from a ride on Tom, the family's pony. After she unsaddled him in the stable, she found that his feed bin was nearly empty and climbed up to the loft to throw some fresh hay down. When she pulled herself up through the hole in the floor, she saw it and screamed. It was the same dreadful sight that her sister had described—a bloated and very dead man was hanging by his neck at the end of a taut rope, his eyes bulging as if in disbelief while his swollen tongue lolled protruding from his mouth. His entire body swung lazily at the end of the rope as if pushed by a gentle breeze.

Agnes lost her grip and fell off the ladder, screaming even as she landed on the hard-packed ground. The girls' big brother John came running out of the house and through the stable doors. Agnes blurted out what she had seen as he carried her into the house. Fortunately, she had not been hurt beyond a few bumps and bruises.

"Now there was no denying it," Miriam said of her sister's experience. "The loft was haunted."

With two of their children as witnesses describing the very same horrible apparition, Miriam's father and mother could no longer doubt that something awful had happened in the old stable. Her father talked to some old-timers who told him the story: a traveling man passing through Devils Lake had taken a room when the house had been a hotel. For reasons no one ever knew, he committed suicide by hanging himself in the stable.

"For many years thereafter this hanging ghost was seen by different persons at various times. He came to be known as an unpleasant hazard," Miriam said in an understatement. "For all I know he is still there."

Is he?

Today's visitors to the city of Devils Lake—population 8,000—usually come for the splendid scenic beauty of the vast nearby lake of the same name, outdoor activities, or perhaps to study at Lake Regions State College. The haunt hunter trying to find the old stable and its attendant revenant might have some success tracking down its location at either the Lake Region Museum or the Old Post Office Museum. However, it seems doubtful that the old house or the stable are still in existence, so it is perhaps safe to say that the hanging man no longer presents an "unpleasant hazard" for unsuspecting children . . . or adults.

Larry, On Stage

The Historic Orpheum Theatre in Sioux Falls, South Dakota, is an active dramatic venue for the locally based Sioux Falls Community Playhouse. With several main-stage productions each year, a Studio Theatre Series and a Youth Education Division, the theatre and its grand old home greatly enhance the cultural life of this city only a few miles from the tricorner region of Minnesota, Iowa, and South Dakota. Virtually all of the acting, directing, and technical work is performed by Sioux Fallians. In recent years, productions have ranged from the Meredith Willson classic "The Music Man," to a stage adaptation of "A Christmas Story"—Jean Shepherd's humorous account of growing up in the 1940s Midwest and of little Ralphie Parker's quest to get his very own Daisy Red Ryder BB rifle. The short story was made into a popular film starring Darren McGavin.

But the one story the theatre has not staged is its very own Ghost Story, for the Orpheum Theatre has a resident spirit.

The tale could begin when the late Sioux Falls actor Ray Loftesness decided to stay late at the theatre way back in 1959. Rehearsals for a mystery/comedy, *The Girls in 509*, had been over for hours but Loftesness wanted to study some particularly difficult stage business and lines that he, and other amateur actors, would be performing in public within a few days.

Now well past midnight, Loftesness was alone, speaking aloud his part as he strode about the set, illuminated only by work lights above the stage. At one place in his role, he had been instructed to look out toward the balcony. On this very late night, however, as he shot a glance toward the darkened gallery . . . something looked back.

"I assumed someone had stayed in the theatre and was playing with the lights," Loftesness remembered. "As I looked up into the balcony there became apparent this very steady glow, which was what I would call an aura, rather of a blue color. I thought for a moment that it was just a blue bulb that someone had turned on, but it began expanding. There was no sound to it. The aura gradually expanded to several feet in diameter and very high. In the center was a man. I could not tell his mode of dress, but he was either pointing or beckoning to me. He seemed to be trying to tell me something."

The mysterious figure made no sound whatsoever.

At about the same moment Loftesness glimpsed the pulsating orb, a stream of cold air enclosed him. It seemed to come from the empty auditorium.

However, the doors had been closed tightly against the chill October air. Loftesness said the icy blast felt as if a freezer door had been suddenly opened, and then slammed shut.

The then-37-year-old amateur actor may have encountered the legendary Larry, a ghost whose origins have been lost in the misty annals of the Orpheum Theatre, the old vaudeville house that is home to the Sioux Falls Community Playhouse. Some accounts say he was a construction worker killed when the building went up around the turn of the century. Or, he might have been a stagehand killed in an accident when the place was host to the top acts in early twentieth-century vaudeville.

But the fact that Ray Loftesness saw a ghostly figure in the balcony may lend credence to a theory that "Larry" fell in love with a married woman and was murdered by a jealous husband . . . in the balcony of the old theatre.

Attempts to trace the ghost's identity have been fruitless. Many newspaper records from earlier in this century were lost in a fire decades ago. Built as a vaudeville house shortly after the turn of the century, the theatre's written history is sketchy, too. The Community Playhouse organization has owned the building since 1954, when the group bought it from Minnesota Amusement Company. The auditorium had been a movie theatre since the 1920s. Sightings of Larry are extremely rare. Ray Loftesness may be the only man who actually saw what he believed was a ghost.

"That feeling of fright began settling into me and I knew I had to leave," Loftesness said of that night decades ago. "I left the theater as hurriedly as possible. I remember going out and locking the door behind me, getting in the car and coming home. I spent a sleepless night."

He returned to the theatre the next morning to see, in his words, "if perhaps someone had been in the theatre after I left." No one had, but the young actor had another surprise waiting for him.

"What did you do down here last night?" the theatre's technical director, Gay Spielman, asked him. Loftesness said he didn't know what Spielman was talking about.

"Well, when I came in here this morning, every fuse in the theater had been blown," Spielman replied.

"I couldn't explain that," Loftesness remembers.

An electrical malfunction was extremely unlikely, as the theater had been re-wired shortly before.

Another incident during dress rehearsals for this same play made Loftesness wonder if, indeed, he wasn't the target for some malevolent entity.

"This happened to be a 'whodunit' show and I was playing the villain," Loftesness said. "One of the actions was that a net was to be dropped down over me, trapping me beneath it.

"We went into dress rehearsals and the scene came and the technicians dropped the net over me. But apparently they hadn't correctly tied a sandbag, which was necessary weight to bring it down correctly over me. The sandbag hit me on the head and knocked me out."

Theatre accidents are not infrequent, and Loftesness, though shaken from the incident, was assured by the crew it would never happen again. Technicians re-adjusted the net and weighted sandbag, hoisted it to a higher level and conducted several more rehearsals to make sure it worked correctly. They had taken "every precaution" Loftesness was told.

But on opening night when the net fell over "villain" Loftesness, the sandbag again went awry, hit him on the head and into unconsciousness. The show was stopped for several minutes until the actor could be revived. No one on the pro-duction staff could explain how the sandbag could have strayed off course. Lof-tesness admits it took him a long time to feel comfortable again on the Community Playhouse's stage.

Interestingly enough, a single, unusual episode of precognition, the ability to "see" future events, involved Ray Loftesness years after he saw "Larry" in the theatre balcony.

Loftesness had a long and distinguished career in show business, broadcasting, and public service. Ten years after his experience with Larry, from 1969 to 1975, he was a manager with Fred Waring and the Pennsylvanians, a popular musical group for nearly 50 years. Waring was known, too, as the inventor of the popular blender that still bears his name.

He was also psychic, according to Loftesness.

"Waring was a remarkable person, of course, with tremendous ability. He led a very interesting life. But very often when I was working closely with him he would make a reference to dreams he had. He would say something 'good' was going to happen today, or something 'bad' will happen. Invariably something of that nature would happen. He was a very deep thinker and he just seemed to have an ability, or some method, to know (future events)," Loftesness said.

Some of Waring's precognitive abilities may have rubbed off on Loftesness. He said that once he did foresee tragedy—near the beginning of a tour by the Penn-sylvanians in 1970.

"I happened to be out on the road ahead of the show. As manager I would contact the theatres in which we were to appear, basically a series of one-nighters. One morning I suddenly saw an image of the tour bus, which Mr. Waring always insisted upon riding in with his 'kids,' literally crawling under a huge semi-trailer truck," Loftesness said.

So clear was the vision that Loftesness thought about calling back to Pennsyl-vania to see if anything bad had taken place. He decided against it because the phone call might have appeared "foolish."

He thought the incident a "personal nightmare" until a phone call from Waring three hours later.

"He said their bus driver had fallen asleep and the bus had slid under a semi-trailer truck. Two people were killed and many members of the cast were injured," Loftesness said. The bus was just leaving Pennsylvania to begin its tour of 200 cities. Waring himself escaped serious injury because he was riding in a rear bed-room compartment.

Loftesness could never erase the prescience of seeing that tour bus slide under the truck and his intuitive sense that something terrible would befall Waring and the Pennsylvanians.

Two very inexplicable brushes with the supernatural left Loftesness with no explanations of why or how the events occurred, only the certainty of their reality.

"I don't understand it, but I do know that something very unusual happened that night (in the theatre). Some people have told me, whenever I bring the subject up, that surely I'm joking. What I say is that I don't understand the experience, but it was as real as any human experience that I've had since. It will always remain with me."

Jack Mortenson of Sioux Falls was once technical director at the Community Playhouse. He, too, confronted the unexplained on the theatre's historic stage.

One stage set had been taken down, "struck," in theatrical parlance, in preparation for a Youth Education Production. Mortenson was going to be that show's technical director. As a final check before starting the new set, Mortenson, like Loftesness before him, found himself alone on the stage late one night.

"I was sweeping the stage before the next day when we were to bring in the kids to start working together (on the set). I had started sweeping from the front of the stage, from left to right. I overlapped the broom about a half-stroke each time to be sure it was clean. Coming back from stage left to stage right on about my fourth or fifth pass, I guess, I sensed a sound behind me, if that sounds reasonable," he remembered.

Mortenson didn't hear anything loudly smashing; rather he seemed to "perceive" that something had happened behind him. He turned around to look and then glanced down. About three steps behind him was a small, square object on the floor that he had just swept clean.

Mortenson walked over and picked up an old tintype photograph. It was of a bearded man who appeared to be in his mid-thirties. His cheeks were tinted rosy, as was the custom in the late nineteenth century. It was slightly larger than a postage stamp.

"I wondered where it had come from because it certainly wasn't in the broom. I had just swept back and forth across the stage and knocked the broom against the floor several times as I went along."

Mortenson turned on the lights, which illuminated the grid above the stage. He thought perhaps someone was hiding up there and had thrown the photograph down as a practical joke. There was no one up there and seemingly little chance that the tintype could have fallen of its own accord.

"I stood there holding this picture, looking at it for what seemed like a long time. Well, the thought of 'Larry' had been there for a time and it suddenly got real cold where I was standing. I just turned and put the tintype on top of the light board, didn't turn off any of the lights, and I walked out very quickly, locked the door, and went home."

Mortenson told his wife about the tintype. She was amazed, and not a little amused, at her husband's story. The next day, Mortenson returned to the theatre. He found the tintype where he had placed it on the lighting panel. Several of his colleagues asked about it and laughed when he revealed its mysterious origins. But they always worked with all the lights on from that day forward. The tintype remained on the light board for many years until a new electrical system was installed. It disappeared after that, but Mortenson thinks it still may lurk somewhere in the theatre—waiting to make another dramatic reappearance.

Where did the tintype come from? Jack Mortenson could not figure it out. As the theatre's technical chief, he had climbed all over the grid above the stage and never seen it. The stage was bare as he pushed the broom across the floor. And, if someone had dropped it earlier, why didn't he see it the first time he brushed that section of the floor? Mortenson had on only the work lights, but it was bright enough to work by.

"There's more doubt in my mind about things that we can't explain," Mortenson said as he reflected on the meaning of the peculiar event. "I'm like the Cowardly Lion. All of a sudden, I do believe!"

Reports of allegedly supernatural events at the Sioux Falls Community Playhouse are very rare and difficult to verify. All good theatres, it is said, should have at least one ghostly inhabitant. Jack Mortenson and the late Ray Loftesness said that, at least in their cases, the supernatural on stage might not be simply a product of imaginative dramatists.

The Sioux Falls Community Playhouse organizes regular theatrical performances in the Historic Orpheum Theatre, 315 North Philips Ave., Sioux Falls. For information about their current performance schedule (or whether Larry has made any recent guest appearances), telephone the theatre at (605) 336-7418.

Banshee of the Badlands

What is it that haunts the desolate Badlands near the place called Watch Dog Butte, South Dakota?

There is a banshee loose in that region, a screeching nightmare in a long, tattered robe and disheveled hair that contorts its arms in strange gestures. On a hillock a mile south of Watch Dog Butte is where this ghost resides. The screams that issue forth from its mouth are said to have chilled the blood of those who have faced all manner of man and beast.

The legend of the Watch Dog banshee is as old as the West itself. Old-timers say it might be the Indian woman who was brutally murdered at the base of the butte. Others maintain it's the ghost of a white woman killed by an Indian war party.

Hunters or hikers unfortunate enough to pass the butte at night frequently find the banshee as a companion. Sudden phosphor flashes warn of her impending visit. She gestures toward them as if asking a question, mouthing words that none can hear. When her unsuspecting hosts suggest they don't understand her appeal, she cries out in a torrent of shrieks that echo from the dry canyon walls. Quickly she is gone, only to reappear on "her" hilltop.

In this land called "hell, with the fires out," a violin-seeking, fleshless skeleton sometimes accompanies the tragic banshee.

He wanders the region after sunset, stopping outside the occasional cabin or isolated ranch house listening for his beloved music. If he hears it, he will stay for hours, his bleached bones swaying to and fro. Should he find a fiddle unattended he takes it up and starts to play a frenetic tune. As the night rushes toward sunrise, the skeleton changes to a mournful passage, growing ever fainter until the first rays of light silence the spectral musician.

Legend warns curious listeners against following the banshee's skeletal escort. The labyrinthine canyons and jagged rocks beneath sudden precipices may doom the unwary tracker, as the intoxicating music slowly drives him mad.

Something Evil on Larabee Street

The haunted house of legend is a Victorian pile, replete with gables and turrets, and windows heavily curtained to ward off prying eyes. A grotesquery of gargoyles crouching along the sagging roofline adds a certain sinister ambiance, as does a weed-choked lawn encircled by a black, wrought-iron fence topped with elaborate scrollwork. Rusty spikes add a nice touch. Then, too, an ancient garden gate must swing on sagging hinges.

But this portrait painted by fictionists should not fool the haunt hunter. It is more accurate to say that even the most tranquil of village neighborhoods may present scenes of inexplicable supernatural terror for the innocent and unwary.

The small town of Horicon, Wisconsin, presents such an attitude, a rural enclave of calm, rational middle-westerners where the biggest yearly event is the arrival of tens of thousands of migrating waterfowl at the famed Horicon Marsh, and the attendant flood of tourists.

The vistas Norman Rockwell might have depicted are deceptive. In a ranch-style bungalow along South Larabee Street—amid the clutter of bicycles and skateboards, lawnmowers and strutting pink flamingo lawn ornaments—there played out a haunting so bizarre that the entire community had an unwilling role to play, and the story eventually captured the attention of media from as far away as Australia and Great Britain. It's a tale of how one family found their lives shattered by what they said were menacing apparitions and psychological horrors so frightening that they fled their home in the middle of an icy January night, literally escaping for their very lives.

Allen and Deborah Tallmann moved their young family into the three-bedroom, ranch-style South Larabee Street home in the spring of 1986. It was their dream come true: a sensible residence affordable even to a factory foreman and his home-maker wife. The house was one of ten built in the neighborhood a few years earlier through the Self-Help Housing Project of Dodge County.

The couple had two children, a boy aged seven and a daughter not quite a year old. We will call them Kenny and Maryann. Deborah was pregnant and would give birth to another daughter, Sarah, later that year.

In every way the Tallmanns were typical of any family in the town. Allen went deer hunting each fall with friends. He worked hard at his job and wanted nothing more than to live in peace with his young family. Deborah devoted her attention to the children and took pride in her tidy, well-ordered home.

The couple was from the area. Parents and grandparents, aunts, uncles, and cousins provided the kind of extended family not unusual for the region. They were content to spend their lives within the confines of a familiar and secure universe.

"When we bought the house we were real excited and happy because it was ours and we owned something for once in our lives. It was a great opportunity . . . at the time," Deborah said about their stake in the community.

Allen qualified for a low-interest, Farmers Home Administration (FmHA) loan because of his income and family size. With the modest mortgage payments, the family figured they would have the house paid for well before his retirement.

Or so they thought.

South Larabee Street is a short roadway, extending only a few blocks at the edge of Horicon near a small wetland. The houses in the development look much the same, primarily one-story ramblers with attached garages. The dominant house color is white. There are no sidewalks. Children scamper across lawns or whiz up and down the street on bicycles and neighbors still visit across backyard fences. Until the early 1980s, the area was best known as a teenager's "lover's lane" and where local police broke up occasional beer parties. Old St. Malachy's Catholic cemetery is two blocks away.

The Tallmanns seemed to fit right in. Deborah was thirty years old, Allen thirty-two.

The first few months in their new home were uneventful. The couple spent their time painting and decorating and getting to know their neighbors. But, within a short time, Deborah and Allen began to notice changes in their home and family, a transformation so subtle that it wasn't until much later that they were able to understand its significance.

"It was after a couple of months," Deborah remembered. "We didn't see anything and nothing unusual happened, but our health started going downhill. I had my kids in the doctor's office at least once a week and sometimes three times. They had everything. Maryann was in the hospital twice, once for chicken pox and once for a cold and an ear infection. Allen had back problems. We were just sick all the time."

At first they thought the illnesses might be traced to building materials used in the house. But a check with building inspectors told them that was not the case. Asbestos or other toxic substances were not present in the house, she said.

Allen's personality, too, began to change. He was easily irritated. When night fell he became "itchy," in Allen's own words, and got "real jittery, short-tempered." He often argued with Deborah over trivial matters. When their second daughter was born that November, he threatened to leave the family and went on a drinking binge. It was uncharacteristic behavior for him. Looking back on the episodes, he can only attribute his mean disposition to their lives in the house on South Larabee Street.

Deborah's mother and sister also seemed to change when they visited.

According to Deborah, "We have real close family relationships, and when we moved in our families would come and visit us all the time. We had a brand-new home and they liked coming here. But it seemed that after a couple of months the visits from our family . . . well, they just didn't want to go there."

During her pregnancy, Deborah was diagnosed with placenta previa, the misplacement of the placenta in an abnormally low position in the uterus. Doctors confined her to her home and cautioned her not to perform housework, or other heavy chores. Her mother came over almost every day until the baby was born.

Deborah eventually found out just how much her mother disliked their "dream home."

"She told me after I had the baby (that) she couldn't wait to leave the house. And the farther away she got, the more relaxed she became because she was so tense in the house. She would tell me, it's a beautiful house, but she just didn't like it."

At about the same time, during the summer and early fall after they moved in, Deborah's sister also stopped visiting. The reasons were the same, a smothering sensation whenever she stepped through the door. "She told me she would love to come over," Deborah said, "but she got headaches whenever she was in our house and actually got sick to her stomach."

The Tallmanns bought a six-month-old kitten—nicknamed Cat—soon after they moved in. It seemed fine for the first few weeks. But then Cat went berserk, Deborah said. "She would actually climb the walls. Sometimes she would come flying across the living room and climb right up a door." Once she crashed into the wall. Cat's rude behavior seemed particularly prevalent after sunset.

Allen started putting the kitten in the bathroom at night, even though she would howl. One night, however, he decided to leave her on the living room couch where she was curled up, sleeping. That was a mistake.

"A couple of hours later," he recalled, "Cat came running across the bed. Deborah had a chest of drawers and a TV set on top with a cable box on it. The cat jumped straight up to the cable TV box."

The cat then leaped for the wall where it hung on the plaster for a few seconds. "Just like an owl," Allen said, shaking his head at the memory.

Cat soon found a new home.

Not long after Cat's antics, another, more perplexing incident happened, yet the couple was still unconvinced that the strange behavior by those who visited—or lived in—the house on South Larabee Street was anything out of the ordinary.

The Tallmanns wanted a night out before their next baby was born. Even more than they wanted to admit, the sicknesses of their two children, the attitudes of in-laws, Allen's shifting demeanor, and the problems with Cat were beginning to weigh upon the couple. The couple just wanted to get away from everything for a few hours.

They hired a baby-sitter, a girl of sixteen who had babysat for them before, and made plans to dine at a favorite restaurant in a nearby city. The evening was pleasant and relaxing, a welcome respite from the growing tension of the past few months.

Their serene evening ended abruptly when they returned home. The baby-sitter rushed to meet them. She blurted out a fantastic story that left Allen and Deborah understandably skeptical. While the girl and seven-year-old Kenny played a board game in the kitchen, a chair at the table started rocking back and forth. It bounced around and then suddenly stopped. The girl was visibly shaken by the incident.

"I just looked at Allen. We didn't want to say she was lying, so we just kind of brushed it off as, well, maybe it did and maybe it didn't," Deborah said. The girl was from a good family and had never said anything even remotely as amazing as the tale she reported that night. Little Kenny corroborated the girl's story when his parents questioned him the next morning. He seemed as upset as the baby-sitter about the incident.

The household seemed to return to normal over the next six months. Deborah gave birth to Sarah in November, Allen went deer hunting with friends, and both tried to adjust to the pattern of life in their home. The children made new friends in the neighborhood. Kenny was in school most of the day, so little Maryann tried to help her mother as best she could with the new baby.

Little Sarah was nearly seven months old when her parents decided that she could begin sharing a room with her big sister. Kenny had been sleeping in the larger of the two children's bedrooms. He moved into the smaller room and the girls were given bunk beds in Kenny's old bedroom.

The room switch by the children seemed to trigger a new round of increasingly violent incidents.

"On the same day we moved Kenny into the room where Maryann had been sleeping, we put a clock radio in there, one with a sleeper alarm," Deborah said. "He had gone to bed with the radio on so it would go off (after) he went to sleep. He came out after a while and said the radio had switched stations. We thought maybe the radio had picked up static, or another station had come in, something on that order. We didn't make too much of it."

Deborah led Kenny by the hand back to his room. She tucked him in, tuned in a radio station, checked the sleep timer and left the room.

Kenny came running back out a few minutes later.

The radio had again changed stations, only this time, Kenny told his mother, he saw the knob turn and the tuning indicator spin across the dial. Deborah and Allen had no way of verifying what Kenny said, but they saw he was very frightened. They wanted to believe him. He was usually a pretty reliable little boy. Deborah took the radio from her son's room and put it in the front closet.

Deborah feared this would add to Kenny's growing irritability. He frequently refused to go to his room alone at bedtime, and rarely slept through the night. He heard "noises" he said, like someone was banging on the water pipes in the basement. Maybe, his mother reasoned, the pressures of a new school, a new neighborhood, and a new sister were causing him to feel some resentment. Deborah had given birth to Kenny before she met and married Allen. Although the boy spent some time with his biological father, the two weren't particularly close.

"We thought maybe this was his way of getting more attention," Deborah said.

A second episode involving a small suitcase stowed under Kenny's bed did nothing to dispel his mother's belief that perhaps he was making up stories to get attention.

Kenny had again fought going to his room that night. After the usual kicking and screaming, Kenny had calmed down enough for his parents to turn off the lights and go back into the living room. A few minutes later, Kenny came running out crying that the suitcase had slid out from underneath his bed. It had zoomed across the floor and then scooted back.

Deborah simply refused to believe him. That just couldn't possibly have happened, she told him. She thought he wanted to stay up late and watch television. Kenny insisted that he had seen the suitcase move. Deborah put him back in bed.

When, in a short time, he ran out repeating the same story, Allen grabbed the suitcase, which was under the bed, and tossed it in the same closet where the radio had been secreted.

All three children had disturbing nighttime experiences during the summer and early fall of 1987.

"Our kids rarely slept straight through the night from the day we moved into that house," Deborah said. "We were up all the time with them; it almost seemed that whatever was in that house would wake the kids up. We could go in and check them and they'd be sound asleep and all of a sudden they'd be crying or fussing. It always seemed to happen about the time we'd crawl into bed. We'd no more than get into bed and the kids would be awake, and they'd stay awake for a long time."

Sometimes her parents heard Maryann, who was now nearly two and one-half years old, apparently talking to someone. "We'd wake up in the middle of the night and we would hear her giggling and talking in there. We never really thought that much about it. We believed she was talking to the doll or her teddy bear," Deborah said. She and Allen joked that their daughter seemed to be having her own little tea party.

Any lightheartedness they felt at Maryann's nocturnal ramblings soon ended, however. The girl's odd conversations soon gave way to nightmares that sent her running to her parents' room.

"She would get to our room and talk about the noises she heard," Deborah said. "She'd say 'Don't you hear it?' We didn't know what it was. She would make the sound 'Shhh Shhh Shhh.' like it was a voice."

Rarely were all three children awake at the same time. When one woke up with a nightmare, the other two slept. While Maryann babbled away, Sarah, in the same room, would not be disturbed. Kenny's separate room kept his own nighttime problems from affecting the girls, and vice versa.

Until September 1987 the peculiar episodes came in irregular patterns. For several days in a row, the children would have restless nights or Allen and Deborah would fight over minor incidents. Then the household would return to normal for a week or so before a new trauma struck the family.

Deborah never heard voices, but there were some occasions when other occurrences startled her. "I heard the garage door open and close. I thought maybe somebody had come in over the fence and went in the back door because we had a freezer full of meat (in the garage). I called up the neighbor next door and said I thought somebody was in the garage and asked her to hang onto the phone while I went to look. There was nobody out there, but the garage door had opened and shut. I heard it."

Violent nightmares also became a problem for Deborah. Like most people, she occasionally had dreams vivid enough to wake her up, but after her move to South Larabee Street they became so violent they made her think she was going mad.

"I'm the kind of person who doesn't have nightmares very often," Deborah said. "But, I had them all the time in the house, one right after another. Horrible nightmares. I'd wake up in the night crying, and I'd ask Allen, am I going to have nightmares like this all my life? They would be terrible, ungodly. I would dream my kids were dying, that Allen was dying, my father would die. People would come up from the basement and line us up along the wall and just shoot us all down. Or, people would kidnap my kids, or they would fall in the river and drown. Over and over again . . . people were going to hurt us."

Deborah can't explain or understand what caused this onslaught of terror-filled dreams, only that they seemed to worsen the longer she lived in the house.

The long nights of soothing their frightened children frazzled the couple's already taut nerves. Only Allen seemed capable of bringing comfort to the children. He would lie on the floor of the girls' room until they settled down, then go into Kenny's room until he fell asleep.

"I heard the banging when I was in there," Allen said. "I told the kids it was the water heater, but I knew the noises I heard didn't come from a water heater. I went down to the basement a lot of times with running hot water upstairs to get the water heater to kick in. You could hear a couple of little plinks and hear the humming from the burner, but the noises I heard the nights I spent in Kenny's room, well it was like mice or rats or something crawling around . . ."

But check as they might, the couple never found evidence of rodents. According to the couple, the house was extremely well-insulated. Allen looked through the low attic and checked around the foundation and in the floorboards for any signs that an animal had somehow gotten inside. Eventually, he dismissed the idea.

For all of the problems the family was facing, Deborah rarely discussed the situation with her husband. "We never talked about the fact that maybe something was going on."

"I fought it," Allen said. "I fought it all the time. Deborah thought there was something in our house. I didn't go for that at first. We used to have some bad arguments."

"But we never really sat down and talked about it," Deborah added. "I mean, just sat down and said this is happening, now what are we going to do about it. Never did we talk about it until . . ."

Until the vague feelings of uneasiness, increasingly cranky children and family tensions gave way to a number of events with one thing in common—they could not be attributed to the imagination.

When the weather started getting cooler, late in September 1987, Allen Tallmann started painting the concrete walls in the basement. It is what's called a "finished" basement, but only used by Deborah for her washer and dryer and as a playroom for the children. The couple had plans to partition the area into a couple of extra rooms.

By now it had become routine for Allen to stay in his daughters' room, stretched out on the floor reading stories until their steady breathing told him they were asleep.

But one night Allen reassessed his skepticism that something unknown and unseen might be loose in their home.

"Deborah asked me to come upstairs," Allen recalled, so he could get the children to sleep. "I took the paint brush and I laid it right across the paint tray. I was upstairs probably a half-hour, forty-five minutes at the most. I told Deb I was going to go back down and paint just a little bit more. It was about 9:30 P.M. Now, up until this point I wasn't scared in the house. Nothing bothered me. Well, I went downstairs and my paint brush had been pulled out of the pan and was jammed upside down in a can of paint."

Allen just stared. The brush was propped absolutely upright, the wooden handle completely immersed in the epoxy paint, like a jokester had placed it there. It hadn't been him, but that was the only thing he knew for certain.

"I didn't say anything. I asked Deb to throw down some towels. I told her I must have knocked the paint brush into the can, but I knew I didn't. I cleaned the paint brush off and painted a little while longer."

A few minutes later he glimpsed what he believed was a shadow flit across the basement. He thought it might have been a passing car's lights throwing silhouettes across the walls and furnace (a basement window faced the street), but he quickly cleaned off the brush and went upstairs.

"A kind of chill went through my spine. That was enough painting for one night." He decided against telling Deborah what had happened.

Another odd incident in the basement almost made the couple believe that it was a prankster and not the supernatural out to harm them. Allen found one of the basement windows removed and sitting on the floor propped against the wall one morning.

Deborah said: "The window was just like it had slid down. Almost like someone had gone into the basement and set it there and crawled back out. We thought somebody had broken into our house. If someone had kicked it in, it would have fallen and crashed. We were home the night before so we would have heard it." Allen had a valuable collection of hunting rifles, power tools, and a chain saw in the basement, but nothing appeared to have been taken. They didn't call the police.

"What we couldn't figure out was, if somebody broke in, how did they get from that high up down to the floor, because they would have had to scoot through the window and jump down. That's okay, I guess, but in order to get back out they would have had to climb on a chair or something. It was real puzzling, but we just put the window back and let it go."

After that, Deborah, in particular, didn't want to go into the basement, especially at night. She admits that a certain paranoia took hold, an almost palpable sense that the family was being watched.

"It would be very warm outside, but we would close all the windows and lock them. We just wouldn't leave them open because we were afraid somebody was going to come in."

The family bought a dog to help foster a sense of security. It was a young shepherd/labrador mix that they were mistakenly told had been housebroken. That wasn't the only problem they had with him.

Deborah said: "The dog barked all night and it messed in the house. The first night we had him there, I had to send it outside to the fenced-in yard. The dog barked at the house, especially when it was night. All day long it would be in the kennel but as soon as the sun started to set, the dog would pace back and forth barking. It just wouldn't shut up. We tried to discipline it. We would bring it in the house, but it just went crazy, scratching at the door wanting to go out. But if you left it outside it would start barking again. We couldn't keep it in and we couldn't keep it out."

Unlike the cat, the dog stayed with the family. The barking problem subsided somewhat with training, although he remained edgy in the house after dark. The Tallmanns found out later that other neighborhood dogs often barked at their house for no apparent reason.

In October 1987, Allen Tallmann was promoted to foreman on the night shift at the manufacturing plant where he worked. Deborah wasn't looking forward to the prospect of staying alone with the children until Allen returned at one or two in the morning.

In late October, Allen became sick with a severe sinus infection and cold. He took medicine, but nothing seemed to improve his condition. The frequent trips with their sick children to the doctor over the past months had been expensive, even with the family's insurance covering part of the cost. Allen was reluctant to seek medical treatment for himself.

One night at about ten o'clock, however, his condition worsened. "I had taken a shower and crawled in bed," Allen remembered. "I was sleeping when I started coughing and then threw up. I got real short of breath."

Deborah called Allen's mother in a panic. She came right over and said she would watch the children while Deborah took Allen to the hospital. He was worse by this time; he had a difficult time catching his breath. Deborah was concerned over her husband's deteriorating condition and called an ambulance.

Hospital personnel stabilized Allen's condition, gave him medication, and sent him home a few hours later.

Allen's mother met the couple at the door, purse and car keys in hand, ready to leave. After a perfunctory inquiry into her son's health, she hurried out. The couple was startled at her rather brusque manner, but they thought she was simply tired from a long day.

However, a telephone conversation sometime later between Allen and his mother indicated another reason entirely. "I asked her if she got a funny feeling when she was at our house because it didn't seem like she wanted to visit us anymore," Allen said. His mother hesitated momentarily and then admitted that, yes, she didn't enjoy coming over at all and, in fact, couldn't wait to leave whenever she was there. She had been especially upset the night Allen went to the hospital.

"That night she was laying on the couch after the kids had gotten settled down and had dozed off," Allen said. "It then seemed like somebody woke her up. She said there were red eyes looking in the window. She blinked and couldn't believe it. She looked again and they were still there." The couch Mrs. Tallmann napped on was directly beneath the living room's wide front window. When she sat up, the staring eyes vanished. Mrs. Tallmann thought someone was looking in through the window, according to her son.

"The only thing that crossed my mind," Deborah Tallmann offered, "is that a car might have driven in the driveway directly across from us. But then she had gone to the window and looked out and she didn't see anybody. You think she would have seen them (neighbors) getting out of their car."

Whatever it was, Allen's mother was very happy to see her son and daughter-in-law return home.

Mrs. Tallmann's description of the red, glowing eyes turned out to be prophetic. That riveting image was to return on several occasions over the next several months.

The most frustrating aspect of the couple's twenty months on Larabee Street was their inability to identify any specific pattern of activity—of something, anything—that would point to a cause for all their problems. They desperately wanted to believe that perhaps it was a prankster that was responsible. The acts were too random, certainly, to connect them with the supernatural. Were the nervous animals simply misbehaving? Did Allen's mother really see taillights? Was Allen confused about where he had left the paint brush? Maybe the children were just being cranky, as children often are.

Or perhaps it was something more, a slowly developing pattern of harassment by some sort of entity that, for whatever reason, had found a haven in the Tallmann home. On Friday, November 19, 1987, Allen, along with his father and brother, left on his annual weekend deer-hunting trip to an area near Wisconsin Rapids, a city in north central Wisconsin. Deborah didn't want to stay alone with the children. Her sister volunteered to stay with her at the house. Both Allen and Deborah weren't entirely convinced that someone wasn't harassing them and went so far as to put a lock on the basement door. Allen still wondered about that mysterious incident with the basement window.

But the house was quiet during Allen's absence, and for the next week. On the following Saturday, November 27, however, an accidentally watched scene from a television show started a new wave of anxiety in the family.

"My mom was baby-sitting for the kids," Deborah said. "Maryann and Kenny were watching television. My mom was flipping through the channels when she turned on a show that had a big bonfire, and out of this fire came running a man wearing a pig's head. It must have been a horror movie of some kind. My mother changed the channel but not before Maryann noticed what was going on."

When Deborah put her to bed later that night, the explicit television scene remained with the little girl. She told her mother that there was a fire in her room and somebody was watching her. She wouldn't settle down. Deborah had to sit with her until she finally fell asleep.

The images of fires and men wearing animal heads plagued Maryann for days afterwards. Fires were on the door, in the windows, and "something" was hiding behind the door ready to pounce when the lights were turned off. A nightly ritual began whereby Maryann took a pitcher from the kitchen cupboard to her bedroom, put all the "monsters" inside and then snapped the lid on the container. She then dumped the "monsters" in the garbage can. Deborah assured her daughter that they were all gone after that.

The problems Allen and Deborah had with Maryann were never discussed with Kenny. "He was fearful enough," Deborah said. "We didn't need to add to that."

Once Maryann sat up so quickly in her lower bunk bed, she hit her head on the bed frame. She cried about "a fire on the door" and came charging down the hallway and jumped into her parents' bed. Neither of the other children heard her cries.

Did the television images contribute to Maryann's nightmares? Her mother thinks that was only part of the problem. Deborah continued to hear her daughter "laughing and giggling," saying something like "hi there" while the rest of the house was silent and dark. When the child became overly frightened and joined her parents in bed, she would say "It's coming" and then state matter-of-factly, "It's here . . . it's here." When her parents asked who—or what—was coming, Maryann got upset and wondered why her parents couldn't hear or see "it."

On the Sunday before Christmas, a new chapter was added to the family's woes, one that would presage their final flight. Eight-year-old Kenny had an encounter with a mysterious figure, a three-foot-tall, hideous-looking, wrinkled old woman.

"Kenny came into our room and said that he woke up to see this lady standing by his door," Deborah said. "When I went with him to his room I didn't see anything. He said she was very old, very ugly, and had a glow around her . . . like a fire. She had long black hair. . . . I tried to tell him it was his imagination and he should go back to sleep. About five minutes later he called to me that she was standing there again."

It was nearly daybreak and Deborah sat up with her son for the rest of the night unable to convince him that it was either his imagination or, as she suggested, an "angel" come to visit him.

"She's too homely to be an angel," Kenny shot back.

When Kenny left for school Monday morning, Allen and Deborah had their first long conversation about the similarities between Maryann's nightmares and Kenny's glowing lady. They also started comparing notes on all the bizarre occurrences over the past eighteen months.

"I told him about Kenny and the little old lady and how she glowed like fire," Deborah said. "We never mentioned anything to Kenny about what was happening to Maryann. The stories were just too similar, too coincidental to ignore. I started talking about how pale Kenny was and how my mom (didn't like) being in the house. . . ."

The couple realized their lives were slowly coming unraveled, their children increasingly disturbed, yet they were at a loss as to what steps should be taken. They considered selling the house, but thought better of it after they calculated the money they might lose in the transaction. Deborah decided that she would call their pastor, the Rev. Wayne Dobratz. "If we had a ghost, the person you would call is a minister," Deborah said. Rev. Dobratz couldn't come over right away, but promised he would stop by as soon as possible.

Other problems surfaced during the couple's discussion that morning at the kitchen table. Allen confided to his wife that he had a growing uneasiness whenever he came into the house. He had the impression "something" was waiting in the garage for him, watching his every movement. When he pulled down the garage door, Allen said it was like "shutting himself in a tomb."

One night as he walked from the garage into the house, he felt a tugging on the lunch pail he held under his arm, as if an unseen hand was trying to pull it away from him. So intense was his dread of entering the house that sometimes he was reluctant to even turn in his driveway.

Deborah remained relatively untouched by the malevolence, but her biggest fear was seeing what was happening to her husband and children. Only they seemed to be the targets of the hostility.

Reverend Dobratz's first visit to the house did not assuage the Tallmanns' fears.

"We told him what was going on," Deborah said. "We asked him if he had ever dealt with anything like this before. It was the devil, he said. Well, that upset us even more. We were already scared enough, but to think that the devil was in our house . . . !"

The pastor wanted to know if anyone in the family had been playing with an Ouija Board, or had held a séance. The Tallmanns hardly knew what to say. They didn't dabble in either activity.

"He convinced us that we had a spirit in our house. It more than likely was not the devil he said, but it was of the devil and our house was cursed," Deborah recalled. "He thought maybe somebody had gotten into our house, someone that had something against us, and put a 'spell' on the house."

Reverend Dobratz told Deborah and Allen to start attending church each Sunday. The family was nominally religious but their attendance hadn't been on a weekly basis. "It seemed like every time Sunday came around, our children were sick or I'd have been up all night and I was exhausted," Deborah said, but the family did start attending church regularly. The minister also suggested that the family recite prayers and read passages from the Bible to rid the house of the evil. They followed his advice.

Allen and Deborah were not convinced the devil, or his minions, were responsible for what was happening to their family. Allen said: "I just couldn't believe in my heart that the Lord would do something of this nature to me. We might not go to church all the time, and I used a little foul language once in a while, but never have I done any bodily harm to anybody or ever threatened anyone. For my pastor to say we've got the devil in our house . . ."

But, at the family's request, Pastor Dobratz returned to South Larabee Street and blessed the house. All was quiet until a few days before Christmas.

Deborah said: "Kenny had been allowed to sleep on the couch in our living room because he was so frightened to go to his room at night. We always left a light on and when he slept he faced our Christmas tree. I could see him from our bedroom. We had all gone to bed as usual when about three-thirty in the morning Kenny called out to me that the ghost was in the living room. I got up to look but didn't see anything. He said she had been right where I was standing. I went back to bed, but no more than five minutes later he said she was back again. She had gotten bigger."

Again, Deborah ran into the living room. Kenny said the figure vanished just as his mother reached him. When it happened a third time, Deborah, frustrated and not a little frightened remained in her bedroom.

"Kenny said she was looking at him," Deborah said. "She was standing by the Christmas tree. When he asked her what she wanted, she just stared at him harder. I heard him say 'Why don't you just go away and leave us alone!' That's when I came back out into the living room. He was so scared, it was like he was paralyzed."

Deborah fully believed her little boy. He was wide awake, she had heard him shouting at something. His fear was too real. But who this phantom woman was, and why she had menaced Kenny, remained a mystery. Perhaps it was the same diminutive figure he had seen some months before, she surmised.

Deborah said: "There was little doubt in our minds after Kenny saw that little lady. I didn't want to put up with any more of it. I had about all that I could take. The kids were paranoid, they wouldn't let me go to the bathroom, they wouldn't go to the bedrooms themselves. I had to constantly take them almost everywhere I went. They always got frightened. After a point you can't explain these things to children anymore. I couldn't tell them not to be afraid, because I was scared myself. The minute it got dark out, the house was in chaos. The girls were screaming, Kenny was yelling. I couldn't put Maryann and Sarah to bed because Kenny wouldn't stay in the living room by himself."

The more Allen thought about what Reverend Dobratz said, the angrier he became, barely able to concentrate at work. He decided to go after the evil himself, if indeed that was the cause of his family's turmoil.

"I came home," Allen said, "and at the top of my lungs I yelled for whatever it was in my house to leave my children alone. I said if it wanted to fight, it could fight with me."

That was not the right approach. Everything just got worse.

"I went to work the next day, but that night I had a dream about a child near a line fence. I didn't know the child, but it was at somebody's farm in the country. As I was driving my car down the road, I stopped to watch him playing around by a barn. I looked across the fields and it was lightning and thundering, so I thought I'd better watch this child because there was no house around.

"I looked up into the sky and saw a funnel cloud come down and start racing across the field. The wind was howling and whistling. I ran to grab the child and got him in the car, but he got back out. He wasn't going with me. About a mile up the road was our house. I couldn't worry about him anymore because he didn't want to come with me. So I drove quickly to my house to get my own children. But when I got there they were gone; there was nobody there. There were no curtains in the window. I kept looking back and the tornado was coming, but there was nothing left in our house."

Allen awakened from the nightmare in a cold sweat, nervous and frightened by the vivid details. What, if anything, did it mean? he asked himself. An innocent child? Howling tornadoes bearing down upon Allen and the little boy? A house deserted? Dreams could foretell the future, he once heard. Could this nightmare so real be connected in some way to the mysterious events plaguing his family?

Allen arrived home from work just before one o'clock a few days later, on Thursday January 7, 1988. The house was dark, save for a dim light kept on in the kitchen. As he put his key in the front door lock, a faint whistling followed by a gust of wind came from the direction of the garage door. The wind became stronger as he turned the door handle to go inside. He thought immediately of his earlier dream.

Suddenly a soft but commanding voice called out, "Come here!"

Allen jumped off the porch and ran to the side of the garage. He thought someone was hiding there trying to scare him. He didn't see anyone near the house. The street was empty at this hour. He strained his ears to catch the sound of running feet but nothing disturbed the cold, bleak night.

"I stood out there maybe five or ten minutes," Allen said. "My wife and children were in the house, but I had to find out where this voice came from. I just couldn't find anything, so I started back up the sidewalk to the porch when it started in again—a howling noise. I started to put my key into the lock when that voice said, 'Come here!' Only it was real loud this time."

Allen quickly looked back over his shoulder.

"I saw this glowing coming from the garage. It got brighter and brighter. I backed off the porch, but it seemed to draw me nearer to it. Flames were coming out of my garage and then the eyes appeared in the overhead door."

Shimmering green eyes punctuated with blood red pupils seemed to float in the wide door—eyes that matched the description of those seen by his mother months before.

"I really don't know how I got the door open so fast, but once I did I ran inside and slammed the door," Allen recalls.

For several seconds, Allen leaned trembling against the doorframe listening to see if the commotion had awakened anyone in the house. It hadn't. But then a horrifying thought occurred to him.

"I said 'Oh, my God, my garage is on fire.' I opened the door and ran back out."

There was no wind, no phantom voice beckoning Allen to move closer. The garage was dark. He walked slowly down the sidewalk toward the attached garage. He really couldn't quite believe what he was seeing . . . nothing out of place, all things quiet and peaceful.

He peered through the garage window but could only see the dim outlines of bicycles, tools, and outdoor furniture stored along the walls. He turned and ran back into the house, bolting the door after him.

"My lunch pail was sitting on the floor by the front door. I picked it up and started walking toward the kitchen when it seemed that something, somebody, came up from behind and slammed against me. My lunch pail went flying across the room, hit the table leg, and opened. My thermos bottle rolled out across the floor."

Allen quickly picked up the spilled contents and ran into the bedroom, sensing all the while that "this thing" was right behind him.

Deborah had finally awakened at the racket Allen was causing in the living room.

"He came flying into the bedroom, threw his keys on the dresser, jumped in bed and just lay there," she said. Allen stared at the yawning doorway as if in anticipation that his tormentor would soon appear.

Suddenly Allen sat up straight. "Can you hear it? Can't you hear that howling?"

Deborah shook her head. She was truly frightened—for herself, for her family, and especially for her husband, who seemed on the verge of collapse. She grabbed him by the arm and demanded to know what it was he heard.

"It sounded like it was growling at me," Allen said later. "But I think it was more the sound of that wind, it was just howling, a whistling noise. It would be real high and then go very low. It was right there in the bedroom. I didn't see anything, but I could hear it, all the time."

Allen got out of bed and turned on every light in the house. The couple stayed awake until dawn. They were scared. None of the children awoke, even though Allen wandered through the house for hours, telling "it" to leave him and his family in peace.

"It seemed like this thing was zeroing in on one person," Allen said. "It would 'tune' everybody else out and keep them sleeping." On this night, the target was Allen.

Remembering that traumatic night, Deborah said: "Allen is not a person that scares very easily, and I'm not either, but he was absolutely terrified."

Allen fell exhausted into bed at daybreak. Deborah stayed up to get Kenny ready for school.

None of the children knew what had happened to their father, although Kenny sensed the next day that his mother was very upset. She refused to tell him what was wrong.

Allen began to contemplate drastic measures. "I can remember one night shortly after this incident at the garage door when I came home thinking that I was right on the edge of losing control. I was going to put shells in my deer rifle and wait for this thing. Blow it to hell. But Deb stopped me. She said, 'It's not something you can shoot, you can't kill it.' "

After Allen's "challenge," he realized the evil force was focusing even more intently . . . on him.

"I'd feel this thing as soon as I got to the door. It was like somebody was trying to shove me back out. I wouldn't even go through the (attached) garage anymore. And once I did get inside, I couldn't sleep, or if I did get to sleep, it would wake me right back up. I'd walk through the house and it seemed like it was always there, but I never could see anything. And that was really working on my mind. I'd be at work and think about it constantly, hour after hour. Everybody was at home and there I was . . . I'd get off work and be fine, but then I'd get down to that street and this thing was there to meet me every night, as soon as I pulled in the driveway. It would never show itself to me, but it was there."

Each night the couple latched all the windows, locked and barricaded the doors going into the basement and garage so they wouldn't rattle in the middle of the night—a regular occurrence that they tried to ignore.

Deborah said: "Allen was going to buy metal bars to put on the basement windows. I told him that whatever was happening, it was not coming from outside our house. Barring the windows wasn't going to keep it away. Locking the doors wasn't going to keep it away. By pushing the chair up against it, the door wasn't going to rattle, but something else was going to happen. It was going to continue to be there, no matter what."

The family had turned from keeping a single light on at night while they watched television to having every lamp in the house ablaze from dusk until dawn. With Allen at work each night, Deborah was dealing with three terrified children, following her even when she went to the kitchen while they watched television.

Deborah had wanted to abandon the house right after Kenny's encounter with the strange woman. She wasn't sure she could last even a few more days. Allen resisted moving. He thought that somehow they could figure out what was going on.

"I told Allen that he went to work and was safe," Deborah said. "He didn't have this happening, this constant pressure."

Allen's attitude toward the events always fluctuated from day to day. When there was a period without odd events, he would settle down and be encouraged that his family could somehow "survive." When the sun shone and the world seemed a bright and cheerful place, the Tallmanns breathed more easily.

Neither did they ever question their own sanity. "We knew that we were all right," Deborah said. "Something was happening to us." The Tallmanns just didn't know what it was.

They were still concerned that someone had a grudge against them and used "black magic" or "witchcraft" to get even. The couple asked Pastor Dobratz his opinion, and he said it was a "possibility."

Try as they could, however, neither Allen nor Deborah could think of anyone who would want to harm them. Especially disturbing was the idea that someone would want to hurt or frighten their children. Though the couple were natives of the region, they were newcomers to Horicon itself and didn't know that many people. With three small children and a modest income they rarely socialized, except at family gatherings and an occasional dinner out.

The family's final days in the house were filled with strange and intense events that became, in the end, their breaking point.

On Friday night, January 8, Jonathan, a sixteen-year-old relative of Allen's, spent the night at the house so the two could get up early the following morning to go ice fishing. At about midnight, the teenager got up to look for a snack in the kitchen. The refrigerator door was standing open.

Deborah was astonished when she heard about the episode the next day: "The refrigerator is tipped so that the door can never stay open. When I put away groceries, the door's banging me in the shoulders all the time, and I keep pushing it back." The two floor levelers at the back of the refrigerator were broken off so the unit actually leaned backwards.

The couple insist that it would be impossible for the refrigerator door to stand open under normal circumstances. But considering all that had happened, they weren't particularly surprised that the refrigerator door suddenly developed an ability to operate on its own accord.

Late Saturday afternoon, after a morning of ice fishing, the teenager was loading a suitcase in the Tallmann's car in the driveway so Allen could drive him home when he saw a floating red light through the garage door window. It seemed to hover near the ceiling of the garage. When he got back inside he asked Allen if he kept a light on in the garage. The answer was no. He and Allen looked but found nothing to account for the shimmering light.

By the end of this day, odd lights would be the least of the Tallmanns' troubles.

After Allen returned from taking Jonathan home Deborah asked him for help in putting the girls to bed.

Deborah said: "I wouldn't go back there by myself to put them in bed. So Allen and I both went. I was praying to let whatever was happening be gone. The girls were almost sleeping. Kenny was in the living room and he kept calling 'Are you coming out?' So I went out there to do some housework and Allen stayed in the room."

The next few minutes were a turning point for the family, according to Allen: "On normal nights when we'd put the girls to bed they would put up a fuss for an hour or so. They would stay awake, or they'd raise their heads up. They'd look to see if we were still there. They didn't want to go to sleep until they got to the point where they just couldn't hold their eyes open anymore.

"Well, for some reason that night the girls were relaxed and they went right to sleep. I was laying on the floor about ready to get up when I heard this high-pitched sound just like I heard the night in the garage. It started out with that whistling, kind of like a vacuum cleaner. I sat right up and looked but it died back down. I laid back down and it came right back. I thought it was something in the furnace pipe."

What Allen heard had nothing to do with furnace pipes or anything else of a mechanical nature. For the first time Allen saw the face of the evil on Larabee Street.

Rising from the carpeted floor came a fog. At first less than a foot in height, the misty substance grew until it reached nearly to the ceiling. Allen shrank against the wall as the vapor took on the form of a body, a human figure shimmering in the center of the room. A head formed, two penetrating red eyes with sickly green pupils fixed intently on Allen. A translucent arm came up and pointed, the entire shape moving inexorably toward him.

A voice as if from the grave spoke to him.

"You're dead!"

As it seemed about to envelop him, the figure dissipated in a burst of flame.

When Allen staggered out of the bedroom, his wife thought he was having a heart attack. He looked stunned, almost paralytic in his movements.

"He was completely white and his lips were purple," Deborah said of her husband. "He stumbled into the wall, ran into the bird cage and he just looked at me, tears coming down his face. He wouldn't tell me what happened. He just kept saying 'leave me alone, leave me alone!'"

Deborah quickly telephoned Pastor Dobratz and begged him to come over. She choked back tears as she described Allen's behavior. Something must have happened to Allen in the bedroom, she told her pastor, but he wouldn't tell her.

Reverend Dobratz said he would be right over.

Deborah returned to her husband, who by now had collapsed in a chair at the kitchen table. Again she asked him what was wrong. This time he told her the entire story.

Within a few minutes their pastor had arrived. The household was in chaos. The children had been awakened by their father's crying and the loud conversation and now they were also crying. Neither of the girls had awakened during their father's ordeal.

Pastor Dobratz urged the couple to leave the house immediately and not to return until after church the next day, Sunday January 10. They quickly packed a couple of suitcases and left for a relative's home. Deborah glanced at the garage as their car pulled out of the driveway. At the top of the garage door glowed a small intense flame. She blinked and looked back. The image was gone. She still isn't sure that what she saw was in any way real, or a by-product of that chaotic night.

The Tallmanns awoke Sunday morning planning to attend church services with Allen's family. However, a half-hour before church Allen discovered he couldn't start the car.

"We even jumped it," Allen said, referring to the process of attaching cables from his car's battery to the battery of another car that was running. "It still wouldn't start. We called the church and told Pastor Dobratz. He said that didn't surprise him."

The pastor suggested the couple wait until after the church service started and then try their car again. At 10:45 A.M., Allen climbed in the car and turned the key. The engine roared to life. The Tallmanns believe the entity pursuing them simply did not want them to go to church.

The family then tried to outwit their unknown adversary.

"We thought that if whatever it was didn't want us to go to church and have communion, we would have the pastor come to our house on Sunday night and give us communion . . . and bless our house."

Pastor Dobratz came Sunday night, administered communion, and led the family in prayers. He also advised them to play religious music all night and handed them a pile of cassette tapes. They followed his advice and, according to Allen, "it was one of the most peaceful nights we had since we moved into the house. The children didn't wake up. I got up a couple of times to check on them and never once did I feel anything was there. It seemed like whatever was there just could not tolerate that church music and just didn't want to come around."

Monday January 11 dawned bright and very cold. It almost seemed that the prayers and recorded church hymns had worked in ridding the house of its evil presence.

Kenny went off to school, Deborah puttered around the house and Allen took care of some chores. Jonathan, who had volunteered to stay with Deborah and the children at night, came over after high school that afternoon. Despite the calm night, Deborah wasn't ready to face the darkness by herself.

This would be the last day the Tallmanns spent on Larabee Street.

Allen left for work at two o'clock. Twilight cast the street in shadows by four-thirty. The sun set at a few minutes before five o'clock in the afternoon.

At six o'clock, Allen called home from work. He asked if the house was quiet, which it was, and had Deborah promise that she would leave the church music playing. She agreed.

Jonathan had taken the children to the rumpus room in the basement. They were playing, having a good time, Deborah told her husband. For once he felt that his children were at ease. Jonathan liked the kids and they in turn enjoyed having a "big brother" to play with.

An hour and a half later, at about seven-thirty, Allen called back. Deborah told him Jonathan had just brought the children upstairs to ready them for bedtime. He promised them he would read and stay in the room until they fell asleep.

Everything was calm, almost too calm, Deborah remembered later. She assured her husband that there had been no unusual sounds, and even Kenny seemed to have settled down.

Allen hung up the phone after promising his wife that he would call again an hour later. He never got the chance. Within forty-five minutes Deborah, Jonathan and the three children were in the car sitting outside Allen's workplace.

Deborah Tallmann relives those final hours:

"I had a habit of getting the kids ready for bed about eight o'clock. But with what happened to Allen Saturday night, I didn't want to go to the room with the kids. Jonathan went back there. I was going to do some housework. God, that had to be the most horrible night of my life! I was doing the dishes and all of a sudden he started screaming. 'Debbie, Debbie, come quick, please come back here!' "

Deborah couldn't move. Jonathan screamed at the top of his lungs, and the little girls were crying. That much Deborah knew, but she just couldn't face whatever had appeared in that bedroom a few yards away.

"I just stood there. I didn't know what to do, but I ran to the phone to try to call the pastor and he wasn't there. I could hear Jonathan crying out 'Debbie, come here quick, oh my God! Oh my God!' I didn't know what was going on."

Kenny had run into the living room. Deborah told him to go back and see what was wrong.

"I can't, I can't," Kenny cried back. Deborah screamed at him to go to the bedroom and come back and tell her what had happened.

"Mom, it's there. I can see it!" Kenny said breathlessly as he ran back into the living room.

Maryann quickly followed Kenny out of the bedroom. "It's Baby Jesus, and he loves you! Don't be afraid!" the child assured her mother, between sobs. Deborah had tried to tell the children that any strange figure appearing in their room was Jesus, hoping the statement would calm them.

This time it didn't work.

"I was running around the house saying, no, that's not Baby Jesus! Finally Jonathan came out of the room. I asked him what happened and he said it was in there. I asked him where Sarah was. He said she was still in the bedroom. I told him to get Sarah, that's it, we're leaving. We were not staying there anymore. I got our coats. The kids were just hysterical. I said we were going to Daddy's work. I turned off all the lights except for the one in Kenny's room. I wouldn't go back there. And one in the living room. I got them in the car with Jonathan. And when I pulled out of the driveway and went past the house Kenny said 'Mom! Mom! It's looking out of the window at us!' "

Deborah dared not turn her head. She took her son's word that something stared after them as they sped down Larabee Street that frigid January night.

The little band of refugees arrived a few minutes later at the factory where Allen worked. Jonathan and the children were crying. They begged Deborah not to leave them alone in the car, but she told them to lock the doors while she went inside to find Allen.

"He came around the corner and I looked at him and said I wasn't going to take it anymore. I didn't care what happened, we were not going back there. I told him he had to come out to the car to talk to the kids," Deborah said. Jonathan was still too upset to describe what had taken place in the bedroom.

Deborah called Pastor Dobratz and he told them to meet him at the church. Allen took Jonathan in the car he had at work and Deborah followed with the children in their other car. As they drove to the church, Jonathan told Allen what had taken place:

Maryann and Sarah had been tucked in bed. A night-light cast a faint glow about the room. Jonathan was stretched out on the floor gazing at the ceiling, a glass of lemonade at his elbow. In the kitchen he could hear his sister-in-law washing dishes, while soft church hymns coming from a cassette player drifted down the short hallway from the living room.

Jonathan yawned and turned over onto his stomach, his face toward the partially open bedroom door. He, too, was getting sleepy, listening to the little girls' even breathing and restful music.

Suddenly Sarah jumped up in bed.

"Hi there!" she called out. "Hi there!!"

Jonathan thought that he must have fallen asleep and that Deborah had slipped into the room. He rolled over onto his back and looked across the room. What he saw wasn't Deborah.

Hovering near Sarah's bed was a human figure, too indistinct to determine its sex, but nearly the same as the one Allen Tallmann witnessed a few days before.

It moved toward Jonathan and, as it did, issued forth the words, "Now, you're involved!" But as it moved forward it seemed to dissipate and was gone before it reached him.

The girls were crying. Jonathan started crying and calling out for Deborah. At the same time, he felt as if he were frozen to the floor, unable to move out of the path of the hideous entity. Kenny had been awakened and caught a brief glimpse of the figure after Deborah asked him to go back into the bedroom.

Jonathan was able to pry himself from the floor and stumble into the living room, upsetting his glass of lemonade in the process. Maryann had gotten out of bed to follow after him, leaving little Sarah alone and frightened. Within minutes, Jonathan had gone back for her and, with Deborah and the other children, had fled the house.

After Allen heard the entire story, he realized that this had been their last night on Larabee Street, but he insisted on driving by the house on their way to his mother's home after their talk with Pastor Dobratz at the church.

Deborah refused to accompany him, still distraught and feeling somewhat guilty over her inability to cope with the trauma of the last few hours.

"I felt real helpless. There my kids are screaming—It could have been hurting the kids, but I didn't have any idea. I figured Kenny had seen it before, so he at least had some idea what it looked like. But you can't go back there (to the bedroom) and shoot it; you can't hit it over the head. Later I felt real bad but someone had said I did the right thing because if I had seen it and something happened to me, what would happen to the kids, you know?

"After we left the church we got to the cars and Allen said he had to go down past the house. I said he was crazy. He said that everything we own is in that house and if it was on fire or something, he had to know. Allen had his car and I had my car and he had Jonathan with him. I wasn't going past it, so I waited at the end of the block.

"He went down the block toward the house and I sat at the end of the street in my car with the kids. I watched him go by the house. He turned around and came back down to where I was parked.

"He said, you're not going to believe this, but every single light was on in that house, every light in the basement, the garage light, all the yard lights were on, bathroom lights, the bedroom lights, the kids' room, everything. He said the house was lit up like a Christmas tree. I didn't leave those lights on."

The family spent the night at Allen's mother's house. Once there, they again called Pastor Dobratz to tell him every light in their house seemed to be on. Allen wanted to go back and turn them off.

Allen said: "Pastor Dobratz said the house was lit up, but it's not costing you a dime, there is no energy there. It's this thing that's giving the house energy to show that there are lights on in the house. No one else can see it from outside. He said if I went back in that house I'd never come back."

Allen decided to wait until daylight to return to Larabee Street.

Early the next morning, Tuesday, January 12, Deborah called the pastor to tell him they had to return to the house to get some belongings. It was their intention to leave, permanently, and stay with relatives until they could figure out what to do with the house. And their lives.

Pastor Dobratz told them to be prepared for anything when they returned to their home. What they did find surprised them, but not in any way they expected.

"We walked in and every light in the house was turned off except for the living room light which I had left on. But the bedroom light that I left on in Kenny's room was switched off," Deborah said.

Allen continues: "I checked every window in the house. I looked down in the basement. To me this whole thing could not be possible, even though I'd seen this thing. It was still mind-boggling. This can't be happening to us, you know, it can't be true. Things can't make my house light up, like the pastor said, and yet have no energy going through the light bulbs."

Allen couldn't find any problem that would account for the glowing lights he saw in and around their house the night before. Each light seemed to work fine when they were switched on.

The Tallmanns took clothes, small pieces of furniture, some children's toys, and Allen gathered up his expensive gun collection. Other than that, they left the other furniture and appliances for another day. Neither one sensed anything odd or unusual in the house that morning, but that didn't surprise them. "It seemed during the day it was like any other house," Deborah emphasized. A few days later Allen, with the help of several church members, packed the rest of the family's possessions. They timed their work so the job would be completed once the sun started setting.

For several days, the Tallmanns wrestled with the question of where they would live and what was to be done with their house. His mother was willing to shelter them until they could find other accommodations.

But on Thursday night, January 21, the problems in the house on South Larabee became general knowledge, and the Tallmanns subjects of intense public and media scrutiny. On that night, Horicon Police Chief Douglas D. Glamann called Allen at work. He had heard rumors of a "ghost house" in Horicon, he told Allen, one that belonged to the Tallmanns. Was that true? After a long pause, Allen admitted that it was true he and his family had fled their house a week before, believing it was haunted.

Chief Glamann suggested that he meet with the family to determine if there was anything his department could do to help. He said there were already reports of cars driving by the house, and curious spectators wandering around the yard. There had even been some inquiries from the media, he said.

"Never did we realize that it would go to this length," Deborah said. "It just floored us completely. The police chief contacting us, people going past our house. At first we couldn't believe it. We had enough problems to deal with and then we had this other stuff going on, too. But nobody knew how to help us. I mean, we didn't know where we were going, but we knew we couldn't go back (to Larabee Street)."

That was just the beginning of the intense skepticism toward the events expressed by Horicon residents, and the sensational media interest in the Tallmanns' experiences.

While the Tallmanns stayed with relatives, the Horicon rumor mills were passing along what allegedly had happened in the house—a driverless snow blower clearing the sidewalks and driveway, a ceiling that dripped blood, coffee cups floating through the air and a fiery hole to Hell that opened in the house. None of those events ever occurred, but their repetition, along with skimpy details of what had actually taken place, was enough to cause lines of cars to crowd Larabee Street. The police had to eventually cordon off the street.

Doug Glamann is a handsome, dark-haired lawman with a penetrating gaze and a no-nonsense manner about him. He was the thirty-two-year-old Horicon Chief of Police and a ten-year veteran of the force when he first met with the Tallmanns and helped them get through their ordeal.

According to Deborah Tallmann, "He was a lifesaver. He is the one that kept us floating through all this. He has done so much. Without him we would have sunk."

Chief Glamann, a Horicon native who had left a factory job because it was "too routine" to become a policeman, first heard about the Tallmanns on January 21.

"One of my night shift officers came in and asked me if I had heard that we have a haunted house in Horicon. I just laughed and carried on with what I was doing. But I bumped into him five minutes later and he said he was serious. It's all over town, he told me. That was early in the morning and all throughout the day wherever I went people were asking me about this. I didn't know anything, you know. I didn't even know where the house was located. I started hearing rumors there was a house with blood running out of the walls and all that stuff."

Late that afternoon, the police department received an anonymous telephone call from someone in the Tallmanns' neighborhood. The caller wanted to know if the police knew about anything "going on" nearby. Chief Glamann eventually discovered that Allen and Deborah Tallmann owned the house being discussed. One neighbor admitted to the chief that the family had left the house, but refused to discuss the situation any further.

With some routine police work, the chief found that Allen was scheduled to work that night.

"I called him at work," the police chief said, "and told him who I was and that I had heard some stories and that I'd like to hear it from the fellow who should know best. His initial response was that he didn't want to talk about it. I asked him why and he said I'd probably lock him up thinking he was crazy. I said, listen, in this business I hear a lot of bizarre stories. I said why don't you just tell me the story and we'll see what we can do for you."

After five or ten minutes of coaxing, Allen told Glamann the general outline of the family's experiences. The veteran officer listened and then suggested that Allen and his wife come down to police headquarters the following morning. After some hesitation, Allen agreed. Chief Glamann wanted the face-to-face meeting so he could "look him (Allen) in the eye and see if this is all on the up-and-up or not."

The couple arrived at police headquarters in the basement below the town library at about nine o'clock the next morning. Their behavior was the first indication for the chief that something was seriously wrong.

"Debbie was kind of high-strung and had a nervous laugh. Al hardly had any eye contact with me. He was always staring at his shoes. It seemed his emotions and his will to survive were just drawn right out of him."

Glamann said Allen looked to be near exhaustion.

"They informed me then that they were working with their pastor on trying to understand the trauma they had gone through," Glamann said. "They were very strong that they wanted to keep it quiet. I said I could do it. If you tell me you don't want something out, we'll do that for you."

Glamann wasn't able to keep his promise. Throughout that Friday and into the weekend, word spread quickly around town about the "ghost house." The crowd at a local high school basketball game Friday night was abuzz with rumors of what had transpired. Scores of cars began crawling down Larabee Street; dozens of people tried the doors and windows of the Tallmanns' house, all hoping to get a peek at what was inside. Police finally erected barricades at either end of the street and made numerous arrests for disorderly conduct or public drunkenness. One man showed up with a Bible in hand promising that he would exorcise the ghosts by shouting "Devil be gone!" He was arrested.

On Sunday night, January 24, WMTV-TV, Madison, Wisconsin, aired the first television report about the haunting. But like the other television, radio and newspaper stories for the first several days, the Tallmanns were not identified by name, nor did they personally speak with any reporter. They were adamant about not wanting publicity. The media seemed satisfied to report rumors of blood-spewing walls and runaway snow throwers without trying to verify any of the happenings.

Glamann attempted to answer requests for all the media interviews he could fit in his schedule. When the number of reporters grew too large, he held a press conference to try and squelch some of the more outrageous speculation.

"I stood up and said there's no blood coming out of the walls and there's no snow blower running around by itself; I'm not telling you the people's names, I'm not giving out the address, and I'm not telling you what we discussed," Glamann recalled.

While he was trying to handle dozens of media inquiries, Glamann also had a family in trouble and wanted to do something to help them.

"We comforted the family as much as we could. We went into the home with the pastor from their church one evening at about nine o'clock," Glamann said of his personal inspection of the Tallmann home on Monday, January 25. Two police officers accompanied Pastor Dobratz. The minister "wanted to do something in there to see if he could get something stirred up, and they went along to be witnesses. I told them to look for any kind of projection devices, or any kind of recorder. They went through the whole house. Both (of the officers) were wearing voice-activated tape recorders through the whole ordeal and nothing unusual came on the tape."

Glamann's officers examined drapery rods to see if the dust which often accumulates there had been disturbed, thus indicating that some sort of "instrument" could have been hidden there producing the ghostly images. The men didn't see anything unusual. The only unsettling incident occurred when the telephone rang several times, but on each occasion the line seemed dead. One officer disabled the receiver—or assumed he had—but the phone rang once more, again with no one on the line.

Chief Glamann and Horicon's mayor, who wanted to see the inside of the house for himself, arrived an hour or two after the officers and Pastor Dobratz examined the house.

"I was in the house for maybe half an hour," Glamann said. "A very warm, cozy little house. A nice house. I was really impressed. The furniture they had was nice, the decoration of the house just made you feel like home. I had some apprehension going in there. You're wondering if something is going to pop out of the wall."

What troubled Glamann the most was not finding any logical explanation for the events, or obvious evidence of the haunting.

"That was the hard part. First of all, this type of complaint most police departments I found out later don't (investigate). Secondly, we're trained to look for the physical things in life, that's part of our job. There's a reason for everything and when you run into something like this it was very frustrating for us. We're seeing their ('Tallmanns') depression and their anxiety, yet we can't help them."

From the chief's first interview with Allen and Deborah, he was convinced that the family had gone through a wrenching, emotionally draining experience. He wasn't willing, however, to accept the notion of a haunting. But neither was he prone to dismiss their story.

"I spent a good deal of time with them and the kids," Glamann said. "The way they looked, they went through some kind of ordeal. I can't tell you exactly what, (but) the way they looked, I can believe that they've either been through it or something strange happened to them."

James B. Nelson was a reporter for *The Milwaukee Sentinel*. He was the first journalist to investigate the haunting and personally interview the Tallmanns. He uncovered their names and where they were staying by using public records at the city clerk's office and at the Dodge County courthouse.

Nelson asked Chief Glamann to intercede with the family on his behalf. The reporter said he would honor the family's wishes not to be identified, at least as long as other media outlets did the same. Glamann believed an interview with the family would put some of the more hideous rumors to rest.

Allen and Deborah Tallmann agreed and met with Nelson on Tuesday evening,

January 26, to tell their story. *The Sentinel* published the first of several stories written by Nelson Wednesday morning.

While Nelson spoke with the parents, Chief Glamann talked with young Kenny Tallmann on the first of several occasions, hoping he could determine some reason that the family had made up the entire yarn. He didn't succeed.

"In talking with him (Kenny), he had no reason to make this up. We could go through it and I could wait a week and run into him again and we'd go through it again, and it (Kenny's story) was identical. I was trying to trip him up because the pressure was on me to find out what was going on here. My first instinct was to look for something with the people."

Glamann also looked into Allen and Deborah's backgrounds.

"I can honestly tell you we didn't even know they were living here so that indicates there were no problems. We never had a complaint against any one of their family members while they were here. They were just going about their business . . . just living their lives. I think Debbie was the one that summed it all up. When they got that house, that was their dream house. They spent all their time working on it, making it the way they liked it. That was their dream come true and they had planned on staying there for a very long time. It didn't work out that way."

The police chief also agreed with the Tallmanns' earlier notion that someone with a personal vendetta against the Tallmanns may be to blame—a person with enough sophistication to make an entire family believe their house was possessed.

"That thought occurred to me. He's a foreman and maybe he got someone mad out there. I talked to his (Allen's) boss in a closed-door session for a good hour and a half. He said Allen had a super attitude, a very likable guy. Everybody liked him there, he's never been a problem with anybody." Glamann dismissed the idea that the events had been the work of a prankster.

Allen's employer had feared losing him, Glamann found out, especially after Allen suggested they might move to another state to avoid the unwanted publicity and initial community scorn. When the family decided to remain in the area, but not in Horicon, Allen returned to work and found his employer and co-workers very supportive.

Glamann also discovered that Allen Tallmann had passed a federal security screening because some of his work involved manufacturing instrumentation for the armed forces. The chief said the government usually does a very thorough job in security investigations and should have turned up any personal problems that might have accounted for the family's plight.

That section of Horicon upon which the Tallmann house was built also came under scrutiny. Glamann noted that Horicon had been a major Indian settlement centuries ago. However, a check with the local historical society turned up nothing unusual ever having been unearthed by archaeologists on Larabee Street.

Ironically, Chief Glamann's father, Don Glamann, was the city's chief of public works in 1988. He told reporters that in his forty years of work in the city, he had never heard of Indian mounds or archaeological digs in the area. Old St. Malachy's Catholic Cemetery, two blocks away from the Tallmanns, is the nearest cemetery.

Several skulls, believed to have been Winnebago Indians, have been unearthed over the years at various construction sites in Horicon and now repose at the historical society. However, none apparently came from the Larabee Street vicinity.

Before houses were built on Larabee Street, Glamann said, the area was on the fringe of a marsh and devoid of structures. It was a popular hangout for teenagers, the chief said, noting that during summer nights the department usually received several phone calls about noisy parties there.

Attitudes of townspeople initially skeptical toward the idea of a "haunted house" in Horicon gradually changed in the days and weeks following the first media reports. At first, the entire episode had been the target of light-hearted banter on Milwaukee and Madison radio and television stations. None of the reporters had been able to interview the Tallmanns, who were still being shielded by Chief Glamann.

He was harsh in his criticism of the media treatment of the story. "I made a comment something like, when a person is on the ground and writhing in pain, are you (the reporters) the type to come up and give them another kick in the belly . . . ?"

Reporter Nelson's accurate, straightforward, sympathetic story in the *Milwaukee Sentinel* on Januaary 27, the first to include comments from Allen and Deborah Tallmann, together with Chief Glamann's tough statement seemed to turn community sentiment toward trying to understand the turmoil the family was going through. Nelson was to talk with the family several times over the following weeks.

By the time media interest waned in late February, the Horicon story had been featured on radio and television talk shows around the world (Glamann was interviewed by both British and Australian radio networks), and written about in newspapers and magazines across the country. NBC Television re-created the haunting, with the family's permission, during a segment on the popular series "Unsolved Mysteries."

When Chief Glamann asked reporters why the intense interest in this story from tiny Horicon, Wisconsin, the answer was always the same: If what happened to the family was serious enough to drive them out of their home in the middle of winter, then it was a story warranting coverage.

Ironically, the local newspaper, the *Horicon Reporter*, didn't write about the events until well after other media had the story. And then their stories were mostly about the "mass hysteria" of the media. The co-owner of the newspaper told a magazine reporter, "it was a non-story. There was no story here; it was a case of herd journalism. Unless something is significant news, we're not going to run a story about it."

Neither did the state's largest newspaper, *The Milwaukee Journal*, find the Tallmanns a legitimate subject for news coverage. That newspaper's science reporter, Paul Hayes, was quoted as saying, ". . . ghosts are a little more preposterous than UFOs—at least there's a percentage of a chance that other forms of life exist out there in the universe. . . . It's far easier to explain this as the imperfectability of the human brain."

Meanwhile, the editor of the nearby *Beaver Dam Daily Citizen* said his newspaper initially treated the story as a joke, but quickly changed its focus to examine the affects on the family. Jeff Hovind thought the story certainly merited coverage: "It's probably the most newsworthy thing to come out of Horicon in as long as I've been here. . . . For anyone to say it's a non-story, when it's the big event in town—that's mind-boggling."

The *Sentinel*'s James Nelson wasn't particularly concerned whether or not the

Tallmanns had seen apparitions, or lived in a "ghost house." He noted that the family had avoided all contact with the media out of fear they would be exploited, first living with relatives, then moving into a motel until they found temporary refuge in a house provided by a parishioner from their church.

"They knew I wasn't going to turn around and make fun of them. I mean, it's not our job to make fun of them," Nelson said. His articles concentrated on the Tallmanns' personal story, rather than an investigation of paranormal events. "I don't care whether they saw a ghost or not . . ." Nelson emphasized.

Chief Glamann called in a trio of psychic investigators to examine the house after his investigation found no physical cause for the incidents the Tallmanns reported. Parapsychologist Carl Schuldt, psychologist Don Mueller, and author Walter Uphoff agreed that there was no evidence of trickery and that the appearances of supernatural beings claimed by the Tallmanns were probably genuine.

Uphoff, a retired professor and author of two books on the paranormal, told a reporter: "They were not lying. They are rational, sane people that would like to get rid of a problem. There is at work there a force that needs to be dealt with and asked to be on its way. If that does not happen, the family will continue to have problems. They did not leave because they were imagining things."

Police Chief Glamann concluded his investigation still unsure about what really happened on South Larabee Street. He was sympathetic to the family's plight, perhaps because he had seen several bizarre things during his police career. When he worked nights, Glamann said he saw mysterious lights in the sky on several occasions. Were they UFOs? He never officially reported them for fear other officers or community residents would think he was "crazy," even though he was with another policeman at the time who also saw the darting sky lights.

What is Glamann's final analysis of the Tallmann haunting? "I wish I knew, I wish I had someone come in and say, this is exactly what we were up against here. . . . I've learned a lot about all these things, parapsychology and things I never knew before. I believe what they told me they honestly believe to be true. Why would they leave, in the middle of the night, and why would they put themselves through all that . . . trouble and just keep running around. There probably are things out there that we cannot actually get a handle on right now, or describe in terms that make everybody happy, with a rational determination of it all."

A few months later, the International Association of Chiefs of Police commended Glamann for his compassionate and professional handling of "a difficult situation."

In early February 1988, Allen and Deborah Tallmann signed over the title for 415 South Larabee Street, their "dream home," to the FmHA, which then had the home appraised and subsequently resold.

The arrangement was unusual because the FmHA usually asks its borrowers to "test the market" before it assumes title to houses.

State FmHA rural housing director George Berger allowed the procedure because "these folks have been under a lot of stress."

Allen Tallmann said the family lost about $3,000 when the FmHA acquired the house for re-sale.

The family that bought the house said nothing unusual has taken place in the home.

After living for several months in an old house provided by church friends, Allen and Deborah bought a small home in another city—financed with a new FmHA loan. Their lives returned to normalcy, but the lingering questions continued to haunt them.

"If there would be some way that we could know why it happened. . . ." Deborah said. "I've always said that everything in life happens for a purpose, and I keep feeling there must have been some purpose behind this. If I could figure out what the reason was . . . or if somebody could come to us and say this was it, we would have an answer. There is no answer, and that's the hard part. I don't know what it was; I guess we were in the wrong place at the wrong time. But I just can't believe that whatever was there came when we came and left when we left. Maybe the house was out to get us, or we were caught between some sort of opposing forces."

[Note: The names of some people in this story have been changed at their request.]

THE SOUTH

Gone Away

The year 2002 marks the Tricentennial of the founding of Mobile, Alabama, one of America's oldest cities and the oldest west of the Appalachians. The Spaniard Hernando DeSoto fought a group of Indians led by the great Tuskaloosa in 1540 at an Indian village called Mobila, but it wasn't for another 162 years, when the French built and occupied Fort Louis of the Mobile as the capital of the Louisiana Territory, that the formal history of the city began to be written. The Frenchmen—led by explorers d'Iberville, Sauvole, and Bienville—also founded a port at Dauphin Island, which shelters Mobile Bay from the Gulf of Mexico.

The Bay also forms the mouth of two prominent Alabama rivers—the Tombigbee along the state's western border, and the Alabama, running southwest out of Montgomery. The Bay has prominently figured in the city's history. Several ghost stories also have their setting on or near that body of water.

The southern United States is replete with infamous haunted mansions, but none may have had such an uncanny reputation as Madison Mansion, which fronted the Bay not far from the city proper. Torn down decades ago, the house provided enough stories to keep the neighborhood wondering what evil had transpired in the old place. It was vacant and boarded up for years before its demise, but even so, the occasional trespasser escaped with harrowing accounts so grisly as to be almost unbelievable. The mansion was built shortly after the American Revolution, apparently by an Englishman named Madison, a rich recluse who lived there with his "daughter," a mentally ill girl no one ever saw. The only other persons in the mansion were several servants, and they were kept well away from the Englishman and his child. He suddenly left for England, wiring back instructions to sell the place. After that, it changed hands many times; no resident ever stayed for very long.

In the old days, fishermen on the Bay were sometimes caught unawares by quick moving storms coming up from the Gulf. They'd head to shore looking for any sort of dry refuge. A particular fishing party of businessmen found themselves in just such a predicament when they put ashore and headed for the Madison Mansion, either blithely innocent of its dismal history or not put off by the tales.

Once inside, the men built a fire, ate a cold supper, and then pulled their woolen cloaks and oilskins tightly around them as they curled up on the floor and tried to sleep. Each one awoke with a start, describing matching, awful dreams of debauchery and murder.

They huddled together as the storm grew in intensity. Lightning flashes through the dust-caked windows illuminated the dank, empty room.

From overhead somewhere came the steady thump of marching feet.

"Who's there," cried one of the fishermen.

The house was quiet again.

The one who cried out felt something splash against his forehead. He wiped the liquid away with his fingertips and held it up close to his eyes. A drop of blood. Then another and another until a widening pool of scarlet spread across the floor.

At that moment, a door was hurled open and pounding footsteps raced around the room, yet nothing could be seen, only the voices of a man screaming as he chased a sobbing woman. Her high heel shoes and his boot prints left clear marks in the bloodstain.

And then they were gone.

Another quiet hour passed. The men huddled together, none daring to close his eyes. From somewhere on the upper floors, wild screams and what sounded like a dozen dancing couples shook the upper floors.

There was maniacal laughter, screams and then, again, sudden quiet.

But not for long.

A scraping and thumping was heard, the sounds of a body being dragged down the staircase, moved slowly and deliberately until it reached the bottom floor. The object was dragged across the entranceway, a door opened and then followed the thud of this invisible something hitting the ground outside.

Not one of the frightened men had the courage to see who or what was then occupying the upper floors of Madison Mansion. The noises gradually subsided, the men finding that their exhaustion sent them into an uneasy slumber from which they fitfully awoke at dawn's first light.

Although thunder sent shudders through the old house and the rain continued to pound against the sagging walls, the men wisely decided to brave the squall rather than risk any more encounters with Madison's unseen caretakers.

As they made their way toward the door, a flash of green light filled the entire house while a clap of thunder seemed to lift off the entire roof.

Up on the staircase landing, a hovering, distorted face stared at the small group struggling to get out the door. One of the men said later the face was so horrible it might have been looking out from hell itself.

Some other nasty *things* lurk in Mobile if one pays attention to city legends.

Back in the late 1930s, the city was rampant with rumors that some sort of "monster" lurked in Fisher's Alley. Every person took it seriously; few who lived in that area failed to leave their homes without a weapon of some sort.

Firefighter Charles Ardoyno claimed to have solved the mystery when he killed an otter outside his home on South Cedar Street. Others weren't so sure the small mammal with brown fur and webbed feet had caused all the commotion.

The tugboat "Red Taylor" sank in January 1952 about twenty miles north of the entrance to Mobile Bay, a quarter mile west of Beacon 12.

Soon after that, the tug became the "ghost of Mobile Bay."

What happened is that the wheelhouse stayed above the waterline after the tug sank. Its location was marked with a light. A storm blew up the next day and the vessel sank. All attempts to find its location failed.

Harbor pilots and other boaters began to find beacons and buoys damaged or mysteriously moved. The superstitious sailors swore that the old "Red Taylor" was sailing along the bottom of the bay each day and then on the surface at night, snagging the floating markers or moving them around so that others would join the ship in Davey Jones' locker.

There are probably hundreds of cemeteries with ghostly legends connected to them. Mobile is no different. In that city, it's the Old Church Street Cemetery, opened in 1819 to replace the city's Spanish burial ground. An iron cross dated 1812 and a child's headstone from 1813 are the oldest relics in the cemetery.

However, the cemetery was full by 1899 and, with but three exceptions, the last one in 1996, there have been no more burials.

The most frequently told tale derives from the time the cemetery's caretaker discovered that a lamp on one of the roadways had burned out. He telephoned a city worker for assistance saying that the light had to be immediately replaced as it worked to keep prowlers and mischief-makers out of the cemetery at night.

He sat down on a tombstone to wait for the worker. Night fell before the city's man arrived. In the dark he found his way to the broken street lamp but nearly jumped out of his skin when a dark, bearded figure rose up from a tombstone and said, "And so, you have arrived at last . . ."

Is that apocryphal? Perhaps. There are those who claim, however, that you can still see the old caretaker rise from his grave in the dead of night.

Face in the Window

The imposing, brick two-story Pickens County Courthouse on the town square in quiet, old Carrollton is perhaps the most unusual seat of local government in all of Alabama. There are courthouses larger and older, quite a few that harbor within their walls stories of Civil War horror and heroism, and not an insubstantial number with ghostly legends. But, for the sheer oddity and grotesqueness of the event, few can match what can be found at the Carrollton Courthouse.

Embedded in a windowpane in a garret window high above the casual pedestrian is the likeness of a human face. To be exact, it is the face of one Henry Wells, a black man accused of burning an earlier courthouse in 1876. How and why Henry Wells's face was etched in that glass for all eternity is a story both sad and bizarre.

On April 5, 1865, Union soldiers under the command of Gen. John T. Croxton burned the University of Alabama at Tuscaloosa, some forty miles east of Carrollton. Gen. Croxton then sent a detachment of troops to destroy the Pickens County Courthouse at Carrollton, although why he issued the order remains a mystery. There was no military value in such an act. The Yankees carried out their mission with soldierly precision and the stately old building burned to the ground.

The people of Pickens County swore to erect a new structure, despite the presence of carpetbaggers and a radical, federally installed government in the county, which made the task doubly difficult. But rebuild it they did, and for twelve years the Courthouse stood, symbolizing, as one writer put it, "the return to law and order in a strife-torn land."

But all that changed on November 17, 1876, not quite twelve years after northern troops torched the first Courthouse. On that late autumn night, two men, one of whom is alleged to have been Henry Wells, a former slave, set fire to the new Pickens County Courthouse.

A newspaper of the era, the *West Alabamian*, contained an account of the fire, on page three, in its November 22, 1876, edition. It said, in part: "The burning was unquestionably the work of an incendiary. It took fire in several places about the same time."

Henry Wells and a companion, Bill Burkhalter, were suspects from the beginning. According to Dan Turnipseed, a Carrollton resident and an expert on the legend, Wells had been accused of raping a white woman and told that if he burned the Courthouse all the records of his arrest would be destroyed and he wouldn't come to trial. Indeed, the fire burned all the books and records of the probate court. However, the "dying confession of Henry Wells," published in the February 6, 1878, issue of the *West Alabamian*, quotes Wells as saying Burkhalter persuaded him to break into the courthouse and steal money. Candles left in the probate court office started the fire, Wells said. Some doubt can be cast on the validity of the well-written confession. Wells could neither read nor write. He signed the "confession" with an "X."

Burkhalter had been indicted for a series of burglaries at about the same time the Courthouse burned, including stores in Reform, Carrollton and Lineburg, all in Alabama, along with three other businesses across the state line in Mississippi.

Both men fled the county before they could be arrested for the courthouse fire.

Two years passed, during which time Pickens County built another new Courthouse. Then, on January 29, 1878, Henry Wells was arrested while working on a plantation owned by Bill McConner near Fairfield, now a western suburb of Birmingham. Wells tried to escape and was shot twice in the legs. The other suspect, Bill Burkhalter, was captured near Tuscaloosa.

The men were returned to Carrollton. The Sheriff feared for their safety and decided to house Wells and Burkhalter and several other prisoners in a garret storeroom. There is no record that Wells was treated for his leg wounds. Word soon spread through the town that the man many thought responsible for burning their Courthouse had been found. A mob gathered on the night after his arrival in Carrollton, intent on imposing their own brand of "justice" on the hapless Wells.

Storm clouds rolled across the sky, bringing intermittent rain and a spectacular lightning display to the mob of whites calling for Wells's hanging. The frightened prisoner stared down from his attic prison, shouting his innocence through the half-opened window. What happened next is part legend and part fact. A tremendous bolt of lightning struck near the Courthouse. The impression of Wells's horrified expression is said to have been permanently etched in the garret window glass.

It remains there to this day.

Although accounts of what finally happened to Henry Wells differ, the generally accepted story is that he died shortly after that loathsome night from wounds inflicted during his capture at Fairfield.

Burkhalter died while serving a sentence at the state prison.

Not long after Wells's death, passersby began to see the distinct image of a man's face on the garret window. One man described it as having a moustache and wearing a black hat.

Carrollton's Dan Turnipseed said it "looks like a negative, when someone sees it from the street." Strangest of all, he said, is that the face cannot be seen when looking out the window from inside. Turnipseed said the face clearly has the look of someone distressed or frightened.

In the mid-1980s the Courthouse was renovated. During the cleaning operation, Turnipseed said the bottom portion of the garret window, where the face is seen, was raised to paint the sill and destroy some beehives. Even with the bottom portion of the window up the face in the top part was visible.

Over the decades many attempts have been made to remove the image from the window by washing or scrubbing the glass, all without success. In recent years the county has decided to leave the window alone. "We don't fool with it," Turnipseed said.

In February 1985, the Atlanta Center for the Continuing Study of the Shroud of Turin took close-up photos of the face in the window using a power company's truck to lift photographers to within a few feet of the image. Copies of the photographs, clearly showing the mysterious face, were sent to the Jet Propulsion Laboratory in Pasadena and a laboratory in West Germany for analysis. A close-up view of the window shows that the face seems iridescent with a variety of colors, reminiscent of an oil slick. One supposition is that the molecular structure of the window changed over time, causing the portion of the glass with the "face" to actually take on a different composition. However, a change of this nature could be caused quickly by heating the glass. Iridescence can occur by shooting an X-ray through glass. Could electrical current, such as that caused by a lightning bolt, also produce such an effect?

Gary Moore, a former student at the University of Alabama, studied the face in the window. In a report, he wrote that lightning is caused by an imbalance of electrical charges between the earth and the sky. Negative electrons in the sky are disproportionately smaller than the positive protons on earth. Lightning is really the larger number of protons rushing upward to correct the imbalanced neutrons in the clouds. Moore speculated that a human face might produce a "very high positive charge, causing protons to flow toward the sky from eyes, nose, mouth, or other features discreetly, until this flow was deflected by the insulation of a windowpane, which then was disfigured."

The window itself has escaped destruction at least once, during the early part of this century, when a hailstorm knocked out every window on the north side of the courthouse save the one with the terrified image of Henry Wells.

Does the ghost of Henry Wells also walk the Pickens County Courthouse? Some say he does, particularly on those nights, like that of a century and more ago, when thunder rockets across the late winter landscape and lightning jabs at the old Courthouse. On those evenings, folks say that the figure of Henry Wells stares out of his garret cell toward the square where the mob called for his quick hanging. If he does appear, or if it is really Henry Wells's face embedded in that window, perhaps it is as a reminder that mob violence does not bring justice, but only sorrow and ruin for those on both ends of the noose.

At last reports, the face is still quite visible on a third floor windowpane, but only when viewed from the ground. Oddly, the face in the window cannot be seen from inside the room with the window. The pane of glass appears clear. On the outside of the building is painted a large arrow that points to the pane of glass many believe contains Henry Wells's portrait frozen for all time.

Hants in the Hollows

Within the 53,187 square miles in the state of Arkansas there may be as many folk beliefs, superstitions, and ghost stories as there are in any other dozen states combined. Perhaps this is due in part to its slow economic development over the past century; the state still has 46 percent of its population considered rural, one of the highest in America, with only forty-nine people per square mile, less than even Missouri and Texas. The late William Johnson, a writer for the *Arkansas Democrat*, wrote that nearly every community, large and small, has or has had a "haunted house." The favorite venue for ghost story telling, he found, was around the fireside "often with the result on the young people's nerves by bedtime that caused them to leap from eleven to sixteen inches into the air if a puff of wind blew out a curtain." Precisely how Johnson knew the height to which listeners' jumped he didn't say, but sitting before a blazing fire in the hearth after dark, in the silence of an isolated hamlet or Ozarks cabin is the perfect venue for any Arkansas tale of the uncanny, including those which date back more than a century:

- From northern Arkansas in the 1880s comes the account of a man who saw several feet of a thin, "fairy-like" substance around the doorknob of his home. His brother is said to have died shortly thereafter. The same family saw the material on two other occasions and both times a family member died a few hours later
- A pioneer Arkansas preacher told the tale of a young boy who fell into a pit of rattlesnakes and died. His body was never found but his screams were heard on starry nights.
- Way back in 1839 young children and teenagers at Van Buren "were seized with a convulsive disorder which affected the mind" according to a contemporary account. Witnesses claimed to have seen two women dancing madly, riding on broomsticks and "balancing on straws."
- A Little Rock attorney told the story of a pioneer Arkansas girl impregnated by a much older man. The girl gave birth, but drowned herself and her child when he refused to marry her. But the cad did not escape his

punishment. The ghost of the baby followed him wherever he went. He lost his mind and committed suicide.

- At Palarm and in Independence County, Arkansas, ghost dogs plagued the population. Near Jamestown Mountain in Independence County, Confederate soldiers allegedly buried a stash of money. It is there that a headless bulldog frightens off treasure seekers. Meanwhile, outside Palarm, the dog breed isn't known that once haunted the old Little Rock-Conway highway. It was frequently seen near an African-American church torn down decades ago. The dog never revealed its purpose for haunting that highway.

But other equally strange stories attest to the singular role Arkansas has played in American ghost lore.

Headless Highwaymen

The roads of Arkansas seem to be filled with revenants in search of their heads. Do they continue to roam about the countryside? Only they know for certain.

Writer Sam Dickson chronicled some of the strangest stories, including one that comes from the vicinity of the Boston Mountains. A homesteader, his wife and young children were loaded down with their meager possessions on an old wagon, headed for a new farmstead. In the evening, with a storm brewing on the western horizon and their two tired mules unable to go any farther, the family pulled their wagon into a deserted house, there to seek shelter for the night. Although the door was closed, a key was still in its lock. It swung open after a solid push. They set up a campsite in the single, large downstairs room that seemed to have served as a dining room, kitchen, and parlor. A collapsing set of steps seemed to lead up to a sleeping area on the second floor.

The young mother cooked a simple supper in the old hearth and then put her children to bed on straw pallets. The thunder rolled in from the west bringing with it a heavy, drenching rain with frequent lightning strikes, though none struck close to their temporary shelter. Her husband said he wanted to go outside to see that the mules were safe. As he left, he closed and locked the door behind him, pocketing the key in his buckskin breeches.

As the storm roiled through the forest, his wife waited patiently for his return. When he didn't come back after some hours she tried to open the door but it would not budge. She ran across the room and managed to pry open the boarded-up window but a sudden gust of wind blew out the single candle sitting on a table. At the same instant from somewhere above, she heard the shuffling of many feet and turned toward the old staircase. The bursts of lightning through the open window illuminated a chilling sight. Three headless men in dusty clothes, shackled together with rusty chains shambled down the steps. She grasped her Bible to her bosom as she knelt beside her slumbering children.

"Don't be scared of us," the ghosts spoke in unison, their voices issuing from their headless shoulders. "It's your husband you ought to be afraid of. Before he married you he killed us for our treasure, but we had buried it before we met up with him. You had better not stay with him any longer. In return we will show you where our gold is hidden."

The specters grew fainter and then were gone.

At last the woman's husband returned to his family. The storm had passed by then and she was curled up next to her children.

"The storm was too dangerous," he apologized as she was startled awake by the key in the lock and the door's slow opening. "I stayed with the mules under that old shed roof."

She would have none of it.

"You weren't worried about your wife and children, but you were scared of lightning!" she cried out. "I will not be married to a coward. You will leave first thing in the morning and never return to me or to my children."

She took the ghosts' warning to heart and didn't sleep for the rest of the night.

At first light, he took one of the mules and rode off.

The headless men kept their pledge and showed her where their money was buried. She repaired the old house, put up curtains in the windows, and lived there with her children for many years.

An old Arkansas ghost tale with something of a religious twist at the end comes from St. Francis County, in the northeast part of the state, about forty-five miles west of Memphis, Tennessee.

A young boy and his mother were walking home from church one Sunday afternoon when some distance down the lane they saw a headless man dressed in his finest suit.

"Look, ma! That man sure appears to be wearing Uncle Walter's suit," the boy cried out as the man drew nearer. "The one he was buried in!"

"That's not possible," his mother said, trying to ease his fear.

The rapidly approaching figure jumped into a ditch when the mother and son passed by. A few moments later he set off after them, keeping pace with their stride but staying several yards behind.

"That sure does look like his suit and the man appears to be about Walter's size," the woman confessed.

But just as she said that, the topless apparition reached into the air as if grabbing at a ladder. Slowly he climbed, hand over hand, each foot stepping up onto an invisible rung, until he disappeared into the heavens.

At the vanished community of Shiloh in Monroe County, about halfway between Pine Bluff and Forrest City, a headless man resting on a bench outside an old schoolhouse gave a start to a young couple that'd just arrived in the region to start a new life.

Outside the schoolhouse stood two tall oak trees and under each one was a long, hand-hewn bench. While his wife stirred the supper stew in an iron pot hung over an open fire, the young man tended to their horses. Her scream brought him running.

"There's a man with no head sitting over there on the bench," she cried, pointing to a torso dressed in rough clothes. Her husband ran over to the figure. He reached out to touch its shoulders but at that moment it vanished.

About midway through their supper, the ghost suddenly appeared on the other bench. This time both the husband and wife ran over and jumped on it but came out holding nothing but each other. They doused the fire, loaded up their wagon and hightailed it for the nearest farmhouse. And it was there they spent the night.

Southwest of Clinton in Van Buren County, is one of several of the state's headless female phantoms. The story goes that her purpose is to guard a buried treasure. Once, two men were digging for it near the base of a magnolia tree when one of them felt a hand drop on his shoulder. He screamed as he turned around and saw a woman in a long, faded dress.

"Why are you searching here?" the men heard a feminine voice ask.

She didn't get an answer. Their legs had already carried them a long way by the time she finished her question. They didn't look back until they got to Scotland. Scotland, Arkansas, that is.

Somewhere in south Arkansas was an old racetrack built well before the Civil War. The ghost of the wife of the plantation owner who had owned the land visited the track. She had fallen off her thoroughbred and crushed her skull during one of the races. Her legendary appearances came on the anniversary of her death as she galloped around the old course aboard her ghostly steed.

The Ozark village of Flippin once boasted of perhaps the strangest headless woman legend in all of Arkansas folklore.

A young woman lived all alone in a house at the edge of town. She vanished one night, never to be seen again. After several months, her distant relatives decided to rent out her old house, but no one would stay long. There were strange and awful sounds from the dank earthen basement and horrible sights which they never specified.

A Texas family moved to the area and heard about the vacant house. They laughed at the idea of ghosts in what, by now, had become the local "haunted" house. At dusk on their first night there they all saw a stunningly beautiful woman float up the sidewalk but fade from sight just as she reached the steps. No one in the family said anything about it the next day for they had convinced themselves it had been an optical illusion.

On the next night she returned in the same shimmering gown and svelte figure ... but above her shoulders there was only empty space.

The third night she came back up the sidewalk. Well, at least part of her did. That half of her from the waist down. By sunrise the house was deserted. That Texas family had loaded their old truck and was halfway back home before the first cock crowed.

Aunt Sissy

Imagine an elderly relative who liked your home so much she wandered around your yard long after her passing.

That's the problem one Benton County family faced for most of the twentieth century with their elderly Aunt Sissy. The kindly old aunt died sometime around the Spanish American War in the late 1890s, but for the next half century and more family members often saw her walking among the trees in the apple orchard or peering around some of the farm's outbuildings. Visitors often asked about the woman they saw as they came up the drive because it seemed odd she didn't exchange their greetings or look in their direction. They were told about the ghost and cautioned not to interfere with her wanderings. Children in the family were told not to chase her or to laugh at her.

Aunt Sissy did have her limitations as a ghost. Not once did she ever go inside the house.

The Killers

Lockesburg is a tiny crossroads community in Sevier County, about thirty-five miles north of Texarkana. Not too much happens there these days, but a hundred years ago the village was ablaze with the story of Dr. Ferdinand Smith and his seven-year-old daughter's encounter with the ghost of a murdered man . . . and his killers.

Originally from Frankford, Missouri, Dr. Smith had arrived in the area with his young family to set up a new medical practice. He had not been able to arrange for housing and feared camping out because his youngest daughter was very ill. A local merchant, R. A. Gillman, told him about a large vacant log house at the edge of town, but then he cautioned him that "nobody has been living there for some time, but maybe you will like it."

Dr. Smith rode to the house on horseback; his wife followed close behind handling the wagon with their three children and furniture. He dismounted, unsaddled the horse and took his bedroll, saddle, and rifle inside. The gloomy interior did indeed look as if the place had been deserted for some time. An open hearth stretched along one wall, while a broken table leaned against another. A couple of backless chairs were piled in a corner. He noticed on the floor near the chairs what appeared to be a large bloodstain. Not wanting to upset his wife and children, he threw his saddle over the blemish and then called his family inside.

For his sick daughter, he piled up several blankets so she could be comfortable. After a cold supper, the family settled in for the night. At about midnight Dr. Smith's daughter awoke with a cry. She said she could see a group of men playing cards in the corner near her father's saddle. They were arguing, she said, staring wide-eyed into the distance. The men seemed to be turning their wrath against one of their companions. Suddenly one of the men pulled a knife and stabbed him repeatedly until he fell in a bloody heap.

Dr. Smith held his sobbing daughter in his arms until at last she settled down. He gave her a sleeping potion and assured the rest of his family that it was nothing more than terrible dreams brought on by their long trip from Missouri and the little girl's feverish condition.

Later the next morning, Dr. Smith rode back into Lockesburg and dropped in again on Gillman at his general store. He described his daughter's strange outburst. The merchant said the girl's description fit with what others had seen.

Everyone who had tried to stay in the cabin had had the same experience. The storekeeper stared intently at Dr. Smith as if assessing the newcomer's ability to comprehend some ghastly secret. He decided to tell him what had happened: Four men had set up camp in the cabin but fell into an argument sometime during the night. No one saw them after that night and assumed they'd left at sunup. A few days later a man's body was discovered in the cabin. He'd died of multiple stab wounds in a way consistent with Dr. Smith's daughter's story.

Although many settlers tried to reclaim the cabin, the place fell into ruins. The problem was that which the young girl sobbed out in her father's arms—a horrifying scene of cold-blooded murder was replayed over and over again for anyone who dared spend a night.

The Little Man of Skeleton Hollow

Somewhere not far from Big Flat, Arkansas, near the confluence of the Buffalo River and North Sylamore Creek is a limestone-rimmed valley with the disquieting name of Skeleton Hollow. It's been described as a pleasant enough place—if you manage to avoid the angry ghosts of two bounty hunters murdered by an itinerant eyeglasses salesman.

The story begins in October 1880 on the morning mysterious Mr. John Smith arrived in the hamlet of Big Flat. His peculiar dress alone was enough to attract the attention of several local wags sitting on the benches and in a few cane-bottomed chairs on the shaded porch of the general store. They chuckled at the stranger as soon as he turned onto the main street. The little man was not even five feet tall but he sported a road-stained cutaway coat, a battered derby hat and brightly polished yellow, high button shoes. But his citified garb was in stark contrast to his other accoutrement—the meanest-looking double-barreled rifle the men had ever seen was cradled on his right arm. He held a battered black satchel in his other hand.

"Good morning gentlemen!" he called out to the small group staring at this peculiar creature. "My name's Smith, John Smith. I'm in your fine community to fit and sell eyeglasses."

"Yer a spectickel peddler?" laughed one of the men. "You shore don't look it."

The man who called himself John Smith didn't answer right away. His unusually small mouth widened just a slight bit as he cracked a tight smile.

"Yes," he allowed, "you might call me that. I wonder if you would be good enough to direct me to the local hostelry."

That question really brought laughter from his appreciative audience.

"The what? Whoeee! It's damn shore yer lost mister!" chortled the old fellow known by one and all as Uncle Mort, sort of the self-appointed spokesman for this informal welcoming committee. "Mebbe you kin find somethin' but I ain't optymistik."

Uncle Mort knew what he was talking about. Smith found that the only available bed would have to be shared with another itinerant traveler. He couldn't do that, he protested, because he had a sickness that prevented him from sleeping soundly.

The storekeeper heard of his plight and offered him the use of the barn out behind the shop. He apologized that all he had was a straw pallet but Smith gladly accepted the offer.

Over the next weeks, the spectacle salesman used the barn as his base of operations. He set off each morning with his satchel and his ever-present long-barrel gun. It was the gun that got the most attention, not only because he was never seen without it, which seemed mighty odd for a peddler, but because of the mismatched barrels. One had been bored for a .44 caliber bullet while the other chamber held a ten-gauge shotgun shell. Someone who got a close look at it one day said it appeared to be of Belgian make.

As far as anyone could tell, Smith never made a sale, nor could folks find anyone upon whom he had called. That really started them wondering what this Mr. John Smith's sudden appearance was really all about. He never volunteered any more information and try as they might, no one in Big Flat could get him to talk about himself.

The weeks slid by until, shortly before Christmas, the salesman showed up back in town one afternoon leading an old mule. His satchel was missing. For the next many weeks, while he let the mule graze behind the barn where he continued to sleep, he took off each morning for the surrounding hills.

"Just hunting," he replied, nodding civilly to anyone who inquired about his destination. And each night everyone noticed that he returned empty-handed, but still held the glistening long gun cradled comfortably in his arms.

On an early spring morning, Ephraim Jones, a farmer who owned a considerable section of woodland along the Buffalo River near the headwaters of North Sylamore Creek, was just pulling on his overhauls when he heard someone step up on his porch and then knock at the door.

"Mornin'," Jones nodded to the little man in a derby hat standing a few feet away.

"My name is John Smith. I see that you own a piece of land that I'd like to build a cabin on and maybe raise a small crop. Would you be willin' to give me the rights?"

Jones thought it over for a minute and then agreed to give Smith squatter's rights. He'd also provide him with some seeds, a plow, a half dozen laying hens, and some provisions until his garden came in that summer.

"All I ask is that you keep a lookout fer fires 'n' timber thieves," Jones said, eyeing his visitor with something akin to puzzlement. But it wasn't for him to figure out the why and wherefore of others, he thought.

The spectacles salesman/homesteader built a shanty cabin with fresh-cut boards from a local sawmill and planted a garden with the seeds from Ephraim Jones. He seemed to settle into the routine of farming, although the folks in Big Flat, especially the boys sitting in the shade of the local mercantile, missed seeing him around town. In fact, he didn't show up again until late summer when he arrived with fresh produce that he traded at the mercantile for coffee, sugar, some household supplies . . . and ammunition and then was quickly on his way out of town.

Travelers coming through Big Flat did occasionally speak of the new settler. By all accounts he was a friendly and gracious host when strangers passing through the countryside saw the lamplight through his windows and asked for an evening's shelter. He invariably gave up his own bed and slept outdoors. He would cook suppers and breakfasts for his unexpected guests before seeing them on their way.

Nearly two years passed and Smith the glasses peddler kept pretty much to himself, except on those occasions every other month when he came into town with his mule loaded down with produce that he would barter for supplies. It did seem that on each visit he appeared ever more bedraggled, his once bright yellow button shoes colorless and his fancy cutaway jacket in tatters. He walked a little more slowly and eventually spoke less and less, which hardly seemed possible.

Then one late winter afternoon when the creeks and rivers were just starting to run free and a few hardy crocuses suddenly appeared in sunny patches, two vicious-looking men rode into Big Flat. The kind of hombres that naturally made dogs yelp and women and children run for cover. Under their high black Stetsons, the pair's flinty-eyed stares were enough to elicit quivering apologies from most anyone who got in their way. And that doesn't even account for the pearl-handled revolvers sticking out of their breeches.

"See any strangers 'round here?" one of them hissed to the storekeeper.

"N-n-n-n-nooo," he stuttered. "Ain't been any folks through here in a month 'a Sundays. That is 'cept you."

The storekeeper's weak laugh died on his lips when one of the men wrapped a meaty fist around his throat.

"Now lissen here," he whispered hard in the storekeeper's face. "We're lookin' fer someone. See, we're hunters. Man hunters. You shore ain't no outsider passed through these parts?"

When the pair were assured by one and all that no one had come through Big Flat they rode on to the northwest across the Buffalo River.

"Woooeee," allowed old Uncle Mort. "I ain't envyin' that man they's chasin. They's shore loaded fer b'ar and a hankerin' fer trouble."

As winter passed into spring and then summer, townspeople noted that John Smith hadn't been seen in town for months, since sometime late the previous fall. Folks remembered that on his last visit he hadn't made eye contact with anyone nor did he nod any greetings. He simply went to the store, traded for some provisions, and then left on foot with his old mule trailing behind.

Ephraim Jones, too, hadn't seen his tenant in many months and decided to check on his whereabouts. He rolled a few provisions into his saddle pack and rode off to the far valley where Smith had settled. It was rugged country so that he didn't near the hollow where Smith had settled until near sunset. The twilight sent a shiver down his back that had more to do with the unnatural quiet as it did anything else. Even his horse snorted in protest at being forced to ride into the hollow. Jones rounded a bend in the dim trail and startled Smith's old mule, that then snorted and took off into the bush.

Jones edged on noting the overgrown garden and rusted plow sitting off to one side. A bedraggled flock of half-wild chickens fluttered up at his approach and ran off in a panicked commotion. The shanty cabin itself was deserted. Its door hung limply on one hinge and a side of its roof had already caved in. Jones dismounted and pushed his way inside fearing that he might find Smith himself dead or dying. But no one had been in there for some time. The farmer looked around and decided that whenever Smith had left it must have been in a hurry for a meal was set on the table and a moldy pot of beans hung in the cold hearth.

He walked back outside "Hallooing!" several times in the hope that Smith might still be alive somewhere close by. Only a distant echo answered his call. He was about to head back to his own cabin before resuming the search the next day when he noted circling buzzards several hundred feet up toward the head of the small valley. He jumped on his horse and made his way through the underbrush toward the limestone bluffs. At the base of one of them he found the cause of the buzzard's presence. Two skeletons lay at the base of the cliff. A cursory look made it clear that neither of the men was the peddler; each of these remains showed a man well over six feet tall. It was equally clear how they died. A single bullet had drilled a neat hole between each man's eyes.

Jones made for the county seat, Yellville, to report his grisly discovery to the sheriff. He rode back to the site with Jones and the county coroner. Together they examined the remains, determining that each of the men had been killed at close range with bullets from either a .44 or .45 caliber revolver. The coroner said the condition of what was left of the bodies showed that they'd been dead for many weeks. The location of the bodies and the preciseness of each killing shot indicated to the sheriff that the men had not been killed in a running gun battle but had probably been captured, lined up next to one another and then summarily executed. The only question was who? The sheriff said only a person or persons unknown committed the murders.

The men were given a respectful burial in a small cemetery, but without their names on grave markers. No one knew their identity.

That was not the case among the locals when it came to guessing who the murderer might be and what had probably happened in that distant hollow. Nearly everyone figured that John Smith was no more John Smith than Uncle Mort was the Duke of York. The two bodies were more than likely those of the mean-looking cusses who had shown up months before. They were lawmen of some sort, or maybe desperadoes looking for Smith, or whatever his name was. Somehow Smith had gotten the drop on them and slayed them where they stood.

It was Uncle Mort who put it in the clear vernacular of northern Arkansas:

"Well, I reckin that there spectickle peddler had us all fooled into believin' he was a harmless critter. Then he up 'n' kilt them fellers in cold blood an' lit a shuck fer parts unknown."

Uncle Mort and his cronies appear to have been correct. John Smith was never heard from again, nor were his remains ever found. His cabin eventually collapsed and disappeared along with any traces of the field in which he had planted a garden.

Skeleton Hollow was returned to nature. With one exception that is. On a certain night in the late spring some folks say a grim scene is replayed at the base of that limestone bluff. A little man in ragged clothes cruelly laughs as he presses a double-barreled long gun against the forehead of a trembling man wearing a black Stetson and then pulls the trigger. But there is no sound as the man falls in a heap next to another body sprawled on the ground. The figures vanish as suddenly as they appear.

The Rinehart Poltergeist

This account might also very well have been titled *The Case of the Haunted Apartment*, for the principal character involved, celebrated mystery writer Mary Roberts Rinehart clearly preferred uncomplicated names for her dozens of short stories and novels. Her work includes pulp fiction, mystery novels, serious fiction, and stage plays. Two of her novels, *The Man in Lower Ten* and *The Circular Staircase*, are among the earliest works of popular entertainment by an American writer still in print. With Avery Hopwood, Mrs. Rinehart wrote a stage adaptation of *The Circular Staircase*. *The Bat* was successful on Broadway and later as a film starring Vincent Price.

We don't know what Mrs. Rinehart would have titled her own tantalizing supernatural mystery. We only know that she detailed the experience in an interesting portion of her autobiography, *My Story*, published in 1931—a narrative certainly worthy of a thoughtfully raised eyebrow for those interested in haunted celebrities.

The Rinehart mystery arose in the first months after she and her husband, Dr. Stanley M. Rinehart, moved into the former Washington, D.C., apartment of the late Pennsylvania Senator Boies Penrose. The Rineharts moved to Washington after Dr. Rinehart took a job as a medical consultant in the early days of the Veterans' Bureau, later the Veterans' Administration.

Her story of the bizarre incidents in the Penrose residence are made even more interesting because of Mrs. Rinehart's professed disbelief in ghosts. As she noted in her memoir: "I have no belief in physical phenomena as a manifestation of survival after death. I have never, either then or now, laid these pranks to the so-called earthbound spirit of Mr. Penrose. But some sort of phenomena we had . . ."

Over the course of several months, her skepticism must have been profoundly challenged. By her own count, there were at least fifteen observable events for which she could offer up little in the way of logical explanation. They all seemed to indicate a classic case of poltergeist activity.

Mary Roberts Rinehart had been born on August 12, 1876, in Pittsburgh, the daughter of a father destined to remain an impecunious dreamer and inventor, and a mother who had to take in boarders to help make ends meet. She attended public high school in the city and graduated from the Pittsburgh Training School for Nurses in 1896. She married Dr. Stanley Rinehart that same year.

Her writing career took off with a series of short stories for pulp magazines and the publication of her first two novels, which many critics contend are her best works in novel form, *The Man in the Lower Ten* (1906) and *The Circular Staircase* (1907). With their success, she never looked back and worked as a full-time writer for the next half century, which would include stints as a Broadway playwright, a World War I *Saturday Evening Post* war correspondent, and as a political reporter at several presidential nominating conventions. She remained one of America's most popular authors until her death in New York City on September 22, 1958.

Mrs. Rinehart effectively blended elements of the unconscious or subconscious with adventure and mystery in much of her writing. One critic noted that she "was alive to the poetic possibilities of the night and the dark. The night is always full of discoveries in Rinehart's work."

The mystery novelist's personal discoveries in that Washington apartment might not have seemed so poetic to her at the time.

The Rineharts, with Mary's mother, moved into the furnished apartment shortly after Senator Penrose died. The Rineharts and the senator had been friends through their mutual Pennsylvania roots and their political persuasions. He had been elected to the Senate in 1906. Born in Philadelphia, Penrose rose to prominence as a lawyer and as a leader of the state's Republican Party. He served for thirteen years in the state legislature before being elected to the United States Senate in 1906. He took over as Pennsylvania Republican leader in 1904 after the death of his benefactor, Matthew S. Quay. Later, in the U.S. Senate, Penrose dominated the influential finance committee and was Republican leader until 1921, when he died in office at the age of 61.

Interestingly, the senator is said to be the originator of the quip, "Public office is the last refuge of a scoundrel," after Samuel Johnson's oft quoted, "Patriotism is the last refuge of a scoundrel."

Mrs. Rinehart's mother had lived with her daughter and her family for some fourteen years following a debilitating stroke.

Mrs. Rinehart was evidently pleased with the apartment's location—she enthused about it "overlooking the city. Rather like Paris, the city, from these windows"—yet she was apparently disturbed by its reminders of Senator Penrose, a bachelor who had used a wheelchair in his last years. He died in the bedroom she used. She sat at his writing desk and on his sofa, and she even had the same telephones with exceedingly long cords so that they could be carried all around the apartment. She predicted, "I did not feel that this was to be a happy new apartment . . . yet those first months, barring certain inexplicable phenomena, were happy and interesting."

Sadly, the unhappiness came about, not because of any paranormal commotion, but from events involving her family. Mrs. Rinehart was a devoted mother to her three sons. Two had left home by that time, including Stanley, who would go on to help found Holt and Rinehart, the prominent New York publishing house. Son Alan was a newspaper reporter who lived with his parents in their Washington apartment.

Her husband was not happy with the Veterans' Bureau. He criticized the Bureau's reluctance to assign experts to treat tuberculosis and mental disorders among the World War I veterans, which he believed the nation had a duty to provide, and was unhappy with the growing number of political scandals tied to various states' attempts to snare government veterans' hospitals.

There was another reason that Dr. Rinehart wasn't happy: He was not pleased with his wife's celebrity status as the "trashy author of popular fiction," as one critic noted. Indeed, and perhaps at his urging, she spent the fifteen years between 1914 and 1929 writing "straight" fiction.

The marriage between the medical doctor and the mystery writer was a difficult one. She loved her sons immensely and was a fine mother. But her attitude toward marriage is manifested in much of her work through loutish husbands who express resentment at the slightest successes of their wives. Though she didn't use the phrase "male chauvinist pig," as it wasn't in use in that more genteel era, it is certainly what she meant.

But the event of most lasting impact on her was the terrible death of her own invalid mother, an event for which she would blame herself for years to come. She had looked after her mother since the older woman's stroke had left her partially paralyzed and without speech.

And so, it was that the Rineharts were, as Mrs. Rinehart writes in her autobiography, cheerful but "not particularly happy" in the apartment.

Her biographers have noted that Mrs. Rinehart was plagued with a series of emotional and physical illnesses during her life, and she admits herself that during their Washington stay she was depressed much of the time. She was "very tired" and "highly nervous," to use her own words. What role her health problems played in her belief that the apartment was the center of unexplained and possibly supernatural phenomena isn't clear, yet the sheer volume of unexplained events and the disparate witnesses would argue against it being the product of her depression or imagination.

She also notes that the events ceased with her mother's death. "Were we being warned?" she asks. "Is it true, after all, that the dead are about us, and that some anxious spirit was there, trying to tell us? Or was some little unseen imp, some child never incarnate, playing at night around our rooms?"

The questions began just as the Rineharts settled into the apartment on their first night there and gone to their bedroom. They both read for a few minutes before switching off their bedside reading lights.

"There was a rush of something through the room," she wrote of the phenomenon. "The effect was as if a large black curtain had been drawn swiftly across, and Dr. Rinehart sat up in bed.

"What on earth was that?" her husband asked.

"We turned on the lights but everything was as it should be. The windows were open, but there was no wind, and the narrow curtains were held flat to the wall by heavy bands and could not blow out under any circumstances."

Nothing further happened that night.

Curiously, there had been some earlier talk by the hotel apartment staff that they thought "the dead man was walking," meaning Senator Penrose, but there's no evidence that Mrs. Rinehart or her husband took the gossip seriously or connected that first night's incident to the senator's ghost. In fact, all during the phenomena, Dr. Rinehart attributed them to his wife's "nervous condition," although it seems improbable that she could have manifested a wind blowing through the bedroom. And he, too, noticed the "rush" and inquired as to whether his wife had felt it.

Mrs. Rinehart took notice of frequent episodes involving apartment buzzers, doorbells and various rappings from odd places, such as on the morning after their first night there.

She employed a maid named Marie who cared for both her and her mother. At 7 A.M., Marie knocked on her employer's bedroom door and entered with a coffeepot and cups.

"It's only seven, Marie," Mrs. Rinehart scolded, still half asleep.

"But you rang, madam. You rang twice," Marie replied. Two short rings was Mrs. Rinehart's signal for Marie to bring coffee.

The bell service continued to cause problems all during their stay in the apartment. It rang so often that, rather than automatically bring a coffee service when the bell sounded, Marie would first check with her employer to make sure she had actually signaled.

In time, Mrs. Rinehart offered three possible causes for the bell's mistaken ringing: there was an electrical short circuit, she herself had rung it in her sleep, or Marie had imagined it.

Over the next month or so, the bell continued ringing with great frequency. One day Mrs. Rinehart thought she'd finally solved the unbearable disturbance.

"I was writing letters . . . in the study, across from Marie's room. My mother was downstairs on the porch of the hotel, and Marie and I were alone in the apartment, she darning stockings in her room across. To my astonishment, the bell from my distant bedroom rang again, twice as usual, and she and I met in the hall, startled."

"Who did that?" Mrs. Rinehart asked.

"She didn't know. My study door had been open, as had been hers. A careful search revealed no one in the apartment, and the only access would have been past the two open doors where we sat."

Mrs. Rinehart thought it certainly meant an electrical short circuit given that there could be no other logical explanation—both women were seventy feet from the bedroom, both women heard it at the same time, and no one else was home.

The electrician she called in found nothing wrong with either the wiring or the bell.

The family accepted the mysteriously ringing bell, the author says, because they "became accustomed to it."

Even when Marie found her alarm clock standing in the middle of the floor one morning, or when she reported that her bedroom door would not stay closed at night, Mrs. Rinehart attributed it to "nervousness" over the bell.

The insight of critics into Mary Roberts Rinehart's affinity for the night was never more accurate than in her recognition that the unexplained phenomena in the apartment were most acute after sunset.

She wrote:

"After a time I began most willingly to believe that something was going on which I did not understand. Working in the study or reading in my bed, there were curious noises, stirrings; sometimes, while reading in bed, through the open door into the living room there came the sound of a chair or table moving, and once there was a crash as if a heavy fern basket had dropped on one of the porches. No basket had dropped, however.

"I am not credulous, and so I tried to attribute the sounds to something I could not comprehend; to the apartment below, to the wind, to the creaking of the metal lath in the walls. I made little investigations, wandering around in my nightdress, pattering in my bare feet so as to come unaware on some mischief-maker. But I could find nothing, nobody."

One night Mrs. Rinehart had a fright that on retrospect might have come from a Laurel and Hardy comedic romp with Boris Karloff through a haunted house. At the time, she probably didn't find anything amusing about it at all.

The incident came about because some time earlier a spiritualist had told her that the next time something untoward took place to speak right up. *See what it wants,* her psychic friend suggested, *so that maybe you can help it.*

So when she heard the window in the living room slamming shut of its own accord, she wrote about her attempt to communicate with the thing: "I edged into the room and with my back against the wall, spoke in a small and quavering voice. Almost immediately, a bell rang down the hall, and continued to ring like a fire alarm. It required some time for me to realize that I was leaning against the bell-push itself on the living room wall!"

One can imagine just such a scene dropped into the middle of a gothic thriller to provide a bit of comic relief. In Mrs. Rinehart's real-life scenario, there was precious little respite from the peculiar events, sometimes piling up almost daily, and at other times so infrequent that it was almost possible to forget anything unusual had happened at all.

The human occupants of Senator Penrose's old place weren't the only ones affected—the Rineharts' bull terrier, Keno, had a sense that something was out of place there. It is not unusual for pets, particularly dogs and cats, to react quite strongly to a sense that something its human masters cannot see also resides in a particular dwelling.

In this situation, Keno regularly sat on Mrs. Rinehart's lap, shaking with fear, his hair bristling as he stared off into a corner. As she looked back on those months in the apartment, Mary Roberts realized that the dog had acted strangely from the beginning. Son Alan Rinehart had a scare on an evening when he was home alone and dressing for a party. He needed to get something from his mother's bedroom and Keno trotted on ahead into the dark room. Almost immediately the terrier came crawling back out, hair again bristling, and whining in what the young man later said was "utter and complete terror." He decided he could do without the item he sought.

Though she resolutely refused to attribute the funny business to the senator's wandering ghost, Mrs. Rinehart knew some sort of phenomena was at play. And she found one particular location in an apartment hallway where it manifested itself quite frequently.

Like a small child, she had taken to sleeping with a light on. Leading away from her bedroom was a small corridor off which were both a bathroom and a separate dressing room her husband used so as not to disturb his sleeping wife. She kept the bathroom light on, with the door open far enough to cast full light in the hallway and across the door to Dr. Rinehart's room.

Her account of one particular late evening is clear and chilling:

"The doctor had been away for ten days, and his room was closed, windows and doors. One night I put down my book about one o'clock, and turned off my light. I was not sleepy, and I lay facing the small corridor and the door to the dressing room, both in bright light. Suddenly there was an imperious knocking on the other side of that closed door. It did not alarm me, for Alan was out at a dance, and I thought he had returned and was having a little amusement with me. There was another door into the dressing room, from the hall.

"I sat up in bed and called:

" 'Come in.'

"The knocking was then vigorously repeated, and I raised my voice.

" 'Come in, Alan.'

"The door swung slowly open, and it was only then that I saw that the dressing room beyond was still dark.

"I shot out of bed and into the main hall, which was lighted, and stood outside the door of the dressing room there. If Alan or any one else was playing a trick on me, I had them trapped. But nothing happened, and at last I opened the door and reaching inside, turned on the light.

"There was nobody there, and all windows were closed and fastened."

A search for explanations yielded unsatisfying results. Dr. Rinehart later found an electric heater hanging on the back of the bathroom door and suggested the forceful rapping came from this as it banged against the door in the draft. But his wife said all the outer windows and doors had been closed and locked. Perhaps the creaking they occasionally heard might have come from the building's structure, plaster over metal lath, they thought. It does seem that Dr. Rinehart did his best to persuade his wife that most of what she said was going on was a product of "hysteria" or some other mental condition.

She didn't agree.

And she particularly didn't think that the small critters that occasionally infiltrated the apartment—a bat and a bird, for instance—were imagined. The home was tightly built, she said, with windows screened, doors kept locked (with the front door fitted for a special, heavy-duty Yale lock), no fireplace or open chimney flue, and no other holes that she could ever find. Interestingly, she was at work on the stage adaptation of *The Circular Staircase* during this time, a play whose title, of course, would be *The Bat*.

A visit by Dr. Rinehart's two sisters offered some additional support for Mrs. Rinehart's contention that "some sort of phenomenon" was taking place in their quarters.

The two older women were given a guest room near the study. Neither woman had been told anything of the mysterious events. On the first night, as the one sister fell asleep quickly, the other was kept awake by her companion's incessant tapping on her bed's headboard. She finally could take it no longer and flipped on the light. Her sister was sleeping soundly, her hands nowhere near the headboard. She turned off the lights. The drumming resumed.

She awoke her sister and together they listened. The rapping had stopped, but through the wall from the study came the clickety-clack of the manual typewriter. They thought it might have been reporter Alan Rinehart working late on a story. The bedside clock read 2 A.M. One of the sisters hopped out of bed to tell him his late night work was keeping them awake. She cast open the door. The study was vacant, the lights unlit.

Although the Rinehart's son Stanley was working in New York publishing, he often came down to Washington for visits with his parents or to attend social gatherings with Alan. His mother had not told him of the occurrences, but he didn't have to be made aware—he found out for himself.

Stanley had come home to attend a dinner party and dance. Only days before, the Rineharts had repainted the hall floor and moved the furniture back in place. On the morning after the party, Mary Roberts got up to find her older son sitting on the floor.

"Come here, mother, I want to show you something," he said to her.

His mother picked up the story at that point:

"He had come in late and gone to sleep at once, to be awakened with a feeling of intense cold and a sense of terror he could not explain. Following that, as he lay there, outside his door in the hall, a heavy piece of furniture had apparently commenced to move, and for an hour it had creaked and moved without stopping.

"Now as he sat there and showed me on the freshly painted floor a series of new scorings around a heavy leather chair; these scorings were very deep, and they covered a space some six inches in diameter. The experiment of moving the chair produced the same sounds he had heard during the night, and again we were left without any explanation."

Mary Roberts thought that on the surface anyway what was loose in the apartment was akin to archetypal poltergeist phenomena, a mischievous force that makes noise or moves objects but is not seen by anyone. The final episode seemed to fit such a pattern because it was "absurd and pointless," she wrote later, which is sometimes the way in which poltergeist activity is described.

Dr. and Mrs. Rinehart, her mother and the maid, Marie, had gone out for a car ride. No one was left in the apartment. When they returned, Mrs. Rinehart found a small pandanus plant sitting in the middle of the living room some thirty feet from where the shrub belonged on a porch that she'd furnished as a kind of hothouse. The plant had been removed from its pot.

No explanation for how the plant took its little voyage was ever given.

The couple's prominence also meant that the story of the Rinehart poltergeist would not remain private. Mrs. Rinehart talked about it one night at a dinner party and the next morning several newspapers ran stories that "the Penrose apartment was haunted and that the dead Senator was still ringing his bell."

Again, she received some unexpected support from outside sources. Several senate staffers told her that the late senator's office bell, the one he rang to summon assistance, continued to ring—*with two short sharp peals*—after he had died. And a senate page told her in confidence that several pages didn't like going into the senator's office—there was a ghost in it.

Sadly, the curious episode of the haunted apartment appears to have ended after the death of her mother. The author had gone to the family ranch and left Marie in charge as she had done many times previously. That evening the maid drew up a bath for the older woman but was called away before she could give her a bath. Somehow, the woman got into the tub and was critically scalded by the water. She could not speak so she could not cry out, neither could she extricate herself from the tub because one arm was paralyzed. She later died of her injuries.

Her death seemed to have a profound affect on Mary Roberts Rinehart. She blamed herself for her mother's death, believing that the move to Washington killed her.

"Why were all our deaths violent ones?" she asks in her memoir, citing the deaths of a baby sister, her father, and others. "And now our mother? Why had our grandmother been killed as she had been, or Laura's child, or that little daughter of the youngest aunt? And there were others. There was Brother Ed, my husband's half-brother, burned to death . . . all my old uncertainties came back. I had no faith in life, no sense of its security. What other people accepted as the normal, safety was and is to me a blessed boon. At night in my prayers I ask for safety for those I care for, not prosperity, not even for salvation. Safety. I have a queer feeling that if I forget to ask for that, something may happen."

As it was with this renowned writer of mysteries, we are left with our own puzzle, our own mystery as it were. Were the phenomena in the old Penrose apartment a warning of another impending tragedy, as Mary Roberts may have suspected, or something else entirely, perhaps the old senator letting the new tenants know he hadn't entirely decided to vacate the premises?

Unlike Mary Roberts's other mysteries, the case of the haunted apartment remains unsolved.

Bridges to the Past

Ghosts are usually associated with structures of one sort or another—houses, hotels, cabins, barns, and even bridges—and for good reason. Many psychic researchers and parapsychologists believe that an individual's emotional imprint can linger in a place with which they were associated long after the earth has claimed their mortal remains. These Florida tales attest to the power of a place to hold onto a person even after he's gone.

"Where's John?"

Her name was Martha. A pretty woman, she had fallen head over heels in love with a local boy whose rugged good looks were accentuated by the dashing mustache fashionable in that late nineteenth-century era. His name was John and he, too, was madly, passionately in love with her. Though their last names have vanished with the passage of time, their story of devotion to one another—and the legend it has created—has not.

The rituals of courtship were much stricter in that era before automobiles and even paved roads. Men routinely saddled up their ponies or hitched up the wagon to pay calls upon their sweethearts, but under the strictest of parental supervision. However, the dense inland backwoods of Gulf Coast Florida of a century and more ago made even that seemingly simple ritual a daunting task. So it was that John, the lover of Martha, had saddled his mare for what he assumed would be another pleasurable visit with his sweetheart—even if her parents sat just inside while the young couple whispered their eternal love for one another as they cuddled demurely on the porch swing. The trail to her home was familiar even in the gathering twilight of an early fall evening. As he neared Fish Hawk Creek the road veered across the bridge he'd taken countless times. But, for some reason, on this evening his horse was more skittish than usual as he reined her onto the bridge. She started to prance from side to side and then tried to back up as he tightened his grip on the bridle and dug his heels into her flanks. She suddenly reared up and threw him onto the bridge deck where he landed awkwardly on his head and shoulders. Death was instantaneous. John had broken his neck.

Meanwhile, Martha waited expectantly. The minutes seemed to crawl by as she gazed down the trail, all the while expecting to hear the recognizable hoof-beats of her sweetheart's horse. All that she heard were the familiar sounds of locusts, crickets and a smattering of bullfrogs from the low swampy ground nearby. Darkness gathered and still John was nowhere to be seen. Then, despite her parents' protests, she took up an oil lantern and headed off down the trail she knew John would have followed. She found her way to the bridge and to the horrible sight of her betrothed crumpled on the ground, his head twisted at an unnatural angle. His horse placidly grazed on the creek bank unaware of the tragedy she brought about.

The young girl fell to her knees and wept. Within minutes, however, she knew what had to be done. Gathering up her skirts she stumbled back up the trail, picking her way along this time without the lamp. She quietly stole into her father's barn, found a sturdy length of rope and fled back toward the bridge. She tied one end of the rope to the bridge side and the other to her neck, carefully judging its length so that her body would not land in the water.

And she jumped. Her reckoning had been correct.

The story might have ended there, with the sad deaths of these lovers, if not for the persistent legend that has built up around John and Martha . . . the story that fifty years to the date of their deaths, Martha's ghost was first seen wandering the old Fish Hawk Creek bridge. Those who saw her said she had but one question on her pale, cold lips:

"Where's John?"

The bridge that John and Martha knew eventually gave way to a railroad trestle over Fish Hawk Creek east of Boyette Road, south of Brandon. But even the tracks disappeared over time and the old trestle bridge was a long walk on rough terrain for anyone pursuing the legendary appearance of Martha's spirit. According to those who have claimed to have seen her, Martha arrives unexpectedly in a flash of phosphorescent green that rises and falls like that of an ocean wave. Materializing out of the haze is her beautiful but lifeless form dressed in the shimmering wedding dress she never wore in life, her arms rising questioningly, beseechingly, as she repeats that single question, Where's John?

This ghost of Boyette Bridge has been a fixture in the region for a half-century or more. Railroad workers in about 1970 were said to have been among the first to report Martha's return. A midnight train had stopped on the trestle when the vaporous form of a woman floated up to the engine and asked the surprised engineer where John was.

A man who claimed to have seen the ghost several times said he found an old man whose mother had been Martha's sister. The fellow confirmed the story of the pair's death.

Martha is said to make appearances on only two dates—Halloween and every Friday the 13th. Whatever the real truth, and it's nearly impossible to discern at such a late date, this tale of love thwarted and a lovely, restless ghost was a welcome diversion for many decades among the rural population of southern Hillsborough County.

Ghost Central

If there is a single Florida city that has spawned more stories of haunted homes and ghostly goings-on, that one place has to be the nearly four hundred and fifty-year-old St. Augustine, America's oldest European-founded settlement. Although Ponce de Leon may have landed near the city during his first voyage in 1513, its recorded history dates from 1564 when Spanish Catholics settled St. Augustine after being driven back from Fort Caroline, on the St. John's River in modern day Jacksonville.

The St. Augustine community of some 12,000 living souls is nestled about a third of the way between Jacksonville and Daytona Beach on Florida's Atlantic coast. With attractions like the Lightner Museum, the Castillo de San Marcos National Monument and the Oldest House in the U.S., St. Augustine is a popular destination for winter-weary northerners and inland Floridians looking for ocean-kissed relief from the dank swamps and piney woods. The red-tiled roofs, iron balconies, and Spanish steeples are permanent reminders of the sixteenth-century blending of Anglo and Spanish influences. A stroll through Old St. Augustine— *San Agustin Antiguo*—is like stepping aboard a time machine and being transported back to a place and epoch when Spain's rule stretched from eastern Florida north to Missouri and thence to the Pacific Ocean.

But there is another side to St. Augustine . . . a side that is the city's other, unseen, history and one so prevalent that entire books and walking tours have been organized around it. It is the story of *haunted* St. Augustine.

Among the reputedly haunted places in this ancient city is the Castillo de San Marcos National Monument, where a "floating head" was reportedly seen. A historian there, however, says the Castillo doesn't track such "folklore." Other haunted sites include a lighthouse, several inns, the city's Catholic cemetery— where a woman in white glides amid the graves—the old Ponce de Leon Hotel, now owned by Flagler College, and several dozen other places.

Pat and Maggie Patterson have owned one of the most enthralling haunted homes. The dwelling dates to the mid-1600s and boasts the ghosts of a calico cat, a sentry, a shadowy white figure . . . and the polite specter of former Spanish governor Don Pedro Benedit de Horruytiner, who lived in the house over three hundred years ago. The word polite is appropriate here, considering how Don Pedro introduced himself to the Pattersons. He suddenly appeared in full formal regalia—black breeches and waistcoat and white ruffled shirt. He bowed formally to Mrs. Patterson, who was so startled she jumped up and ran from the room.

The Pattersons told a reporter that the apparitions in their home were playful sorts who preferred practical tricks, like hiding jewelry, moving furniture and turning on the lights. In fact, the Pattersons discovered the ghosts in their house with an exhibition of spirited fun. Shortly after they moved into their house in 1981, Mrs. Patterson, who had heard stories about ghosts in the house, announced aloud and to no one in particular that she would like to meet them.

"If there are any ghosts in here I wish they would give us a sign!" she reportedly said, half-jokingly.

Lights suddenly popped on at the home's entrance and on the staircase.

"It's an exciting house to live in," Mrs. Patterson said in a published interview. And made even more exciting, perhaps, by those things which even a ghost might find a bit discomforting—such as a coffin on the third floor, a memento of those years when a doctor lived there and kept a couple of them handy just in case his patients didn't survive the treatments!

Smoke and Mirrors

The methods by which families cope with ghosts or other indications of a haunting vary a good deal and often depend upon how threatening the behavior. Some families live happily with their house ghost while others flee in fear for their lives. These extremes of behavior are illustrated in two Florida stories from opposite corners of the state.

The ghost in one Pensacola home was a big man who favored plaid shirts and work pants. Though nearly six feet tall, no one in the family was able to identify this working-class gentleman because his face was shrouded in an indistinct haze.

The father in the family was the first to see the ghost, though he managed to keep it a secret from his children and even his wife for nearly two years. His name was George Glines. The story unfolded on a night he stayed home when the city had a hurricane warning. As he rested on a couch he sensed that someone was standing nearby. He lifted himself up onto his elbows and looked to see a husky older man staring at him. George got up to chase after the intruder—for he thought a burglar had gotten in—but the man took a step back and faded away. George turned on the lights and searched his house for some sign of entry but found nothing. Despite the suddenness of the appearance, George never felt threatened or frightened. However, he decided to be discrete and avoid talking about the incident, especially with his own family.

He never mentioned it, he later told a Mississippi newspaper reporter, "because I didn't want to upset the rest of the family."

He was successful. Not until two years later, during the visit of a daughter's possible future husband, did the ghost visit again in person.

The young man George's daughter was introducing to her family—James Boone—was asleep alone in an upstairs bedroom when he awoke to see the same man standing near the bed. And as before, there were no intimations that the ghost had any intention of harming Boone or anyone else in the house. "He just stood there watching," Boone said later.

When Boone shakily related his story to the family the next morning, George Glines listened intently then held up his hand, interrupting to correctly say that the man Boone saw was wearing khaki pants and had on a plaid shirt.

Boone acknowledged that that was absolutely correct.

Mrs. Glines demanded to know how her husband could possibly know that information. It was then he told her and the family about his experience two years earlier.

"I think we've got a ghost in the house," he concluded matter-of-factly.

The prospective son-in-law and father George were not the only ones to have brushes with the ghost.

Mrs. Glines told the reporter that her two-year-old son George Jr. had a habit of playing on the staircase. When she told him to be careful of the steep steps, he said that "Puki" was there, too, and would keep him from falling down. He went on to describe a tall man in khakis and a plaid shirt. The little boy couldn't see the man's face very well, though. "It isn't clear," he said.

During the four years they lived in the Pensacola house, the Glines found that the ghost could also produce knockings and footsteps. Each night at about 11 P.M., a rhythmic tap came from one living room wall. The family asked their landlord to tear out the wall but that didn't reveal any reason for the sound. When the wall was rebuilt, the tapping resumed. The footfalls of a running man were not localized to any specific room and became so routine the family hardly noticed.

After the house burned, the Glines family moved back to Mississippi. Before they left, however, Little George Jr. said "Puki" told him that he was upset that the house was gone. But he told the little boy he might come back when it was "all fixed up again." The Glines declined to stick around to see if he was true to his word.

The Glines' experience with their benign visitor was in stark contrast to what happened to Mary Winters in her North West 22nd Avenue Miami home. Although the house was torn down long ago when the avenue was widened, Mrs. Winters remembered many years later, and with startling clarity, the evil she experienced there.

The strange series of events began almost routinely—for a haunting—with chairs tipping over and lights snapping on and off but then they took on far nastier dimensions. Her pet cat would not walk around the yard. A tree oozed blood after it was hit by lightning, according to Mrs. Winters, who had been recently divorced at the time of the haunting.

Unfortunately, all that was but prelude to her late night encounter with a homicidal cloud of smoke.

Mrs. Winters told a Miami newspaper reporter that shortly before midnight she was sitting on the edge of her bed taking off her shoes. The room itself was in darkness, but the hallway light was on and shone around the slightly open door.

"Suddenly a cloud of smoke seeped into the room and slowly rose to the ceiling," Mrs. Winters was quoted as saying. "Like a large, turbulent cloud. I figured there had to be an explanation, but I jumped into bed and pulled the covers over my head."

She stayed hidden for several minutes. When she peeked over her blankets, the cloud was hovering near the ceiling. Then it slowly started to descend. She made the quick decision to escape but as she attempted to get up off the bed, two arm-like extensions emerged from the cloud and grabbed her around the throat. She fell to the floor with the "thing" on her back and its arms squeezing tightly around her.

"They felt like ice. I was paralyzed, and I could hardly breathe," she said.

She thought that if she could get to the light switch and turn it on the monstrous cloud might release its grip. But she was nearly unconscious from the pressure, her head spinning in dizziness.

Abruptly, a voice that she described as soft and low came out of the crushing mass. "Aaaaaaaah!" it seemed to say, like an extended exhalation of breath.

"It transmitted a thought to me that, after it had dealt with me, it would go for my son, sleeping in another bedroom," Mrs. Winters recalled.

The idea that her eight-year-old son might be in danger gave the young woman the power to pull herself across the bedroom floor and then to reach up and turn on the lights. The cloud disappeared. She rushed to her son's room where she found him asleep and undisturbed.

She telephoned a friend to tell him what had happened and he offered to come over.

Though he didn't completely believe her, he suggested that they try to repeat the exact circumstances as those she encountered earlier.

"We turned the light off, leaving the one on in the hall. We sat and waited. After an hour or so, the cloud of smoke came in through the door. My friend was a big, brave man, but he rushed for the light switch. Again, the cloud disappeared, but we were both so shaken we sat up all night drinking coffee," she said.

What are we to make of the story? Mary Winters moved away from the house and it was eventually torn down. The identity of whoever or whatever was responsible for the haunting was never discovered. She remarried and moved with her new husband to West Miami. She said whatever it was that accosted her on that night never again bothered her. The idea of blood oozing from trees and vicious clouds is nearly incomprehensible, yet Mrs. Winters insisted she was a sane and sober witness to the events. And so convincing was her telling of the events that it won a ghost story contest sponsored by a Florida newspaper.

On the Old Kolb Farm

Katherine and James Tatum always considered themselves rational, practical, stable people. Their marriage had been solid, they traveled widely both in the United States and abroad and enjoyed a wide circle of friends. James was a retired army officer. Katherine was an accountant who was, in her own words, "used to analyzing the cause and effect of things in my work."

Therefore it was frustrating when they weren't able to find a "normal" explanation for an extraordinary series of events which thrust them into an encounter with the supernatural.

Their story began, just as it has for thousands of older Americans like the Tatums, with a search for just the right community in which to retire. After traveling the world courtesy of Uncle Sam, the couple first settled in Florida upon James's retirement. However, the extremely hot summers there soon persuaded them to look elsewhere. They also missed the change of seasons of more northern climes. That's when they discovered Marietta, Georgia, and a new housing development that was being built on what had been known as the Kolb Creek Farm, a tract of ground that had been under cultivation since well before the Civil War. Amid the wooded, rolling hills a few miles northwest of Atlanta, Katherine and James Tatum were among the first families to build a house in the exclusive subdivision. They moved to Kolb Ridge Court in the late 1980s, just down the road from the original historic log-sided Kolb Creek farmhouse.

For the first year the Tatums' enjoyed their lovely, two-story contemporary-style home. They often entertained new acquaintances in Marietta and old friends often dropped in for visits. But their idyllic retirement took a decidedly unexpected turn soon thereafter.

Katherine Tatum remembered quite clearly how it all began.

"A little over a year after the house was built, we began to experience strange events," she said.

What transpired were over a half-dozen events so perplexing they would be "hard for anyone to believe . . . unless they experienced it themselves," Katherine said.

And it might be even harder for the uninitiated to comprehend how it all began since it started in almost a clichéd manner . . . in the middle of a quiet night.

"My husband and I had gotten up to go to the bathroom at the same time, about 2:30 A.M.," Katherine recalled. "Our bedroom is upstairs. My husband used the bedroom bath and I went into the hall bath. The bathroom door was open. I saw a man walking down the hall in front of the open bathroom door. I assumed it was my husband looking for me. I called out to him. He didn't answer. I thought he'd gone downstairs (since) he had not heard me call out."

She briefly followed after the figure toward the staircase, calling out all the while since she still believed it was James. By the time she got to the stairs the figure had disappeared. That's when she turned around and returned to the master bedroom . . . and found James settled back in bed.

"He couldn't figure out why I kept calling out," she said.

Katherine told her husband that she had seen a man going down the hall toward the stairs. James grabbed a gun he kept next to the bed and quickly checked all the windows and doors in the entire house. There was no sign of an intruder.

That upset Katherine Tatum even more.

"It was almost impossible for me to go to sleep. I spent the rest of the night going over and over the incident. I came to realize that when the man walked past me there had been no sound, as you would normally hear whenever someone is walking down the hall."

The more she concentrated on the figure she had seen, the more she remembered. The figure had had his head slightly tilted. He seemed to be wearing a long coat of some sort and a hat pulled low over his head.

He was in shadow because a high-intensity flood light on the side of their house was throwing light through a hall window directly opposite the bathroom.

"He was a solid figure," Katherine remembered. "I couldn't tell what he was wearing because I was on the dark side of him. He was walking like he was going somewhere, not shuffling. And he was swinging his arms as he went by. Like he had some place to go."

"I became afraid," Katherine said. "I started trying to rationalize what had happened. What did I see? That's when I realized I didn't hear anything when the figure went by."

What did James think of his wife's encounter with a phantom? "At first he thought somebody was in the house. And then he didn't know what to think."

She and her husband did not need to exchange words to understand the implication of the incident—the figure in the hallway was not human.

Not human.

Two simple words, but for Katherine Tatum they spelled what seemed almost impossible—their new house in suburban Marietta was not quite what it seemed. And yet Katherine's commonsense approach to life and her work experience told her to look for the logical explanation, the facts behind this real nightmare. But before she could reach a satisfactory answer other equally perplexing episodes caused the couple to nearly question their own rationality.

James Tatum had undertaken a small carpentry project involving a problem with attic steps that could be pulled down from the ceiling in the upstairs hallway. Every time the stairs were lowered from the ceiling, the bottom posts dug into the hallway carpeting. James was going to bolt a board across the bottom to prevent any further damage.

Katherine Tatum takes up the account:

"He had his tools and a power drill up there. One time I called him for dinner. He laid the drill to the side and came down intending to go back and finish later. Well, he forgot about it and started watching a television program. Later on I went upstairs to our bedroom to lie down and read. I had turned away from the bedroom door when I heard the drill. It was real loud, as though someone was playing around with it, turning it on and off. I thought that James was trying to scare me with it. I tried to ignore it and continued to read my book. After a while I had had enough of his 'playfulness' so I ran out to the hallway."

The drill lay on its side, propped up against the wall just as James must have left it several hours before. Katherine found it cold to the touch. She ran down the stairs to find her husband. He hadn't heard anything.

"He was sympathetic," Katherine said, "yet not quite able to believe me. I was one shaky woman."

The house was quiet for some time. The Tatums could almost have believed the earlier episodes were an aberration, somehow explainable—if only they could figure out how to explain them.

"I had just about gotten over the drill business," Katherine said, "when I went upstairs to watch television one night. I was completely engrossed in a TV drama when I began to hear what sounded like static electricity in the middle of the room. A kind of popping in the air."

She turned off the television set to concentrate. Try as she might, however, there didn't appear to be any clear source for the mysterious sound. But as she walked around the room the noise seemed to move toward her.

"I backed up clear to the corner and it came right up to my face. I had no alternative but to duck under and run down the stairs."

The noise stayed in the room and did not follow her. At Katherine's insistence, James checked through the room, but by this time all was quiet. Whatever had caused Katherine's fright had vanished.

"This began to make me quite fearful of what was happening in our home," Katherine emphasized.

A few days later, the Tatums left on a long-planned two-month vacation to the West Coast and Alaska. Katherine, in particular, felt a desperate need to get away for a while.

"When we returned home everything was quiet. I was hoping that it was the end of it," she said.

It wasn't.

The Tatums' were readying themselves for a short trip to Florida several weeks after their return from the West Coast when Katherine had a close encounter with their uninvited tenant.

"I was in a rush to get things picked up and packed away. We were going to take our motor home down there. I was bent over putting a casserole in the microwave when I felt two distinct tugs on the bottom of my blouse. I turned around thinking that it was my husband. He was outside."

They left for Florida the next day.

Katherine did have other physical reactions to the haunting.

"I always felt a cold spot in the upstairs hallway and one of the guest bedrooms. The hair stood up on the back of my neck in the bedroom. It almost felt like I was infringing upon someone else's room," she recalled. Katherine had a desk in that guest bedroom at which she would sometimes work. But she doesn't linger there. "It's just not comfortable for me, yet it's a very comfortable room."

James Tatum had been only indirectly involved in the strange goings-on at his home. He never doubted his wife's sincerity, yet he didn't have any explicit proof of the events his wife described. All that would change in a series of irritating occurrences with a small angel bell the couple kept in a second guest bedroom.

"My husband gets up quite early each morning," Katherine explains. He would usually dress and go downstairs for coffee and to read the morning newspaper in the family room. She would stay in bed.

"I ring the little angel bell that we keep in the guest bedroom whenever I need him," Katherine said. "The family room is so far away that it's difficult for him to hear me when I call out. It's easier for him to hear the bell. One morning he heard the bell ringing and came upstairs. But I was still asleep. He couldn't figure it out."

When Katherine awoke later, James told her the bell rang that morning. She denied ringing it and, indeed, to James it seemed totally out of character that his wife would pull such a prank. He jokingly told her that the "ghost" was behind it. A few days later, the couple wasn't laughing anymore.

"It happened again, and he ran up the stairs. As soon as he hit the top step the bell stopped. He looked in the guest bedroom and the bell was still in there. He started back down the stairs when the bell rang again, as if he was being teased," Katherine said.

That morning at breakfast, James told his wife that he had no intention of running up the stairs again when the bell rang unless the couple could adopt some sort of code. He wanted to be sure it was his wife whose hand held the bell. Katherine told him she would ring the bell three times to let him know that it was she.

"You know what happened, of course," she laughed. "The next time it rang, it rang three times. He checked on the bell again. And it started ringing as he left the room. After that he told me that if the bell rings again, he wasn't going to answer. He said you'll have to come and get me. The bell never rang again."

The "ghost" remained dormant for some four months. The couple believed whatever was responsible for the activities had left the house. The next May their hopes were dashed.

Katherine Tatum was again the center of the incident.

"I had gone upstairs to read before going to bed. It was quite late, and my face was turned away from the door so that I could read by the bedside lamp. My husband keeps a little wooden bowl on the chest of drawers so that he can put his pocket change in it before going to bed. I heard the money dropping into the bowl a coin at a time. I turned to look at him, but he wasn't there. Yet I could hear the change being dropped in the bowl. It was just as clear and as loud as can be."

She ran downstairs to find James, but by the time they got back to the bedroom all was quiet.

"He was ready to shoot 'it,' " Katherine said. "I told him you can't shoot something you can't see. Whatever we have in this house, everything it does seems to be some sort of teasing. As long as I'm alert and looking for something to happen, it doesn't. It seems to happen only when I forget about it, or I'm engrossed in something else."

An incident involving a pack of TUMS and a glass of water Katherine kept on a tray on her nightstand is an example of the "teasing" nature of the haunting. It was late evening and Katherine had just turned off the bedside lamp. James was still downstairs.

"First I could hear the tray moving around and the glass being lifted up and put back down. I knew exactly what was going on. It was like listening to a bunch of rats playing around," she said. "And then when I didn't turn over (to look), the TUMS started dropping down on the tray—1, 2, 3, 4, 5, just like that." As soon as she started paying attention to the annoying noises, they ceased nearly as suddenly as they had begun.

The Tatums rarely told anyone of their experiences. However, two of their long-time friends may have had an inadvertent brush with their prankish spirit. James and Katherine had arranged to "house-switch" with the couple—they would stay at their friends' house in Florida for a week while their friends visited the Atlanta area by staying in the Tatums' home. Neither James nor Katherine told them they thought their house was haunted.

Surprisingly, they didn't hear any reports of oddities in their home until well after their friends' departure.

"About two months later we were talking to them on the telephone when I asked if anything strange had happened to them while they stayed here," Katherine said. "He (the husband) said something very odd had happened and he wondered what had caused it."

It seems that three nights after the Tatums left, the visiting couple were jarred awake in the guest bedroom very early in the morning by a loud, persistent ringing. Though it sounded like an alarm clock, they couldn't figure out where it was coming from. Eventually they found it was an electric alarm clock in the master bedroom. Somehow, it had gone off this particular morning . . . seventy-two hours after the Tatums had left.

The next morning, the husband, an electronics technician at Disney World, examined the clock but couldn't figure out what had made it ring in the middle of the night.

In their phone conversation, Katherine told their friends about the inexplicable events in their house and said it was probably another example of the mischievous spirit.

Katherine and James Tatum were able to find a possible explanation for the ghostly activity when they researched local history. Not only was their house built on a very old homestead, but the farm was the site of Civil War combat. The Battle of Kolb Farm took place at about the same time as the more famous Battle of Kennesaw Mountain, Georgia, during which 13,000 Union troops under the command of Gen. William Tecumseh Sherman stormed Confederate forces dug in across the mountain. Sherman failed to dislodge Confederate Gen. Joe Johnston's troops, and lost several thousand men in the process. It didn't deter him, however, from continuing his march toward Atlanta.

The skirmish at Kolb Farm is a historical footnote to most who know about it, but for Katherine Tatum its legacy may account for all of the inexplicable events she and her husband endured. The quick, probably painful death of a soldier nearly a century and a half ago might provide a clue to the haunting. The lingering presence of one who died so suddenly may still be embedded in the land upon which the Tatums built their home. Katherine can't be sure that the man she saw in her upstairs hallway was a soldier from the Civil War, but his long coat and floppy hat seemed to fit the period.

So far it's the only reason she can come up with for the haunting on the old Kolb Farm.

Katherine also understood for the first time what it meant to go through such an experience.

"It's hard for anyone to believe this phenomena unless they experience it themselves. It's mostly aggravating, but I do get frightened when it happens. It just doesn't make sense."

The Conjure Chest
and Other Tales

An elegant mahogany veneer chest of drawers, hand-carved by an African-American slave 150 years ago, has resided in the Kentucky History Museum at Frankfort. Crafted in the Empire Style, the chest has glass knobs on its four drawers. Nothing about its outward appearance gives any hint that tragedy has stalked its existence—that those who know its story term it the "conjure" chest.

Two decades before the Civil War, the family of one Jacob Cooley lived a sumptuous life as wealthy Southern planters. Jacob owned many slaves and farmed thousands of acres. He was also a despicable man who frequently beat his slaves for the slightest infraction of his harsh rules.

Cooley ordered one of his slaves, an excellent furniture maker named Hosea, to build an exquisite chest for his first-born child. For a reason known only to himself, Cooley was displeased with Hosea's result and beat him so savagely that he died a few days later.

The other slaves, led by an old "conjure man," placed a curse on Hosea's chest for all future generations. One drawer was sprinkled with dried owl's blood; a "conjure" chant was sung. Legend has it that all those associated with the chest—except Jacob himself—fell victim to the curse's evil power.

The baby for whom the chest was built died soon after birth. The chest was in his nursery. The dead child's brother inherited the chest. His personal servant stabbed him to death.

Jacob Cooley had another son, John, who inherited one of his father's many plantations. The young man led a serene bachelor's life until a vivacious young woman, barely out of her teens, came into his life. Her name was Ellie and she soon married John, who was nearly three times her age.

The couple inherited the conjure chest. Knowing of the tragedies that had befallen her husband's siblings, she put it away in the attic.

Meanwhile, Jacob Cooley's youngest daughter, Melinda, eloped with an Irish rascal named Sean. With nowhere to live, Melinda turned to her sister-in-law Ellie for help. John and Ellie had done well and had amassed several farms in neighboring Tennessee. They turned over one of them to Sean and Melinda to work.

While Melinda bore her young husband a brood of children and worked from sunrise to sunset, Sean came to loathe the monotony of farm life.

Ellie Cooley tried to help, but Sean's rebuffs made her presence unwelcome. To try to bring some beauty into Melinda's dreary existence, Ellie sent over Jacob Cooley's chest, even though she had learned of the curse. It had been in her attic for a very long time and nothing had happened. Perhaps the "curse" was only a lot of idle talk. It wasn't.

Within days, Sean deserted his wife for the bright lamps of New Orleans. Melinda was disconsolate. She took to her bed with an "ailment." Melinda soon died, an exhausted, gray-haired woman not yet forty years of age.

Shortly after his wife's death, Sean was struck in the head and killed by a steamboat's gangplank.

The conjure chest had claimed its third and fourth victims.

John Cooley was given the job of traveling to Tennessee to assign the orphaned children to other family members. The youngest, a baby named Evelyn, ran up to him, her tiny arms outstretched. John took her to live with his own family.

Little Evelyn grew into a beautiful and intelligent young woman. When she turned sixteen, she passed an examination that provided her with a teaching certificate with which she took over a one-room schoolhouse.

She met and married Malcolm Johnson barely two months after she began teaching. As a wedding present, Ellie presented her niece with Jacob Cooley's handsome chest.

Evelyn Johnson had children, and even adopted a young orphan girl with the beautiful name of Arabella.

The curse was all but forgotten. Evelyn had the chest but didn't find it necessary to use right away. However, after Arabella married some years later, Evelyn put the girl's bridal gown in the chest. Shortly thereafter, Arabella's husband suddenly died.

That was the beginning of a series of horrible events visited upon the Cooley family.

Arabella's child died after her baby clothes had been put in the chest.

Evelyn's daughter-in-law, Esther, married to her oldest son, put her wedding attire in the chest. She died.

Evelyn's Aunt Sarah knitted a scarf and gloves to give her son for Christmas. While walking along a train trestle, he fell off and was killed a few days before Christmas. Two other tragedies befell Evelyn's immediate family—a son-in-law deserted his wife and a child was crippled for life in a bizarre accident.

Yet Evelyn's husband, Malcolm, was a success. A small man, always courteous to those around him, he parlayed a shrewd Scottish sense of thrift into a burgeoning business empire that, at its height, consisted of mills, several houses, a coal yard, a river wharf and a dry goods store.

Malcolm was an extraordinarily wealthy man when he died a natural death. Despite her material comfort, his wife was haunted by the memories of those around her struck down or stricken in some other way by hardship. Evelyn Cooley Johnson could not control her personal demons and committed suicide.

Eleven persons who had possessed the conjure chest had died unnatural deaths. Coincidence? Or was the curse of the conjure chest taking its toll?

As the twentieth century unfolded, Virginia Cary Hudson inherited the chest from her grandmother, Evelyn Johnson. Mrs. Hudson thought tales of the "curse" were hearsay.

Her first baby's clothes were put in the chest. The child died. Another child's clothes were tucked in one of the drawers and she contracted infantile paralysis. Another daughter's wedding dress was stored there, and her first husband ran off. A son was stabbed in the hand—he had some clothes in the chest.

A friend of the family put hunting clothes in it. He was shot in a hunting accident.

And so it went. Sixteen victims in all, with one thing in common: some of their personal clothing had been put in the cursed chest.

Mrs. Hudson wanted to put an end to the tragedies. She found what she hoped would be the solution in the presence of an old friend of hers, an African-American woman named Annie.

Annie understood curses and conjures. The spell cast by Hosea's faithful companions would be broken only when three conditions were met:

First, Mrs. Hudson would have to be given a dead owl without her having to ask for one.

Second, the green leaves of a willow tree must be boiled from sunup to sundown. The dead owl had to remain in sight of the boiling leaves.

Third, the boiled liquid was then to be buried in a jug with its handle facing east, toward the rising sun, below a flowering bush.

A stuffed owl given to Mrs. Hudson's son by a friend accomplished the first requirement. Mrs. Hudson plucked leaves from a nearby willow tree and boiled them in a large, black pot. The owl kept its silent watch from a kitchen counter. At dusk, old Annie and Mrs. Hudson dug a deep hole beneath a flowering lilac bush outside the kitchen window and buried the jug with its handle pointed east.

Annie said they would only know if the curse had been broken if one of them died before the first full days of fall.

Annie died in early September, the seventeenth, and last, known victim.

The final private owner of the conjure chest was Mrs. Hudson's daughter, Virginia C. Mayne. Though she may have been skeptical of the curse, and knew fully the story of its "lifting" by Annie and her mother, she never stored anything in the chest and kept it hidden in a corner of her attic.

Mrs. Mayne donated it to the Kentucky History Museum in 1976. According to museum registrar Mike Hudson, "The chest is in storage in our vaults, awaiting the time when it fits into a new exhibit. Supposedly, the curse has been removed."

Has it? Tucked safely in the top chest drawer is an envelope . . . with a cluster of owl feathers inside.

The museum isn't taking any chances.

Witch Leah

The old woods known as Lapland, near Battletown, Kentucky, is a dangerous place to visit. Locals advise you to venture through the dense forest with a knowledgeable guide and then only in the fall or winter, when the deadly rattlesnakes are in hibernation.

But there may be another reason to be cautious in the old forest and it has nothing to do with the natural world.

The ghost of one Leah Smock, an accused witch who died mysteriously 150 years ago, haunts the old Betsy Daily Cemetery that holds her mortal remains. Some claim Witch Leah is the oldest haunting in all of Kentucky.

A reliable sighting came from a hunter who told a longtime area resident that he believed he had seen Leah's ghost hovering near her grave in the abandoned cemetery.

The apparition had long black hair, he said, and was swathed in a white robe set off with black ties at her waist and throat. A purple light seemed to envelop her incomplete form.

The life of Leah Smock is difficult to detach from the legend that has grown up around her. The facts are sparse. She was born about 1818, reputedly the daughter of another powerful Kentucky witch. As a child, she preferred to be alone, strolling for hours upon end in the woods searching for fruits and berries to eat.

She had few friends and seldom visited with other neighborhood children. Once, while playing at a neighbor's cabin, she encountered their black cat scratching wildly at the walls. When Leah opened the front door, the cat ran screeching from the house never to be seen again.

Leah was also a fortune-teller. She frequently "predicted" the deaths of critically ill people. As she was frequently right, her reputation for "knowing" the future spread through the frontier community. It's *not* known how many times her predictions were wrong!

Her death, when she was barely into her twenties, on August 21, 1840, is also shrouded in mystery. Some accounts say she starved to death in the woods. Other reports have it that she was burned to death when her house caught fire. Her little more than two decades on earth, however, live on in the ghost legend that continues to this day among the older residents of Meade County.

An area resident once led a reporter and two companions to Leah's grave. Battling through the dense underbrush, pistols at the ready to thwart any belligerent rattlesnakes, they found the old hilltop Betsy Daily Cemetery deep within a grove of trees. Forsaken for decades, the graveyard's seventy or so plots were covered with pine needles, leaves, and moss. Leah's grave was the only one with a pointed headstone. Nothing stirred there; it was still daylight.

The visitors did find one peculiar detail during their visit. Shortly after Leah Smock died, locals who claimed to have seen her ghost piled a two-foot-high stack of small boulders on her grave. To keep her in her coffin, they hoped. For over a century, that pile of stones had remained intact.

On this day, however, the rocks were in disarray. About half of them had been removed. By whom? For what purpose?

Witch Leah surely knows the answer.

Bloody Polly

Frances Clara Brown was a strikingly beautiful woman. Tall and slender at age eighteen with a sweet disposition and a gentle face, her flaxen hair framed a creamy complexion set off by large, expressive brown eyes. She lived with her father, Frederick Brown, her mother and brothers and sisters in a log cabin a few miles from Lancaster, in Garrard County. Mr. Brown had taken his brood to the rough Kentucky wilderness from Maryland in 1815.

He soon turned their frontier cabin and few acres of land into a large and thriving plantation. His mules broke the earth for crops and a mill built with his own hands separated hemp from flax for spinning.

Life was good until the day Harry Geiss showed up.

Now Frances Clara had a sister two years her elder. Polly Brown had coal black hair, flashing eyes, and a fiery temper; she usually got her way.

Polly's worst fear was becoming an "old maid," she told anyone who would listen. Women usually married by their late teens on the wilderness frontier, so at twenty years of age her prospects were already looking a bit faint.

When Harry Geiss came along—single and evidently on his way to becoming a prosperous merchant—Polly Brown set her sights upon him. They became engaged, but it wasn't long before his attentions wavered—he seemed much more interested in Polly's younger sister, Frances Clara. Perhaps it was Polly's temper that made the young bachelor have second thoughts. Everyone in the neighborhood could clearly see that the handsome Harry would soon marry vivacious "Fanny Clary," as her family had nicknamed her

Apparent to all, that is, except Polly Brown.

Enraged at the thought of losing Harry to her sister, Polly's devious mind created a scheme so horrible that years passed before its full impact was known.

The fateful series of events began one morning when merchant Geiss set out on a business trip to Maysville, Kentucky, on the Ohio River. There was no transportation into the deep wilderness surrounding Lancaster, so goods were transported from Philadelphia to Maysville where they were off-loaded and toted by mule or wagon to pioneer communities such as Lancaster. Geiss periodically made the several-hundred-mile round-trip, taking several days to complete the journey. On this day however, as he bade farewell to Frances Clara, he had no way of knowing that it would be the last time the two would ever be together.

A few hours after Geiss's departure, Polly Brown found her sister upstairs at her loom weaving. Polly cheerfully persuaded her sister to accompany her to a Mrs. Brassfield's, there to examine a new quilt pattern the woman was completing. The two young women plunged through the thick forest. In a grove of papaw trees Polly remarked that Frances Clara's hair was coming loose. She would pin it up, she said, guiding her sister to a log.

Frances Clara should never have turned her back. As soon as she did, Polly Brown drew a hatchet from beneath her skirts and, grasping her sister's hair firmly in her left hand, brought the sharpened blade down in a mighty swing toward her sister's pale neck. Blow after blow rained down on the helpless girl as her own sister crazily swung the bloody hatchet in a murderous rage. Frances Clara managed to cry out for mercy but Polly didn't stop until her sister's crushed head rolled off her lifeless torso.

The murder had been carefully planned; savagely executed. Polly Brown had picked the precise part of the forest in which to carry out her deed. She dragged her sister's remains to a nearby sinkhole and buried them in the soft earth, being careful to obliterate any signs of a struggle. So meticulous had been her scheme that she had secreted a change of clothing nearby so as not to call attention to her own bloodstained garments.

Unbeknownst to Polly, however, three young slaves worked in a field some distance away. But Abe, Tom, and Pomp all heard Frances Clara's screams carry through the woods, "Polly, don't kill me!"

Abe, the oldest, dashed forward and hid behind a bush. He saw Polly inflict the final, fatal blows. Quickly retreating, he told his companions what he had seen. He made them swear never to reveal what had occurred. All three were fearful they would be blamed for the murder.

For the rest of that day, Polly Brown quietly gathered up her sister's saddle, good clothing, and personal effects from their home and stashed them in another area of the forest several hundred yards away from her sister's makeshift grave. She calmly returned home and awaited the discovery of Frances Clara's absence. The murderess had an explanation for that prepared, too.

As twilight descended, Frances Clara's parents did indeed wonder what had become of their daughter. Polly slyly stepped forward and offered the opinion that she must have run away with Harry Geiss as he had left for Maysville that morning. She pointed to the fact that Frances Clara's saddle and "Sunday clothes" were missing, sure signs that Geiss had persuaded her to leave with him. The hint of a self-satisfied smile must have slipped across Polly's face. She knew that it would be days or weeks before Geiss returned with his merchandise. By that time, she hoped, he would have forgotten her rival and would turn his attention to her.

Polly Brown's plan would have succeeded but for a macabre discovery by several small boys a few weeks later. Sent to gather papaws in the woods, a wild pig chewing at something on the ground startled Claiborne Lear, Joshua Comely, and Sammy Johnson. When they got closer, they were scared witless to see that the pig's snack was actually a thin, pale white hand sticking out of the sandy soil.

The boys raced home to tell their parents of the awful discovery. Within hours, several dozen neighbors had gathered at the papaw patch. They unearthed the remains of the headless Frances Clara Brown. Her parents reburied her on the plantation grounds.

The whereabouts of Frances Clara's good clothing and saddle remained a mystery. A psychic named Ramsey who lived in nearby Lancaster predicted that the missing items would be found precisely 440 yards south of the Brown home. Another family friend, Thompson Arnold, measured out the distance and found the material only a few inches below ground.

The devious plan hatched by Polly Brown succeeded in keeping anyone from suspecting her, but failed at winning Harry Geiss's affection. He eventually left town.

When they heard the news of Frances Clara's murder, the owners of the slaves grew suspicious. They recalled that the youths had been working near where Polly's body was found. Eventually, Tom and Pomp were arrested and jailed. Perhaps someone overheard one of them talking about the murder, or maybe they were confused by Abe's orders to keep quiet. Whatever the reason, they were tried for murder. Their jailer—who claimed to have heard one of them say, "The first lick didn't kill her"—presented the only evidence. He may, of course, have overheard Abe say just such a thing as he was an eyewitness to the hapless girl's death throes.

Justice was nonexistent for African-American slaves and any pretense of fairness a mockery. The boys were found guilty on December 13, 1820. Tom was hung on January 7, 1821. Pomp was sent to the gallows two weeks later. Nothing is known of Abe's fate.

Polly Brown didn't raise a hand to prevent the tragic hanging of two innocent young men. The blood of three and possibly four persons now stained her hands.

It was all too much even for the twisted mind of Polly Brown. Her family moved away to Indianapolis, leaving her behind. It isn't known why. Perhaps it was her turning toward herbs as cures for disease, or her long walks in the woods by herself—particularly near the old papaw trees where her sister's body lay for so long.

She moved into a small cabin when Josiah Burnside purchased the Brown farm. Mr. and Mrs. Logan Harris also lived there and more or less looked after her.

One night many years later, Polly Brown was returning through the woods after a visit with a sick "patient." Her herbal medicines were popular during a frontier era when a physician may have been hundreds of miles distant. On this evening, however, even the strongest drugs would not have helped her. Coming at her was the ghost of Frances Clara, her arms outstretched as if to grab at her tormentor. But where the apparition's head should have been there was only a bloody stump.

Polly turned and ran, shaking uncontrollably at the sight of her reanimated sister. When she stumbled into the Harris cabin babbling about ghosts, the couple immediately put her to bed. From that night forward, Polly Brown descended into madness. Eventually she was chained to her bed after she was caught attempting to break into her old home. Her gray hair fell in long, unkempt strands about her shoulders; her once dancing eyes grew dull and sunken. Mr. and Mrs. Harris could only keep her in a rough-sewn sack dress.

The truth was eventually learned. As she lay dying, Polly Brown confessed to the murder of her sister, and expressed her sorrow for the wrongful deaths of Pomp and Tom. She amazed Mr. and Mrs. Harris by appearing completely lucid on her deathbed.

Josiah Burnside and his wife Almira raised a large family on the old Brown plantation. Regular appearances by the ghost of Frances Clara became a part of the family's tradition. She would playfully pull covers from the bed or rush through the front door, slamming it as she entered. The soft rustle of her skirts could be heard ascending the stairs to her old loom room.

The last vestiges of the Brown homestead reportedly burned to the ground in about 1940. Did the ghost of Frances Clara Brown vanish with the last of her old home? Most of the folks in the vicinity think so but others, well, other people familiar with the tragic tale just aren't so sure. They think Frances Clara is still out there somewhere, looking for her head.

Ghost Lovers

Old Noel Sympson wasn't known for spreading wild tales even though he was a fisherman who sometimes made exaggerated claims about the "one that got away."

That's why the story he told one day at Greenfield's Store was so improbable that the local philosophers gathered around the wood stove thought he'd taken to drink. Or worse.

"Better change your brand of whisky, Noel," they hooted. "Ain't no ghosts on the Barren River—ain't no ghosts anywhere—and you well know it."

He left the little store a few miles from Bowling Green, but told the hecklers he would return with another eyewitness. And so he did, about a week later, this time with Hosiah Hathaway in tow. Both men claimed to have seen a boy and girl, ghostly lovers floating down the Barren River in a small boat. They tried to get up a small band of "detectives" to prove their statements.

Only Schoolmaster Lindley was persuaded to accompany Sympson and

Hathaway back to the river. The trio boarded Sympson's rowboat at sunset and floated off downstream. They slipped past cedar trees clinging to the steep banks while bats swooped low to pick off tasty dragonflies dancing on the water's surface. The stream narrowed so that stands of quivering sycamores formed a canopy over the water.

At last they came to Hammel's Cliff. While Hathaway rowed and Sympson kept a sharp lookout ahead, the schoolmaster peered back upstream. He suddenly gave a sharp cry and collapsed in the bottom of the boat. Bearing down on them in the dusky twilight was a translucent skiff being rowed by a wan, black-haired young man. Admiring his muscular physique was a lovely young blonde, her skin milky white, with her back resting against the bow of the boat, her arms draped atop the gunwales. She was smiling at her beau's effortless rhythm with the oars. The opposite shore was clearly visible through them.

Neither the girl nor boy took any notice of the three men watching the phantom rowboat, which made no sound as it swept by. Suddenly the girl stood up and put her arms around the young man. The boat quickly vanished beneath the surface. Nary a ripple stirred the river's calm surface.

Days later, Lindley began asking around if anyone might know who the ghostly boaters might have been. The Widow Overton nodded her head knowingly when she heard the question. Yes, she told the schoolmaster, that must have been Harry Stonewall and Annatte Bellmont, who had eloped. They'd set off down the Barren River in Annatte's boat.

They were last seen near Hammel's Cliff.

The Horseman of Sinking Fork

In the years before the Civil War, Oldham County, Kentucky, northeast of Louisville along the Ohio River, had its share of slave traders. They would park their big, black wagons near a crossroads and load them with African-Americans purchased in the region and destined for the slave markets of New Orleans and Atlanta.

Ironically, just a few yards away slaves attended the Cross Roads Methodist Church. After the war a new church, the Sinking Fork Church, was built some distance away. But not everyone believed the terror engendered by the slave traders was gone with the winds of war.

A story is told of one old woman who walked to church with her granddaughter one Sunday morning. Although it was much shorter to go by way of the crossroads, grandmother insisted they take the long, winding route so as to avoid "the horseman" and then told her granddaughter the story of this frightening specter:

On a night when Sinking Fork Church was new and the old woman a teenager, she had taken the route past the crossroads. Pounding hooves warned her that a slaver on his black horse was bearing down on her. She ran for her life, fearful that he would snatch her up and sell her down river. So close was he that she could feel the sting of his whip against her back.

She made it to the crossroads in time to meet a group of folks carrying lanterns and also going to Sinking Fork Church. The horseman sped by and vanished in a cloud of smoke.

For the remainder of her days, and she lived well past the age of ninety, the old grandmother never ventured close to the crossroads. Only when she died and her coffin was carried on a black wagon past the crossroads to Sinking Fork Church did she ever get near that wicked place.

Shadow of the Unknown

The Cumberland Lake region of south-central Kentucky is rich in tales of the supernatural. Perhaps it is the mountainous terrain and isolated settlements that give rise to such beliefs, but stories of ghosts and haunted places are plentiful.

Eddy Pierce had an eerie experience several years ago that he recounted for writer Helen Price Stacy.

Pierce said he and his wife had just finished supper when the telephone rang. A man's deep voice advised him that if he would meet him at a certain house not too far distant, Pierce might find one of the best ghost stories he'd ever heard.

He jumped in his car and headed for the abandoned farmhouse, one that he had passed many times before. The man met Pierce at the front door, and guided him inside. To his amazement, Pierce found oil lamps lighting rooms furnished in turn-of-the-century style.

Suddenly, the soft rustle of skirts and a slight cry caused him to glance at the staircase. Coming down the steps was a lovely young woman in a long dress with petticoats.

Pierce's nameless host explained that the girl had lived in the house with her widowed mother. When she remarried, her husband began beating his step-daughter in frequent drunken rages. Then one day he killed her with a sharp blow to the head.

The girl's mother accepted her husband's explanation that the girl had fallen from a horse. Or at least she didn't ask questions.

"But the girl's soul has never rested in peace," the man told Pierce.

He watched as his mysterious host and the young woman walked out the front door. Pierce rushed to follow, but they'd vanished. Pierce knocked on the door of a lighted farmhouse across the street to ask if he might use the telephone. He called his wife and asked her to bring his camera.

Minutes later, as the couple walked toward the house, they noticed that all the lights had been turned out. The front door, which Pierce had left open, was now firmly closed. He put his shoulder to it and after several tries finally forced it open. The rooms were empty. Dust covered the floor and windows, massive cob-webs hung from the ceiling. There was no sign of the furniture and lighted lamps Pierce had seen only minutes before.

The farmer across the street said he had seen only Pierce go into the house. He had not seen any lights in the vacant house.

Eddy Pierce never solved the mystery of what had happened to him that night. To him it always remained the time he walked into "the shadow of the unknown."

Mrs. A.

Never annoy a nice old lady who wants to keep her home just the way it was . . . *when she was alive.*

That's the lesson one young man learned when he set out to remodel a mansion in Lexington's old Northside district that had fallen into disrepair. The imposing three story 1880s Victorian pile on North Broadway was noted for its impressive Corinthian columns at the entrance. Eight bedrooms inside, a solarium, a rooftop terrace, and an elevator reminded visitors of the opulence that once marked American gothic architecture. Cherry and white walnut wood was used throughout. The wood reportedly came from central Kentucky plantation holdings of the house's builders, the Headley family. They used it as a sort of nineteenth-century townhouse—but certainly not with the same meaning as today.

The twenty-five-year-old Lexington man bought the place in the early 1970s, after it had sat empty, forlorn and neglected for three years. In nearly every room, wallpaper hung in shreds and light fixtures had been taken away or stolen over the years. Some immediate restoration began on the elaborate staircase, carved mantle and a sagging back porch. A new roof stopped years of water leakage.

A ghost in such an Addams Family-esque manor seemed quite appropriate, and for the young renovator it meant having to explain to relatives and friends just whom it was running up and down an upstairs hallway or why the substantial front door creaked open and slammed shut when everyone could plainly see it had been bolted securely.

The instigator of these shenanigans seemed to be a former owner referred to only as Mrs. A. She lived there for a quarter of a century, until sometime late in the 1950s. Even thought she died in a hospital, her spirit seems to have never left home.

The old woman must have really liked her house, the owner thought, since she was apparently still in residence. The owner and his roommate discovered her presence when they heard someone running in the house. They thought someone had broken in. A search proved fruitless. A few weeks later, a carpenter hired to do some renovations was so unnerved that he left work and brought back his wife to keep him company.

Mrs. A. continually let the new owner know about her preferences. She seemed to thump and bash about if some change displeased her. She particularly seemed to disdain female guests and family members. On several occasions, a woman spending the night in the mansion would be startled awake by a sharp slap to the face. The young owner's grandmother was surprised early one morning by something clutching at her knee.

While the new owner filled his home with assorted Victorian bric-a-brac—including brass chandeliers, loveseats, statues, busts, figurines, and more—he arrived at a sort of truce with Mrs. A., a peace that included a promise not to have her exorcised.

"We have an agreement," the owner told a local reporter. "I told (Mrs. A.) she could stay as long as she did not harm anyone and so everything has been very congenial."

She seemed to keep her promise.

Her Good Husband's Arms

The young bicyclist dropped to his knees and brushed away the dirt that obscured the carved, weather-beaten words on the flat tombstone nearly lost in the old Bloomfield Cemetery's high grass. He looked closely at what it said:

In memory of
Jereboam O. Beauchamp
Born Sept. 24, 1802,
and Anna, his wife,
Born Feb. 7, 1786,
Who both left this world
July 7, 1826

Below, the barely discernible epitaph:

Entomb'd below in one another's arms/The husband and the wife repose/
    Safe from life's never-ending storms/Secure from all their cruel foes.
A child of evil fate she lived–/A villain's wile her peace had crossed/The
    husband of her heart revived/The happiness she long had lost.
He heard her tale of matchless woe/And burning for revenge arose/He laid
    her base betrayer low/And struck dismay to virtue's foes.
Reader, if honour's generous blood/Ere warmed thy heart, here drop a tear/
    And let thy sympathetic flood/Deep in thy mind its traces wear.
A brother or a sister thou/Dishonoured see thy sister dear;/Then turn and
    see the villain low/And here let fall a grateful tear.
Daughter, if virtue grant the tear/That love and honour's tomb may claim/
    In your defense the husband here/Laid down in youth his life and
    fame.
His wife disdained a life forlorn/Reft from her Heart's beloved Lord/Then
    reader here their fortunes mourn/Who for their love their life blood
    poured.

He leaned back and folded his arms trying not to notice a prickling of the small
hairs on the back of his neck or the slightly elevated thumping of his heart. As
he looked around, taking in the filtered light of a midsummer's afternoon, he
knew instinctively that there was absolutely no other living soul anywhere near.

This whole incident now seemed to be the culmination of something quite
impossible. A dream, hallucinations brought on by the exertion of his steady ped-
aling for so many miles in so short a time.

And yet how could he have seen the woman *three times?* How could he have
been so certain of her *reality?* How could he have followed after her into the
cemetery only seconds behind and yet find now that she had *vanished so completely?*

The bewildered man in the cemetery was a Louisville native who, like many others
in the 1890s, had discovered the exhilarating pleasures of zipping about the countryside on the innovative, leg-propelled machines that were being referred to as
bicycles. Now that Englishman James Starley had patented his "safety bicycle"
with wheels of about the same diameter and a sprocket-chain connecting the
pedals to the rear wheel, the League of American Wheelmen was actively en-
couraging city-dwellers to take to the country.

On this day, the young League member had left Louisville for a jaunt to Bardstown, by way of Taylorsville and Bloomfield, in preparation for the group's 1896
national meet in his hometown. He had hoped to make Bardstown by dusk. His
route over the next few days would take him to Shakertown, at Pleasant Hill,

southwest of Lexington, and then back to Louisville—an ambitious jaunt. So far, on this first day, the twenty to thirty miles on the dusty roads had passed uneventfully enough, but with few marked roads and still fewer road signs, he lost his bearings several miles outside Bloomfield.

The best he could hope for was a farmhouse where he might confirm with the friendly occupants that he was riding in the correct direction. He saw a small farm off in the distance, but at nearly the same moment he rounded a slight curve in the road and noticed a woman striding along the edge of the roadway, her long skirt sending up swirls of dust. She looked to be barely five feet tall and quite slim. He thought she seemed smartly dressed for a countrywoman. As he slowed to draw alongside of her, he noted with pleasure the delight of using the new coaster brakes instead of dragging one's feet to stop his forward motion. She turned timidly to him with what seemed to be a distant sort of look in her eyes but with the hint of a smile. He thought she appeared quite youthful for a woman of apparent middle age. Shimmering auburn hair fell in long whorls about her shoulders. Despite her pallid complexion, surprisingly she wore no bonnet or scarf on her head.

"Pardon me, am I on the correct way for Bloomfield?" he asked, bowing slightly and noting that she was even frailer than he had originally thought.

She hesitated for a moment.

"I must return to my good husband's arms," she whispered.

He thought she must have misunderstood.

"I asked if this is the way to Bloomfield? Do you know?"

Again, she repeated that same, peculiar phrase in her soft, airy voice.

He apologized and pedaled on. This one's a bit soft in the head, he thought.

Farther on, he sighted another farmhouse where he could check directions. On the side of the road a lone figure was standing quite still. The person turned toward him at the sound of his tires on the gravel roadway. It was the same peculiar young woman he had seen a mile or so before.

"How is this possible?" he muttered to himself as he decided to coast on past her.

"I must return to my good husband's arms," she called out, as if to remind him of her objective but, of course, he had absolutely no idea what she meant.

This time he did not attempt conversation, he did not stop and he did not look back. He continued right past as fast as his legs could push the pedals.

Within a few miles, he knew that he'd not misjudged his route after all; he came within view of a small cemetery and then just beyond a sprinkling of buildings that he took to be Bloomfield. As he neared the cemetery, however, he blinked back amazement for the *same young woman* stood by its solitary entrance. But this time she seemed quite preoccupied and took no notice of his approach. She turned quickly and walked up a pathway and on into the graveyard. He coasted to a stop and watched her, a dozen or so yards away from him, moving now with a purposeful stride. She abruptly turned to her right and appeared to glide into a bank of tall weeds that quickly obscured her figure.

He got off the bicycle, pushed it down into some roadside bushes and hurriedly made off after her, his immense curiosity overcoming his mounting belief that he really must be dreaming the entire episode. He plowed into the underbrush, pausing briefly to look around and listen for someone moving on ahead. There was no one to see and nothing to hear save his own rapid intakes of breath.

He set off again, stepping gingerly through the growth, and nearly tripping over a raised slab of stone that apparently covered an all-but-forgotten grave. He recovered his balance and kneeled down to read its words. . . .

The visitor stood up, brushed off his wool trousers and thought it was all too much. The woman's impossible appearances alongside the road . . . the old cemetery . . . and now this strange verse—somehow he must learn more about this couple interred in the same grave and whatever their story might be.

The fifteen some miles of roadway between Bloomfield and Bardstown rapidly passed beneath his pneumatic tires and he found a comfortable inn in which to pass the night. At dinner, he struck up a circumspect conversation with the proprietor about his unusual encounter earlier in the day. When he mentioned the names of the couple etched into the tombstone, the owner allowed as how he knew the story of Anna and Jereboam but had never heard of anything like this stranger's tale.

The innkeeper's story began over in Simpson County, southwest of Bowling Green on the Tennessee border, in the early 1800s when the family of Anna Cooke fell upon hard times. They'd been prominent farmers and landowners outside Franklin. Most of her family died within a short time of one another. Her father had been Mordecai Cooke, descended from an old and respected Virginia family. Her mother was born Alicia Payne, also from a Virginia family prominent in Fairfax and Loudoun counties.

Anna was particularly devastated by the family's sudden poverty and pledged her intent to regain the family's honor and wealth. She was a beautiful woman eagerly courted by many young men, but instead she sought out a young lawyer/politician named Colonel Solomon Sharp. He courted her, but in the end absconded when she became pregnant with his child, which was later stillborn. Gossip about his affair with Anna had spread through the region so that later, when he met the woman he wanted to marry, he forged a document denying he was the father of the child and claimed that Anna had become pregnant by an African-American. But the rumors continued to hound him even during his later political campaigns.

The years passed. Anna had no immediate family remaining and so moved alone to a farm close by another owned by Thomas Beauchamp, the father of ambitious Jereboam Orville Beauchamp, a young man still in his early twenties who had been studying law since the age of sixteen. Jereboam had been a friend of Colonel Sharp and had considered studying law under him. A friend of Jereboam related Anna's story to him and he felt pity for her. On his next visit home, he dropped in at her farm, ostensibly to have the loan of a book from her extensive library. Their casual friendship blossomed into love even though she was some seventeen years his senior.

He persuaded her to marry him, but she agreed only after extracting his promise that he would seek out and slay the man she still reviled for deserting her—Colonel Solomon Sharp, who had by now risen to prominence in Kentucky politics, first as attorney general, and soon to be sworn in as speaker of the state's house of representatives.

Jereboam set off immediately for Sharp's offices in Bowling Green to fulfill his promise to her. He confronted the politician with Anna's charges and challenged him to a duel to avenge the sullied honor of Anna Cooke. Sharp again denied his culpability. He told Jereboam that not only would he not participate in a duel, but that he would decline to even raise a hand in self-defense if the young man attacked him unprovoked. Sharp, however, fled town the next day after Jereboam said he would return to horsewhip him.

Anna then schemed to kill Sharp. She made contact with him and asked that he meet her to discuss the issues that divided them. He suspected a plot and declined her invitation.

Jereboam and Anna quietly married. Anna continually reminded her young husband of the promise he had made. So it was that he set off for Frankfort to track down his wife's former paramour and fulfill his pledge. He cleverly disguised himself with a tight-fitting black mask so that anyone passing him at night would think he was African-American. On his feet he wore heavy wool socks so that no footprints would be detectable. Early on the morning of November 6, 1825, Beauchamp armed himself with a butcher knife whose tip Anna had dipped in poison. He had it hidden in his shirt when he banged on Solomon Sharp's door. When the politician answered, Beauchamp threw off his mask so that Sharp would know who it was who killed him, drew out the knife and plunged it into the much older man's chest just below his heart. Sharp crumpled on his doorstep.

According to later testimony, Beauchamp ran but a block away before hiding in a doorway and watching to make certain that the colonel was dead. He then returned to Anna and his home, confident the murder would go unsolved. The couple had made plans to move to Missouri, which they now scrapped so confident were they that suspicion would not fall upon them.

But that was not to happen. Colonel Sharp had been embroiled in a bitter political battle and suspicion fell upon the opposition . . . and Jereboam O. Beauchamp was named its head and arrested for Sharp's murder.

Sharp's affair with Anna Cooke Beauchamp had continued to be the subject of quiet gossip, especially during this campaign. Anna was questioned but eventually let go when it was clear she had not been in Frankfort at the time of the killing.

Jereboam was convicted of Sharp's murder and sentenced to hang at dawn on July 7, 1826. Anna pleaded to stay with her young husband in his cell on the night before his scheduled execution, a wish that was granted by prison officials. What they didn't know was that she and her husband did not plan to wait for the hangman's noose. She secreted in her long skirts two instruments of their anticipated destruction: laudanum, a tincture of opium used to treat stomach disorders; and a long knife. The laudanum only succeeded in making them sick. Anna then drew out the knife and pleaded with her husband to plunge it into his heart and then she would follow him with her own self-inflicted fatal wound. He did as she directed, falling to the cold stone floor. She pulled out the knife and gripped it in her unsteady hand and with all the force she could gather thrust it into her stomach. She drew it out and plunged it in a second time. As the life drained from Anna's body, Jereboam's sudden cries at the pain brought jailers running to the cell and he was dragged away to the small infirmary where he was bandaged and kept under close watch until the execution a few hours later.

At the appointed time, the warden allowed Beauchamp to ride astride his own casket to the gallows. He waved to the people on the street as he passed by. As a lone fiddler played "Bonaparte's Retreat," he stood up on his casket, allowed the noose to be placed around his neck and gave the signal for the cart to be driven away. He happily joined his Anna in death.

The couple left detailed instructions for their burial. They were to be interred together in the same casket at Bloomfield Cemetery and their tombstone should bear the verse the cyclist had read earlier in the day.

The young man from Louisville left the inn's dining room still dazed by this day's baffling adventure. Halfway up the steps to his room he suddenly stopped.

July 7, 1826.

But, of course.

He hurried back downstairs and confirmed with the innkeeper what he knew had to be true.

That *today* was also July seven. But the year was 1896—the seventieth anniversary of the passing into death of Anna Cooke Beauchamp and Jereboam Orville Beauchamp.

The heartrending story of the Beauchamps has been told in scores of pamphlets, memoirs, novels, and plays. The novel *World Enough and Time* by Robert Penn Warren was based on Anna and Jereboam's short life together. The original horizontal tombstone remains to this day, although the words on it have been nearly worn away by time. A newer vertical tombstone was placed next to it a few years ago. The ghost of Anna Cooke Beauchamp has not been seen on the streets and lanes of Bloomfield for some time.

Damp Things

Louisiana ghost lore seems to be of two persuasions.

Deep in Cajun country, for example, far removed from the steamy alleys and crushing tourism of New Orleans, ghosts can be gentler sorts who would rather gaze idly through wispy drapes at the occasional passerby than to wrap their bony hands around the nearest warm neck or to scare the bejeebers out of a wandering sightseer. That's not to say those sudden frights don't occur, it's just that they seem a bit rare.

New Orleans tales, however, have a definite strain of the macabre with overtones of the undeniable, albeit fictional, romanticism of the antebellum South. Perhaps that schizophrenia attests to the city's multiple personalities—the birthplace of blues and jazz and its modern incarnations in the bawdy revelries of Bourbon Street; the historic terminus of riverboats carrying gentlemen gamblers, plantation overseers, and crinoline-clad belles to the genteel society of the old city; the uninhibited glamour and excitement typified by Mardi Gras . . .

. . . and the mysterious, chilling legacy of voodoo and slavery.

Though not all of the stories originate in the French Quarter, that most exotic of all American neighborhoods does seem to have more ghosts per square block than any other part of any city.

There is, for example, Marie Laveau.

When she died on June 15, 1881, Marie was New Orleans's most famous voodoo priestess. Her grave in St. Louis Cemetery Number One, on North Rampart Street, is on a popular tour sponsored by the aptly named Voodoo Museum. Curiously, her tomb is often marked with little "x's" drawn in the brick dust, while shells, coins and beads are strewn around its base, along with occasional flowers and scribbled notes all seeking Marie's intercession in some temporal difficulty.

Unfortunately, their devotion to the dead voodoo queen may be misplaced. Many folks believe that Marie is actually buried in an unmarked grave in St. Louis Cemetery Number Two; it's really Marie's daughter in the tomb at the first cemetery.

Whichever grave holds the remains of Marie Laveau, *mere*, it is indisputable that her life has passed into New Orleans legend. Fact and fiction have blended to create a figure of almost mythic proportions.

Those New Orleans historians who believe there were, indeed, two Marie Laveaus—mother and daughter—say mama Marie died in the early 1880s. Her place was taken by her daughter, also named Marie, who had her own voodoo practice until the turn of the century.

But others cling to the belief that only one Marie Laveau existed.

Their Marie was born sometime in the early 1800s and was practicing voodoo as early as 1830, in Congo Square. Her home was at what is now 1020 St. Ann Street. African-Americans, Cajuns, and Anglos flocked to her door to ask special favors. From charms that cured diseases, to love potions, poisons and spells, Marie could accommodate almost any request. A portrait of her in the House of Voodoo, 739 Bourbon Street, depicts her as a wrinkled old hag with blazingly white hair. One long strand curls down the side of her face and ends in a serpent's head at her neck.

What may be most fascinating, however, is the legend that Marie never really died, in a paranormal sense anyway.

Reports have placed her ghost in the vicinity of St. Louis Cemetery Number Two on several occasions. One man said she slapped him as he walked by the graveyard.

Her old home on St. Ann Street has been the subject of tales of wild voodoo ceremonies practiced by the ghostly Marie and her followers.

Curiously, another house may also harbor Marie's ghost. In the late 1980s, a family that lived on Chartres Street told reporters that their house contained "a diaphanous form" that seemed to hover in the living room near the fireplace. The house was built in 1807 by Pierre de La Ronde. According to legend, Marie Laveau lived there for some time. Also, a murder may have been committed under its roof, according to psychics consulted by the owners. The owner of the house told the newspaper writer he wasn't sure the ghost was that of Marie Laveau. "In New Orleans, the ghosts are part of the package. We just move in and they usually make room for us," he noted serenely.

However, it may not be all that difficult to contact Marie Laveau. One legend has it that she turned herself into a large black crow when she sensed that she was dying. That bird can still be seen flying noisily around her final resting place.

If you're fortunate enough to see Marie herself, and want her to perform a small miracle, be forewarned. She will expect to be paid well for her services. But whatever you do, don't disappoint her. Death does not rob a voodoo priestess of her powers over the forces of darkness.

A Strange Request

There are two well-known New Orleans stories involving the old French Opera House. Though each takes place in the last century, their tales of love and loss resonate through the decades.

The young man was paying a visit to his first Mardi Gras celebration. His childhood in a large Eastern city had not prepared him in any way for such an uninhibited, colorful pageant as he saw unfolding before him. All during Carnival, he had taken in as much as he could and now, on Shrove Tuesday night, he sat transfixed in the French Opera House watching the Mardi Gras Ball swirl across the stage. Tomorrow there would be fasting and prayer as Lent began, but tonight was still for revelries.

Then the young man saw her—the loveliest woman he had ever seen—and sitting only a few rows away. His gaze slid lovingly over her slim form, and her dark Creole features, both contrasting sharply with the shimmering white silk gown she wore. From that moment on, the gaudy spectacle on stage might as well have been taking place a thousand miles away, so taken was he by her ravishing beauty.

At some point during the evening, and the young man could never quite remember when, their eyes met. He smiled. She smiled, slightly. His friends barely noticed when he excused himself to go to the lobby.

A few minutes later, the Creole girl swept through the curtained doorway into the grand foyer of the Opera House where he waited patiently. Somehow he knew she would join him there.

He did all the talking. She seemed very shy, a not unappealing blush creeping up her neck as he began to speak. All that he recalled of that first encounter is that he asked her to accompany him on a walk in the spring night air. She demurely nodded her assent.

Once on the sidewalk, however, her demeanor changed quite dramatically. He had compelled her to leave her opera seat, she said, though she couldn't quite explain how that might have occurred since she left of her own volition. Further, she stated, her fiancé, with whom she was seated, would be very upset to know that she was talking to this impertinent young man.

If that was the case, the chivalrous suitor said, then it was incumbent upon him to marry her to save her reputation. What her words were in reply are not known, but she never returned to the ball.

So this strangest of all Mardi Gras courtships began with the simplest of words, the recitation of their names, and moved swiftly forward as he suggested they might have dinner at a nearby Royal Street restaurant. Again, she agreed, not yet quite understanding how she could fall so swiftly and completely under the spell of this handsome stranger.

At the restaurant, the couple exchanged the kind of personal information most lovers reveal over the course of weeks or months. Quiet conversation mixed with gentle laughter over childhood memories as they revealed their family backgrounds and their dreams for the future. The hours passed quickly, food and wine satiating their more earthly hunger.

Dawn found them on the steps of St. Louis Cathedral for Ash Wednesday services. They would not wait any longer to exchange wedding vows and sought out a priest who proceeded to marry them that very morning.

The couple then went to her home to assure her worried parents that she was safe and, to their surprise, married to a man whom they had never met. Despite the highly unorthodox courtship, her family grew to accept the young husband as part of their family, even though they knew the couple would be living in the east so that he could continue in business.

The story does not have a fairy-tale ending. Within weeks of the couple's return to his home and business, the young wife succumbed to an unknown illness. She was buried far from her grieving New Orleans family.

At the next Mardi Gras, the owner of the Royal Street restaurant where the couple had first dined received a letter from the sad young widower. In it he asked that the same dinner be set out as was served to him and his Creole bride on their first, and only, Shrove Tuesday together in New Orleans. He included a check to cover the costs. The restaurant manager complied with the request in all its details. No one showed up to eat the elaborate meal.

For more than two decades, the man sent a check so that a similar meal could be prepared at the restaurant. When he died a wealthy widower, his will contained a bequest that the tradition continue "as long as the restaurant remained in business." In this way he could celebrate his enduring love for the woman who died too young.

Is the story true?

Cynics suggest it is fiction, but the restaurant on Royal Street continued to set out its most delicious dinners at two empty places for many decades. A centerpiece of bright flowers and Carnival decorations complemented the fine food. The attentive wine steward filled the goblets with the finest French champagne, while a silent waiter didn't think it odd that course after course was never consumed. No one at the restaurant even knew the couple's names.

The ghost dinner became a commemoration of a love that transcended death and time.

The Witch of the French Opera

She was an ancient hag, with white hair and blazing red eyes looming from a bony, ashen face. In 1907, witnesses swear she descended the front steps of the French Opera House, walked to the intersection of St. Ann and Royal Streets and thence into a rooming house. Boarders who met her in the hallway found new accommodations the next day!

The ghost was thought to be that of a woman who had fallen in love with a much younger man. When she discovered that her beloved had made love to a younger woman, she committed suicide.

Soon thereafter, the young couple was mysteriously asphyxiated in the rooming house when a gas jet was somehow turned on in their room. It was the old woman's ghost who did the dirty deed, several residents avowed.

The wraith haunted the neighborhood for many years until the serendipitous discovery of an old letter. It seems that a boarder in the couple's old room found the missive, a love letter from the old woman to her youthful lover, secreted between the chimney and mantel. After she read it, the boarder threw it on the fire.

Suddenly, the ghost materialized and tried unsuccessfully to retrieve the letter from the flames. With a vengeful cry, she swirled about the room and vanished. Forever.

The Devil's Mistress

The ornate mansion at 1319 Saint Charles Avenue was to be avoided at all costs. At this address, the Devil once took up residence in New Orleans.

Built sometime in the 1820s, the so-called Devil's Mansion took form, according to legend, literally overnight. Satan needed the house for his beautiful lover Madeleine Frenau.

So quickly did the house go up, however, that each room was at a different level—steps led up or down to every room. Even so, the mansion was outfitted with the best Satan's money could buy. Crystal chandeliers hung above carved mahogany furniture, while the finest dinner china and silverware were set for visitors who never came. Strangely, no servants were ever employed there. Not even dust dared gather in the Devil's own kingdom.

Mademoiselle quickly tired of being left alone to wander the lifeless rooms while the Devil plied his "trade" on the wicked streets. Sometimes he would be gone for several days at a time.

Eventually, she found another lover. His name was Alcide Cancienne, a vain and handsome Creole man who found in Madeleine such physical pleasure as he had never known. Again and again he came to Saint Charles Avenue to lose himself in Madeleine's charms. Alcide was unaware that he had a rival who would stop at nothing to destroy the illicit liaison.

One day Alcide was particularly morose. As was the couple's habit when the Devil was away, they were eating dinner in the elegant dining room. Madeleine asked him the cause of his melancholy. He told her of his experience a few hours earlier. On the sidewalk outside the mansion he had been accosted by a dark-haired man attired in a great cape and top hat. The stranger asked him if he knew Madeleine Frenau. Alcide said truthfully that she was his lover. He was on his way to see her at that very moment.

The stranger laughed merrily and said that he, too, was her lover but that he had grown tired of her. Alcide could have her, but on one condition. The couple would leave with a million pounds of gold, the stranger promised, if Alcide promised to change their names to "Monsieur and Madame L."

Alcide told Madeleine that he was puzzled as to what the "L" stood for. She evaded answering for a few moments, but at last she acknowledged that the "L" symbolized Lucifer. To leave St. Charles Avenue they would have to become the "Devil's couple."

Despite the conditions, Madeleine begged to leave with Alcide. She had had enough of the Devil's insatiable depravity.

Alcide just laughed at her. He had no intention of taking Madeleine anywhere. The Devil was right. He, too, was growing tired of her. And she was growing old, he added. There were many other younger and more beautiful women he could have. Besides, a mistress would never make a proper wife.

Mademoiselle Frenau was furious. She grabbed a long cloth napkin and before Alcide could act she had twisted it about his throat, crushing an artery. Blood spewed from the dying man's mouth, soaking Madeleine's hands and gown. Alcide slid off the chair and fell in a heap on the lush carpet, a pool of blood forming beside his head.

For the rest of the night, Madeleine tried to wash the blood from her body and clothing. It would not go away. At last the Devil returned from his rounds. Madeleine told him of the events, but he simply chuckled in merriment. His plans were progressing nicely, he thought.

He hoisted Alcide's corpse over his shoulder, grabbed the struggling Madeleine by the arm, and climbed to the roof. Grinning, he told Madeleine that he had not had a decent meal all day. With that he began to devour Alcide's body, leaving only a few bloodied shreds of skin. He threw those to the alley below for the neighborhood cats. His hunger was still not satiated. He turned to Madeleine . . .

For many years the three-story house stood vacant, its bottom windows barred, moss growing on the pillars. A family finally moved in during the 1840s, but with them came the ghosts of Madeleine and Alcide. It was always the same. In the dining room, a large table would materialize. Seated at it were the diaphanous figures of the young couple. Soon there was a scream and Madeleine's ghost lunged for the deceitful Alcide. As she twisted the napkin around his throat, the entire scene faded away. That family, and many others after it, found the horrible scenario too upsetting to stay for long.

The only family to stay was Charles B. Larendon and his wife, Laura (Beauregard) Larendon, the daughter of Civil War General Toutant-Beauregard. The Larendons saw the ghostly murder take place many times, but grew to accept the Uninvited Ones. They loved the house and remained for many years. Sadly, the Larendon's infant daughter died there. Mrs. Larendon passed away soon after. Charles remained a virtual recluse, keeping meticulous diaries of his experiences there. It was he who was responsible for gathering the house's incredible early history.

A Mrs. Jacques and her family later lived in the Devil's Mansion but the haunting overwhelmed them. Not only did the spectacle in the dining room frequently turn up, but often there was the acrid smell of smoke when no fire was set in one of the numerous Italian carved fireplaces, doorknobs would be twisted by unseen hands and disembodied footsteps raced up and down the hallways.

To passersby familiar with the house, the weirdest sight of all was the head of the Devil himself embedded in the gable. Some said it was simply a hideous gargoyle made of stone or bronze, but those who really knew said it was the head of the living Devil himself. How did they know? If you watched carefully, the eyes would follow your path and its lips would pull back in a snarl, revealing long, spiked teeth soaked in human blood.

The house was razed long ago.

Buyer Beware

Would you knowingly buy a haunted house?

And if you did, how would you go about appeasing the resident specters?

In New Orleans, making peace with the nearly departed can be an all-consuming chore because, it seems, almost every old house in the city harbors its share of ghostly tenants. Quite a few have become designated historic sites or museums, so the ghosts can wander unimpeded, knowing their routines won't be upset.

The strikingly austere Le Pretre House, at the corner of Dauphine and Orlean Streets, for instance, would come with a sultan and his five translucent wives—if it were on the market. In 1792, the unlucky Arab and his comely retinue were all murdered in their sleep. Despite that definite end, their ghosts continue partying well past midnight on certain dismal nights.

At the French Quarter's Hermann-Grima Historic House, 820 St. Louis Street, resident ghosts are of a kindly nature. On chilly winter mornings, they will light the fireplaces and scatter the pleasant essences of lavender and roses about the parlor.

For the sheer number of ghosts in residence, however, the Beauregard-Keyes House, 1113 Chartres Street, is the clear winner. It's hard to ignore the clattering footsteps of an entire phantom army regiment!

Gen. Pierre Beauregard leads the invisible Rebels in a re-enactment of the Battle of Shiloh in the various rooms of his magnificent house. The soldiers materialize out of the paneled walls on those foggy, moonlit nights reminiscent of the bloody Civil War battle. Gen. Beauregard, of course, went down to bitter defeat in the final minutes of the Shiloh bloodletting.

Why the good general chooses to re-enact his worst hour in his former New Orleans mansion rather than at the original battlefield is anyone's guess.

A local historian said there is another legend at the Beauregard-Keyes House. Dancers and a fiddle player stage ghostly soirees in the ballroom.

Interestingly, caretakers deny that anything unusual has ever been documented. Nevertheless, the Beauregard-Keyes House is a strong contender for the city's most haunted mansion.

A house in the 700 block of Royal Street is noted for the beautiful female ghost that walks across its roof. And she's an x-rated wraith at that!

The girl was a young slave who fell in love with a handsome Creole lad. He promised to marry her if she would prove her love by spending the night on the roof of his house naked.

On a cold December night, she obeyed his bizarre demand, for she was hopelessly in love with the man. She stripped off her clothing and walked back and forth on the roof. Her fiancé found her frozen to death the next morning.

Neighbors say the young woman re-enacts her fatal devotion whenever December nights turn especially chilly; her nude form is clearly visible against the moonlit sky.

Nakedness also plays a role in another famous New Orleans ghost story, although the perpetrator was very human. But the cause was quite clearly something else again.

In this case, a policeman watched wide-eyed as a young man, naked as a jaybird and covered with soapy water, raced by him on St. Peter Street. After a short chase, he caught the streaker a few steps up Royal Street. The cop hastily threw an overcoat about the man's shoulders . . . and then asked what in blazes was going on.

Doctor Deschamps was at fault, the young man stammered to the cop. It seems that he was lounging in his bath when the doctor dropped by his old apartment.

That is to say his head did.

In midair.

And directly above the terrified bather.

The startled cop and most of New Orleans knew all about the ghost of Doctor Deschamps. He was the dentist from hell.

Some years before, at his apartment/office at 714 St. Peter Street, Doctor Deschamps had carried out a hideous plan. He had somehow become obsessed with a treasure he claimed was hidden somewhere nearby. He enticed a young girl to act as a medium so he could find the treasure. He hypnotized her day after day, but each time failed to get from her any of the information he demanded. Hypnosis gave way to torture and, finally, murder when he smothered her with a towel doused in chloroform.

Doctor Deschamps was found guilty of murder and hanged.

For decades, occupants of the doctor's old apartment said his ghost and that of the innocent young girl played out their fateful scene. Doctor Deschamp's ghost was "a burly, muscular man with hairy, apelike arms," one witness said. The girl's ghost cringes in a corner as her torturer rages about the room. At one time, the haunting supposedly frightened the author Oliver La Farge.

What of the young man who encountered the incredulous police officer? After he told the authorities what he had seen, he never again set foot inside 714 St. Peter Street. Friends bravely cleared the apartment of his clothing and furniture.

La maison est hantée

The French and Spanish in the old Quarter knew the place all right. *La maison est hantée*, they whispered. *The house is haunted*. And not just any house. This address, 1140 Royal Street, is the most notorious haunted house in all of New Orleans, and perhaps in all of Louisiana as well.

On Royal Street was the 1830s home of the Madame Delphine Macarty Lalaurie, a monstrous purveyor of torture and death, wrapped in the guise of a beautiful, sophisticated society belle known throughout the city for her lavish entertainments and grand balls.

The most famous names in early New Orleans frequented Madame Lalaurie's salon. New Orleans' raconteur and author Lyle Saxon said that as late as the 1920s Madame's old mansion was "the largest and finest in the neighborhood, rich and beautiful in detail."

But her public demeanor was a hideous charade. Lurking behind the charming smile and crinoline skirts was the soul of a sadist, a woman who reveled in unspeakable cruelties and slow, agonizing death; the exact number of helpless slaves ripped and sliced apart on her instruments of torture will never be known. Madame Lalaurie may have been the most prolific murderess in early American history.

Those unlucky enough to have heard or seen the ghosts of her victims claim they are far removed from anything else the supernatural world might inflict upon the living. The twisted, translucent forms are missing limbs, or a length of intestine might dangle from a gaping stomach wound, maybe an eye or a pair of lips might be sewn shut with heavy black thread. Blood spews from the severed buttocks of one particularly hideous specter.

For a few unfortunate pedestrians, a casual stroll past 1140 Royal Street has included witnessing the suicide of a young black girl as she plummets from the mansion's roof, her dying screams lingering in the still, humid night air. Knowing it is all a ghostly reenactment of an actual suicide does not lessen the terrible suddenness of the event. Some say it was murder.

The house of Madame Lalaurie is old enough to harbor many ghosts. One tradition is that Jean and Henri de Remairie built it in 1773 on land they received through a royal grant from the French Crown. The forty-room mansion passed through various hands until Delphine de Macarty inherited it. She was married three times, the last to Doctor Leonard Louis Nicolas Lalaurie in 1825.

Other historians, however, point to conflicting legal records. A court record seems to show that Madame Lalaurie bought the site in 1831 and had the house built and ready for occupancy in 1832. Old City Hall records declare that Louis and Delphine (Macarty) Lalaurie bought the house from Edmond Soniat du Fossat on August 13, 1831.

Believe what you will of the mansion's origin, Doctor and Madame Lalaurie's magnificent house was all that early New Orleans society could have wanted in a center for lively galas.

The exterior of the three-story mansion, though almost plain to the point of severity, is graced by delicate lace ironwork around the second-floor balcony and by street-level arched windows.

If the outside was undistinguished, the interior was lavish even by the excessive standards of the antebellum South. The house was made for grand parties. Mahogany doors with hand-carved panels of flowers and cherubic, human faces opened to parlors and dining rooms lighted by crystal chandeliers aglow with hundreds of candles. Fireplaces taller than a man warmed almost every room, while the finest products of Eastern and European furniture-makers rimmed the walls. Fabrics of satin and velvet were draped in dazzling array from the walls. Guests dined from delicate, European china.

The charming and beautiful Madame Lalaurie knew how to impress New Orleans society and they, in return, made her mansion on Royal Street reverberate with hundreds of voices laughing in earthly delight. Night after night the pampered rich in their slippered feet strode through the front portico and across the marble floor of the entrance hallway and preened before the great, gilded mirrors. Their attentive hostess bustled about the rooms seeing to their comforts.

But beneath the veneer of sophistication was the cursed institution of slavery, practiced with special gusto by Delphine Lalaurie.

Attending to the house and its luxurious furnishings were dozens of slaves. A small black girl helped dress Madame; another dusted the downstairs rooms and served the petit fours. A large black man whose name may have been Carlos fetched Madame's foodstuffs. Another slave was the wine steward and still others washed Madame's clothes, or swept the courtyard. One had the exclusive task to bathe Madame's favorite poodle!

Ironically, it was Madame Lalaurie's personal maid whose suicide gave the public its first inkling of her mistress's secret life.

Her name was Lia. She leaped from the mansion's roof one afternoon. Her body smashed into a long banquette on the sidewalk outside the house, missing by only inches a startled passerby who alerted authorities.

Before Lia's suicide, there had been some quiet conversations about how Madame's servants seemed to never stay long in her employ. A new young girl would replace the parlor maid with no explanation as to her whereabouts, or the slave who groomed Doctor and Madame's horses suddenly disappeared from the stable—never to be seen again.

Understandably, Madame Lalaurie had a very difficult time explaining away Lia's death. Suspicions were raised, but after all, Madame insisted, the girl was nothing more than a piece of property to be used or gotten rid of. And yet . . . the first whisperings of unease from Madame's old friends were being heard. A few party invitations declined, a dinner abruptly cancelled, a night at the theatre called off . . .

On April 10, 1834, however, all doubts about Madame Lalaurie were expunged. The full story of Madame Lalaurie's cruelties were revealed in particulars so disgusting that people from the shores of Lake Ponchartrain to the Old Spanish Trail talked about it for decades.

On that otherwise pleasant spring day, a small fire brought the city's fire brigade to the mansion. An elderly black woman, who herself may have started the fire in a desperate attempt to attract attention, begged the firemen to unlock the door leading to a garret apartment. Human beings were captives up there, she cried.

At the top of the uppermost flight of stairs they found the room—Madame Lalaurie's chamber of horror. Even the most hardened of the firemen cried out in anguish at the depravity of anyone who could have created such an abomination.

The April 11, 1834 edition of the *New Orleans Bee* reported the event in the typically verbose style of nineteenth-century journalism:

"The flames having spread with alarming rapidity, and the horrible suspicion being entertained among the spectators that some of the inmates (sic) of the premises where it originated were incarcerated therein, the doors were forced open for the purpose of liberating them . . . Upon entering one of the apartments, the most appalling spectacle met their eyes—seven slaves more or less horribly mutilated, were seen suspended by the neck, with their limbs apparently stretched and torn from one extremity to the other. Language is powerless and inadequate to give a proper conception of the horror that a scene like this must have inspired. We shall not attempt it, but leave it rather to the reader's imagination to picture what it was."

". . . They had been confined by her (Madame Lalaurie) for several months in the situation from which they had thus providentially been rescued, and had been merely kept in existence to prolong their suffering and to make them taste all that the most refined cruelty could inflict. . . ."

It was left to witnesses other than the *Bee*'s anonymous reporter to catalogue the tortures found in Madame Lalaurie's secret chamber.

All of the victims were naked and chained to the walls. Some of the women had their stomachs sliced open and their intestines wrapped around their waists. Other females were covered with black ants, supping on gobs of honey spread over their bodies. One had had her mouth stuffed with animal excrement and then sewn shut.

The men were in even more hideous condition. Fingernails had been ripped off, eyes poked out, or buttocks and ears sliced away. One poor soul hung lifeless from his shackles, a stick protruding from a gaping hole that had been drilled into the top of his skull. It had evidently been used to "stir" his brains.

Several had their mouths pinned shut.

One man had his severed hand stitched to his stomach.

All of the prisoners wore heavy iron collars about their necks and their feet were in shackles, according to one newspaper account.

The torture had been carefully administered so as not to bring quick death. Nevertheless, some of the slaves had apparently been dead for some time. Others were unconscious. One or two were crying in incomprehensible pain, begging to be killed and thus relieved of their agony. At least two of those rescued died of their injuries later in the day.

Just how many slaves were found in Madame's torture chambers during and after the fire is not certain. Some of the servants who had "vanished," or supposedly been sold to other owners, actually never made it out of the house.

While Madame Lalaurie's grisly hideaways were being searched, and the small fire doused, she apparently stayed in the mansion. But even in the slave-holding South of the 1830s, her barbarism was too much for the city.

The *New Orleans Daily Picayune* detailed what happened next in an 1892 history of the events:

"A silence fell upon the faubourg, but it was the ominous silence that precedes the outburst of the smoldering wrath of an outraged public. During the morning, an idle crowd hung about the Lalaurie mansion, the numbers increased toward midday and by evening the throng was so dense that standing room was almost impossible upon the pavement. They hissed and hooted and some cried out for satisfaction. Madame Lalaurie did not mistake the meaning and conceived and executed a bold plan for flight.

"Promptly at the hour at which she was accustomed to take her usual drive her carriage drove up before the door and Madame, dressed in her usual elegant style, stepped out upon the sidewalk and entered the vehicle. In a second more the horses were going at full speed over the clean, smooth shells of Bayou Road. Madame was taking her last drive in the fashionable quarter, and it was a drive for life itself. It took but an instant for the crowd to recover from her masterful stroke of audacity, and in another moment they were at her back, yelling and hooting and screaming: 'Stop that carriage!' 'She is running away!' 'Drag her out!' 'Shoot her!' 'Shoot the horses!' but in vain; the coachman drove furiously on; the horses went at a break-neck speed; they had borne their mistress before and would not fail her now, and fashionable New Orleans stopped its carriages and watched in blank amazement . . .

"Mrs. Lalaurie, it is said, took refuge for ten days near the spot where the Claiborne cottage stands in Covington, whence she made her way to the Mobile and thence to Paris."

Madame Delphine Lalaurie's eventual fate is in dispute. The *Daily Picayune*'s history of the Lalaurie mansion states that she lived all her final years in Paris, in a handsome mansion that, like its New Orleans predecessor, grew to become a favorite of the cultured and elite of the city. She died, the newspaper said, "in her own home, surrounded by her family."

Another account, however, published in the 1940s, alleges that Madame Lalaurie secretly returned to New Orleans some years later and settled in a home "on the Bayou Road." She called herself "the Widow Blanque." A record may actually exist showing a "Mrs. N. L. Lalaurie" freed a slave in 1849 in that same district.

Wherever the fiend of Royal Street finally came to rest, there is no record of any legal proceedings being taken against her for the crimes she so wantonly committed. And nothing shows that she ever again saw her New Orleans mansion.

The same cannot be said of those she butchered.

The ghosts swirling about 1140 Royal Street have been the stuff of legend virtually from the day Madame Lalaurie's carriage pulled away from her front door for the last time.

A local agent, apparently on the instructions of Madame herself, placed the mansion on the market. Records indicate that it was sold in 1837 to a man who kept it only three months. He was plagued with strange noises—cries and groans and rattling chains—so that he was unable to spend a single peaceful night there. The nameless gentleman also tried to rent out several of the two-score rooms, but tenants only stayed a few days. Neighbors reported seeing the front door swing open on its own, and windows rise up and down without assistance.

A furniture store and barber shop may have also occupied the premises, but again, for just a very short time.

One particularly unnerving episode took place above the old stables some years after Madame Lalaurie fled for her life. A black servant was spending the night there when he was suddenly awakened by someone choking him. Bending over him in the dim light was a pale woman with black hair, a terrible look of anger on her face. She had his throat firmly in her grasp. As he was nearing unconsciousness, another pair of hands, black hands, appeared and pried the woman's fingers from his throat. Both the assailant and the servant's savior faded away in the murky darkness.

Following the Civil War, Reconstruction found the Lalaurie Mansion turned into an integrated high school "for the girls of the lower district."

In 1874, the notorious White League succeeded in forcing the black children to leave the school. Later, a segregationist Democratic school board made the school for black children only, but that lasted only a year.

After a period of vacancy, the Lalaurie mansion again found itself the center of society when an English dance teacher opened a "conservatory of music and fashionable dancing school" in 1882.

However, the resident ghosts seemed to have other ideas.

All went well for several weeks. The teacher was very popular, drawing the best young ladies and gentlemen of New Orleans society. A newspaper wrote of that wistful time: "Music and light and laughter filled the great apartments, and it was pretty of a spring evening . . . to watch the girls in their light and graceful costumes flitting about the great rooms and over the broad balcony to the measured strains of music, while the voices of a tenor or contralto trilled through the apartments and floated out upon the dreamy street."

The dream ended abruptly. A local newspaper apparently printed an accusation against the teacher, perhaps alleging improprieties with one of his young charges, just before a grand soiree was to take place at the mansion. Students and guests stayed away and the school closed the next day. The spirits hanging about the old mansion undoubtedly danced well into the night at such wonderful news.

Not everyone was driven out of the haunted mansion. Rumors of lost treasure at 1140 Royal Street surfaced in 1892 after the death of Jules Vignie, the eccentric offspring of a prominent French family.

Vignie lived in the Lalaurie house virtually unnoticed in the late 1880s and early 1890s. Indeed, those who had known Vignie after the Civil War were surprised at the news; they had assumed him dead long before. He was a studious collector of antique furniture, fine paintings and bric-a-brac of all sorts, and had worked for a prominent New Orleans auctioneer for years.

Vignie's body was found on a tattered cot in the attic by neighbors curious at recent signs of activity in the house. They were amazed at the beautiful furnishings Vignie had managed to acquire. A bag containing several hundred dollars was found near his body. Quick searches revealed another $2,000 secreted in his mattress.

Vignie's possessions were sold off and the house stayed vacant until immigrant Italian families sought housing in the Old Quarter. The Lalaurie Mansion became an apartment complex for several dozen families. For many of them, their lives in the Lalaurie mansion were anything but peaceful. The ghosts would not be stilled:

- A towering black man wrapped in chains confronted a fruit peddler on the staircase and then vanished on the bottom step;

- Strange figures wrapped in shrouds flailed away with riding crops;
- A young mother screamed when she confronted a white woman in elegant clothes bending over her sleeping infant.
- Stabled mules died mysteriously after being visited by a white-robed woman; dogs and cats were found strangled and torn in two. And always, always the groans and screams from the attic rooms.

It was never easy to keep tenants in the old house, and that was made even more difficult after one owner decided to perform some remodeling.

Workmen discovered several skeletons under the old cypress floors. The remains were found not in orderly graves, but as if they had been dumped unceremoniously into the ground. Well, the owner tried to reason, the house had been built on old Spanish and Indian burial grounds. True enough, but his response was dismissed when authorities said the bones were of relatively recent origin, certainly buried after the house was built.

What was found, officials concluded, was nothing less than Madame Lalaurie's own private graveyard. She had removed sections of the house's floor, dug shallow graves and thrown the bodies of her tortured slaves in them so as to avoid having to answer for their deaths. The mystery of the sudden disappearance of Madame's slaves was finally solved.

The twentieth century has seen the mansion on Royal Street renovated and become, for now, a favorite sight on tours of the Old French Quarter.

But sad Lia still plummets from the towering roof on moonlit nights, the groaning of tortured souls can be too much to bear, and no one stays long in this evil house. The ghosts of the innocent men and women Madame Delphine Lalaurie sent to premature graves may be too numerous to ever go peacefully from this world.

Loup Garou

The marsh known as Honey Island Swamp is the reputed hunting ground of a legendary creature known as the *loup garou*, the swamp thing. If not precisely a ghost, it is certainly an oft-reported creature not known for its sociability.

The mysterious wetlands near Slidell have given rise to all sorts of tales—people who have gone for a day hike never to return and, in the nineteenth century, of escaped slaves building new lives somewhere in the impenetrable water wilderness.

The swamp thing, a sort of big-foot creature said to look much like the Sasquatch of the Pacific Northwest, was even once reported along Interstate Highway 10 after severe flooding of the Pearl River. Hunters have claimed the thing chased them until they were nearly prostrate with exhaustion. More level-headed observers, however, claim the reports are the product of too much drink and too little skepticism.

But the stories of *loup garou* will not go away. Popular hikes into the swamp—with a guarantee of a safe return—always include tales of Louisiana's own missing link.

Miserly Mr. Holt

Far removed from the steamy alleyways and boulevards of New Orleans reside other wraiths known for gentler, kinder hauntings.

Just why this should be the case is a mystery. Perhaps these courteous old plantation revenants were taught in life to respect the privacy of others. Why shouldn't the wellborn retain their dignity even if they have been dead for over a century?

Take kindly old Mr. Holt for example.

For most of his life, he was secretary to Frederick Conrad, the popular owner of The Cottage, a lush plantation that once graced the Great River Road landscape south of Baton Rouge. In the decades before the Civil War, Conrad entertained the likes of Zachary Taylor, the Marquis de Lafayette, Jefferson Davis, and Henry Clay. Francis Parkinson Keyes wrote *The River Road* while living there. Long before it burned down three decades ago, and even today, various ghostly tableaus have been played out in its stately rooms.

The most well-known tales concerned Mr. Holt himself. He was born in 1802 and died in 1880, but that's not the least of it. As far as is known, he is the only Louisiana ghost to have had his photograph taken . . . a half-century after his death!

But first about the man himself.

Mr. Holt was devoted to Frederick Conrad, so that when Federal troops occupied The Cottage in the waning days of the Civil War it isn't surprising that both men were tossed in prison. Conrad died there, but Mr. Holt was at last released and returned to The Cottage to live out his remaining years.

Prison apparently warped Mr. Holt's mind. In the dozen years or so that he lived at The Cottage, he developed a pathological fear of poverty. As the lone tenant of the old mansion, he saw to it that each shred of cloth was carefully stored away, unused pieces of twine wrapped on a spindle, and even spare biscuits tucked away for some future repast. Long after his death in 1880, Mr. Holt's insurance against indigence was being discovered by The Cottage's subsequent owners.

Added to his odd behavior was the appearance of Mr. Holt himself. The occasional visitor would report that the old man was an insomniac who wandered through the plantation's hallways all night long in a tattered white nightshirt, his scraggly beard splayed across his narrow chest. All the while he took great pains not to alarm guests or call undue attention to himself. A true gentlemen's gentleman.

Beginning in 1880, shortly after Mr. Holt's demise, his ghost reenacted his nocturnal wanderings. Right up to The Cottage's conflagration in 1960, the old man's countenance peered mournfully from the mansion's ancient windows. It was at one of those windows that a photographer caught what was said to have been the ghost of shy Mr. Holt staring through the glass. The picture was published in *The Elks Magazine*.

Mr. Holt may not have been the only spirit at The Cottage. Vague dancing forms and faint fiddle and banjo music occasionally graced the generous front verandah on quiet, humid evenings. But these were musicales performed by ghostly slaves at some ethereal soirée. Long after The Cottage was nothing more than a charred ruin passersby noted the occasional laugh or patter of tapping feet coming from what was once a grand and glorious place.

Headless Ghosts

Louisiana is home to at least four topless wraiths that haunt three different plantations.

Lacy Branch Plantation, near Natchitoches in northwest Louisiana, can be thankful the ghost who haunts the nearby road hasn't yet made an appearance near the mansion grounds. Those who have seen him, it, don't forget the sight—a headless body appearing suddenly from the ditch to scare the wits out of motorists and late-night pedestrians. Sometimes the thing is on horseback. No one seems to know under what circumstances the ghost lost its head, or even who the hapless victim was.

An aimless, headless man shuffles about Skolfield House, near Baton Rouge, harmlessly looking for the rest of his being. His identity, too, is unknown. An earlier Skolfield specter was so nice—she was the wife of a former owner who resented her husband's new bride. Around the kitchen this woman-ghost scorned would rattle, knocking pots and pans to the floor and slamming doors. She vanished when death claimed her former husband. Their battles on "the other side" are probably dreadful affairs.

Kenilworth Plantation, below New Orleans, is a poignant reminder that true love knows not even earthly bounds.

A man and a woman, ghost lovers, stroll hand in hand through the rooms and hallways. Sometimes his arm is about her corseted waist. Both are dressed in elegant antebellum clothing. Neither speaks a word, nor can they. Each is absent its head!

Treasure Seekers

At least two Louisiana plantations have intriguing stories of legendary buried treasure connected with them.

A bevy of specters haunt ancient St. Maurice Plantation, outside St. Maurice, between Shreveport and Alexandria, including an intriguing fellow who hovers a few yards from the house, supposedly over the location of secret treasure.

However, a number of years ago the plantation's owner tried digging in the earth there. His metal detector indicated the presence of metal. A few feet down he found . . . a pickax.

The visitor may have more success in spotting one of St. Maurice's other ghosts—a lady in the attic, several playful children and a former caretaker. The plantation has been open for tours in recent years.

Saint Bernard Parish is on a desolate peninsula southeast of New Orleans. The Mississippi River Gulf Outlet Canal slices through the area, while the Biloxi Wildlife Area stretches across the parish's thumb near Lake Borgne. There are no settlements east of tiny Yscloskey.

One of Louisiana's most gruesome lost treasure tales arises from this dismal region, at the old Mercier Plantation, and dates back over a hundred years.

An old black woman who worked as a cook there nearly collided with the ghost of her former owner, Mr. Mercier himself, when she stepped out onto the porch one humid summer night. He called her by name—"Sarah"—and told her to meet him behind the milk house that night. He would show her where a fortune in gold was buried.

Not only did she not want to meet him anywhere, but she screamed her head off at the sight of the dead man, summoning nearly everyone else in the household to her side. As she stammered out her story, everyone else's eyes blazed with the thought of hidden riches.

News of the episode soon reached the ears of a black minister who volunteered to lead a delegation to the milk house treasure. The group met at eleven o'clock at night—the ghostly Mr. Mercier's stated time—and the preacher began to dig. Suddenly, he dropped his shovel and screamed in pain. He said the Devil had grabbed him; witnesses said they could hear the sound of a whip striking the poor man. Awful welts rose on his back; blood oozed through the fresh rips in the preacher's shirt.

Sarah pushed through the throng. She could "see" Mr. Mercier, she cried out, it was he who wielded the whip. He was angry that Sarah had disobeyed him and allowed others to search for the treasure.

Within minutes the minister was unconscious. He died of the terrible injuries a few days later. No one knows what became of the gold supposedly buried at Mercier Plantation.

Strolling Phantoms

Not all of Louisiana's ghosts live in antebellum homes and ancient plantations. Some mysterious things have been seen in the desolate countryside of the Pelican State.

The old Roddy Road in Ascension Parish, about twenty miles south of Baton Rouge, was once called the Lighted Lane of Gonzales. Fascinating, dancing lights were often seen there late at night. Witnesses said they saw what looked like a match being struck, with the light then moving alongside the roadway. One legend maintained that a young woman was buried along this road and a light placed over her grave to keep the night away.

Sheriff Hickley Waguespack reportedly saw the strange light in April 1951, according to newspaper accounts. He said it had a "yellowish cast" but didn't create a distinct beam. The light wouldn't let anyone approach it.

Swamp gas, or phosphorous fire, is said to be prevalent in this part of Louisiana. Caused by rotting vegetation, the swamp gas is sometimes seen as a shimmering light in rural areas.

Ponchatoula is a small town in southern Tangipahoa Parish, thirty miles north of Lake Pontchartrain. There is a haunted gum tree there that weeps with the pearl-like tears of a young woman who committed suicide under its branches.

The ghosts of soldiers buried in unmarked graves haunt the woods near Marksville, on the Red River in east central Louisiana. An old legend holds that a Civil War battle was fought on the road near the woods and the dead buried in a trench. At night the men still march among the trees . . . headless.

An avenue of oak trees leading to Parlange Plantation in Pointe Coupee Parish is the setting for a particularly poignant ghost story.

The Marquis Vincent de Ternant of Dans-ville-sur-Meuse built the mansion. He obtained the land from the French crown.

The Marquis' son, Claude Vincent de Ternant, had four children with his second wife, Virginia Trahan. One of their daughters, a beautiful girl named Julie, went mad on her wedding night. As hundreds of guests looked on, she started screaming and ran hysterically down the oak alley pursued by her distraught husband. She collapsed and died several hundred feet from the house. Her sobbing specter is seen on moonlit nights running down that very same path at Parlange.

Madisonville boasts two ghosts on its old streets.

A depressed druggist rented a room at a St. Mary Street boardinghouse operated by a Mrs. Puis. Sometime in 1911, he retired to his room and promptly shot himself in the temple. Students at St. Anselm's Church school reported for many years that they could see his ghost through the window of his old room or walking back and forth in front of the boardinghouse.

The Silk Lady appears only at night and only at the western end of Johnson Street, in the Palmetto Flat area. Sadly, no one knows her origins or what she seeks.

A Good Night's Eternal Sleep

Is it any wonder that a man who built his own coffin and regularly slept in it at night haunted his old home?

That was precisely the case at Oakland Plantation, near Haughton, in Boosier Parish. Ex-Confederate Colonel Sutton believed firmly in the importance of providing for one's own future. He placed the burnished wood casket in his own bedroom and regularly passed the nights in peaceful slumber within its cozy interior.

Don't believe such a thing could happen? Neither did the two handymen employed at Oakland years ago. That changed when they swore old Colonel Sutton's regular stroll across the squeaky floorboards of his bedroom ended when he climbed in the coffin. From that night on, the men slept behind locked doors with an ax and a pick as their only companions.

Colonel Sutton doesn't seem to have any connection with the other legendary ghosts at Oakland Plantation, a quartet of ghostly horsemen who charge their mounts around the grounds. An amazing sight it must have been one evening after nightfall when the horsemen clambered onto the verandah still mounted, pounded through the doorway, down the long hall and out the back door. The veracity of the story may be questioned owing to the fact that the horses have never left behind any telltale reminders of their unpredictable visits.

Sad Little Cygnet

Hampton Mansion, north of Baltimore, is filled with grief and sadness and the phantoms of seven generations of one family who lived and died on the vast estate for a century and a half.

Charles Ridgely, a member of the Maryland House of Burgesses from 1773 to 1789, built this grand Georgian mansion. He was also a member of the committee appointed to frame a constitution for the state. On 2,000 acres of land willed to him in 1772, Ridgely built his legacy, the largest house in the United States at the time of its completion in 1790. It is one of the largest and most magnificent mansions of the post-Revolutionary War era. Its two and a half-story main section is capped with a cupola and flanked by one-story wings. Ridgely died only six months after its completion.

The estate passed to his nephew, Charles Ridgely Carnan. To conform to an odd provision of the will, Carnan changed his name to Charles Carnan Ridgely. This "new" Charles Ridgely served as governor of Maryland from 1815 to 1818 and it was he who brought national attention to Hampton Mansion with several grand additions. Formal gardens enhanced the grounds, stables were filled with the swiftest horses, and elaborate dinner parties were held for the state's aristocracy.

But Hampton Mansion brought no happiness to the governor's wife, Priscilla. Although she bore eleven children, she seemed to take little interest in them, or anything else for that matter. Indeed, she felt imprisoned within the great stone walls of a benign fortress. While her husband entertained important guests, Mrs. Ridgely remained in seclusion upstairs, reading her Bible for hours on end. Sadly, even her religion brought her no comfort. Thirty-two years after entering Hampton Mansion, Priscilla Dorsey Ridgely died a lonely, mentally unbalanced woman.

But she may be traipsing now through the passages and rooms she avoided in life. Servants and family friends reported seeing Priscilla on a number of occasions in various parts of the mansion, always dressed in a gray gown.

On a winter's day, years after Priscilla's death, a new bride in the Ridgely family heard a faint tapping at the front door. She opened it to find a thin, frail woman shivering on the doorstep. She wore no coat, only a plain cap on her head.

"Won't you come in and warm yourself by the fire?" asked this Mrs. Ridgely.

The stranger hesitated, peered through the open doorway, then turned abruptly and vanished into the crisp night air. A servant told the young bride that it was the spirit of Priscilla, still searching for the happiness that eluded her in life.

Over the years, a haunted chandelier has foretold the deaths of Hampton's first ladies. Everyone in the mansion at the time hears the crash of the ceiling fixture as it falls to the floor, spraying shards of glass and bits of plaster in all directions. Trouble is, servants never find anything disturbed in any of the rooms. All the beautiful crystal chandeliers are always hanging in place.

The fifth mistress of Hampton Mansion was enjoying the company of her family one spring-like Easter Sunday when they heard the dreaded crash. The children and housekeeper scattered in all directions. They searched every room, but found nothing amiss. However, this Mrs. Ridgely was dead within twenty-four hours, perhaps giving rise to the legend of the chandelier.

It is not only the women of Hampton whose deaths have been foretold by psychic phenomena. Legend has it that whenever a master of the mansion dies away from home, his soul returns in a spectral coach.

Charles Ridgely IV had taken his young sons to England to enroll them in a boarding school, after which he proceeded to the Continent to vacation in Italy. One wintry night during his absence, tinkling sleigh bells and the thud of horses' hooves on the packed snow awakened the caretaker's wife. She arose and peered out the window. The landscape was an unbroken and glistening white in the moonlight. There was no sleigh. There were no horses. The next day word reached Hampton Mansion that "Mr. Charles" had died in Rome. His family was already in mourning.

Of all the tales of haunting associated with Hampton Mansion the most poignant swirls around Governor Swann's beautiful daughter who died at the mansion in the nineteenth century. Miss Swann had recently recovered from an illness and Hampton's first lady, Eliza Ridgely, invited her to the mansion. Eliza was very fond of the girl and always called her Cygnet, or, "little swan." The fresh country air might help to restore her strength.

Sadly, that was not to be the case.

One morning the girl appeared at the breakfast table looking quite pale. Dark circles rimmed little Cygnet's blue eyes and her long golden hair lay in tangles about her face. Eliza feared she'd taken a turn for the worst, but the child assured her hostess that she felt well. It was just that she'd had a nightmare, she said, a terrible dream of death.

An old man with a scythe had chased her through endless fields of wheat, she said of her nightmare, and after she narrowly escaped his desperate clutches, he shouted, "I'll get you yet, my golden-haired beauty!"

In the suddenly silent dining room, Eliza alone spoke as she reached out to pat Cygnet's cold hand: "It's nonsense, child. Everyone has bad dreams once in a while. They mean nothing. Come now, we'll sit outside on the terrace and rest."

That evening, Eliza staged a ball to cheer the sickly child. But when she failed to appear, a servant was sent up to her room. Poor little Cygnet was slumped over the dressing table, one hand still clutching her hairbrush. A doctor called her death "mysterious," but no investigation ever looked into the circumstances.

Visitors to Hampton Mansion over the years claim to have seen Cygnet in her northwest bedroom. She sits in her satin ball gown, combing her golden locks.

The ghosts of Priscilla and Cygnet may not be the only ones in the mansion.

One raw January afternoon about seventy years ago, a young woman interested in historic mansions stopped at Hampton.

She'd been invited by the Ridgelys to "stop anytime."

A formally dressed butler answered her knock and said that, although the family was not in residence that day, he'd be pleased to show her around. As he escorted the guest from room to room, she became amazed at his knowledge of the Ridgely family history. He identified portraits hanging on the walls and spun stories of by-gone days. Finally, when the woman started to leave, she tried to offer him a tip for his kindness.

"Thank you, ma'am," he said, shaking his head, "but I need for nothing. Nothing . . ." His voice trailed off.

Several days later, the woman telephoned Mrs. Ridgely.

"I'm sorry you weren't home the day I stopped at Hampton," she apologized. "But I want you to know how much I appreciated the wonderful tour of your home with your butler. He seemed so devoted and so knowledgeable about the family."

"My butler?" exclaimed Mrs. Ridgely, completely mystified. "But I have no butler. As you must know, it's very hard to find help these days."

The unexpected caller described the butler down to his formal clothing and kindly manner. Mrs. Ridgely said, "That must have been old Tom. He was born on the place and served us well for many years."

She paused.

"But Tom died thirty years ago."

The Ridgely family occupied Hampton Mansion for more than 150 years, but no one ever determined the identity of the ghost who roams the mansion at midnight opening doors.

People say they hear latches lifted, bolts withdrawn, and doors opened. A check of the premises finds no disturbances. In any old house, floorboards may squeak under human weight, a certain window may rattle in a high wind, but at Hampton Mansion it's the metallic clank of the bar over the south portico door that brings alarm. This door opens into the Great Hall and was never used late at night. Anyone arriving home late used another door.

One night, when young John and Stewart Ridgely were sleeping in a room on the south side of the mansion, they were awakened by the scrape of an iron bar.

Burglars!

Shivering with excitement, tinged with fear, the boys climbed out of their beds, grabbed a flashlight and tiptoed through the quiet hallway. At the top of the staircase, the boys hesitated, then descended one step at a time, each clutching the other's arm.

Inside the Great Hall, John snapped off the flashlight and threw on the light switch. In the sudden blaze of light, the huge room appeared in order. The ponderous hasp on the outside door had not been disturbed.

In 1948, the Avalon Foundation, a philanthropic organization, acquired Hampton Mansion and donated it to the federal government. The Society for the Preservation of Maryland Antiquities acts as custodian. Hampton Mansion was designated a National Historic Site on June 22, 1948, and is operated by the National Park Service. The mansion and its approximately sixty-two acres in Towson, Maryland are open to the public.

The haunting continues.

Park Service employees staying in the mansion have heard harpsichord music coming from the bedroom where sad Cygnet died, but, according to all available records, no harpsichord has ever been in the mansion.

On one occasion, the Great Hall was used for an exhibition. In the middle of the night the ranger on duty was awakened by a terrifying crash. Rushing into the Hall, he found all the display racks thrown to the floor. The incident was never explained.

But the old tack room may be the busiest and certainly the noisiest of all the "empty" rooms. Rangers have heard chains beating against the walls, and when they look in they see saddles and harnesses swinging back and forth from pegs in the walls. The windows and doors are kept tightly closed.

Some speculate that Jehu Howell, Hampton Mansion's builder, has returned to take one more ride. Howell had received more than $6,000 and sixty-eight quarts of rum for his labors, but he didn't live to enjoy his financial and liquid windfall. One night in November 1787, Howell rode his horse into a rain-swollen creek. He may have misjudged the water's depth or, more likely perhaps, imbibed too much of his payment. No one will ever know.

In the morning, Jehu Howell and his horse were found dead on the stream's bank.

The Simpsonville Case

Those people who believe that only deserted mansions and ancient ruins harbor the ghosts of today might be forgiven their foolishness, for without this deception how else would real estate agents be able to sell new homes? The truth of the matter is that *any* dwelling may well provide refuge for shadowy bits and pieces of lives past.

The furthest thought from Mildred Trevey's mind was that her own brick, split-foyer house in Simpsonville, Maryland, would be one of those sanctuaries.

Mildred, her husband, and their three children were the first to live in the four-bedroom home on Seneca Drive in an area that had been named Arrowhead. Simpsonville has since been incorporated into Columbia.

"It was a new development," Mildred, a lifelong resident of Howard County, remembers. "We had half an acre, a beautiful lot. It had all been farmland before the houses were built."

Just eight homes lined Seneca Drive when the Treveys moved in. Even at that, the family had to work hard to clear their large lot. "There were a lot of rocks and stones there. I think I pulled up enough rocks to build a quarry," she laughs. "All of that part of Howard County was full of rocks and quarries anyhow. I was surprised they could even build houses because it was solid rock."

Mildred lived there for fourteen years. She worked for many years at a local radio station where she was office manager and secretary to the president. Later, she held a job at a British car distributor. Even though she is now past retirement age, she works part-time for a food distributor.

For the first five years, life in the Arrowhead area was normal for the Treveys. However, all that changed when Mildred and her husband divorced. By that time, her daughter had married and her two stepsons had gone out on their own. Since it was a big house, Mildred asked a long-time and recently widowed friend, Margaret, to move in with her own two young children, which she did.

But their lives would be anything but uneventful. Mildred doesn't recall anything out of the ordinary until several years after Margaret and her daughters moved in. "That's when we started to hear odd things. There would be footsteps up and down the hallway. They'd go down to the front door, but you'd never hear the door open. They just stopped. We heard it any number of times, but after a while we just didn't pay much attention to it."

The house had a carpeted hallway but hardwood floors underneath and in the various rooms. The bedrooms had scatter rugs on the floors. A small foyer with a solid slate floor was just inside the front door. Sometimes the stealthy footfalls provided some unintended surprises for houseguests.

"My friends June and Ed stayed with me for about three months while they were waiting for their apartment to be finished. I had a little dog at that time, a poodle that weighed about twelve pounds. Well, June said one morning, 'My, for a little dog, Sylvester makes a lot of noise going up and down the hall!' I had to tell her the dog had never gotten off my bed," Mildred says.

A light switch in the hallway of the lower level provided additional puzzlement.

"When you went downstairs to the family room, you could make a left turn in the little hallway. There were doors to the bathroom, the laundry room and the fourth bedroom. There was a little light switch in the hallway. I never saw the switch move, but I did see the light go on and off by itself. No one was near it. I hired an electrician to come out for something else and I had him check that switch and the wiring. He said there was nothing wrong with it. He asked me why I wanted it checked. I said, oh, just check it. There was no sense in telling him and have him broadcast it all over the world."

The misbehaving light became something of a running joke.

"Gus was the man my friend Margaret went with for so long. Once we were sitting in the kitchen and Margaret's girls were going to bed—they had the bedroom downstairs. Margaret reminded them to turn off the light in the hall. Gus piped up and said it won't make any difference because 'somebody' will come along turn it back on. He didn't put it that delicately, but that's what he meant," Mildred chuckles.

Even under ordinary circumstances, what is *perceived* to have taken place and what has *actually* taken place can be easily confused. But that is especially true when one believes that she is living in a haunted place. It happened to Mildred Trevey in, of all places, her very own kitchen. Her friend Margaret's oldest daughter was eating breakfast. Mildred and Margaret were also at the table.

"Mom," the young girl blurted out, "I just saw that frying pan move! It raised up."

Because the older women had experiences with unusual events in the house, they didn't want to alarm the girl.

"No," Margaret told her daughter. "Many times when you look at something long enough it seems to you like it moves."

"No, mom," the girl replied, shaking her head. "I saw it move!"

Mildred Trevey understood why they had to tell the white lie, but she also knew the girl just might have been right. "I had seen the same thing a few times before," she says.

Unexplained noises and moving objects are often associated with poltergeists, literally the German for "noisy ghosts." In some cases, a possible haunting moves from this type of activity to . . . something more. For Mildred, that change came about when she caught sight of a distinctly human form.

"At least twice, when Margaret and I were in the den watching television, I looked up and saw a shadow in the doorway. As fast as I saw it, it disappeared. It was always a man. Now when that happened, my toy poodle jumped up and ran over to me. He'd curl against my legs shaking as though he was chilled,"

Mildred recalls, adding that at other times a sort of formless, gray mist floated in the air. She thinks the vapor might have been connected to the man she saw.

Margaret had her own eerie run-in with the male specter. Two sets of steps in the foyer at the front door led either upward to the main, first floor or down to the lower level. Once, as Margaret walked up the steps to the main floor, she looked up to see a shadowy form with a distinctly male appearance. Before the figure vanished, she noted that he wore what seemed to be an old felt hat on his head.

When Margaret later related the story to her, Mildred found the description particularly interesting. "I never saw my dad without a hat, ever," she says.

An inevitable task in such circumstances is to try and establish the identity of the entity haunting one's home. And that was no less the case with this modern home on Seneca Avenue. Although she was ultimately unsuccessful at establishing a link between a formerly-living person and the ghost in her home, Mildred Trevey had some theories.

"We understood that on the ground where my house and the one next to it stood, there had been some violence. I don't know the specific details, but the story was that a man had murdered his wife there. But it was never proven. It was just a story that had come down through the years," she says. A farmstead had stood where the Arrowhead development was later built.

The more likely explanation Mildred thinks, is that the specter the women saw may have been either Margaret's or her own father "keeping an eye on us."

"We often smelled cigar smoke in the family room. It would be quite strong at times. No one was in the house that smoked cigars. Margaret said that her father used to smoke those big, black Havana cigars. She thought it was his presence that we felt."

It might have been Mildred's father, however, because he wore a hat when he was alive, as did the specter Margaret saw. He died shortly after the Treveys moved into their home.

But there is an even stronger reason that Mildred believes there was a protectiveness about the wandering soul in her home—it was gentle. "Our ghost was friendly. It never did anything to us. Somebody told me it was probably a poltergeist, but I don't think it was because they can be very nasty. I never felt threatened at any time. Maybe I didn't have enough sense at the time because I don't know how I'd feel now."

Nevertheless, there was one summer evening that she thought her pleasant guest had decided to take a nasty turn. The house had a walk-out patio from the den/family room on the lower level. On this night, Mildred, Margaret and her friend Gus, and her other friends June and Ed had just wrapped up a cookout on the grill, which was on the patio reached through a set of sliding glass doors. It was just beginning to get dark—around eight thirty or nine o'clock, Mildred says—and the small company had retired indoors to listen to music.

"We put a stack of records on the stereo," Mildred recalls of that day before the advent of CDs. "We were talking and listening to the music when the fireplace tongs kind of moved; they 'jangled' a little bit. June asked Ed if he'd seen that. He said he hadn't. I said oh, maybe the air was moving, but we didn't have air conditioning."

June insisted she'd seen them move. But that was but prelude to what happened next. An Early American-style rocker situated next to the fireplace started to gently sway back and forth, as if someone had just sat down in it. At the same time, the chair began inching toward a corner of the room.

"It couldn't get around that corner of paneling," Mildred says. The rocker armrests struck against the wall. "The day I moved there were still pieces chipped out of the arms. The scars were also on the edge of the paneling where the wooden arms kept banging against it. I guess it must have rocked like that for twenty or twenty-five minutes."

Margaret's friend Gus got up from where he was sitting and went over to sit down in the rocker.

"He said 'I'll fix this s.o.b.' " Mildred says, "but it threw him out right into the middle of the floor. Margaret and I were in hysterics, we were laughing so hard we had tears running down our faces."

Although uproarious amusement is hardly the response one would expect in such a situation, Mildred and her circle of friends were quite used to such abrupt activity. "We were laughing because it didn't surprise us at all. Margaret's sister was a medium so she'd been living with the supernatural all her life."

June was petrified, Mildred says. "She was sitting on the sofa closest to that corner. I said, June, it's coming after you because you don't believe in it. We nearly scared that poor girl to death!"

As the rocker continued its erratic behavior, the small group got their next surprise when the stereo plug sailed out of the electrical socket. "It was just like somebody took hold of it and pulled it straight out. I said, our ghost doesn't like the music we're playing. I plugged it back in, but about five minutes later, it came straight out again, like you'd taken your hand and pulled it. Then the fireplace shovel and brush came right out of their holder and scattered on the floor."

Margaret's two children were roused from their sleep in the nearby bedroom by the noise. "They wanted to know what all the noise was . . . and we told them we were having a party," Mildred says.

After that episode, the house was quiet for a while. There were still the occasional footsteps and hovering gray mists, but nothing nearly so disturbing as that night in the family den.

That was not to be the end of it.

Enter the "crying woman."

"Margaret hadn't been working because she had been ill. She told me she heard a woman crying. She said it quite unnerved her. Now, she was a complete believer in the supernatural and I thought perhaps she was hearing an animal. But then, once around midnight, I was in bed and awake and I heard it, too. Now, I thought maybe it was Julie, the girl next door. I went outside to see if she was crying or something, to make sure she was okay. But there was nobody home there. I just couldn't place it. It sounded like it could be outside, although I was never really sure. Margaret heard it three or four times," Mildred says today, still not entirely certain who or what caused the weeping her friend said she heard.

Mildred Trevey now says her decision to sell her home in 1978 was "one of the worst ones I ever made in my life." Although the haunting was not a factor in her decision to leave, she was honest in telling the buyers, Bob and his wife Betty, what she and others had experienced. Surprisingly, Betty said it didn't bother her because she'd had similar types of experiences.

And it seems that the gentle haunting continued for the new owners. But this time a new element was added.

Mildred had given the new owners her pet Siamese cat, Koko, because her new home was quite near a busy highway and she was worried that the cat would wander onto it. Regrettably, someone poisoned the cat just six months later. It was buried at the end of the backyard where, Mildred notes, a veritable pet cemetery had developed over the years she and her children lived there.

"Their two little grandsons were visiting when both of them said they'd seen Koko in the laundry room," Mildred says. She had always fed Koko from bowls in the corner of the laundry room.

"Bob told them they couldn't have seen Koko because he'd gone to 'cat heaven.' But Betty said she didn't know if they might really have seen him because she had felt him walk across the bed many mornings after Bob had gone to work."

Later that same summer, the couple's daughter, son-in-law and their boys went on vacation and Betty agreed to keep their cat while they were out of town.

"Betty thought she would feed her own 'boarder' in the same place," Mildred remembers being told. "But she said the cat would go only as far as the water heater, which was also in the laundry room, then stop and arch her back and hiss. She just wouldn't go any farther, so Betty had to feed her in another part of the laundry room. She also told me that when she kept her neighbor's golden retriever, the dog wouldn't sleep on the bed in one of the guest rooms. It was in that same room that we heard strange noises when we lived there."

Were the animals sensitive to some unseen forces in that house? Was Koko the cat still crouched beside her food bowl . . . even though she was in 'cat heaven'? Mildred thinks that it was possible.

Bob and Betty sold the home in 1984 and moved away. Mildred Trevey has lost track of who now owns her old home. "Perhaps the ghosts moved when the house was sold the last time," she sighs. It is apparent that the mystery continues to fascinate her though over two decades have passed since the last of the extraordinary events she described occurred.

Her memories of life on Seneca Drive remain warm and vivid.

"It was a beautiful home; I wish I was still there. I was never afraid in that house. The ghost never did anything to us. I have no idea of who it was, but except for the crying woman and the time it didn't like the records we were playing, the ghost seemed to be friendly."

She wonders if the spirit could have indeed been either her own father or Margaret's dad keeping an eye on them.

Perhaps Mildred Trevey's regrets come also in knowing she may never solve that enigma.

The Story Man

Not all endangered species are members of the animal and plant kingdoms. A persuasive argument can be prepared that in the twenty-first century we also face the imminent loss of the informal sharing of stories, particularly those unique within each family or those which have been passed down through the generations.

One doesn't need to look far to discover that other priorities occupy whatever time the modern family has to itself. Yet, in the face of unprecedented threats to American society perhaps it is more important now than ever before to understand who we are and where we came from, and how that has been shaped by the stories kept within limited familial or geographical confines.

In other words, our stories make us who we are. And we must know who we are if we are to make intelligent decisions about the future.

There have always been those resilient souls who have endeavored in their own corners of North America to preserve their regional traditions and legends by assembling those primarily oral tales, writing them down and then passing them along to anyone willing to sit still for a few minutes.

And listen.

Listen, for example, to Michael Renegar.

He is one of those people.

A soft-spoken native of East Bend, North Carolina, Michael has lived in that hamlet of 619 folks hard by the Yadkin River all of his thirty-two years; well, all of it except for the few years he attended Appalachian State University in Boone. He was a history major thinking about being a schoolteacher, but it "didn't work out . . . I ran out of money." Besides, he quickly realized he didn't have the patience to work with teenagers.

Now, he's in a partnership of musicians who write and play gospel, country, and old time rock 'n' roll. Buddy Holly's niece has recorded a demo of their music. He's also a photographer specializing in promotional work and portraits.

But it's his love for history, and particularly North Carolina history, that motivates him the most. His special passion has been in collecting the legends and stories indigenous to his patch of earth, that part of North Carolina west of Winston-Salem to the Tennessee border and north up to Virginia. There you'll

find towns like Roaring Gap, Deep Gap, and Lowgap. There's Tobaccoville. Andy
Griffith's hometown and the real-life model for Mayberry is Mount Airy, and that's
up in Surry County, one county north of where Michael lives.

The region is rich with lore—Daniel Boone explored it when it was still wilderness, and it's where that poor boy who was going to die, Tom Dula (Dooley),
paid with his life for the crime that became the basis for the famous folk song.

He's a particular enthusiast for tales of the supernatural in that mountainous
northwest section of his home state. It's an area, he says, where children sometimes still don't go out to play for fear of the boogeyman. Elders, who are reluctant
to discuss such things with outsiders, take the suggestion of "haints" very seriously.

"When I was little, my cousins and I used to sit around outside on summer
evenings and listen to the ghost stories the older folks told," Michael recalls. "My
great grandpa on my dad's side was named Shober. They said he could really tell
some good tales. I never heard them straight from him, but some of the stories
I have are things he told my older cousins, my parents, and their siblings when
they were much younger. Stories about the Cox ghost light and a headless hitchhiker.

"After he passed away, a young boy and girl were walking through the woods.
They came out of the woods and saw my uncle walking down the road. They told
my uncle that they'd heard something in the woods. My uncle told them that
was just great-grandpa Shober taking down his still.

" 'But we thought he was dead.'

" 'He is,' my uncle replied."

Not unlike most teenagers, when Michael was that age he began to doubt what
adults told him and lost his interest in ghost stories. It wasn't until he left for
Appalachian State that his interest was rekindled. "Things haven't been the same
since," he says.

He formed an unofficial club at the university called the "Ghost Chasers" and
in small groups they'd visit haunted places in western North Carolina. He even
lived in a haunted residence hall on campus and wrote of his experiences for the
college newspaper.

Michael's zeal for the supernatural "haints" of his region is stronger than ever.
He's made it one of his life's missions to preserve in written form as many of the
stories he's heard aloud as he can. He also knows that it's getting more difficult
with each passing year.

"There's just not much storytelling going on. A lot of the older folks in my
family have passed on. We don't get together as much as we used to, people seem
busier now and have their own things going on. There aren't many family get-
togethers anymore. It's sad because I think many of those stories will be gone.
Who knows how many already have been lost. That's why I collect them and write
them down. To keep them alive."

The singer/storyteller says there may be several unique characteristics of North
Carolina ghost stories. There are an abundance of ghost lights in North Carolina
and lots of vanishing hitchhikers.

"I've heard of five vanishing hitchhikers within just a hundred miles of my
home. There's one that's a little bit different, too. That one's out on old Highway
64 in Randolph County. The story is that a woman was driving too fast down a
hill through there and she ran off the road and was killed. Now if you're on that

old highway and you're going too fast, that girl will show up in the seat next to you and tell you to slow down. Personally, I'd be afraid to see if it's true by driving fast down that hill. That ghost might show up and tell me to slow down. You might get in a wreck just from the shock of it all."

The custom of moonshining plays a substantial role in some of the stories, Michael says. He tells one anecdote of a moonshiner near Yadkinville whom the law was chasing. He crashed at the end of a dead-end road noted for two trees growing together in the form of a cross. Ever since then anyone driving down that road and turning around to go back will be followed by the dead man in his phantom automobile. If you stop, he'll stop, too. As far as Michael knows, no one has gone back to see what kind of game that ghost is playing.

"A lot of the stories are based on mountain lore, but then, of course, you find that in Tennessee, too. Then, too, I think there's also a particular flair of the storytellers here," he says.

When Michael Renegar is asked to tell some of his favorite stories, these are often the ones he chooses:

Valle Crucis is a quiet village, named after the cross formed by the rivers there in the North Carolina mountains. Located on old North Carolina Route 194, the town is best known for the Mast General Store, Camp Broadstone, and St. John's Episcopal Church.

The small wooden church sits on an isolated knoll, reached by navigating a dirt road. The Anglican Mission opened St. John's more than a century ago, but its congregation has moved on. The Mission keeps up the building; opening it occasionally for weddings, reunions, and other limited functions.

A ghost lives there, too.

The story of the church is that many years ago, a young minister arrived at St. John's with visions of reviving the congregation. The minister's new ways and ideas didn't go over with the simple folk of Valle Crucis. Attendance at the church fell until only a handful of people showed up for Sunday services.

The minister couldn't understand why he'd failed. Depression overwhelmed him, and one day he took a rope, fashioned a noose, and hanged himself, although just where the deed took place is in dispute. It might have been in the bell tower or from one of the three big trees in front of the church. Now his broken-hearted spirit wanders around St. John's still trying to understand why his congregation left.

The story of the young reverend has been retold for so long that it's become a popular legend.

Unfortunately, the story is not true.

The preacher who is the subject of the tale is Reverend William Skiles. He was neither new nor young when he came to Valle Crucis and St. John's. He didn't drive away his congregation with his fresh views, nor did he commit suicide. He didn't even die in Valle Crucis. Reverend Skiles moved to Linville to help care for a man wounded in the Civil War. He died there on December 8, 1861, probably of cancer or consumption.

If the original story is not true, does that mean there is no ghost at St. John's?

It may not be a spectral, suicidal minister, but something strange goes on at the church. Too many people have seen and heard things that can't easily be explained.

And whatever it is, it scares the daylights out of people.

A group of Appalachian State University students left the church in a hurry one night when every one of their flashlights went out at the same time.

Another student drove his girlfriend out to Valle Crucis after dinner. Dusk had fallen, but there was still enough light to see by. Mitch turned down the old road that led to St. John's and parked beside some bushes near the church. He smiled at Rhonda as he shut off the car engine. He leaned over to kiss her.

"Look!" Rhonda gasped.

"What?"

"There's a man watching us," she said. Rhonda pointed out the window. "Over there at the church."

A man stood on the church steps. Though Mitch couldn't make out the details of his face, he could tell he had been disgusted by what the two college students had been about to do. The man wore a black coat and hat. He turned his back and walked into the church.

Mitch felt guilty. He hadn't meant to offend anyone. He hadn't even realized they'd parked that near the church.

"Must be a preacher from Holy Cross," Mitch said. "I'd better go apologize."

Rhonda protested that she was scared and wanted to get away.

Mitch ignored her, got out of the car, and walked over to the church. The lights were on inside. He went up the steps and through the door.

"Hello," he called. "Hello, Reverend."

The chapel seemed to be vacant.

He looked around, walked up to the pulpit, but there was simply no one there. Puzzling. The door was unlocked, the lights on, and he'd seen the man go inside.

That's when he felt a coldness beginning to encircle him. It seemed to go right through him. It made the hair on the back of his neck stand up.

"I'm sorry for what you saw!" he cried out loud as he ran back outside and to his car.

"Mitch, what happened?" Rhonda asked as he jumped behind the wheel and turned the key.

"I apologized."

He slammed the car into reverse.

But he didn't add that he'd made the apology to an empty church.

As he drove off, Mitch looked in the rearview mirror. The lights of the church were off, but he again saw the man in black on the top steps, watching. Mitch stomped on the gas.

What Mitch and Rhonda saw that night, and what others have seen and heard, has become part of the legend of St. John's. Much to the caretaker's chagrin.

The year 1919 began more peacefully than had the previous year. Although civil conflict raged in Russia between the Bolsheviks and the White Army, the fighting that would later be known as World War One, the war to end all wars, had come to an end in November 1918. The American soldiers—doughboys—started coming home shortly after the armistice.

For one family in East Bend, North Carolina, there would be no happy ending.

Shortly after rumors reached them that the war would soon be over, they learned their son John had been killed in France as his unit attempted to storm a German trench. His body could not be recovered.

The young soldier's mother suffered a breakdown. His father tried his best to be strong and show how proud he was of his son's willingness to sacrifice his life for his country. But he could not hide his pain.

John's younger brother, Jacob, simply refused to accept the truth that his big brother would never come home.

Weeks passed. The war ended. The family's life went on as best it could. John's mother slowly recovered. His final words to her before he left gave her some comfort: *Don't worry, mother. No matter what, I'll always be with you.*

Jacob continued to hope that it was all a mistake. His parents worried about him. They told him what the army had said, that John's unit had been destroyed. Still, they were gentle with him for they did not want to crush the boy's spirit.

One late winter day, Jacob's good friend Everett came over to play checkers. The weather was unsettled, a strong wind whipped the clouds across the sky. The day grew dark as a thunderstorm rolled in bringing with it a cold rain. Everett stayed for supper and waited for the rain to let up.

But the storm grew ever more intense. Peals of thunder crashed around the house like artillery shells.

Mother served the meal. Jacob asked the blessing which, as always, included a prayer that his brother return safely home.

While the menfolk began eating, mother walked around to the stove where she had a pot of stew simmering. She pushed back the curtains and saw that the rain was still heavy, and now mixed with sleet. But through the lightning flashes, she saw something else, something familiar. A horse and its rider were coming down the road.

Mother dropped the pot of stew. Her hands flew to her mouth.

"Dearest God!" she cried, tears rolling down her cheek.

Her husband rushed to her side.

"What is it?"

She pointed out the window. He looked. Tears welled in his eyes.

Jacob and Everett crowded under the adults and peeked out the window. Little Jacob's face lit up.

"It's Johnny! It's Johnny! See, I told ya' he'd come home."

"Is it possible," father said, holding his head in his hands. He hugged his wife as they cried in one another's arms.

The small group watched as John got off his horse, opened the barn door, and led the animal inside.

"I'm going to meet him," Jacob yelled.

"Sure, go ahead," father called out. "No, wait I'll go. It's sleeting out."

He wiped his eyes and took a deep breath.

"I'll take care of his horse and send him on in here."

Father pulled on his heavy coat and turned up the collar as he tumbled out the door.

Minutes passed.

"Where is he?" Jacob demanded, watching through the window all the while.

He saw his father come out of the barn and head back to the house.

"Where's Johnny?" Jacob persisted as his father came through the door.

His father's face was pale. He shook his head.

"I—I don't know," he wavered. He pointed to the barn. "He ain't in there. And there ain't no horse."

Mother cried.

Jacob couldn't understand. He went out to look for himself.

Only Everett seemed to recognize what might have happened. They all wanted to see John so much that their minds had played a collective trick on them. True, he'd seen the figure on horseback, too, but he'd been caught up in the joy of the moment.

The sleet turned to snow. Everett decided to stay overnight. Mother and father went off to bed, but Everett and Jacob stayed up late, talking about what they'd seen. Jacob still could not understand why his brother had been there one moment and gone the next.

Everett made himself a pallet with two blankets, close to the roaring fireplace. He curled up and soon fell asleep.

He awoke with a start. The fire had burned down to orange embers and the room was dark. He got up to add some logs but quickly drew back. Someone was with him in the room. A presence.

Suddenly flames leaped from the dying embers. John stood before the fireplace, his arms reaching toward the warmth of the blaze as if trying to shake off the cold.

Everett knew there was no mistake this time. It was John. He saw his face clearly in the firelight, he saw his peaceful expression. He saw—the uniform.

The tattered uniform.

The bullet holes.

Everett didn't really know what to do, so he waited.

Presently, the flames burned down but then leaped up again.

The young doughboy was gone.

Now Everett moved. He searched in vain for some way into or out of the house that he did not know about. There was no one in the old house except for his pal Jacob and his parents.

Everett stoked the fire, then went into Jacob's room.

Jacob saw his friend sitting in the rocking chair when he woke up early the next morning.

"What's wrong, Everett?"

The boy did not reply, but quietly gathered up his few things and left. He didn't tell anyone about what had happened that night for many, many years.

The house is gone. A church softball field is there now. Few are left alive who remember the boy who wanted to be with his family, always.

The Story Man never knew John, of course. But Michael Renegar so cherishes this tale of familial devotion he refuses to let it disappear from the hearts of folks in his native North Carolina.

Katie James

Susan Woolf really didn't know what to expect on that hot, Oklahoma summer night a quarter-century ago. A senior history major at Southwestern State College at Weatherford, she was especially interested in the lore and legends of Oklahoma. The last thing she suspected was that the evening marked the beginning of her efforts to solve a seventy-year-old murder mystery . . . and in the process confront her own skepticism about the existence of such things as ghosts and haunted places.

Several weeks earlier, a classmate had told Woolf that there was a place not far from Weatherford where "you could see a ghost." Although she didn't pay close attention to the details, except something about a "dead woman," her curiosity was aroused. A self-described "smart-aleck" at that time of her life, Woolf really didn't expect a "real" ghost to show up. But she agreed to go anyway.

The weather was still hot and sticky even at nine o'clock at night. Woolf asked her friend to drive her car. He knew the way, after all, and besides, she didn't know how stalwart a ghost hunter she would turn out to be.

Woolf climbed into the passenger seat and set off with her friend for an area about six miles northeast of Weatherford, near a bridge over Big Deer Creek.

"We drove to a portion of a farm field that abutted a creek bed," Woolf remembered. "The field was cleared, and we drove in and turned to the right, parking the car facing the creek bed, a deep cut-out, sort of a small canyon. Both sides were heavily overgrown with trees and brush.

"The theory was that one drove in, parked facing the creek bed, and waited for the ghost to appear. I recall being told that if you were brave enough to await the ghost's approach to some close proximity, then the car's ignition, radio, and electrical system would fail.

"We turned in and parked and waited for not very long, around ten or fifteen minutes. . . ."

Woolf's skepticism was unfounded. Something did show up. She remembers it as a luminous blue light of "no particular shape or description, rising from out of the creek bed and slowly coming toward us."

The light was clearly visible . . . and coming directly toward them, across the farm field. That was close enough. Woolf told her friend to start the car and leave. Fortunately, the ignition worked and they sped away.

While that one experience with a mystery light might have been enough for most people, Woolf decided that her innate curiosity was stronger than any fear of what might lurk in the old creek bed.

"We returned the next afternoon," Woolf said. "I wanted to try to find out what had caused the light. We checked the trees and other vegetation in the stream bed. We could find no obvious source."

There were no electric wires anywhere near where the light danced toward them, nor anything else that might have produced what is commonly known as a will-o'-the-wisp, or marsh gas. They didn't notice any great quantities of rotting vegetation, sometimes said to be responsible for visible gaseous vapors.

During their search, however, they did find something interesting. A small plaque was affixed to the old bridge:

"Dead Woman's Crossing, 1905"

So her friend had been correct. A "dead woman" had something to do with this place on Big Deer Creek.

Susan Woolf found the mystery deepening: Who was this anonymous woman? Could it have been her ghost that haunted this otherwise pastoral scene?

The answers to those questions came slowly. During a lengthy, personal investigation, Woolf uncovered the woman's identity and the circumstances of her death . . . one of the Oklahoma Territory's grisliest unsolved murders.

Woolf never returned to the bridge to see if the ghost would reappear. Not out of fear, she emphasized, but because of her real-life quest to solve an old murder.

"The fact is, we were becoming absorbed in what we were finding out about the woman who had given the crossing its name. And, too, I think it was because the more we learned about what had happened in that field, the more disinclined we were to trifle with whatever might have been there."

If ever a ghost had the right to haunt, the spirit of Katie James should wander the banks of Big Deer Creek forever. She was twenty-nine in 1905 and the mother of an infant child, Lulu Belle, when she was brutally murdered, her body dumped near Dead Woman's Crossing. But the true identity of her murderer is still unknown.

From a distance of nearly nine decades, the facts are not easy to ascertain. Even in 1905, many pieces to the puzzling murder were missing. What Woolf found out though, and later published in an issue of the *Chronicles of Oklahoma*, was the compelling story of a woman mysteriously slain . . . and the origin of an enduring Oklahoma ghost legend.

Katie DeWitt James was not a happy woman on July 7, 1905, when she and fourteen-month-old Lulu Belle boarded the train at Custer City, Oklahoma. Although she was a respected member of the community and a former schoolteacher, her marriage was crumbling.

On July 6, she had filed for divorce from her husband of four years, Martin Luther James. The reasons for the divorce are not known, but they must have been serious enough to cause Mrs. James to want to leave Custer City for a period of time. She was on her way to Ripley, in north central Oklahoma, to spend some time with the family of her cousin, Wellington Knight.

Martin James was not at the station to see his wife off. Katie's father, Henry DeWitt, had traveled the thirty miles from his farm near Taloga to bid farewell to his daughter and granddaughter. It would be the last time he saw Katie alive.

Katie James and her daughter never made it to her cousin's home in Ripley, but their disappearance wasn't reported until her father became concerned when he didn't hear from her. It was her habit to write to her father nearly every day whenever she traveled. Several weeks had passed and DeWitt had not received a single letter from Katie to let him know she had arrived safely at her destination.

Strangely, the record doesn't show that DeWitt ever contacted Martin James. He was still on the farm that Katie had homesteaded before her marriage—and which would have reverted to her after her divorce. Rather, DeWitt went to the state capital, Oklahoma City, to ask Sheriff Garrison for help in finding a detective who might assist him in finding his daughter and grandchild.

Garrison recommended a detective, Sam Bartell. He and DeWitt decided to begin the search in Clinton, the first large city Katie James would have passed through on the train to Ripley. No one remembered a woman with a baby getting off the train in Clinton on the date Katie disappeared.

While Henry DeWitt had to return to his ranch, Bartell went on to Weatherford, next on the train's scheduled stops. He got there on July 28, 1905. A wide-open city of 15,000, Weatherford boasted eighteen saloons and seventeen gambling houses. In this raucous milieu almost any activity—legal or otherwise—was tolerated, if not actively promoted.

Bartell met with his first success. A woman answering Katie James's description had been seen in Weatherford in the company of one Mrs. Fannie Norton of Clinton. According to these accounts, Katie James, little Lulu Belle, and Mrs. Norton had spent the night with Mrs. Norton's brother-in-law, William Moore. The following morning, Mrs. Norton, with Katie and the child, had left the Moore home in a buggy heading in a generally northeast direction. That was the last time anyone saw Katie James. Mrs. Norton returned to Weatherford alone, returned the rig to the livery and took the next train back to Clinton.

Katie had evidently met Fannie Norton on the train. For unknown reasons, she had gotten off the train in Weatherford with Mrs. Norton and agreed to spend the night with her at Moore's house outside town.

Little is known about the background of Fannie Norton. During Susan Woolf's modern-day investigation, she found evidence that Mrs. Norton had a reputation of having been a prostitute. That only deepens the mystery as to why a woman of Katie's upstanding reputation would strike up an acquaintanceship with a woman of such dubious character.

Detective Bartell discovered the route the women had taken when they left William Moore's house and followed it. Near Big Deer Creek he found a witness who had seen Mrs. Norton's buggy in a field near the creek. Later, according to Bartell's testimony, Mrs. Norton stopped at the farm home of Peter Birscheid and left a baby with them, assuring the Birscheids she would pick up the child when "she returned from a trip." Katie James was not with her. The child was Lulu Belle. Her clothing and blanket were stained with blood. When Bartell later returned to town and examined the buggy Mrs. Norton rented, he found bloodstains on one wheel.

Bartell telegraphed Henry DeWitt of his findings and the baby's location—she was still with the Birscheids—and returned to Oklahoma City. He had determined that after returning to Clinton to gather up her four children, Mrs. Norton had gone on to Guthrie, Oklahoma, where she enrolled her children in a private school, and went on herself to Shawnee.

Some time later, Bartell met DeWitt in Shawnee and reported their case to the police who found and arrested Mrs. Norton. There is some evidence that Mrs. Norton was not unknown to authorities. She had been accused of shooting a Weatherford bartender in the back with her own .38 caliber pistol, but had been acquitted for some reason.

She admitted knowing Katie James, but told a "rambling story" about the events of July 7 and 8. She claimed Katie had gone off with a man in a covered wagon when they reached Big Deer Creek. A small woman dressed in poor clothing, Mrs. Norton adamantly denied murdering Mrs. James, but Bartell was convinced otherwise.

He would never have the chance to prove it.

As she sat unguarded in a jail corridor, Mrs. Norton started vomiting and lost consciousness. Less than an hour latter Fannie Norton was dead. An autopsy showed she had taken poison, either morphine, cocaine, or strychnine, according to various sources.

But Katie James was still missing. A murder had apparently been committed, but still there was no hard evidence of the crime.

Rewards were offered for finding Katie—alive or dead; the territorial governor said the state would pay $300 for information leading to the "arrest of the person or persons who murdered Mrs. Katie James."

Two separate, ultimately unsuccessful, searches were mounted along both branches of Big Deer Creek near where Fannie Norton was last seen with Mrs. James and her daughter. Then, on August 31, 1905, nearly two months later, her remains were found.

The discovery was purely by chance. A lawyer named G. W. Cornell had taken his boys fishing at the creek and stumbled across the skeleton when he got out of the buggy. The remains were in plain sight near a well-used wagon crossing. The skull, with a bullet hole behind the right ear, was several feet away from the rest of the body. A .38 caliber bullet was still lodged in the skull, and the revolver itself was found nearby. Buggy tracks were still visible near the body. It looked like Katie James had been shot while she rode in the buggy and her body pushed out.

Lawyer Cornell's son remembered the event decades later both because of its inherent drama . . . and because his father used the reward money to buy him a pony.

Henry DeWitt identified his daughter's remains through the worn but recognizable clothing, her hat, a comb she wore in her hair, her shoes, and a gold wedding band upon her left hand. She was buried in Lot 1, Block 35, of the Weatherford Cemetery.

The circumstances of her brutal murder, however, were not so easy to discover. A coroner's inquest concluded on September 2, three days after the body was discovered, that Katie James died "by means of a gunshot wound fired from a .38 caliber pistol in the hands of Mrs. Fannie Norton . . . on or about the eighth day of July 1905." Robbery was the motive, the coroner found. No other culprits were named, but there was plenty of speculation.

Why wasn't the body found during two earlier, organized searches? The reward money even motivated a number of individuals to conduct their own surveys near Big Deer Creek. Yet the body was found in the open, without any attempt at concealment, in an area that had been subjected to earlier sweeps by investigators.

Did Fannie Norton have an accomplice? The most likely candidate, townspeople suspected, was Katie's estranged husband, Martin James. Newspaper accounts say he didn't take part in any of the searches and showed little remorse when his wife's body was found. However, he had airtight alibis for the time of his wife's murder.

A court eventually awarded him half of Katie's estate, the other half going to little Lulu Belle. In March 1907 Martin married a seventeen-year-old girl, was given custody of Lulu Belle, and soon thereafter sold the farm and left Oklahoma. Neither he nor his daughter was ever heard from again.

The rest of the many questions remain unanswered.

Why did Katie James go with Fannie Norton in the first place? The women were apparent strangers to one another. Perhaps the women were drawn together on the train ride because each was having marital problems. If Mrs. Norton was in league with Martin James, maybe she deliberately struck up an acquaintance-ship with the young mother. But Katie was hardly a naive girl. She was a home-steader, former schoolteacher, and respected member of the community. At the age of twenty-nine, with a young daughter to care for, it seems very strange that she would change her plans so dramatically by going off with a woman she had known for less than a day. Yet that is what the evidence shows.

Was robbery really the motive, as the coroner concluded? Testimony suggested that Mrs. Norton had seen Katie open her purse and thus might have spied the twenty-three dollars she was carrying. There is no indication whether any money was found in Katie's purse lying near her body. If robbery was really the motive, why was the five-dollar gold ring still on the corpse's finger?

As the brutal murderess she was portrayed to be, Fannie Norton behaved oddly. When she was arrested in Shawnee, she was nervous and gave conflicting stories of her relationship with Katie James.

And why commit suicide? A month had passed since the murder and no body had been found. She was certainly not afraid to resort to violence, as her acquittal in the bartender shooting attested. And, she had four children to support in a private school. Unless, the speculation was, she had an accomplice, someone she was so afraid of that she took her own life rather than being forced to confess.

Did Martin James know Fannie Norton? Was he the mastermind behind the murder? He had an alibi for the time of the murder. However, he certainly had a lot to lose with the divorce. The farm would have reverted to his wife, Lulu Belle would have gone with her mother, and he would have been left with very little. A possibility exists that he entered into a conspiracy with Mrs. Norton and, perhaps, another unidentified person to kill his wife. Virtually nothing is known about James's personal life or his acquaintances before his marriage. It's conceivable that he had known Mrs. Norton, a woman of dubious reputation to say the least. She may have been a prostitute . . . as well as a killer.

The likelihood of an accomplice is strengthened by the fact that the field near Big Deer Creek had been gone over at least twice by posses searching for Katie's remains. The body may have been concealed by a person or persons unknown and, after Mrs. Norton's suicide, returned to where it was eventually discovered.

Susan Woolf's original intention was to find out why a bridge over a rural Oklahoma creek was called "Dead Woman's Crossing." In the process, Woolf thinks far more was accomplished:

"I do not know if the ghost still appears at the crossing, although I think it does not. I think there was a ghost, and that it is no more. I had the very strong feeling that we were researching something that was intended to let the woman rest. It was because of that feeling that we worked so hard to try to solve the murder. I honestly believe that the ghost ceased its appearance, at least during that time, because something was being done to let it rest."

But there was another incident that caused Woolf to wonder whether the ghost of Katie James was not somehow closer to her than she suspected:

"I was spending one weekend at my parents' during that summer when we were tracking down the mystery of Katie James. I got up in the middle of the night . . . I happened to glance into the mirror that was on my dresser. I have the distinct recollection of having seen a woman's face in the mirror. I recall looking at the whatever-it-was for a minute or so, and then calmly going back to bed.

"For me to have calmly looked at a disembodied head in a mirror and then gone back to sleep is incredible, as I suspect it would be for most people. I must admit that I have a great deal of difficulty in admitting to such, or to my belief in such an experience. But, were I under oath on a witness stand, I would have to swear that I definitely recall seeing something in that mirror and being absolutely unafraid."

Woolf doesn't know if the image was that of Katie James. She does know that she saw something that night. But, she hastens to add, "I have never, ever seen such a thing since."

A dancing blue light that frightened two college students, an unsolved murder at the turn of the century, and a ghostly face in a mirror. All mysterious events that may show how a restless ghost found peace at last . . . through the tireless efforts of a sympathetic historian named Susan Woolf.

Abiding Love

Miss Fenwick's Curse

The eerie cry of swooping sea birds is not the only sound some folks hear on Johns Island, southwest of Charleston, South Carolina. Since before the days of the American Revolution, the ghost of the beautiful daughter of Edward Fenwick has stirred more than the imaginations of those who encountered her at old Fenwick Hall.

How the lovely and unconventional Miss Fenwick came to haunt her ancestral home is the story of an ill-fated romance, a tyrannical father, and the legacy of one of the legendary families of which she was a part.

The Hall was the pre-Revolution home of the British Fenwick family, wealthy planters celebrated for their fast thoroughbreds and beautiful women. The seventh Earl, John Fenwick, built the main part of the Hall in 1730. Two decades later, his son Edward Fenwick added brick flankers to the main house, a coach house, and elaborate stables for the racehorses. Records indicate that Edward eventually acquired a 3,000-acre tract of land along the Stono River on Johns Island. He bought most of the land from Robert Gibbes in the early 1700s.

The legend of the Fenwick ghost begins in those years between 1730 and 1776. Edward Fenwick had several beautiful daughters, of course, all courted by dashing young men who would ride their own thoroughbreds to the Hall in hopes of winning the hand of one of the young maidens. During the summer season it was not unusual for the Hall to see scores of dinners and dances for the young men and women of the countryside.

The most striking of all of Edward's daughters, however, had the misfortune to fall in love with her father's groomsman. Knowing full well that the Earl would never allow such a union to take place, the couple eloped on the back of one of the swiftest race horses in the Fenwick stable.

Their flight was brief.

They were delayed at the Stono ferry long enough for a posse of family members, led by Edward Fenwick himself, to catch up with the young people and drag them back to the Hall. Edward locked his daughter in her upstairs room. He then hauled her lover to the courtyard below her window where he organized an ersatz court of Fenwick men and sympathizers. They quickly tried the young man. Not surprisingly, they found him guilty of kidnapping and sentenced him to be hanged.

Despite Miss Fenwick's frantic screams, her lover had a noose put around his neck and then, with his hands tied behind his back, was loaded onto the same horse on which he'd made his desperate dash for happiness. Edward himself threw the rope over a stout oak limb, tied it off and slapped the horse's flanks. The groomsman's neck snapped as he was wrenched from the horse.

Edward Fenwick's revenge was neither sweet nor long-lived.

At the instant her beloved died at her father's hands, Miss Fenwick collapsed on the floor of her room. She was carried to her bed, but the horror of the day apparently destroyed her mind. Her utterances were reduced to nonsensical babble, her behavior constantly monitored for fear that she would harm herself or, should she somehow escape, her father.

She never recovered from the shock and, according to the legend, died a short time later. But not before a brief moment of sanity when she cursed her family for depriving her of sweet love.

She seems to have exacted her revenge.

The Fenwicks remained British Loyalists during the Revolutionary War. But while the Crown was in control of Charleston in early 1782, the General Assembly of South Carolina's Revolutionary Government was formed at Jacksonboro, a settlement on the Edisto River. Beginning on February 26, 1782, they compiled lists of Loyalists whose estates were to be confiscated by the Rebel Assembly.

The first list was published on March 20, 1782, in Charlestown's *Royal Gazette* that, despite its name, was a Rebel newspaper.

Among those names were Edward Fenwick, who "congratulated Earl Cornwallis on the victory gained at Camden," and Thomas Fenwicke (sic) who bore a "commission, civil or military, under the British government, wince the conquest of this Province."

The Fenwicks were ultimately banished from the Carolinas.

The old Hall stood abandoned for some time. No caretaker would stay for more than a few nights—young Miss Fenwick and her handsome English groomsman were far too much in evidence. Soft footsteps beneath the rustle of silken skirts brushed across the old floors, a dusty rocker creaked from a locked and empty room, and a pool of dank well water sometimes reflected the sad face of a striking girl in high lace collar and golden hair.

And once in a very great while, along old Stono Avenue itself, the reflection of warm spring moonlight is cast on the girl and her lover strolling hand in hand within the comforting shadows of ancient oaks, their love transcending the boundaries of time.

Sad Mary Clark

In the long-ago days before high tides and hurricanes dramatically altered the landscape of Edisto Island, more than a score of airy, two-story antebellum homes lined the broad beach at Edingsville where planters' families and their slave servants passed the hot summer months being cooled by the Atlantic breezes.

Though little remains of Edingsville but the name, the legendary and restive spirit of a sea captain's wife walks the sand of Edisto Beach, reminding those she chances to encounter that not everyone who passes this way becomes ashes and dust.

Europeans settled Edisto because the Earl of Shaftsbury knew a good deal when he saw one.

Records indicate that the Earl, one of the Lord Proprietors, bought the island from the Edistow Indians in 1674 for beads, hatchets, cloth, and other goods. The manufacture of world-famous Sea Island cotton became its most prominent industry, but a boll weevil infestation after the Civil War destroyed the cotton crop. The island never recovered.

But in the century and more before that time, cotton enabled the rich plantation owners to build fabulous mansions filled with the finest of European furniture, art, and priceless books. Some of them remain to this day and can be viewed by tourists.

The Edistow tribe was not so nearly as fortunate.

Though little is known about this group of Native Americans, its miniscule estimated population of 1,000 in 1600 is one reason for its precarious existence, particularly after being introduced to Europeans in 1562 when they helped the Huguenots try to build a colony at Port Royal.

The tribe battled the Spanish at Fort San Felipe, after which they migrated to Edisto Island. They were friendlier to the English exploring parties, but by 1715 the tribe was decimated by European diseases for which they had no immunity and from brutal skirmishes with other nearby tribes.

The Edisto people are extinct, gone in bone and in spirit.

Not so for Mary Clark.

In the heyday of Sea Island cotton, when the plantation gentry withdrew to Edingsville for some respite from oppressive inland heat and humidity, grand summer weddings were an honored and much anticipated tradition. Each family tried to outdo one another to stage the most magnificent union of man and woman that enclave had ever seen.

So it was for the marriage of sea captain John Fickling and young Mary Clark. Both were children of prominent Lowland families, both had grown to adulthood on Edisto. They had been childhood sweethearts.

Each family was wealthy and so no expense was spared—inside St. Stephens Church an archway of fresh green myrtle and white yucca blossoms framed the happy couple as they exchanged their wedding vows. Some distance away, and down a path strewn with fresh flowers and lit with burning torches, a splendid party for hundreds of guests was held on the beach, where dining tables heavy with food awaited them. Bonfires cast flickering glows on the dancing and laughing guests.

The couple was enormously happy, but in time, Captain Fickling had to leave for a several-month-long voyage to the West Indies in command of a trading schooner.

Summer weeks passed into months. Mary watched the days slip by, marking each day until John's return. By September, it was time for him to return.

Now, late summer and fall is hurricane season on the Carolina coast. There were no warning systems a century and a half ago as there are today when such storms threaten this low-lying country.

On a day when Mary thought her husband might return, the wind grew strong and the waves high. That night, a hurricane struck the island with a force like nothing that anyone who survived had ever remembered.

At dawn, the ocean had returned to a placid, glass-like sheen. But on the island, the storm's aftermath was clear to any observer. Houses were destroyed, the roofs torn off many others. Palm trees lay twisted on the ground. Crops were flattened. Debris washed up on the beaches. Some of it seemed to be pieces of buildings and other manmade objects that had taken flight with the wind, but then had dropped from the sky only to be thrown back onto the land.

Onto the littered beach walked Mary Fickling, gazing seaward and praying that her dear husband had somehow managed to survive the storm.

It was not to be.

A single dark object washed gently landward and, in time, was recognized as a body. Mary rushed to the water and dragged the corpse onto the sand. Strangely, the face was unmarked. And it was that of her husband.

No survivors of his vessel were ever found.

It is said that on those nights after a storm on Edingsville Beach, the ghost of Mary Clark Fickling reappears to grimly repeat her single, final act of tenderness— she gently pulls Captain John Fickling's body from the sea, cradles his head in her lap and cries over the only man she ever loved.

The Candle

The rambling mansion on King Street in colonial Charles Town burned to the ground in the 1860s, but until it did the story of a father's tragic mistake and how it caused the place to be haunted was repeated by all who lived in the oldest parts of that historic city.

This was yet another wedding day during the Revolutionary War. The bride and groom were both the children of wealthy merchant families. And like the marriage ceremony at Edingsville, this was to be the grandest event the city of Charles Town had seen in some time. The War, of course, did affect the planning. Instead of being held in a church, the marriage was planned for the bride's spacious home on King Street.

Her father ostensibly sided with the Loyalists, but was secretly assisting the Patriot cause with money and provisions. Early on, he had agreed to hide military supplies in his generous basement, including barrels of gunpowder that had been labeled "sand."

But that was months ago and today was a time for rejoicing.

As the guests arrived, they were directed into the home's airy parlor, there to await the nuptials. The father busied himself checking that his guests were comfortable and that the servants were attentive to the large meal planned for immediately afterwards. He noticed that the wine choices seemed unforgivably meager for such an event and directed a maid to go to the basement and retrieve several fresh bottles from his well-stocked wine cellar. She picked up a candle to light her way.

He hurried back to greet his guests at the front door—but without shaking hands with even a single additional couple, he gave a sharp cry and ran back to the cellar door. He had forgotten about the caskets of gunpowder stockpiled in the same room in which he kept his precious wine.

Meanwhile, the maid had made her way carefully down the basement steps, across the damp floor to the wine cellar door, pulled it open, and gone in.

The desperate father raced through the house, pounded down the basement steps but pulled up short when in the distance he saw the dim flicker of the maid's candle. However, coming toward him, her arms full of wine bottles, was the young girl.

Hardly daring to breathe, he asked her why she'd left the candle behind.

"Well, sir," she panted, "I didn't have arms enough to carry it and all these bottles as well."

He stared at her, his words forming in his brain but sticking in the dryness of his mouth.

"Where . . . where did you put it?" he asked.

"I just stuck it in one of those barrels what are sand you've got back there. I'll go right back to get it soon as I've taken these to the kitchen, sir."

He angrily waved her up the stairs. His worst fears had been realized.

He carefully made his way back to where the flickering candle had been stuck in the gunpowder, its flame hardly visible above the volatile mixture. A slender wick extended upward from the flame, burned black, yet somehow had managed not to fall over. He knew that the slightest spark would ignite the gunpowder and blast him and his houseful of family and guests to hell and beyond.

He carefully placed the palm of each hand on either side of the flame and slowly brought them together. At the moment his palms would have touched the flame, he quickly clapped them together and at the same moment raised his clasped hands into the air, pulling the wick safely out of the gunpowder.

Staggering back toward the staircase, his hands still gripping the charred wick, his body started shaking convulsively and then his mouth opened in powerful gales of hysterical laughter. The guests heard him and rushed to his aid. They found him crawling up the steps, his nonsensical words about fire and death meaningless to all. His family and friends would never know that this man had saved so many from a horrific death.

It had all been too much for him. His mind snapped. He died within the week, in the bed to which his family carried him. He was never able to explain what had occurred in that dank basement to cause his derangement.

That was not to be his *eternal* end, however.

When the house was destroyed by fire sometime in the early 1860s—some in Charles Town said they knew why. For decades, nightly passersby strolling past the old house swore they heard someone's frenzied laughter from inside and when they stopped to look, a pinprick of light such as that which might come from a distant, nearly extinguished candle flame could be seen through a basement window.

And there simply came a time when the old man was unable to save his beloved home and family.

The Fatal Bracelet

The city of Georgetown had never seen such wedding preparations. Though old Mr. Withers was less than enchanted with his prospective son-in-law, his daughter's happiness was all that mattered to him. So, he had agreed to this union between his divinely beautiful and talented only child Constance and the rugged sea captain with whom she had fallen in love.

When he learned of the couple's love, however, he had issued a single caveat: The couple must not marry quickly, but rather had to wait until the captain returned from his next, long voyage to the Far East. If they still wanted to marry, he would give his blessing. Further, he promised, the wedding plans would move forward in the months and weeks before his future son-in-law's scheduled return.

This was but a small price for Constance to pay. If her father thought his daughter might find another to love as equally well, he would be disappointed. Between her studies of several foreign languages and her piano studies, the girl busied herself until the time came to begin the marriage ceremony arrangements.

Her wedding gown of white satin was designed and made by the best dressmaker in Charles Town, garlands of fresh flowers were ordered for every room in the home while cords of vines were draped over the mantels and up the stairway. A veritable army of bakers and chefs sent wave upon wave of delicious smells floating through the house days in advance as they prepared the ham and chicken, vegetables, desserts, breads and pastries that would be served to hundreds of guests.

The captain returned less than a day before the wedding was to take place. He swept his bride-to-be in his arms and kissed her.

"Darling," he said. "Here is my gift to you."

He took out from his pocket a small wooden box wrapped in blue cloth.

Constance unwrapped the cloth and opened the box. Inside was the most beautiful bracelet she had ever seen. Small rubies had been linked to an oval of pure gold so that it formed what looked like a beetle. Small gold links joined each ruby to the larger diamond.

"Oh, it takes my breath away," she cried, and threw her arms about his neck. "Wherever did you get it?"

"On my last port o' call an old salt brought it to me as I dined in a tavern. He was tipsy, so I don't know how much stock to put into what he said, but he claimed it came from Egypt. He muttered something about the tomb of a pharaoh's princess. And then he said, well . . . he . . ."

"Yes, darling?" his bride-to-be urged. "What else did he say?"

"Only that it had brought him nothing but ill-luck and that he was glad to be rid of it."

"Do you believe him?"

"Nothing so beautiful could be so evil," he smiled back at her. "He staggered to my table when he sold it to me—I almost asked that he be thrown out—so I'd wager he wanted nothing more than drink with my coins."

She held the bracelet and worked at the clasp, but it would not budge. She said she'd have her clever maid open it, kissed her fiancé and rushed to her room to prepare for the ceremony.

Later that afternoon, in carriages and on horseback, the elite of Georgetown society arrived for the wedding. They gathered in the splendid parlor of the Withers' house while the bridegroom waited in the hallway.

The small musical ensemble had just begun to play the ceremony prelude when terrifying screams rained down from somewhere upstairs. The bridegroom sprang to the staircase. At the top, he saw Constance, screaming and grabbing at her wrist. The wrist on which she wore his precious gift.

Before he could move to reach her, she lurched forward and fell headfirst down the staircase.

The beautiful Constance lay broken on the floor, like a rag doll thrown aside by an angry child, her head twisted at an unnatural angle.

He bent over her and raised the wrist around which the bracelet was wrapped. He had intended to check for a pulse but instead saw blood oozing from underneath the bracelet, running in narrow rivulets across her silky white skin. Thin metal pins, shaped like claws, had extended from underneath the jeweled beetle and punctured her skin. He carefully removed the bracelet; the claws drew back inside the strange bracelet.

The dead girl's maid, Clara, sobbed out to the bereaved captain the story of what had happened moments before the joyous occasion was to take place.

She had easily opened the clasp on the bracelet. Her mistress wrapped it around her thin wrist and snapped it shut. As she held it up to admire the sparkling jewels, she screamed in agony. Grabbing at her wrist, she cried for Clara to help her take it off but neither could remove it. The hysterical girl ran from the room to the top of the staircase and there . . .

He knew the rest of the story, but not *why*.

A chemist analyzed the bracelet. He found that an ingenious series of small pins, each one no thicker than a single thread, had been carefully built into the bottom of the bracelet. When the warmth of the wearer's skin reached the mechanism, the pins extended downward piercing the wrist. He also found that the pins were laced with a deadly concoction found only in the Far East.

The sea captain was never charged with any crime for it was clear that he had no knowledge of his deadly gift.

Sadly, his beautiful never-to-be bride paid the highest price.

On late afternoons before a night of the full moon, she walked the halls of what came to be known as the Withers-Powell home. If the weather was warm enough, her shadowy form in veil and lace might have been glimpsed gliding through the gardens or rocking gently on the wide veranda.

The Camden Gray Lady

The most notorious herald of disaster along the South Carolina coast is the Gray Man of Pawleys Island, a sliver of beach joined to the state's mainland by two short causeways. He first appeared before the hurricane of 1822, then again in 1893 when he showed up at the door of the wealthy Lachicotte family, long-time residents there. The family fled their home, but most others stayed. Most were not as fortunate as the Lachicottes and were killed by the hurricane that soon swept over the island. His most recent appearance was in September 1989, before Hurricane Hugo decimated the Grand Strand, of which Pawleys Island is a part.

There is another, albeit lesser known, gray-clad harbinger of tragedy in South Carolina, a lady whose legendary appearances were part of Camden folklore for many years.

The story begins in France during the Wars of Religion between the Protestant Huguenots and the Catholics, from about 1562 to 1598. Families, precincts, and even entire towns were torn apart by rivalries among those who advocated for

Protestant rights and those who wanted to maintain the old order of Catholic supremacy.

Among those affected by the turbulence were the ancestors of the DeSaussures family, which later immigrated to Camden and founded a hotel later known to coastal tourists as the Court Inn.

In the sixteenth century, however, the political and religious warfare pitted DeSaussures against DeSaussures. There were five in the family: father Henri; his wife, Charlotte; two sons, Jules and Raoul; and a daughter, Eloise.

Only Henri was a devoted Catholic. Everyone else in the family, most particularly his two sons, was a Huguenot.

Eloise fell in love with a gallant but hotheaded Huguenot boy. When her father discovered the affair, he set off to find and murder the young man. Only with Eloise's pleas did her father agree to spare his life.

Her life was not to be the same ever again.

Henri dragged his only daughter off to a particularly strict convent where he ordered the nuns to keep her under lock and key until she came to her senses.

She did not and died within the year, but not before summoning her father to her room.

"On you my father and on all of your descendants I leave a curse of heaven upon your heads," she cried out on her deathbed.

Charlotte DeSaussures was as devastated by her husband's ruthless act as was her daughter. She, too, cursed her husband. Her death came shortly after Eloise's.

Henri's grief was too great and he took his own life.

Raoul and Jules were left alone to manage the family's affairs.

One night as they went over their accounts, a scuffling as if from slippered feet drew their attention to a corner. To their astonishment, they saw that it was their sister who glided toward them, her slim form draped in a gray cloak, a hood draped about her shoulders. Her arms were outstretched beseechingly; her mouth formed words but no sound came forth. She glowered as if in anger that she could not be heard. Moments later she faded from view.

Both men retired for the night. Jules fell quickly asleep. Raoul, however, had a most puzzling incident occur in his room. In the middle of his bedroom floor he found a bundle of cloth. He picked it up and saw that it was a monk's habit.

Early the next morning, a band of radical Catholic soldiers began a massacre of Protestants. Jules was killed, but Raoul slipped on the monk's robe. In this disguise, he stole out of the city.

Raoul DeSaussures eventually reached America. His son settled in Camden, building the Lausanne hotel, named after the family's ancestral Swiss home, which he later changed to the Court Inn.

His sister Eloise—the Gray Lady—accompanied him. Though the family long ago gave up any connection to the hotels, her appearance at the old Lausanne and the newer Court Inn portended disaster for someone in the family or connected to the hotel.

ENTR'ACTE—
THE LUMINARIES

The Luminaries

They are termed ghost lights, mystery lights, spook lights, corpse candles, spirit lights, UFO lights, arrows of flame, and any one of a dozen other names, but by whatever phrase these mysterious, luminous phenomena are known, their beguiling presence in North America and Europe has been documented for centuries. Appearing sometimes as a point of light or as a radiating sphere, these anomalous spectacles usually appear to roam about a specific geographic area, usually with what witnesses describe as a kind of ingenuity. Often they vanish when observers approach them.

In those regions of the country where the lights have been reported for decades, as in the Marfa lights of Texas, the Brown Mountain lights of North Carolina, the Chapel Hill light in Tennessee, or the Hornet Spook Light of southwestern Missouri and eastern Oklahoma, legends have built up around their presence. The traditions are usually quite gruesome, involving, in many cases, the search by a railroad conductor or brakeman for his missing head, lost when he was run over by the very train upon which he was working. The light is said to be the lantern he holds while he conducts his futile explorations. There were other legends as well. Author Jerome Clark reports that in 1909, the citizens of Stockton, Pennsylvania, noted a mysterious arrow of light on a mountainside where the mutilated body of a woman had been discovered two years earlier. A newspaper account said some villagers thought "it is the avenging spirit of the slain woman come back to keep alive the history of the crime so that the murderers may some day be apprehended." Thus, ghost lights are often said to be of supernatural or unearthly origin. In this view, the locales themselves are haunted with the revenants of the human being whose spirit is responsible for the light.

Efforts to apply scientific scrutiny to these odd lights have met with only mixed success. In some cases, careful observation has shown them to be automobile headlights reflected over a great distance—as in the Paulding light of Michigan's Upper Peninsula. In other instances, the lights have been found to be the reflections of the moon and stars caused by changes in atmospheric density. "Swamp gas"—a luminescence produced by decaying organic matter—is offered as another explanation, although many such ghost lights occur in dry, mountainous regions.

Canadian scientist Dr. Michael Persinger has published controversial research suggesting that these lights are connected to "intense electromagnetic fields . . . systematically associated with tectonic strain within the earth's crusts." Further, Persinger says such lights can produce traumatic changes in an observer's memory and behavior.

So while many so-called ghost lights can be readily explained, others continue to puzzle and mystify observers. What follows is a consideration of diverse North American mystery lights.

Chapel Hill in the Moonlight

"That's one of my fondest childhood memories."

Nancy Hicks is not speaking of a visit to the circus or a special birthday celebration. Rather her memory is about the evening she watched her father's panicked reaction to an unexpectedly close encounter with Tennessee's legendary Chapel Hill mystery light.

"All the way down there, my father was complaining that the trip was a waste of gas and time. He didn't know why he'd let us talk him into the trip. And I'm thinking, oh, please God, if that light's going to show up, make it tonight."

Nancy got her wish.

Her dad parked the car directly across the old railroad tracks where the light was said to appear. With only a single freight train lumbering through each day, there wasn't much danger of being struck. He was still "yammering" away, she said, when his manner suddenly changed.

"Nell," he screamed to his wife, "What's that!"

A few feet outside his closed window, a ball of yellow light hovered in the air. It didn't throw off any illumination but seemed to be a glowing, self-contained sphere that pulsated a bit in the air.

"It had a kind of warm glow, but it didn't light up the car," Nancy says. "You couldn't see through it, but you could see above, below and to its sides. It was just a solid yellow glow. Now, my dad's trying to start the car and he's yelling. Finally, that light just went 'poof' and went over to my mother's side of the car. She's sort of waving at it and it's just bobbing up and down next to her. Dad's still screaming. Just as my dad got the car started, the light blinked out and reappeared way down the tracks."

The story of the haunted tracks of Chapel Hill, about thirty miles south of Nashville, goes back perhaps a century. As with many other ghost lights connected to old railways, the Chapel Hill light is said to have originated when a clumsy brakeman slipped from his perch on a freight car and fell under the train wheels. He was decapitated. The light is from his lantern as he searches for his crushed cranium.

Interestingly, the Chapel Hill light has moved beyond mere legend because many people claim to have seen it, including Nancy Hicks, her boyfriend, and several members of her own family.

But there have been others as well. Lillian Cantrell lived in Chapel Hill all of her life and had heard the legend many times when she had her first sighting of the ghost light. That came about on a misty, gloomy night when she and her three children went out to see if they could spot it. They parked next to the old

Chapel Hill Depot, which by then had been converted into a feed store.

"We hadn't been there too long when here it came," she said. "First it bobbed a while on one side of the tracks, then it crossed over. It bobbed on that side for a while. Shortly, it started coming toward us and the children screamed and wanted to go home."

Cantrell's description matches that of Nancy Hicks. The light is noticed at the outset as a small, white pinpoint that seems to emanate from a position several miles down the railbed, a long straightaway at that spot. It seems to bounce around on the tracks, but then will look as if it's jumped into the trees near the tracks, before leaping back down to ground level.

The light as the glowing yellow ball Nancy Hicks's family encountered is more unusual, but one that the young woman had seen before that memorable trip with her family. All told, she made about five visits to the area, the first time during her senior year at a Nashville high school. But although she didn't see the ghost light on that particular occasion, she discovered that floating lanterns weren't the only disquieting feature in that particular rural neighborhood.

"My boyfriend, Doug, went to Middle Tennessee State University and some of his friends there had told him about the ghost light and a haunted church," she remembers. The church is about a mile from the tracks. Doug and a couple of his buddies had earlier found the church and haunted tracks. "It's out on a two-lane highway that meanders through the hills. You really had to know somebody who'd been there before to give you directions. The trees made a canopy over the little narrow, gravel roadway that led to the church. It was a decrepit tarpaper, tin-roofed, one-room church with one of those old cemeteries with it. The doors were off their hinges and the place had holes in the wall."

Nancy and Doug made the trip on a September weekend afternoon. Their plan was to wait until dark to see if they could detect anything at the church and then drive on to the tracks where the ghost light appeared.

"There was a car already sitting there, backed into the front of the old church-yard. We thought it was some local couple, necking. We drove on down this gravel road and it was starting to get dark when here comes a car up behind us going like a bat out of hell. Doug said he thought it was the same car we saw parked at the church and I said it sure looked like it. So, we made a U-turn back to the church. Then we waited for it to get good and dark because we were going to go in the church to look at it," Nancy says.

The minutes rolled by. Doug was growing fidgety and told her he had to use the outdoor facilities.

"He went outside and I sat there and sat there. The darkness was total. About the time I was wondering how long it took this fella' to pee, he jumped back in the car in a total panic. He tore out of there so fast I nearly hit the dashboard. Several minutes later and several miles away he pulled over and told me what he'd seen."

Doug told her he'd been standing, facing the church and had seen a glow coming through one of the broken windows. He'd decided it must have been an outdoor light coming from a distant farmhouse when it blinked out as though someone had blocked out the hole. When it came back on again he realized there seemed to be somebody inside the church passing the hole in the wall.

"Then he swore he saw a tall figure standing in the church's doorway," Nancy says. "It was very dark, but he said he could make out a white collar and an outstretched hand that seemed to be beckoning to him. He also thought the figure was holding something in his other hand."

Doug told her it was all he could do *not* to carry out the dark figure's bidding. He raced back to his car and the couple sped off.

As they sat in the dark and Doug stammered out his incredible story, Nancy remembered something he had told her about his first visit there with his friends.

"I reminded him that he had a piece of one of the church's pews he'd collected on his previous visit in the back of the car. I said he should get rid of it right then," she says. Doug had taken a broken leg off one of the pews and thrown it into his trunk a few weeks earlier. Both of them got out and opened the trunk. The piece of wood was missing. A search of the rest of the car was not any more successful.

"I said maybe that's what it was beckoning you for, it wanted its piece of church back," Nancy adds. The couple decided against staying to look for the mysterious light—the incident at the church was excitement enough for one night.

But a couple of weeks later, Doug told her that he wanted to go back. He said he wanted to conquer his fears of the church and try this time to find the storied Chapel Hill light.

"We went through the church in daylight this time," Nancy says. "That was about all I could manage. The place gave off really bad feelings; you just didn't want to be there."

As darkness approached, they drove to the railroad tracks and waited.

"We stood there in the dark. We saw this little light, it looked to be about the size of a flashlight, only it wasn't radiating light out into a cone," Nancy says of her first look at the Chapel Hill light. "It was bobbing around in the trees way down the tracks. Then it would be down on the tracks, and then it bounced back up into the treetops. It glowed like a lantern and then changed to blue. That's all it did."

Nancy was disappointed. She had heard the light sometimes came right up to an observer, but it kept its distance on this night.

The next weekend Doug and Nancy returned with her cousin. A professor from Middle Tennessee State and several of his students were already there, apparently coming to see the light for themselves, Nancy recalls.

"We all stood in a little wad on the tracks," she says. "The light appeared as before, a long ways down the track, bobbing a few feet above the ground, then going into the trees."

But then the group got an unanticipated personal visit from the light.

"Suddenly the light blinked out and then reappeared only a few feet in front of us. None of us felt any fear. It was at waist height, about the size of a softball, and had a warm, amber glow. We couldn't see through it, but we could see the tracks underneath. It wasn't radiating any light as such."

Several members of the small group began walking toward the light, but it kept moving away down the middle of the track. "It would keep an equidistant space between itself and us. If we ran, it moved that much farther. We followed it up the tracks for a few hundred feet and then it just disappeared. Then we saw it down at the far end of the tracks."

The group waited for some time to see if the light would venture back in their direction, but it didn't and everyone eventually drifted away.

"That's when I told my mother, father and brother about what I'd seen," Nancy says of that fourth trip to Chapel Hill, the one that remains such a favored childhood recollection. "It seems like that light had some sense of humor. I've always wondered about it. I was praying for it to show up" so her father would stop complaining about making the trip.

A final visit a few weeks later by Doug, Nancy, her mother, and her brother—her father refused to go back—ended abruptly when a local deputy sheriff ordered them away. "He told us that folks around there were tired of visitors 'snooping around' and to leave and never come back," she says. "We just left at that point and never went back."

What is the Chapel Hill ghost light? As with the experience Lillian Cantrell had, the light most commonly appears on nights with drizzle or mist. It's certainly not the reflection from car lights. As Nancy Hicks noted, that part of rural Tennessee "makes Mayberry look like a metropolis. Maybe raccoons passing by would be as much traffic as that place would get. You couldn't see traffic. You couldn't see a house. This was out in the woods."

Perhaps it is phosphorescent gas produced by rotting organic matter roiling along and above the railroad tracks, but that wouldn't explain the light's ability to move toward or away from an observer with a kind of intelligence. If one is to believe the witnesses to this particular light, its explanation is as enigmatic today as it ever has been.

The Hebron Light

HEBRON—A weird ball of light which grows bright as an automobile headlight, then vanishes as you come close to it, put in another ghostly appearance last night on a back road near here.

Lt. C. C. Serman of the Maryland State Police and three troopers were eyewitnesses to the eerie light last night. They tried to approach it. The light went dim and disappeared. Police say they are baffled to explain the phenomenon.

Old timers will vouch for such a light having been seen on scores of occasions. It has been a legend around here for at least 50 years.

About 20 carloads of people and troopers in two police cars were attracted to the location last night. The light picks a spot on the Church St. Extended Road, about a mile west of Hebron, near Route 50 . . .

Salisbury *Daily Times*, July 10, 1952.

Hebron is a small community on Maryland's Eastern Shore, approximately seven miles northwest of Salisbury. For most of the twentieth century, a section of highway known as Old Railroad Road was the scene of some bizarre encounters with one of the most elusive of East Coast ghost lights. In fact, so notorious was this mysterious glow that Old Railroad Road is the newer name of that thoroughfare—locals had informally known it as Ghost Light Road!

As with many ghost light traditions, it is often difficult to distinguish between fact and fiction. What is known is that there was a brief flurry of official activity in the early 1950s involving the State Police, followed by several newspaper stories based upon those encounters between the light and law enforcement personnel.

Since that time, anecdotal evidence suggests the light is still a lively tradition in Wicomico County, while others go one step further and claim to have seen the Hebron light in more recent years.

The most credible reports of what the Hebron light *was* came from that period in July 1952 when police chased the glowing beacon and several hundred people subsequently camped out on what was then the Church Street Extended Road, about a mile west of Hebron. Police had received several reports of the light.

Two squad cars were sent out to investigate on Wednesday night, July 9. One squad car held State Police Lieutenant C. C. Serman and Trooper Robert Weir, while in another were Troopers Robert W. Burkhardt and Edward Bracey. Burkhardt had investigated the light on earlier occasions.

Lt. Sherman, with his partner in one car and the other two troopers in their own vehicle, tried to box in the light, but as they moved in the light faded. According to their later report, the men spent about two hours observing and chasing the light that night.

Burkhardt said the light was about the size of a bathroom sink, and the same color and height off the ground as a car headlight. He said the light seemed to bounce across the road, into a field and then into nearby woods. He and Trooper Bracey chased it in their squad car for about a half-mile before it changed direction and flew into a farm field, moving at what they estimated to be about fifty miles per hour.

On the previous Friday night, July 4, Burkhardt said he watched as the light approached his car. He had to swerve to avoid a collision with what he thought at the time might have been a wagon with a dim light or lantern hanging from its sideboard. His car ended up at the side of the road. The light hovered about twenty feet away. Burkhardt pressed the accelerator and steered toward the pulsing orb. But as he did so, the light moved away keeping an even distance all the while. The light disappeared into the woods when the speedometer ticked by forty miles per hour. He searched the area, figuring someone might have been playing a practical joke; he didn't find any evidence of a hoax or pranksters. Throughout the chase, the light never rose above the level of his headlights.

Burkhardt had a closer encounter with the light on another night. He was parked on the road waiting for its appearance when his attention was caught by a glare in his rearview mirror. The light was cautiously approaching from behind. He jumped out and ran toward it. "It was just like a neon tube when you turn it out," he said. "It faded slowly into a reddish glow which finally went out."

During that same summer, a *Life Magazine* photographer showed up to try and capture the light on film. On July 12, Albert Fenn joined several hundred onlookers as they anxiously awaited the light's antics. Despite a variety of cameras and film and an all-night vigil with Trooper Burkhardt, the photographer left disappointed—the light chose not to make an appearance.

Lieutenant Serman voiced the wishes of many when he told a newspaper at the time that he wished someone would step forward to provide a scientific explanation for the phenomenon.

Although an explanation satisfactory to all has never been offered, several theories have been expounded over the years.

A sort of explanation might have been provided by a Johns Hopkins University professor, who refused to be publicly identified in the news articles quoting him and said the light may have been "nothing more than swamp gas."

"There must be a marsh out there, or perhaps a peat bog," he claimed. "The gas is generated by decaying vegetable matter, seeps up to the surface, gathers in a sort of pocket and is moved around by gusts of wind. It seems a shame to have the State Police sitting out there all night trying to catch a little bag of gas."

However, there is no indication the professor even visited Hebron or its environs.

Based on the troopers' reports, a "little bag of gas" would hardly be expected to zip down the road at forty to fifty miles per hour before careening off into a field. Neither would it explain how the light kept apace with Trooper Burkhardt's squad car.

Another theory rested with the fact that it was a dirt road on which the light appeared. The county tarred it in 1953, widened and rebuilt it in 1958, and black-topped the expanse in 1974. Reports of the light greatly diminished after that, leading some to suspect the light may have been the reflection of dust in automobile headlights. However, it is hard to imagine that such an investigation as that launched by the State Police would be based on nothing more than road dust, hardly a unique substance in rural America.

And there are many who believe the ghost of a murdered man generated the light. How was he murdered? The folklore of the region includes several possibilities: it's the revenant of a railroader killed by a train; the ghost of a man who committed suicide by hanging in the nearby woods, but whose body wasn't found until the next spring; or the light is generated by a man killed by gamblers when he refused to pay his debt.

Whatever the cause of the Hebron ghost light, it continues to fascinate the rural enclaves of Maryland's Eastern Shore.

The Cemetery at Silver Cliff

May 1882. The miners' whoops and hollers echoed through Wet Mountain Valley as the buckboard lurched over the stony trail. It had been a good night of carousing—the drinks were hard, the women were soft.

Now, the men were on their way home to Silver Cliff, one of Colorado's great silver mining camps. As the carriage rolled past the local cemetery, Jake Daniels, who'd been swigging from a whisky bottle, drooped it and shrieked, "Holy Mary, Mother of Jesus, look at them lights!"

A hush came over the revelers. Bright blue flames danced on top of the scattered gravestones, chasing one another, disappearing, and then reappearing. There were too many to count. Or were the men seeing the same ones over and over again? They couldn't tell.

Jake tumbled to the ground and his tipsy pals followed. Staggering over the ground, with arms outstretched as if beseeching the lights to come to them, the men tried to catch the elusive lights, but as soon as they got close to one it vanished. They stumbled, fell, got up again.

"The ghost got me!" screamed one man, falling facedown and narrowly escaping hitting his head on the corner of a granite marker. His buddies helped him into the buckboard and climbed in after him.

The next morning the miners told their story of the mysterious lights to the bemused townsfolk. Everyone laughed. A bunch of drunks might just as well have seen the prancing devil himself. Yet a few persons were curious enough to check out the report.

Several nights later, a small band walked the half-mile to the old graveyard to

conduct what they called a "scientific" investigation. Jake Daniels led the expedition. Joining him were: Harold Parsons, an assayer; attorney Hulbert Cowles;
Ephraim Ballew, a photographer; saloon keeper Spike Norton; and sisters Anna
and Emma Turner, milliners.

Though Daniels was the ostensible leader, the women took charge. They
marched up and down between each row of tombstones, swinging their lanterns
toward every stone and calling out the names chiseled on each, as if to summon
all the spirits of the dead. The men stood in a knot and scanned the dark sky,
waiting for the lights to appear.

The day had been warm, but the night had grown cold; the ground was damp
from a recent rain. Cowles felt the dampness seep through the soles of his boots
and stomped his feet to keep warm. He should have worn a sweater under his
thin cotton duster.

"All right, Daniels," Cowles snorted, "where are those damn lights?"

"I dunno'," shot back the miner, shrugging his shoulders, "but they sure were
here the other night."

Anna held her lantern up to his face. "Jake Daniels, you have done nothing
but lead us on a wild goose chase and we are leaving."

"Good night!" put in Emma.

Arm in arm, the Turners started back to town. The men watched them go but
said nothing. Then shortly after they'd left, each man, singly, drifted away from
the cemetery, angry that an ordinary miner had duped him.

Daniels stood alone now, hands deep in his pockets. Where *were* the lights?
They had been there, of that he was, well, *almost* certain. He walked the perimeter
of the cemetery and neither saw nor heard anything. Just as he turned to leave,
he caught a bright flicker out of the corner of his eye. He swung around. A blue
light danced atop a tombstone, then another and another, almost as if they were
taunting him. Trembling with excitement, he cupped his hands to his mouth and
shouted, "The lights! The lights!"

The skeptics heard his cries, quickly retraced their steps and stood slack-jawed
at the sight before them. Soon scores of blue lights swarmed like moths over the
tombstones. Curiosity replaced fear as each man tried unsuccessfully to catch a
tiny light as it floated past. The women, learning about the sighting the next
morning, lived to regret their hasty departure. They never once saw the lights.

In the twelve decades since their first recorded appearance, those dancing lights
have been the subject of endless speculation and numerous theories. Some said
the lights were St. Elmo's fire, an electrical phenomenon that sometimes appears
on ships' masts and other pointed objects before a storm. Yet the sightings at
Silver Cliff did not presage a storm.

Others thought the lights were will-o'-the-wisps, a phosphorescent light caused
by the spontaneous combustion of gases from rotting organic matter. Except that
will-o'-the-wisps occur in swamps and marshes and the Silver Cliff cemetery is on
a rise of land grown up with yucca and cacti.

A reflection, perhaps from lights in Silver Cliff? Doubtful. There were no electric lights in 1882, and even as late as 1963, when all electric lights were turned
off in several nearby communities the lights still appeared.

Longtime Silver Cliff resident Francis Wernette took a young man from Denver out to the cemetery. The visitor was convinced that the lights were nothing

but reflections. He had a blanket with him and, seeing a light on the top of a stone, threw the blanket over it. Within seconds, the light popped up behind him.

Folklorist and anthropologist Dale Ferguson took a different approach to the puzzle of the lights. He says that the Cheyenne and other Plains people buried their dead on hilltops, and a number of Native American legends mention dancing blue lights on these sites. But unless there is a prehistoric burial site far below earth level, the Silver Cliff site was used mainly by the German and English settlers.

After all these theories were discussed and dismissed, the residents of Wet Mountain Valley concluded that the lights were on the helmets of long-dead miners, still seeking frantically for silver on the hillside. The ghost theory prevailed.

But wherever you find ghost stories, you find pranksters and charlatans.

One dark evening two young girls in black clothing prowled the cemetery, carrying small lanterns with blue-tinted globes. Their deception was soon discovered when a man who'd seen them head for the cemetery got there first. He leaped out of a fresh dug grave, and the girls ran for their lives.

A spiritualist from Pueblo hawked pieces of smoked glass that he said would enable the viewer to see a tiny human form in the center of each light. It isn't known how many gullible buyers, if any, bought the magic glass, but the quack was quickly driven out of town.

Folklorist Wernette recalled stories his uncle told of going to dances by horse and buggy. As the rigs neared the cemetery the drivers beat the frightened animals to get past the place as quickly as possible.

Wernette added that the best weather in which to see the lights was in the snow or rain, or on nights of heavy cloud cover. "There's no explanation for them," he said, "and as far as I know they've been out there with Geiger counters and I don't know what all, trying to find out what causes them."

Kathy Williams, after a visit to the cemetery, said, ". . . the rocks beside the road glowed as well as [the] many, many lights."

The lights might have remained only curious local phenomena had they not been dignified by reports in The New York Times and National Geographic magazine.

After the publication of the Times account, tourists from all over the country flocked to the little burial ground to see for themselves what all the fuss was about. Some saw the lights and pondered their significance; others went away disappointed.

The Times correspondent, W. T. Little, said, "I know they [the lights] are not all myth, for I, too, have seen them."

Later, Edward J. Linehan, assistant editor of National Geographic, toured the cemetery with Bill Kleine, a local campground manager who said he'd seen the lights many times.

"This is a good night for them—overcast, no moon," Kleine reportedly said, as he and Linehan climbed out of their car and waited. Linehan strained to see something—anything—and, as his eyes grew accustomed to the darkness, he discerned the jagged rows of weathered tombstones.

Suddenly, the lights appeared.

"I saw them, too," wrote Linehan. "Dim, round spots of blue-white light glowed ethereally among the graves. I found another, and stepped forward for a better look. They vanished. I aimed my flashlight at one eerie glow and switched it on.

It revealed only a tombstone. . . . No doubt someone, someday, will prove there's nothing at all supernatural in the luminous manifestations of Silver Cliff's cemetery. And I will feel a tinge of disappointment. . . ."

Some 322 year-round residents live in Silver Cliff, and few speak of the cemetery lights. Newcomers, too, have been attracted to the beautiful and peaceful valley set in the Sangre de Cristo Mountains. Because of lights from new homes and ranch lights burning from dusk to dawn, the mystery flames are often difficult to see. And when they are visible, they seem to cluster around six tombstones, all circa 1912.

Moody's Light

What is the peculiar shimmering orb, reported by so many people, fifteen miles west of Francesville, and not far from Rensselear, in northwest Indiana? The glowing, evanescent light in an isolated wood mutates in color from red to white, chases cars and people and, according to local folklore, is connected to several deaths.

The story of the Francesville light, or Moody's light as it is sometimes known, begins in the middle part of the last century. Its specific origin is unknown, as is its cause. Although it has reportedly been investigated by scientists from several universities and the air force, it is most widely known in the folklore of northern Indiana.

The light is hard to locate. It is not listed on county maps, of course, making it necessary to ask a local for directions. Although the light sometimes appears over a nearby road, it is most often sighted in a dank woodlot, across an open field. It will flash red to white and back again. Once, a young woman watching the light with some friends said it shot across the field with the speed of a bullet. The light was so bright, the young woman and her friends had to shield their eyes. The edges of the sphere were clearly visible to the viewers.

Several viewers have said the light looks quite like an automobile's headlights, but he didn't see how that was possible. "We've been out there when it will come right up to the car and it illuminates the whole area. It's scary. It sits way out in the woods and as it comes close it changes colors back and forth from white to red. It scares you to death when it comes up like that," one witness told a folklore researcher.

Another man said it looked like a car light. "But then it will disappear and come back red, and flash back white, and so on. Sometimes it comes all the way up to (you) and gets real bright, and then everything shines. We've flashed our car lights at it before, and it flashes back at you," he said.

There are several legends connected to the light itself and the surrounding countryside. The name Moody's light seems to have originated with a family by that name who lived in the neighborhood. Late one night, the father returned home to find his house burning with his family trapped inside. The light is said to be the father swinging his lantern, searching for his lost family.

Some investigators say the light is probably caused by rotting organic matter, light reflecting from a fog bank, or periodic emissions of natural gas.

Whatever its origin, Moody's light adds a touch of the unknown to the rolling farm country of rural Indiana.

St. Mary's Beacon

When darkness blankets the Iowa prairie, the tapestry of fields is stitched together by lights burning in barns and farmhouses. A half-mile south of St. Mary's in Warren County, a different sort of light illuminated the landscape for many years.

Beginning in 1874, a glowing light was seen floating like a globe along the perimeter of a 160-acre tract of the Storz family farm. The light was described as about fifteen or twenty inches in diameter, bright red at its center, and shading to orange at the edge. It flashed bright, intermittent signals, and then dimmed. Although it usually traveled in the same horizontal plane close to the ground, some observers said they saw it shoot straight up into the sky. Several young people tried to catch the light at various times, but none was successful.

For seventy years people tried to explain the light's origin. Realists insisted it was swamp gas, ball lightning, or reflections from the moon. Others said it was the spirit of a young girl who had died a violent death. Or was it, as some thought, the spirit of a certain Mrs. Wallace who had supposedly burned to death in a house that once stood on the Storz land? Neither story has been satisfactorily documented.

In the 1930s the light was especially active. C. A. McNair, proprietor at the time of the general store and café at St. Mary's, was driving home one night when he glanced out the window of his Model T Ford. Seeing the light hanging in the sky at the south end of the Storz farm, McNair floorboarded the gas pedal. He later told friends: "That old car never traveled so fast!" In the opposite direction from the light, it must be added.

Orval Benning was a local farmer who saw the light on a number of occasions. Once, he wished he hadn't. At one-thirty one wintry morning, Berning was walking home from a card game with some neighborhood cronies. As he passed the Storz place, he noticed a light floating along slowly, just insides the fence line. Berning covered the rest of his way home in record time.

In the morning, Berning told everyone who would listen, "That light was no more than twenty-five feet from me. There was no moon and there was no one in the field with a lantern."

Berning insisted he'd seen the light many times from a window of his own house, which was three-quarters of a mile east of the Storzes. He said it would flit about until one or two o'clock in the morning, going along the ground, and then soaring away above the treetops.

Witnesses to the light told news reporters the fiery orb never left the Storz place, but it apparently did, at least once. Nobel Nixon was riding past one evening when his horse suddenly bolted. Nixon pulled on the reins and swung around in his saddle. The light was bobbing down the middle of the road . . . right in his direction. It increased its speed . . . and so did Nixon's old mare. The farmer hunched in the saddle holding on for dear life. He didn't remember reaching home and he never forgot his wild ride. Neither did the horse; she refused to leave the corral for a week.

By the 1940s Bill Brentano was farming the Storz land. He claimed he'd never seen the light, knew no one who had, and was an unyielding skeptic. However, by this time tales of the mysterious radiance had spread far beyond tiny St. Mary's, some twenty-five miles south of Des Moines. At the conclusion of World War II when gas rationing was lifted, amateur ghost hunters came from far and near to see the spirit light for themselves. Carloads of visitors descended upon Brentano's farm and made his life miserable, trampling his shrubbery, uprooting trees, and stealing his chickens. The sheriff had to disperse the crowds on several occasions.

Some visitors claimed to have seen the light and didn't know what to make of it. Sixty-year-old Roy Whitehead, of Indianola, Iowa, did. In 1947, he made a startling observation. While standing at the edge of a field watching the light bob and blink along its accustomed route, Whitehead claims he heard the "cry of a lost earthbound soul" coming from inside the bouncing object.

There is little talk today about the mystery light at St. Mary's. Either it has ceased its prowling or the people of St. Mary's have been too busy to notice. But in the dark of the moon when autumn winds crack the dry stubble of cornstalks in the fields, a few of the old-timers may sit by their windows, watching and waiting. . . .

The Hornet Spook Light

The Seneca Light. The Neosho Mystery Light. The Devil Light. Devil's Promenade. The Indian Light. The Missouri Mystery Light—

Missouri's most famous unexplained light is called many things in this region twelve miles southwest of Joplin, near the Missouri-Oklahoma state line. That's where an obscure, east-west gravel lane, not quite four miles long, slices through a canyon of blackjack oak. Even though most of Spook Light Road, or the Devil's Promenade, as it is known locally, lies in Oklahoma, just beyond the former border village of Hornet, Missouri, the spook light is generally tied to Neosho, Missouri, because the road is a few miles northwest of there.

The road is similar to other lanes in the Ozark foothills. Except at night. When darkness falls, a mysterious light appears, bobbing along from west to east. It has been seen almost every night from dusk to dawn for over a century. Early pioneers called it the Indian Light, but it is now more commonly known as the Hornet Spook Light.

The orb of light, varying from baseball-sized to larger than a bushel basket, spins down the center of the road at great speed, rises to treetop level and hovers, then always retreats, as if its scouting expedition is over. At other times, it sways from side to side and up and down like a lantern is being carried by some mysterious hand.

The light can be silver, red, or yellow. Sometimes blue or green. It is usually seen as a single glow, but one woman said she saw it "burst like a bubble, scattering sparks in all directions." If it's chased, the light seems to go out, only to reappear somewhere else later on. One man drove his car directly at the light. Witnesses said the pulsating light landed on the roof.

Although the mystery light has never been known to harm anyone, many people say they've had frightening encounters with it. Gregory Briones, while driving his car early one morning, happened to turn around and saw the spook light sitting on the top of his trunk. "It throwed off a good bit of light, like an electric bulb close up to you," he told a news reporter. "I took off in one big hurry."

A man walking along the Devil's Promenade said the light swung past him so closely that he felt its searing heat.

Another fellow swore that he saw the figure of an old crone tottering down the road with the light riding on her shoulders where her head should have been. The man claimed to be sober.

When Bill Youngblood lived near the area, he said the light bouncing around outside his bedroom window kept him awake.

Garland Middleton, who operated the Spook Light Museum, claimed the light had chased him home several times.

Other people reported seeing the light dip through open automobile windows. One car supposedly caught fire when that happened.

On at least two occasions, the light was observed six miles beyond the western end of Spook Light Road, near Quapaw, Oklahoma.

Chester McMinn, who farmed near there, was working his fields late one summer evening when the spook light appeared overhead, illuminating his acreage with silvered brilliance. McMinn was grateful for the unanticipated assistance.

Louise Graham rode home in a school bus after attending a carnival at Quapaw. The light suddenly materialized at the rear window. The brilliant light appeared as a yellow fireball, frightening Louise and her schoolmates. The driver was nearly blinded by the bright light and had to pull over. Only then did the light drift away to continue its mischief-making.

Generations of local people believe that the Hornet Spook Light is a ghost, or "ha'nt," in the local vernacular. There are countless legends to account for the queer glow.

A popular one is similar to many other lover's leap yarns.

The area was once the home of the Quapaw Indians. A maiden and a young brave fell in love. The girl's father, a greedy sort, demanded a larger dowry than the young man could afford. Unable to marry with the tribe's blessing and unwilling to separate, the lovers ran away together. Their absence was soon discovered and a party of warriors set off in pursuit. Overtaken on a bluff above the Spring River, the couple joined hands and leaped to their deaths.

Shortly afterwards, in 1886, the light first appeared; it was thought to be the spirits of the young lovers. It created such a panic in the village of Hornet that many people abandoned their homes and farms and moved away. The light was a "hoodoo," they thought, one that brought death and disease.

And then there's the "likker" story:

During Prohibition (1920–1933), when law forbade alcoholic beverages, stills operated in the Ozark hills. With some regularity, federal agents, or revenuers, tramped the countryside, flushing out moonshiners. Eventually they caught old Uncle Dick Hunt, purveyor of the finest "corn likker" in all of the hills. It was so fine, in fact, that Uncle Dick refused to pour it into bottles that had contained any blended stuff. He used bottles of only the best brands or the buyer's own stone jug. But after the "feds" raided him and broke up his still several times, Uncle Dick got smart. He mounted the still on the rear of an old spring buckboard wagon. Then whenever the agents were snooping around, Uncle Dick moved the still to the safety of a nearby cave. The spook light is Uncle Dick Hunt's still, jouncing around the old trails heading for cover.

Over the years, the light has been studied, prodded, poked, photographed, and even shot at with high-powered rifles in efforts to identify and explain it.

So, the question is: What *is* it?

Marsh gas? Probably not. Winds fail to disperse the fireball as they do conventional marsh gas.

A will-o'-the-wisp? The light is far more intense than the luminescence created by rotting matter.

Glowing minerals from the numerous piles of mine tailings in the region? Maybe.

A pocket of natural gas ignited by lightning and once worshipped as a fire-god by Indians of the area? Not likely. Natural gas flames and, in time, burns out.

Some experts believe that lights, such as this one in Missouri, are electrical atmospheric charges generated by the shifting and grinding of rocks deep below the earth's crust (although such lights are frequently associated with earthquakes, their presence does not necessarily forecast quakes). The distorted electrical field that results from these charges can make the light appear to act in an intelligent way, changing direction and altitude and giving chase. And physical encounters with the electrical field can make a person fearful and apprehensive. Sleep difficulties, skin burns, nausea, and temporary blindness may follow.

Joplin, Missouri, just north of the spook light area, lies on a great fault line running from east of New Madrid, Missouri, westward into Oklahoma. At least four earthquakes during the eighteenth century were followed by a devastating series of quakes that convulsed this area in 1811–1812. Strange lights may have accompanied these quakes, but it was not until 1886 that the Hornet Spook Light was first reliably reported. Although the appearance of the light has not been accompanied by any major quake in this century, seismologists consider this region of Missouri one of the most unstable areas in the country, and the generation of an electrical atmospheric charge may possibly explain the Spook Light.

Yet, some authorities have a different opinion. Teams of investigators who have studied the lights conclude that they are those of automobiles driving east on a U.S. highway, about five miles away in a direct line with the Devil's Promenade, but at a slightly lower elevation. A high ridge lies between the two roads. The density and rarity of the atmosphere as it rises over the ridge causes the light to bend, creating the eerie effects.

Old-timers smile and shake their heads in disagreement. They know the mystery light was seen decades ago at the same point in these woods long before the automobile was invented and modern highways were developed.

"I was coming here in horse and buggy days and saw the light then," said L. W. Robertson some years ago.

Whatever the Hornet Spook Light may be, it attracts thousands of spectators each year. Cars often park bumper-to-bumper on the narrow gravel road, while drivers wait and watch for that strange light that swings and sways and bobs along in the night sky. It is, as they say in that region, one of nature's great unexplained mysteries.

The Brown Mountain Lights

The mountain peaks of western North Carolina bear fanciful and sometimes unforgettable names: Blowing Rock, Grandfather Mountain, Clingmans Dome, and Rattlesnake Knob. There's Chimney Rock, from which the Cherokee people once sent smoke signals.

But the most famous mountain of all goes by the more pedestrian name of Brown Mountain. Hardly qualifying as a mountain at all, it spreads across the Blue Ridge foothills at an elevation of a mere 2,600 feet and straddles Burke and Caldwell counties, about fourteen miles northwest of Morganton. Long and flat as a tabletop, Brown Mountain lacks any distinguishing characteristic—except at night. Then lights of various colors rise above the treetops, shimmering and dancing, disappearing, then reappearing.

The lights have been seen in this way for over 150 years.

Descriptions vary from one observer to another. One person reported seeing a bright red light that vanished in less than a minute. Another said he watched a pale white light whirl inside a halo, disappear for twenty minutes and then reappear. A minister described the light as cone-shaped and larger than a star. When two more arose, he and his sons, who were with him, watched through field glasses. The lights rose high in the sky and terminated. Other persons said they saw yellow lights that moved upward, downward, or horizontally. Sometimes clusters of lights appear and rise so fast that it's impossible to count them. When viewed through a telescope, the lights resemble balls of fire.

No one knows when the mysterious lights first appeared, but legend says they were visible well before the Civil War, possibly as early as 1850. In that year a woman of the region disappeared. Neighbors suspected that her abusive husband had murdered her. Shortly afterwards, while search parties scoured Brown Mountain in search of her body, strange lights bobbed above them in the night sky. Some of the more superstitious among the searchers suspected the victim's spirit had returned to haunt her murderer; others thought the lights had been sent as a warning to end the search. The woman's remains were eventually found under a cliff. It wasn't clear if she had jumped, fallen, or been pushed to her death.

Ever since that time, the lights have appeared with some regularity. They are well-known to North Carolinians and to increasing numbers of out-of-state visitors.

Many theories have been advanced to explain this weird anomaly. At first the lights were thought to be a will-o'-the-wisp, a phosphorescent light hovering or flitting over swampy ground at night, possibly caused by the combustion of gas emitted by rotting organic matter. However, there is no marshy ground in that section of Burke and Caldwell counties.

Could it be foxfire, produced by certain fungi found on rotting wood? Probably not. Foxfire is usually a weak, pale light that would not appear as colored globes floating in the sky, as has been reported at Brown Mountain.

An amateur explorer once reported that he'd found at one end of the mountain a piece of pitchblende, a radium ore. But the rays from the radium are, of course, invisible. And geologists have since confirmed that Brown Mountain is composed of ordinary cranberry granite.

Another proffered idea was connected to the prevalence of moonshiners, who once operated near Brown Mountain. They screened their stills to conceal the fires, but when the covers were removed and the fires raked out, clouds of rising steam reflected the firelight from below. But the era of moonshining has long since passed and the lights still appear.

St. Elmo's fire was yet another theory set forth. This is an electrical discharge from sharp-pointed objects during a thunderstorm. Sailors are well acquainted with it because it often appears at the tip of a mast during a storm. But the phenomenon requires a solid conductor and never occurs in midair. Also, the

Brown Mountain lights appear on clear nights with no storms brewing anywhere in the area.

Interestingly, the lights do not appear after a long drought.

For a time, an observation made in the Andes Mountains of South America was offered as an explanation for these North Carolina lights. The so-called Andes Lights incidents were observed in these high Chilean mountains when silent discharges of electricity passed through clouds and onto the mountain peaks. These discharges often produced round, shimmering lights that could be seen sometimes for more than three hundred miles. However, that idea was eventually dismissed when it was determined that this phenomenon occurred only at elevations over fifteen thousand feet, not at the much lower altitude of the Blue Ridge foothills.

The U.S. Geological Survey has made at least two formal studies of Brown Mountain. The first geologist determined that the lights were caused by headlights of locomotives and automobiles in the Catawba Valley, south of Brown Mountain. But three years after his report, a massive flood washed out railroad tracks and bridges and turned the primitive roads into quagmires. No traffic of any kind moved, yet the lights appeared as usual.

Later, a second geologist came to Burke County to survey the lights. He carried with him an impressive array of scientific equipment: a fifteen-inch plane table, a telescopic alidade, field glasses, topographic maps, a barometer, compasses, camera, flashlights and other research aids. Each time the lights were sighted, their appearance was checked with the train schedules. After two weeks of diligent work, the investigator completed his study. He found that 47 percent of the lights originated from automobile headlights; 33 percent from locomotive headlamps; 10 percent from fixed lights; and 10 percent from brushfires. The geologist believed that the lights originated in a deep valley several miles away and that atmospheric conditions caused the lights to appear to rise over Brown Mountain. Mist and dust particles rendered the lights colorful.

Despite these prosaic scientific explanations, at least some of the mountain folk continue to believe the lights are of divine origin.

John Harden, in his book *The Devil's Tramping Ground*, quotes from an account written by J. L. Hartley, a state fire warden. Hartley said: "If God could make Brown Mountain, could he not also make the lights? . . . I have fought forest fires on every mountain from Linville Falls to Blowing Rock at all times of the night and have seen these lights a great many times from Grandfather Mountain above any human habitation. It is true there were hunters with lanterns, but please tell me whoever saw a lantern ascend up into the elements where no game exists . . . ?"

Summer evenings after eight o'clock are the best days on which to look for these particular mystery lights. There are three popular vantage points: Beacon Heights, just off the Blue Ridge Parkway near Grandfather Mountain; Wiseman's View, on North Carolina Route 105 near Morganton; and on the scenic North Carolina Route 181, also near Morganton. At the latter location, the U.S. Forest Service has erected a sign detailing the story of the Brown Mountain lights.

Joe Baldwin's Lantern

It had rained hard all day and now, in the darkness of the night, only a fine drizzle fell, like a beaded curtain. The freight train rattled along between scrub pines and deep underbrush, headed for the village of Wilmington, near the southeastern North Carolina coast.

To conductor Joe Baldwin the chugging of the old steam engine made a comforting sound, especially as the train neared the end of its long day's journey. Joe liked his job on the Wilmington-Florence-Augusta line and felt fortunate to have secured such a fine position. Some of his friends who had returned with him after the Civil War were not so fortunate.

Although tonight there were no scheduled pickups or drop-offs of freight before Wilmington, Joe called out each station in turn. That was his job. Now as the train neared Maco Station, he slid open the rear door of the next-to-last car and expertly leaped across the network of pins and couplers. But as soon as landed on the last car he knew something was wrong. It had lost momentum. Beads of sweat stood out on his forehead. With sickening dread, he realized what had happened. The last car had become uncoupled and was rolling to a stop. He also knew a passenger express train was only minutes behind.

Joe seized his lantern firmly in one hand and jerked open the rear door of the car. Then, stepping out onto the platform, he peered down the tracks. The headlamp from the oncoming passenger train grew, first as a pinprick in the far distance and soon, all too soon, as an enveloping bath of blinding light. He frantically swung his light in great arcs to signal the oncoming engineer. His screams were cut off as the screech of metal striking metal punctured the night air; soot and sparks showered the brush on either side of the glistening rails.

Joe Baldwin was decapitated. His mangled torso was found sprawled across the tracks. His head was never found. He was the only person killed.

Not long after that tragic accident in 1867, a mysterious light appeared by the tracks near Maco Station, a scattered handful of farmhouses a dozen miles west of Wilmington. It was unlike anything that had ever been seen in the area. After newspapers picked up the story, throngs of people converged upon the little outpost each evening to watch for the eerie glow. Many hundreds of people claimed to have seen the light.

Some witnesses believed the light to be Joe Baldwin's railroad lantern still swinging its futile warning to the approaching train. Others think the light was the conductor himself—searching for his head. One observer claimed to have seen the light in a swamp near the place where his lantern had been found on that fatal night.

John Harden was a newsman and a collector of Carolina legends. He said, "The (Maco) light is first seen at some distance down the track, maybe a mile away. It starts with a flicker over the left rail, very much as if someone had struck a match. Then it grows a little brighter, and begins creeping up the track toward you. As it becomes brighter, it increases in momentum. Then it dashes forward with a rather incredible velocity, at the same time swinging faster from side to side. Finally, it comes to a sudden halt some seventy-five yards away, glows there like a fiery eye, and then speeds backwards down the track, as if retreating from some unseen danger. It stops where it made its first appearance, hangs there ominously for a moment, like a moon in miniature, and then vanishes into nothingness."

The Maco Light's appearance was unpredictable at best. It might show itself night after night, especially if a fine mist was falling or, again, it would disappear for weeks at a time.

In 1873, a second light suddenly began appearing. This one traveled west rather than east, and the two sometimes met. More than one frightened engineer, believing another train was coming toward him on the track, yelled at his brakeman, squeezed his eyes tightly shut and prayed. At the dreaded moment of impact, the light rapidly vanished. Finally, signalmen began carrying both red and green lanterns. Given a green light, an engineer could push fearlessly down the tracks past Maco Station.

In 1886, an earthquake jolted southeastern North Carolina and the strange light disappeared. But three years later, it returned.

One day during that year, President Grover Cleveland was riding a train toward Wilmington when it stopped at Maco Station to take on coal and water. While waiting, the president decided to take a stroll down the tracks. Seeing a signalman swinging a green lantern in one hand a red one in the other, he asked about the curious signal. He was then told the story of old Joe Baldwin and the legend of the Maco Light.

Numerous attempts have been made to explain the phenomenon. Reflections from automobile headlights coming from nearby roads have always been a popular explanation for anomalous lights. On one occasion at midnight, all roads near Maco were cordoned off for an hour with guards posted to turn back motorists. The light still appeared, hovering about three feet above the tracks and traveling east.

At least one attempt was made to destroy the light. A machine gun detachment from the United States Army's installation at Fort Bragg was sent out to investigate. The men fired repeatedly at the light, but were unable to hit it as it hopscotched ahead of them down the track.

The tracks were torn up in 1977, and the light once again went away. But no one can say for certain if this time the Maco Light has been extinguished for all time.

The Old Cox Light

Some of North Carolina storyteller Michael Renegar's favorite tales are those he heard as a little boy sitting in the yard with his elderly relatives on a hot summer night.

"We'd be outside under the stars," Renegar says. "Sometimes we'd have a little marshmallow roast going on and I'd listen to my aunts and uncles telling stories. My parents, too. They talked about all the things they saw or what had happened to them in the old days."

A favorite story on those summer nights was one told by Michael's elderly Great-Aunt Nat, who claimed to have actually seen what was known in that region as the Cox ghost light.

This is the story Michael learned from his great aunt:

Nat was the daughter of Michael's great-grandfather Charles Renegar, who lived on Lone Hickory Road, across from the South Oak Ridge Baptist Church cemetery. Nat's brother was George, who would become Michael's grandfather. Nat, George, and their siblings got their first view of the Cox ghost light from a window in their house on Lone Hickory Road.

That old road meanders from U.S. Highway 601, south of Yadkinville in Yadkin County, west on to U.S. Highway 21. Lone Hickory Road was part of the Old Coach Road, or Old Wagon Road, that used to connect Winston with Salem, North Carolina.

On this lonely road was the Cox place. No house had been on the property in living memory, but there was an old abandoned graveyard in the nearby woods.

Legend had that African-American slaves had been buried there. No headstones remained, but the ground was sunken where it's thought the graves were located. An open well was also on the property.

By the time Michael's Aunt Nat was born in 1914, the tales of the Cox light were already widespread. She had her own experience with it one night when she was little and couldn't sleep. She sat up in bed and looked out the window. The Cox light rose in the distant darkness directly above where she knew the open well to be. The light moved along the road and then arced over the old graveyard.

Nat was frightened and tried to wake her father, Charles, but he grumbled, rolled over and went back to sleep. She ran to the window to see if the light was still there. It was.

Her running around woke up her brother George, who got up himself and looked out the window.

"Pap, get up. It's the light!" George called out to his daddy.

His father got out of bed, pulled on his pants and shirt, took down his rifle, and went outside. George trailed behind, pulling on his own clothes as he ran.

They trailed the light, but no matter how hard they tried, they couldn't get near it. Presently they gave up, realizing they'd encountered the mysterious Cox ghost light.

Many other folks in that part of North Carolina claim to have seen the light, either hovering over the old well, or jumping about in the old cemetery, or moving down the road. No one could get near it. No one could ever explain it. And no one could figure out why it rambled about as it did.

Michael's Aunt Nat claimed that someone must have fallen into the old well and drowned. She thought the Cox light was the spirit of that unfortunate soul, trying to let passersby know there was a body down there.

The story is that the light finally disappeared when new owners filled in that old well on Lone Hickory Road.

Lighted Ohio

A statistician would undoubtedly be required to determine which of the fifty American states and thirteen Canadian provinces and territories has the greatest number of mystery lights, but it is not presumptuous to suggest that Ohio might very well finish high in this atypical competition. Here are a half-dozen of the most well-known Ohio mystery lights:

The Lake Erie & Western freight train roared through the night a few miles outside the village of Arcadia. Dense woods there formed an arc over the steel rails and gravel roadbed. All had been routine on this run between Sandusky and Lima, until conductor Jimmie Welsh was suddenly jolted from his position at the caboose's side window. He knew from experience that a coupling had come loose and the train had broken into two sections.

Welsh left the caboose and clambered forward, nimbly navigating the freight car ladders. He held his balance atop the car leading the rear, broken section and was starting down the ladder above the broken coupling when he heard the squealing of the steam engine's iron wheels against the tracks and saw sparks fly as the engineer applied steam to brake the train. He knew what that meant. The doomed conductor watched helplessly as the lead train rapidly slowed. The impact would be awful as the broken section he clung to hurtled toward the lead cars. The crash threw him to the roadbed. Before he could twist out of the way, Jimmie Welsh's head was severed by one of the massive wheels.

And thus began the legend of Arcadia's phantom conductor.

Beginning in November 1890, shortly after Welsh's horrific death, engineers and conductors on the midnight passenger train from Sandusky going west to Findlay complained that his ghost roamed the tracks about eight miles east of Findlay, near Arcadia. They said that scarcely a night passed when the headless apparition of Jimmie Welsh was not seen coming out of the woods carrying a lantern, which he waved back and forth as though searching the ground for his missing head. As the train screamed by, the ghost turned and walked back into the woods, disappearing into a blue mist.

Two train crews were said to have requested a change of assignment after they saw the specter. An engineer in mid-January 1890 was so badly frightened one night that it took considerable persuasion to keep him aboard the train until it reached Lima.

"I won't make that run again for all the money the president of this road possesses," he declared.

The engineer's conductor and brakeman apparently concurred in the story. They saw the apparition nearly every night their train passed the scene of the accident.

"On bright moonlight nights the apparition is not so plainly outlined as when the nights are dark and rainy, as has been the rule of the past month," one contemporaneous witness claimed. "On such occasions the phantom conductor comes out clear and distinct having all the semblance of a man minus his head, while the lantern in his hand gives out a fitful, uncanny sort of illumination that freezes the blood in the veins of the boldest railroader on the line."

Crewmen aboard the midnight passenger express were the only railroaders affected by the apparition. That was because each night the train passed the site at the time of the grisly accident.

An ominous warning in an account of the haunting seemed to predict the continuing presence of headless Jimmie Welsh: Unless the spirit of the dead conductor was appeased in some way it would be difficult to get men to make the midnight run between Sandusky and Lima.

A trainman grasping a swinging lantern while he searches for missing body parts is not an unusual beginning to mystery light stories. That's also the case with headless motorcyclists, as in this story from Elmore, Ohio, recalled by Richard Gill.

The recently discharged army veteran was mad as hell. He stormed out of his girlfriend's house on a farm near Elmore when he learned that while he had served his country during World War I she'd become engaged to another man. He jumped on his new motorcycle and roared off down the driveway and onto the twisting county road she lived on. Less than a mile away, the road curved before it crossed a bridge. He lost control and crashed through the bridge railing. Searchers found his headless corpse in the shallow creek. The cycle lay crumpled on his body. Curiously, the headlamp was missing.

According to Gill, the motorcyclist reappears every vernal equinox, about March 21—but only if certain "conditions" are met will a visitor see him.

One must park one's car on the far side of the bridge facing the farmhouse. The car lights must be turned on and off three times, and the horn honked thrice. A light appears at the abandoned farmhouse, hurtles down the driveway to the road, and then vanishes when it reaches the place on the bridge where the motorcycle went over into the creek bed.

Would it be possible to verify the existence of the Elmore Light? Richard Gill claimed to have done just that with the assistance of a friend. This is his account:

"On March 21, 1968, a friend and I decided to test the truth of this legend. We went to the site near Elmore, Ohio, with two cameras, one a movie camera, the other a still camera timed to take a series of time exposures, and a tape recorder. The cameras were placed on the far side of the bridge facing toward the farmhouse. We then got into the car, which was parked in the appointed place, and blinked the lights three times, then honked the horn three times. The light appeared at the farmhouse, moved down the driveway, down the road and disappeared in the middle of the bridge. My friend then tied a piece of string across the road in the middle of the bridge. We returned to the car, blinked the lights three times, and honked the horn three times. The light appeared again, moved down the road and disappeared in the center of the bridge. We got out and found that the string was intact. My friend then decided to stand in the middle of the road, and I went back to the car to blink the lights . . . then honk the horn . . . the light appeared, moved down the road and disappeared in the center of the bridge. I waited, and when my friend did not return to the car, I went out to investigate. He had disappeared from the center of the road. I found him in a ditch by the side of the road, badly beaten. When I brought him around, he had no recollection of what had happened. At first, I thought he was faking it but, knowing him, that didn't make a great of sense to me. For our fourth experiment, we moved the car into the road on the near side of the bridge, facing away from the farmhouse. We blinked the lights . . . and honked the horn. . . . As the light appeared, we started the car moving. The light came up from behind, passed through the car and went in front of us to disappear in the center of the bridge. It was at that time that I began to believe in ghosts. My friend wanted to stay and perform other experiments but, since it was my car, we kept going. The movie film showed nothing. The still camera showed a light source of some kind. And, the tape recorder, one which records high-pitched sounds not heard by human beings, picked up a humming sound."

Is the story true? Perhaps. And then again, perhaps not. Gill did not pinpoint the location of the house nor could he remember the name of his friend.

From a farm outside Oak Harbor, just up the Portage River from Port Clinton, comes a ghost light story that in all likelihood *was* the result of natural causes.

A farmer finishing up in his fields at dusk was startled to see a bright, white light floating along the hedgerow about twenty feet in the air. The light appeared the next night and for several nights thereafter. Soon, carloads of the curious— and not a few young lovers looking for something exciting to do during those Depression years—clogged the roads around the farm field. It's said the light continued to appear for three years before it blinked out.

Wakeman lies a few miles south of the Ohio Turnpike in Huron County. It's also where a traveling lantern marked the favorite path of one Grandfather Harrison.

The old man had emigrated from Ireland and married a Native American girl. He died a wealthy landowner and left his three children a sizable estate. The family cemetery is located on Harrison Road, west of Wakeman near U.S. Highway 20.

Grandfather Harrison tended a nice vineyard. As it happened, a trail led from the cemetery to the vineyard. After he died, family members swore they saw his familiar red lantern swinging along the footpath from the cemetery to the vineyard and back again.

Some fifteen miles east of Cincinnati is the suburban community of Batavia, in Clermont County. It's the location of about the only legend of a haunted flashlight to be found anywhere.

An old man lived in a rickety shack built over a deep cellar. What he had in the dank pit was his, and only his, secret. Neighbors assumed he hid money or perhaps an illegal still in its depths. The more anxious folks around claimed that he killed and butchered livestock down there.

He used only kerosene lamps to light his way when he descended the steep ladder from under a trap door in his one room cabin. Townsfolk were surprised then, when he showed up at the hardware store and bought a big old flashlight.

Neighborhood kids gave him no end of trouble. They knocked on his door at night, spied on him during the day and generally made his life miserable. He'd chase them away with an old Indian hatchet. One day on a dare from her mischievous older brother, an especially brave little girl sneaked in the unlatched front door. She looked around. Inexplicably, the flashlight lay on the floor next to the open trap door. She nearly fainted when a guttural roar came up from the cellar and she heard the ladder creaking as someone climbed up. She kicked the flashlight into the hole. She didn't look back even though the old man—for that's who it *must have been* down there—screamed.

No one dared go near the cabin after that. A few days later, however, a neighbor peered in through a window. The place was empty, the trap door open. He went in and shone his own light into the hole. Nearly ten feet below, he saw the crumpled form of the old man, his head twisted at an unnatural angle. The hatchet was in one hand. The flashlight lay next to his head. It must have knocked him off the ladder and he'd broken his neck in the fall.

The country graveyard where he was buried was never the same. That flashlight beam was seen all the time. Some said it was the old man looking for a mean little girl. Others claimed the beam was trying to guide him out of the grave and back to his cabin.

Over in St. Paris, Ohio, some fifty miles west of Columbus, curious crowds tried to fathom just what exactly was happening to a tombstone in a local cemetery.

The stone marker was over the McMorran family gravesite at Evergreen Cemetery in Johnson Township. Reports were that as many a thousand people in a single night visited the cemetery in the 1970s trying to figure out what caused the faint glow or light that seemed to discharge from the marker. The problem was that as one drew closer the light faded away. Reflections from St. Paris or some sort of glowing fungus were offered as solutions to the mystery.

The Curious Grave

The oldest reported mystery light in North America may well be the one sighted at Narragansett, Rhode Island, in the late winter and early spring of 1722.

According to contemporary reports, as many as twenty people saw the light flitting about a fresh grave. They had gathered one evening for that express purpose. The story combines the grimness of death by smallpox in this colonial settlement, the acknowledged strangeness of unexplained night-lights, and the unsophisticated scientific understanding of early American settlers.

The story of the Narragansett light begins in the winter of 1721–1722 when an unnamed woman died of the smallpox and was buried in the small cemetery. Within days, what looked to be a fire appeared over her grave at about ten o'clock each night. Sometimes the firelight bounced to a barn and a stand of trees next to the cemetery, and sometimes it broke apart into several smaller blazing lights. The light grew in size over the course of the evening until it was so large that it quite literally illuminated the tree bark, grass and tombstones. When it was at its maximum height, witnesses claimed they could see sparks fly from it, like sparks from a fire. Most jarringly of all, the image of a person seemed to appear in the middle of the light, as if wrapped in a sheet with its arms folded.

The light—or whatever it was—moved with incredible swiftness, sometimes the distance of half a mile from one place to another in the twinkling of an eye, one report said, continuing with its rapid, but aimless roaming until daybreak.

Tabor Cemetery

In the rolling farmland some seventeen miles northeast of Esterhazy, Saskatchewan, the old Tabor Cemetery was the center of episodes involving a flickering, pinkish light that created such a stir an armed posse of farmers actually patrolled the roads nearby.

One such farmer blasted away at the light with a twelve-gauge shotgun as it seemed to take off down the snow-packed road toward him. He ran toward the spot where the light seemed to originate, but all he found was hard packed snow.

Another eyewitness claimed to have raised his own shotgun to his shoulder to fire at it when the glowing orb suddenly blinked away.

R. A. Fraser told the Canadian Press news service the light had been around for several years.

"At first I thought it was someone with a lamp," said Fraser, "then as I drove faster and it stayed the same distance away from me, I couldn't figure out what it might be. It's there all right."

In this particular case, one expert who was consulted on the matter dismissed marsh gas—natural methane produced from damp, rotting vegetation—because the light most often occurred in the winter when the ground was frozen and snow-covered. A more likely explanation, but hardly one to satisfy those keen on finding a supernatural source, is that the dry, frosty air was producing some sort of electrical discharge. The pinkish glow could have been produced by nitrogen in the air, which glows pink when excited by a charge of electricity.

Dr. Gordon Shrum, a physics professor at the University of British Columbia at the time, said, "a dry, freezing wind blowing past a hilltop might conceivably produce an electrical discharge. The mechanics of such a discharge are still a bit vague . . ."

However, his uncertainty was enough to keep doubts alive in that lonely corner of eastern Saskatchewan.

The Marfa Lights

On a lightly traveled road east of Marfa, Texas, in 1973, Samuel Whatley saw lights coming toward him. Strange, he thought, because he seldom met a car at this predawn hour as he drove home from his job as a computer operator. Perhaps it was a tourist traveling all night to avoid the heat of the day. Whatley rolled down the window of his pickup truck to wave a greeting.

A reddish orange ball of light the size of a watermelon appeared outside the truck window. The lights ahead of him had vanished. There was no other vehicle on the road. He floored the accelerator, but the light moved along beside the truck. If Whatley slowed, the light slowed. His hands were damp on the wheel.

"Hell, I was scared," Whatley told a reporter. "I was crawling out of my skin." He estimated the light had stayed with him for two miles before vanishing.

That same year, geologists John P. Kenney and Elwood Wright were prospecting for uranium in the region. They saw the light on several occasions and became so fascinated by it that they kept a journal of their sightings.

What had these three men seen?

For more than a century, the so-called Marfa Lights have been seen in the Mitchell Flat area between Alpine and Marfa, Texas. They vary in intensity, sometimes appearing as stars sparkling over a mountaintop in the Chinati Range and at other times as one huge globe shining so brightly that they can be seen for fifty miles. Motorists driving the thirty-five mile stretch of U.S. Highway 90 between Alpine and Marfa frequently see the lights.

Robert Ellison is the first non-Indian credited with seeing the lights. That came in 1883 when he saw what he thought was an Apache campfire. After scouting the countryside on horseback, he realized the lights were not those of a campfire or a homestead. On his many cattle drives from Alpine west to Marfa, Ellison saw the strange lights. But he never feared them, nor did his son-in-law, Lee Plumbley, who saw the lights for the first time in 1921.

Plumbley told author Nancy Roberts that he considered the lights a "welcome, familiar sight" in a vast and empty land. He was not the least bit afraid of them.

Early settlers would have understood Plumbley's feelings. They called the lights ghost lights, and superstitions needed no explanation. Some believed the Indians' story that the lights were the spirit of a Chisos Apache warrior who was sealed into a cave to guard stolen gold. Later, white men thought the lights were Pancho Villa and his men moving supplies across the Rio Grande after dark.

But modern man is certain a rational explanation for the lights is possible and that science will provide it—of course.

The Marfa Lights have been around for so long that each new generation tries to find its own explanation for their existence.

During the First World War, the beacons were thought to be guidelights to detect enemy invasion from the south. Of course, no invasion ever took place.

The same notion fired the imagination of one Major Davidson, who, it is said, during World War II sent up pilots from a nearby air base to investigate. When the pilots buzzed the lights, the orbs floated into Mexico, and then winked out. Finally, the pilots were ordered to bomb the lights with bags of flour to serve as source markers. In the morning, nothing was found except white powder covering the landscape.

The army and the air force conducted endless investigations, while reporters from every major Southwest news medium jostled one another in their haste to scoop the story. There was no story, save the Pentagon's final directive to the armed forces—leave the lights alone.

Science, however, has presented some plausible explanations for the lights.

One theory was offered by John Derr, a geophysicist, who thinks that what are seen near Marfa may be earthquake lights—electrical atmospheric charges generated by the shifting and grinding of rocks deep below the earth's crust. Although such lights are frequently associated with seismic activity, their presence does not necessarily predict quakes. As far as can be determined, this region of Texas has had no recent quakes.

Odd atmospheric effects may have something to do with the phenomena. Mirages are common in that part of Texas. More than one person has reported seeing false mountain ranges shining in the distance. Because Marfa is in a basin between mountain ranges, it does have a lot of unusual weather.

The automobile headlight explanation is advanced for nearly every case of mystery lights ever reported. In this instance, the lights are said to be coming from cars and trucks approaching a hill on U.S. Highway 90. But the lights glow steadily, unlike a car's headlights that flash by in seconds, or appear, disappear and reappear as they move across the landscape. And, of course, no mechanized traffic existed in the nineteenth century.

Astronomers at McDonald Observatory postulated that the lights might be caused by the Novaya Zemlya effect, in which light beams are bent by adjacent layers of air at different temperatures and carried over long distances.

Other scientists suggest that they are of electromagnetic origin, perhaps related to the geomagnetic field's response to sunspot activity. But, as more than one researcher has noted, that doesn't explain why the lights are seen in only a few specific places and only on some occasions.

An investigation sponsored by the television series "Unsolved Mysteries" sought to solve, finally, the Marfa Lights enigma. A trio of scientists—an astronomer, a geologist, and a chemist—set up a series of infrared video and film cameras to record the lights' appearance. Precise steps were taken to avoid mistaking car lights on a highway in the Chinati Mountains with the ghost lights. Powerful marker beams were placed at either end of the highway so that any light appearing between them could be accounted for. A radio beacon tower visible in the mountains was duly noted.

At 11:59 P.M., the century-old lights became visible—far outside the path of the highway, in an area known to be uninhabited. The images were recorded on video and film as slightly greenish orbs that seemed to pulsate, expand slightly and then vanish, reappearing a few minutes later.

The scientists agreed that the lights were something of natural origin, but were unable to offer a unanimous opinion as to what that might be. Perhaps it was refracted starlight or, possibly, luminous gases being released through thin fissures in the earth during earth tremors so slight they are undetected by scientific instrumentation.

Gary Cartwright was convinced "something's out there." On an August night, Cartwright and a group of skeptical writers gathered on the highway halfway between Marfa and Alpine, looking across an abandoned air base toward the Chinati Mountains. Cartwright later wrote in Texas Monthly that "when the first point of light appeared where there had been only darkness, there were some nervous giggles and a fluttering of rationalizations, and when a second came dancing above and to the right of the first, I swear something ice-cold moved across my skin. The points of light appeared one or two or sometimes three at a time, moving diagonally and sometimes horizontally for ten to fifteen seconds. They would vanish and then reappear in some new location. They could have been a mile away, or twenty or thirty . . . No one spoke for a long while."

A San Antonio poet along on the trip told Cartwright the experience had changed her life. Some of her dreams were directed at trying to figure out how to get to the lights.

One man *did* get to the lights, and his experience remains the most bizarre of the many legends surrounding the Marfa lights. Years ago a rancher living near Shafter, in the Chinati Mountains, often had to climb high to reach strayed stock. Late one day as he was climbing, a blizzard caught him. Snow pelted down and the wind knifed through him as darkness fell. He knew there was no chance of making it safely back to his cabin. But if he stopped walking, he'd freeze to death. On a bend in the trail a huge outcrop blocked his way. He was lost.

Flashing lights suddenly confronted him and seemed to speak to him, although he could never explain how. He understood that he was far off his route and close to a precipice. He must follow the lights or he would surely die.

The lights led the rancher to a small cave, and as he crawled inside, glad to be out of the howling snowstorm, a large light followed him in and remained close enough to warm him with its heat. A smaller light accompanied the larger one.

The lights somehow made the man understand that they were spirits from an ancient time who had come to save him. The man slept, and when he awoke, the lights were gone and the sun was shining. The abyss lay just beyond the outcrop where the lights had confronted him.

A hallucination by a half-frozen and delirious rancher? He did survive and the rancher's daughter repeated the story scores of times. She had some firsthand experience. She said the lights came down in their pasture all the time . . . and they were always friendly.

The Moorefield Mystery

The origins of countless enigmatic lights are in the melancholic events surrounding unsolved or suspicious deaths. In the Cole Mountain region outside Moorefield, West Virginia, a community in the state's northeast Appalachian Mountains, a phantom light has been seen on and off since before the Civil War. Yet, reports of encounters with the light continue on to the present day.

The story begins in the 1850s with a nighttime coon-hunting outing on Cole Mountain by a prominent, local landowner, Charles Jones, and one of his African-American slaves. The much younger slave carried a lantern so that they could keep up with the hounds. Soon, the dogs began yapping loudly and took off running. The men trailed behind as best they could, the slave with his lantern in the lead.

When the slave got to the dogs, he discovered that Jones was missing. He doubled back swinging his lantern back and forth and calling out. He spent the rest of the night and into the morning searching, but he found no sign of the older man. Leashing the dogs, the young slave made his way back home with the sad news. Mrs. Jones organized her own search party, with the slave guiding the way back to where he'd last seen the missing man. The fruitless search lasted for a week before Mrs.

Jones reluctantly called the men in and accepted the fact that her husband was dead, his remains lost forever.

On the one-year anniversary of Charles Jones's disappearance, the slave set off again to look for him, carrying the same lantern he had the year before. He was never seen again, nor was *his* body ever found.

And that began the tale of the Cole Mountain mystery light. It is the slave's lantern light bobbing through the woods still looking for his vanished companion. The light has turned from yellow to red over the subsequent decades.

According to writer Ruth Ann Musick, the lantern glow is still very much in evidence on that Appalachian mountainside.

One night, an adventurous young suitor had driven his girlfriend to a popular lover's lane alongside the foot of the mountain. He had only just turned off the motor when a bright red light appeared outside his driver's side window. He thought someone was trying to trick him, so he threw open the door and jumped out. The red orb hovered in midair only a few feet away. It moved in close to him, roamed down his face and body and then vanished. The young man hadn't believed in the Cole Mountain light until that moment.

A Moorefield schoolteacher reportedly saw the light shimmering on the mountainside, but he thought it was the moon that night reflecting on a stream. He later checked the locale but found there was no water where he'd seen the glow.

If the light is indeed the ghost of the slave searching for his master, as legend has it, then it would surely have a particular distaste for modern coon hunters. Two Maryland men were on the mountain with their coonhounds when their dogs abruptly took off barking through the woods. The men lost sight of them and sat down to plan their next move. A hovering red light eased out from behind a tree and buzzed toward them. As they backed up, one of the men fired his shotgun at the light. It let out a scream and flew toward them. They dropped their weapons and hightailed it out of the woods, the light bobbing and weaving only a few feet behind them. As the hunters piled into their truck, the light stayed behind, closer to the edge of the woods. And then it seemed to draw itself into a tiny pinprick and was gone.

A Question of Perspective

The summer visitor turns off an old gravel road about four miles north of Watersmeet, Michigan, drives up a slight hill and parks his car. If it's a good night, a dim, glowing orb of white light will appear in the far distance. The light may vanish for a time, but then reappear moments later. Sometimes other lights of various colors appear with it. During the winter and the early spring, the light appears more infrequently.

That's what thousands of visitors will attest they have done at what has been termed alternately the Paulding Light, the Watersmeet Light, the Dog Meadow Light or, simply, the Mystery Light. For at least three decades, the light has brought the curious to this point north of Eagle River, Wisconsin, on U.S. 45 and then through Watersmeet, to a point about a dozen miles north of the Wisconsin state line. The light appears after dark on that lonely road, seemingly rising from the horizon, glowing like a beacon, and then splitting, changing color and mysteriously disappearing as quickly as it came.

The mystery light is usually traced no further back than to the mid-1960s when a carload of teenagers stopped one clear evening on that gravel road near the bog swamp known as Dog Meadow. Suddenly, the teens claimed, brightness filled the car's interior and lit the power lines paralleling the road. They were so frightened they fled back to town and told their story to the local sheriff.

One of the earliest verified sightings came in the late 1970s in a story recounted by two Wisconsin men, Elmer Lenz and Harold Nowak, who had been skeptical of supernatural explanations. The men parked their car on the road and the light appeared in the distance as a bright spotlight shining directly at them. The light moved closer, backed away, and even appeared at an angle from time to time. Lenz, who had grown up near a railyard, said the light looked just like the headlamp of a locomotive.

The men said a smaller light glowed below and slightly to the right of the larger, white light. "The two, at times, seemed to move together, then part, one or the other disappearing, then showing again," Lenz said. The smaller light was red, though they claim to have also seen a green light.

They got out of their car and walked toward the light. As they approached, it seemed to disappear down over the next rise, but continued to cast a bright glow in the night sky.

After walking a half-mile and finding nothing that might explain the mystery, the pair turned around. As they walked back, however, the lights reappeared over the rise. When they got back to their car, other observers at the site told them that in the men's absence they'd seen a large red light above a small white one in the middle of the road a block ahead of them. If the reports were accurate, the lights would have been between the men and their car.

The men drove ahead for some distance, parked, and shut off their car lights. The mysterious light reappeared with a smaller one beneath it and shining down the middle of the road. A minute later, the larger light vanished, and the smaller light, Lenz said, "seemed to touch down and burst into three" orbs. The outer two lights disappeared, but the third remained about 200 feet away. Nowak snapped on his headlights but the light in the road didn't move. Minutes later, the men claimed this single light rose four to five feet in the air.

Journalists, too, have tried to explain the Paulding light. *Milwaukee Journal Sentinel* reporter Harry S. Pease described it in this way: "We had chosen the hill above Dog Meadow because it's easiest to find in the dark. You just drive north from Watersmeet on (U.S.) 45 about four miles, turn left onto the town road and stop on the high ground. Our eyes and ears sharpened with the passage of the minutes. We could hear cars a long way away on the highway. We could see a dimness—not so much a bigger as a less dark **V**—as we looked ahead down the road and the powerline that ran beside it. Then we saw the light. Right ahead of us, it began as a diffuse glow and then condensed into a hard knot of brilliant white. You had the feeling that maybe it was moving, but you couldn't be sure you weren't moving your head instead. It could have been big and distant or small and close. There was no way to tell. The silence remained unbroken."

The accounts by Pease, Lenz, and Nowak coincide with one of the legends of the origin of the Paulding Light. In the early twentieth century, a railroad switchman with lantern in hand was crushed between two rail cars while attempting to signal the train's engineer. Another tale holds that a trainman was murdered along the old railroad grade outside Paulding where the light appears.

A third account asserts that a rural mail carrier and his sled dogs were mysteriously slain at Dog Meadow in the early 1800s, below the vantage point from which the light can best be seen. The modern road through the region was built on the Civil War-era military road from Fort Howard in Green Bay to Fort Wilkins at Copper Harbor. Federal troops during the war guarded copper supplies moving along the path. But much earlier, men with teams of sled dogs delivered mail to isolated communities using old trails. The light, it is said, is the lantern held by the mail messenger looking for the men who murdered him.

Ezra Zeitler first heard about the Paulding light when he was a student at Minocqua, Wisconsin's, Lakeland Union High School. "On Monday mornings students would come back and say they had seen the Paulding light over the weekend and it was real scary and mysterious," he said.

Despite the captivating stories, Ezra didn't make the 120-mile round trip to the Upper Peninsula until 2000.

His younger brother, Micah, later heard similar stories. "There's not much to do . . . so we'd all go see the light. I was guaranteed to see it so that's the only reason I went," he said. He was impressed with what he saw and heard, including the legends of the dead trainman and murdered mailman.

But Micah and Ezra decided to take their interest one step further and, with their university geography professor, set off to try and solve the mystery of the light. Their results may finally explain the origins of this particular light, at least for those willing to accept something short of a paranormal justification.

The Zeitler brothers met Dr. Don Petzold, a professor of geography at the University of Wisconsin—River Falls, when they took one of his classes. They told him about the light and he became intrigued with the story.

"When Micah came back from his first experience (of seeing the light), I was immediately skeptical," Dr. Petzold said. He started asking Micah questions about how long the lights had been reported and whether they predated automobiles.

"I found out someone said it dated back to Indian times but, of course it wouldn't then be associated with the ghost of a wrecked train because there weren't any trains there either. And who could document that it dates back that long? I was determined . . . to see the light."

Dr. Petzold arranged a trip to Paulding with Micah and Ezra . . . and a good set of topographical maps for the Upper Peninsula.

The three men drove to the site on a summer Saturday night in 2000. About ten or fifteen vehicles were already there. With a pair of strong binoculars, they walked over to the fence, near where the gravel road ends. The first thing they noticed was that a power line right-of-way extends in the same northerly direction from which the light appears. Then they saw the light itself.

"It was in the right-of-way," Ezra said. "It did look like it was hovering around. A red light appeared. I can't remember if I could identify them as moving up and down, but it looked as if they were hovering."

Complete darkness had not fallen so the researchers could still detect the skyline in the distance. It didn't take them long to realize what they were looking at: car lights.

"I could tell they were headlights of cars, taillights of cars," Ezra said. "After that we kept passing the binoculars among us. Each of us agreed."

It was not as easy to pinpoint how far away from them the light was.

With the help of their topographic maps, the trio figured the car lights were from U.S. Highway 45 since no other road in the area would have so much traffic.

"There's a straight line of sight right down the cut for the power line," Dr. Petzold points out. "The highway is really straight, with one short exception. So, we thought the light appearing must have had something to do with the cars coming up and over this hill that's about a mile beyond Paulding, but that's a distance of about seven miles from the viewpoint. The white light does appear as one large light, but over (such a) distance the headlights converge because of refraction and temperature differences in the atmosphere to look like one, large light. Then as the cars come down the hill, it gives the appearance of coming closer to you, but then all of a sudden it disappears at one point. But that's when the light dips below the trees or some lower elevation. As a climatologist, I attribute the movement of the lights to refraction in the lower part of the atmosphere. I think it would really be quite different if the car lights producing this effect would be closer."

The red lights, Dr. Petzold reasoned, are occasional taillights going north out of Paulding, then up a grade known locally as Cemetery Hill. With binoculars, he could pick out two red lights, confirming his suspicion that they were taillights.

To confirm their hypothesis, Dr. Petzold and his students got back in their car and headed north on U.S. 45. "On the other side of Paulding," Ezra Zeitler said, "the highway goes up a gradual incline on a long, straight hill. Toward the top of the hill I could see in my rearview mirror the headlights of the cars that were stopping at the viewing point. That's when we really knew that seeing the Paulding light was not a real mystery."

Dr. Petzold said an understanding of the Paulding light was not difficult to arrive at. He shakes his head in bemusement at the simplicity of it all.

"We can't possibly be the first people to have looked at a scale map and said, 'Ah, ha! This is a pretty straight road and there is this gradual incline . . .' It would be neat to stop traffic for a period of time and go up there with headlights and flash a signal," he said.

There is an equally simple explanation for the light's supposed irregularity. For example, when Micah Zeitler first visited on a night in early spring, it took some fifteen to twenty minutes for the light to come out. The reason is that there is not much traffic in the remote Upper Peninsula of Michigan on early spring nights. But it's a different story during the height of tourist season.

Another reason people who see the Paulding light may not consider U.S. Highway 45 as part of the answer is that one must turn *left* off the highway onto the gravel road which leads to the viewing area. That would seem to mean they would be looking west to the lights, and thus into dense wilderness. In reality, the gravel road veers around so that one is actually looking *north* toward the U.S. highway. The hill north of Paulding is at Maple Hill Cemetery, over ten miles from where the light is best viewed. The cemetery is at 1,315 feet above sea level, while Paulding, south of it, is in a depression. Thus, observers pick up the car lights going up or down Cemetery Hill and then lose them as they descend into Paulding. Lights from the village itself may account for some reports that the bright lights are followed by radiance as they disappear from view.

Any rational explanation does not diminish Dr. Petzold's fascination.

"There is this incredible combination of topography, geography, the alignment of the highway, and this power line. I suppose it could be reproduced somewhere else, but I don't know. This would not happen if it were a much shorter distance because then you would be able to separate the two headlights easily. But seven miles is a long distance for light to travel in a straight line, over terrain of forest and hills. It's just the right combination of natural and manmade effects."

The geography professor hasn't found a duplicate convergence of lights anywhere else, but he's still looking. "It's not often that you can see traffic for seven miles in the distance," he adds.

Logical explanations will not, of course, deter those who prefer to believe the lights are produced by something other than natural causes. Even the government has entered the fray by erecting a sign giving the history of the Paulding light. Local tourism officials have found it to be good for business. On a warm summer night it is not unusual for dozens of people, some sitting in lawn chairs with camcorders at the ready, to watch and wait for the lights to appear and disappear.

Side Lights

Alabama
Some two miles northwest of Molloy, Alabama, a mystery light has been seen off and on since the late 1890s. Little is know about its origins, other than that it occurs in a predominantly rural area. Molloy is on State Highway 12.

Arkansas
The Kans Wilson Light appears as a ball of fire near Farmington, Arkansas, which is about three miles southwest of Fayetteville. The light is supposed to be the work of an old woman who died in about 1895.

Florida
In the dense, swampy Apalachicola National Forest of the Florida panhandle there is said to exist one of the most mysterious phantom lights ever reported in the United States.

Variously termed the Great Florida Mystery or the Wakulla Volcano when it was extensively reported in the media of a century ago, the mystery object appeared as a plume of spiraling smoke during the day and as a sharp shaft of light shooting up from the earth after dark. Tallahassee is about thirty miles to the northeast, but even at that distance some folks on the outskirts of the city told reporters they'd seen the light from their homes. The exact location of the light has eluded most searchers . . . and locals are suspicious of outsiders snooping around that part of the Florida backwoods. One estimate is that it's close to a line drawn between Medart, at the junction of U.S. Highways 98 and 319, and Sumatra, about forty miles due west. The problem is that no highway runs directly between the two small towns and the region is virtually impenetrable.

Georgia
Not far from where the rich and powerful vacation on St. Simon's Island there is a graveyard with a poignant tale which is the origin of a ghost light legend. At Christ Church Cemetery, the eerie glow of a candle is sometimes reported next to the grave of a young woman who died in the late nineteenth century. She was terrified of the night and always kept candles burning in her bedroom. Upon her death, candles were placed next to her grave. Though her family and friends have long since died, ghostly candlelight keeps the dark away.

Hawaii

A strange light was seen on Saddle Road before the 1955 eruption of Kilauea Volcano. In Hawaii, this light was attributed to Madame Pele, the goddess of volcanoes. Henry Macomber and his family saw the light. They were cruising down the road on January 31, 1955, when their truck shuddered as if it had been hit with strong wind gusts—except there was only a slight breeze at the time. A little while later, they saw strangely shimmering lights near the highway. Several government officials traveling along the same section of highway some days later reported that they, too, had seen lights dancing along the road.

Nebraska

Seward is a small city of some six thousand persons some twenty miles west of Lincoln and the home of Concordia University. Not much happens there on a regular basis, but that certainly wasn't the case in 1875 and 1876 when the Seward Flame Light made its first appearance.

About six miles east of town, on Middle Creek, a fifteen-foot-high column of fire appeared every Tuesday night at about ten o'clock. The neighborhood was described as being somewhat nervous over the singular sight. The first man to see the flame was one August Meier, as he was driving home during the summer of 1875 in his horse-team on a road between the farms of George Libert and Robert Mankel. Actually, his horses were the first to spot the flame. They stopped dead in the road and refused to go any farther until it vanished. The flame reappeared in January 1876 when Meier and Christ Gaustman saw the flame at the same time. Witnesses said that although the flame appeared to be about a story and a half tall, it was only a few feet in diameter and visible for a few moments at a time. Meier said the flame bent over and disappeared.

Texas

The Marfa Lights are not the only odd nightly illuminations in the Lone Star State. Saratoga is a small community of some 1,200 residents about thirty miles northwest of the Beaumont/Port Arthur area. The Big Thicket National Preserve is a massive region of swampland brush. On summer nights sightseers thronged Bragg Road north of Saratoga when fireballs bounced through the impenetrable thickets. Sometimes the lights were pure white or colored globes, intensely bright and skimming along quite close to the ground. It got so bad one year that the Hardin County sheriff had to post signs prohibiting the discharge of firearms along the road—it seems that folks were trying to blast the fireballs to smithereens with buckshot and rifle fire. No one was successful.

Brit Bailey was buried standing up. That's what he wanted when he died in 1833 at a place known as Bailey's Prairie, about five miles west of Angleton, or forty miles south of Houston. Since that time, a spherical object that glows as if with incandescent paint hovers near Brit's grave. Legend has it that curious onlookers have chased the orb across the prairie. Another tale encourages visitors to his grave to stand directly on top of it so that they can hear a low, deep rumbling coming from within the earth. Perhaps it is Brit Bailey himself trying to lie down.

Virginia

The Great Dismal Swamp in southeast Virginia is the location of an infrequent mystery light similar to others reported around the world—it appears as a single beam, sometimes described as looking like an automobile headlight. Travelers along rural Jackson Road south of Suffolk say it swerves off the road when one drives toward it, but then darts back on the road once it's passed. The light has been reported for more than a century.

THE WEST

Fort Ghost

Army Colonel Roy Strom was sound asleep in a bedroom of old Carleton House at historic Fort Huachuca, now incorporated into the city of Sierra Vista in southeastern Arizona. Colonel Strom's wife was out of town for a few days and his daughters had returned to school.

Suddenly, a loud crash that sounded as if it had come from somewhere in the house startled him awake. Colonel Strom climbed out of bed and set about trying to locate the source of the disturbance. It didn't take him long. In his daughter's now-vacant room he found an Oriental jewelry box face down in the middle of the floor. The lacquered box's five drawers were still closed. When he picked it up, the drawers and their contents spilled out onto the floor.

Colonel Strom was perplexed. He had bought the jewelry box for his daughters during a tour of duty in the Far East. It had been sitting on the fireplace mantel a half-dozen feet from where he found it lying. How did it land on the floor? It would have been impossible for it to have slid off and land where he found it. Earth tremors were ruled out since nothing else in the house had been disturbed.

Colonel Strom, a former deputy commander of the U.S. Army Intelligence Center and School at Fort Huachuca, calls the flying jewelry box incident the most puzzling occurrence during his stay at Carleton House. Or as he discovered . . . the *haunted* Carleton House.

Built as the post hospital in 1880, Carleton House performed that role for only a few years before being turned into officers' quarters, an officers' mess, post headquarters, a cafe and then a schoolhouse. In more recent years, the house has been the post residence of the hospital commander or other officers assigned to the base.

Fort Huachuca itself dates from February 1877 when Colonel August B. Kautz, the commander of the Department of Arizona, established a camp in the Huachuca Mountains to protect settlers and travelers in southeastern Arizona. Army records indicate a temporary camp was located at the present site of the fort on March third, 1877. Fort Huachuca played an integral role in the Indian Wars of the 1870s and 1880s. Its location was central to blocking Apache escape routes to Mexico and served as advance headquarters and supply base for the Geronimo campaign.

Later, the 10th Cavalry headquartered at Fort Huachuca joined General John Pershing's punitive campaign into Mexico to find notorious Pancho Villa in 1916. The fort was also home to the four regiments now known collectively as "Buffalo Soldiers," segregated regular Army units of African-Americans during the nineteenth and early twentieth centuries.

Carleton House is the oldest building on the base and named after Brigadier General James H. Carleton, the famed leader of the "California Column" during the Civil War. When the fort was temporarily turned over to the State of Arizona from 1947 to 1951, Governors Sidney P. Osborn and Dan E. Garvey used Carleton House as a retreat. The Army Engineers reactivated the fort during the Korean War. The fort is the key military installation in Arizona and of strategic importance in the American West.

Tales of ghostly apparitions and peculiar incidents have been reported by several of the families that have occupied Carleton House. But the Strom family was the first to attach an identity to the elusive spirit.

"I never believed in ghosts. And I didn't change my mind because of 'Charlotte,'" said Strom, who was promoted to general after his tenure at Fort Huachuca.

The general's wife, Joan Strom, was the first to attach the name Charlotte to their resident specter. There seems to be no historical connection between the ghost and anyone named Charlotte, other than it being "a nice 1800s sort of name," Mrs. Strom said. She wanted to be able to call the ghost by name, particularly on those occasions when the family wanted to blame "someone" for mischievous activities in the house.

On the very first day the Strom family moved in, the house's reputation was impressed upon them when they met several local men who had been hired to help the moving company unload furniture. One worker in particular seemed jittery. He carried boxes only to the front door, where he sat them down. His cohorts were upset with his apparent laziness.

"I'm just not going in there," he advised them. "That house is haunted." He didn't explain how or why he knew about Carleton House.

On that same day, the Stroms piled boxes in what had been the hospital's morgue, now a bedroom a few steps below the level of the rest of the house. Sometime that evening all the boxes were torn open and the contents strewn about the room.

The family's dog is generally blamed for that piece of mischief, but Roy Strom really isn't convinced it couldn't have been something else, something more elusive.

A day or so later, Strom was home alone when the doorbell rang. He answered but no one was outside. Twenty minutes later the bell rang again. This time, he checked all four entrances to the house, each with a doorbell, but again didn't find anyone. A few minutes later, the doorbell buzzed a third time. Strom figured it might be some kids pulling a prank, so he raced around the house trying to catch whoever was out there. Again unsuccessful, Strom arrived at his own solution a half-hour later when the bell rang once more. He disconnected the wiring from each and every doorbell!

Four chandeliers in the cavernous knotty-pine living room, a wardroom when the building had been used as a hospital, also seem to cause occasional problems. Two separate switches control each pair of lights so that to have all four chandeliers lighted both switches must be flipped on. On the day the Stroms moved in, all four lights worked. But that night Roy tried them again. Three of the chandeliers worked fine, but a fourth refused to operate. The next morning all four worked fine once again. That pattern was repeated throughout the family's stay at Carleton House. Lights developed sudden, albeit sporadic, electrical problems.

Soon after they moved in, the Stroms hung a number of pictures in the dining room. The adobe walls made the job difficult, but they finished the task after a few false starts. On the night after they finished hanging the pictures, they all fell down, including one that had a solid brass Oriental trivet. It was bent nearly in half. Roy tried to straighten it by hand the next day, and failed.

"I think I can explain almost everything that happened to us in the house," contends Roy, citing poor wiring for the electrical problems and weak walls for the pictures falling. But he still can't understand how the brass trivet became so badly twisted.

His wife Joan sectioned off a portion of the living room she called "Charlotte's corner." The area is perceptibly colder than the rest of the house (which Roy says is caused by it being close to a stairwell) and the overhead chandelier is the one that always refused to work at night.

Joan thought the ghost might be that of a woman who died when the house was a hospital in the 1880s. The woman may have died in childbirth, along with her newborn child. Joan believed that the ghost doesn't think her dead child was properly buried. While she lived in the house, Joan unsuccessfully searched Fort Huachuca records and a local cemetery trying to find evidence of a mother and child's death. However, records were sketchy during the frontier era, or they may have been lost over the decades. Sometimes those who died simply were buried in unmarked graves.

Two other peculiar events at Carleton House directly involved Joan Strom. Early one morning, she was at a table in the kitchen when she saw her teenage daughter, Amy, walking down an adjacent hallway. Joan called out to her, but Amy didn't stop or return her greeting, which her mother thought very unusual. She got up from her desk and went into her daughter's bedroom. Amy was fast asleep, as were her two sisters. Joan doesn't think it was Amy that she saw in the hallway that morning.

One of the eeriest experiences of Joan's life in the house, according to Roy Strom, took place one afternoon as she took freshly washed linen to a bathroom closet. A swirling miasma, a kind of whitish fog, enveloped her. Joan said it wasn't hot or cold, dark or damp. She couldn't feel anything, she reported.

Although the legend of the Carleton House haunting has been around for many years, only a few people, perhaps including Joan Strom, have reportedly seen the ghost. One of the first sightings involves the ten-year-old son of a neighbor family who had been sent to deliver a message to the Koenig family, residents of Carleton House before Roy and Joan Strom. The boy didn't know that the house's front door was actually located at the side. Instead, he went up the front steps and knocked. He later told his parents that Margaret Koenig walked right down the hall toward him but ignored his raps. She had blond hair and wore a long dressing gown.

Puzzled by her neighbor's rude behavior, the boy's mother later telephoned. Mrs. Koenig insisted she and her family had only just recently returned home. No one had been in the house at the time of the boy's visit. But the child insisted that a woman had been in the hallway of Carleton House.

One of Margaret Koenig's teenage daughters may also have seen Charlotte's ghost in an incident eerily reminiscent of the one Joan Strom had. Nancy Koenig had been out late on a date. Earlier that evening, her mother had asked her to "check in" when she returned home. Nancy got home, went into the paneled living room and saw her mother standing at the end of the hallway. "Hi mom," Nancy called out. "I'm home." She then went to bed. The next morning Mrs. Koenig scolded her daughter for not letting her know when she got home. Nancy insisted she had and described how she had seen her mother in the hall.

Col. Warren Todd, his wife Nancy, and their two sons lived in Carleton House for several years. If the Stroms took a somewhat lighthearted view of the house's ghostly reputation, Warren and Nancy Todd became reluctant believers that the story of Charlotte may have been something more than make-believe.

Warren Todd was the post's hospital commander. He is a pediatrician and mechanical engineer. "I like to look at things and try to make sense out of them," he insists.

Within a month of the family moving in, Dr. Todd's belief in rational explanations to all events was thoroughly tested.

"Something happened to the hot water heater," he remembered. The unit was located in a small room under the house reached through a door near the front steps. "I got a key, went into the room and walked about ten feet before I said, 'I don't like it in here at all.' I never got to the hot water heater. I guess you could say I was 'psyched out.' That room was the only place that I've never wanted to go into. Nothing really happened. I just said that if I didn't have to go in there I wasn't going to."

According to several psychics who contacted Dr. Todd after the incident was publicized, the little child that Charlotte is said to be looking for may have been buried in that room. Dr. Todd said his sense of dread upon entering that isolated cellar room was palpable.

Several additional events convinced the Todds that reasonable and logical explanations for what went on in Carleton House might not always have been possible.

The first took place very early in the morning, Dr. Todd estimates it at about 3:30 A.M., as he studied for a class in health services administration he was taking at the University of Arizona. He sat in the kitchen; the door going into the dining room was shut.

Suddenly a voice that seemed to come from some distance beyond the door to the dining room called out:

"Father!"

"Father!"

Dr. Todd jerked his head toward the childish voice, worried that his six-year-old son wanted something. But his son never called him "father," always "dad" or "daddy."

The voice, clearly like that of a child, again rang out even more insistent than before:

"Father!"

"FATHER!"

Dr. Todd jumped up from the table, shoved the door open and raced for his son's room, some twenty feet down the hallway. There he found his son Drew safely tucked in bed. He had clearly not been the source of the voice in the night.

The Todd's dachshund was never comfortable in Carleton House. He seemed to have a sixth sense that something unseen roamed through his territory.

Nancy Todd clearly remembered his behavior.

"His hackles would go right up for no reason at all. We would be in the TV room and he would go racing down the hallway, barking all the time. He 'dug' a hole in the rug at one particular spot in the hallway. There was something about that area he didn't like at all. We finally had to put chicken wire over that part of the carpet. This went on the entire time we had the dog, not just for a few days. He would quiet down for a few hours and then be back at it. There was never anything any of us could see, smell, or hear that would cause him to do that."

Nancy also heard a peculiar voice in the house. "I was out on the porch very early one morning, about five o'clock. And I heard something. I looked out to see if a jogger or walker was going by but I couldn't see anyone. The only way I can describe what I heard was that it was like a computer voice, sort of mechanical sounding. It seemed to be saying something like 'Sleep . . . sleep.'"

Her stepson lived with the family during their stay at Fort Huachuca and reported another strange encounter. The boy's bedroom was down a short flight of steps, in the lower level that was formerly the hospital morgue.

"He had to cross the front paneled living room, the one with Charlotte's corner," Nancy Todd explained, "in order to get to his room. Well, he had fallen asleep in the TV room and was going back to his bedroom through the living room when he looked to his left and saw a dress. There wasn't any *body* connected to it, just a long dress that seemed to be standing all by itself."

The next morning he drew a picture for his stepmother of what he had seen: a light-colored gown with ruffled edges around the sleeves and hemline. Just the type of dress a young woman on the Arizona frontier of the 1880s might have worn, Mrs. Todd observed.

Nancy Todd even decorated the portion of the living room she termed "Charlotte's corner" with a rocking chair occupied by a baby doll. No one ever sat in the chair. Mrs. Todd thought the chair and doll might help out the young woman's ghost on those lonely nights when the "search" for her baby seemed particularly hopeless.

"Charlotte is like a young puppy dog," Mrs. Todd said. "She would never do anything with a lot of people in the house."

Despite the many brushes with supernatural overtones, Mrs. Todd never thought about moving out of the historic house, even if the ghosts were quite close.

"In the TV room I definitely got the feeling that somebody was standing there, or walking near me. But, I never felt uncomfortable in that house. I was always very secure, even though I don't particularly like being alone. It never felt eerie, and I never wished that I didn't live there," she maintained.

For his part, Warren Todd doesn't disbelieve in ghosts as much as he once did. "If it had not been for that one early morning episode with the child's voice and with our dog's strange behavior, I would have said it's a cute story but that's all." He wanted to "meet" Charlotte, hoping that he could talk to her and find out what she wanted. He regrets that the meeting never took place. But he does think the house remains intriguing and might be "worthy of inspection" by reputable parapsychologists.

Fort Huachuca is operated by the U.S. Army Intelligence Center. It's the location of the Army Intelligence Center and School and the Army's Information Systems Command. All C130 flight training for NATO has taken place at the fort, as did training for the Israeli army and air force.

The Fort Huachuca Historical Museum in Building 41401 contains a history of the U.S. Army in the Southwest and is open free of charge to the military and civilian public seven days a week.

The partially reconstructed army post known as Fort Lowell, in northeast Tucson near the confluence of the Rillito River, Tanque Verde Creek, and Pantano Wash, is also home to a legendary ghost tale from turn-of-the-century Arizona. The historic post was in operation from 1873 to 1891, primarily for campaigns against the Apache Indians, including Chief Geronimo. By April 1891, all the troops at Fort Lowell had left for New Mexico's Fort Wingate.

Numerous families continued to live near the abandoned fort, and it was their reports that first attracted the attention of frontier Arizona newspaper editors. On December 14, 1900, the *Arizona Daily Citizen* wrote that "reputable citizens have told the story of their adventures with the ghost and today one of the residents of the Rillito came to secure a quantity of ammunition for the final attack upon the visitor should he appear tonight."

The account describes the ghost as coming out of the ruins at night and fading into the crumbling adobe walls when pursued. The ghost did not take kindly to being interrupted as "one of the residents of the fort was within twenty yards of the ghost when it suddenly turned on him and fired a volley of stones at the pursuer."

Over the next few days, the *Daily Citizen* and then the *Arizona Republic* of Phoenix chronicled the adventuresome specter. On December 16, the Phoenix newspaper described the figure as of "unusual stature, wearing high boots and the uniform of a soldier." Although several people shot at the figure, it eluded capture.

The *Daily Citizen* of December 28 reported a Christmas Eve sighting: "It (the ghost) emerged from the adobe ruins of the old fort and stole a turkey from a rancher. The ghosts of the fort enjoyed a turkey dinner at the expense of the rancher, but the sacrifice was not begrudged as ghosts who throw stones must eat, even though but once a year."

Finally, on April 13, 1901, the Tucson paper carried the last known account of the Fort Lowell ghost. "A Mexican resident . . . was sitting beside his fireplace when a gust of smoke came down the chimney and spread out into the room. . . . A man formed in the smoke and stood gazing with fixed eyes upon the frightened Mexican. When he could control himself, the Mexican spoke a few words of welcome in Spanish to the strange visitor, but no reply came. . . . The phantom vanished as it had appeared, taking with it the cloud of smoke and no one has since heard or seen anything of it."

Perhaps the winter nights were long and the reporters bored in frontier Arizona.

High Spirits

Although storytellers have been collecting Colorado ghost stories for countless years, it appears there is little danger they'll deplete this (un)natural resource. There is the a Rollinsville cabin haunted by a little boy, a pleasant gray-haired lady materializing in a Colorado Springs home, an elevator that moves by itself in a Littleton art center, and the embarrassment of ghostly riches in storied Cripple Creek and Victor, and all are part of Colorado's abundant heritage of supernatural lore.

Where the West Still Lives

If there are any Colorado communities in which the Old West seems as close as that hitching post yer' leaning against, they're fabled Victor and Cripple Creek, about six miles away from one another and some 25 miles southwest of Colorado Springs by rugged mountain road. On clear days, 14,110-foot Pikes Peak seems within spittin' distance. The little communities are of such importance to the nations' Western heritage that their few thousand and some permanent residents must content themselves to live in officially designated historic areas. But based upon what writer Charles Clifton found out, the towns might well be advised to stake a claim to having as many ghosts per square frontier block as any other community in the Centennial State.

There is the ghost of Maggie, looking like a Gibson girl from the 1890s—a great-looking, willowy brunette in her twenties wearing a white shirtwaist, long dark skirt, and high-heeled boots. Her hair's done up in a fashionable bun . . . well, at least fashionable a century ago. That's when Maggie lived. But that's not the last time she was seen. No, that came decades later. When she ought to have been quite dead.

The apparition of this young woman was a pleasant spirit who made herself at home in a four-story brick building that takes up a huge chunk of real estate at Bennett and Third Street in Cripple Creek. The business is known by the name of the undertakers who once operated out of the basement, Fairley Bros. & Lampman. As with many buildings in Western towns, the place was home to several enterprises, including physicians, chiropractors, and even housed the ballroom of a fraternal organization.

Maggie's origins are obscure, although some people think she may have been associated with one of the doctors who operated out of second-floor offices years ago. That's because among the ghostly sounds reported in the building was the clicking of keys on a manual typewriter and the agreeable aroma of rose-scented perfume. Maggie might have been a receptionist or secretary. The haunting goes back to at least the 1960s when artist Charles Frizzell owned an art gallery in the building. He often let hippies coming through town "crash" in empty upstairs rooms. But Frizzell said they didn't stay long. Murmuring voices kept them awake most of the night.

The third-floor ballroom that stretched across the rear of the building also puzzled Frizzell, although at the time he worked there the room was vacant. He and his wife heard laughter and dancing coming from the deserted ballroom on several occasions. Odd blue lights sometimes came skipping down the staircase to the second floor. The Frizzells futilely tried to keep out the lights by closing the double doors leading to the staircase and then twisting coat hanger wire around the doorknobs. But when they checked back in a short while, the hangers had been untwined. The doors stood wide open.

But Maggie the ghost seemed to settle down some years later when building co-owner Katherine Hartz had a little talk with her on that same staircase. It began on a late fall day as Mrs. Hartz was closing up the building for the winter. As she walked down a second-floor hallway she detected someone walking above her, on the third floor, but from the position of the footfalls, the individual would have to be walking through walls! As she ran up the stairs, coming *down* the steps was a wispy young woman. That would be Maggie. Mrs. Hartz said hello. The woman telepathically said 'Hello!' back to her. That's when Mrs. Hartz made her deal with the ghost: "You are welcome to stay in this building as long as you protect it, take care of it, and as long as you're here only for the good."

Maggie apparently agreed with the rules—for the most part. There were those odd little pranks now and then. Once she hid some money that was supposed to be in a cash register. One winter, Katherine Hartz and her husband Kenneth received several small electric bills when the building should have been vacant and shuttered and the power shut down. When they investigated, the local police chief and a shopkeeper across the street said they'd seen lights on. A search proved fruitless; the main power switch had indeed been turned off. Mrs. Hartz tried a different tact with their ghost just before they left the building. "Maggie," she called out. "Quit wasting electricity. Go to bed before dark!"

It worked. The lights stayed off.

Did the soaring form of a ravishing female ghost crying out "I'm free!" rise through the flames when the Welty Block and the Cripple Creek Market burned the night of March 4, 1977?

That's what at least some firefighters who battled the blaze seemed to think. The history of that particular section of Cripple Creek would certainly support the theory that enough odd things had happened there to think its destruction might vanquish a ghost or two.

The Welty Block was huge, with fifty rooms and a Masonic Hall. The bottom floor held a bar and restaurant and a grocery. The wife of a former owner said lots of "spooky" things went on when she and her husband lived there. Her bed shook in the middle of the night and her dog growled at nothing she could see. A parade of comely apparitions dressed à la Lillian Russell disturbed the sleep of some overnight guests.

All that is prelude, however, to that cold March night when the Cripple Creek and Victor volunteer firefighters tried and failed to save the old block from destruction. Part of the problem was the subzero temperatures—fire hydrants froze and the men themselves looked like "living icicles" according to onlookers.

One new firefighter reported that someone had died in the building. He heard screaming. The building was locked and vacant at that time of the year. Another veteran firefighter—a man who had done carpentry work in the building and said his tools would often turn up in places he hadn't left them—had his own eerie experience the night of the conflagration. He swore that as the rear wall and roof collapsed, he heard a scream from inside the burning building. But the scream was one of release. The words he heard were "I'm free! I'm free at last!"

That recollection jibes with other witnesses who said they saw the apparition of a beautiful woman rising through the smoke, toward the heavens.

Robert Lays had decided that a late night/early morning mid-summer cleaning at his Palace Hotel would spiff up the place for the remainder of the high tourist season. So it was that he was shampooing the lobby carpet at about 3 A.M. when he got the "weird feeling" that he wasn't alone. He shut off the machine and looked around. Standing farther down the lobby was the specter of a woman with long hair, dressed in a nightgown with puffy sleeves.

Her name was Kitty Chambers.

That much Robert knew. Why she decided to haunt his hotel on Bennett Avenue was just one of those many unexplained mysteries in Cripple Creek. She was the wife of Dr. W. H. Chambers and together they owned the hotel, a former pharmacy—not connected to the original, larger Palace Hotel in the city—at the turn of the century. Her premature death in 1908 occurred in the hotel's Room 3.

Mrs. Kitty's brief appearance to Robert Lays that one night was not the only indication of her presence. There were countless times when the "extrarational" Lays, as he described himself, either sensed that she was around or found products of her playfulness. One of her favorite tricks, he said, was to light candles on tables in the closed bar or in one of the shuttered dining rooms when he was working elsewhere in the hotel.

This former owner seemed to remain connected to the room in which she passed away, Room 3. Passersby on the street below reported they'd see lights in that room in the off-season. During tourist season, the Palace provided many guest amenities, but turning down sheets for guests wasn't one of them. Yet, those staying in Room 3 found their bedsheets turned down.

She might have had a (translucent) hand in Robert's problems with room keys. They'd continually disappear, especially those for Room 9. Why Room 9? No one seemed entirely sure. One year, during the first thirteen days the hotel was open for the season Robert lost six keys for Room 9. None was ever recovered.

Going Down?

Going to work, for most people, often means grabbing a briefcase, jumping in the car, and hoping that no one has taken your reserved parking space. The day is spent at a desk pouring over forms, answering telephone calls, and maybe trying to squeeze in an extra few minutes for lunch. That seemed to be the life for those at the Littleton, Colorado, Town Hall Arts Center, but according to published reports folks there sometimes got more than they bargained for.

What they found in the circa 1919 structure, built as a combination town hall, fire station, and community center, were some decidedly unusual activities that some said meant the place was haunted. They cited such things as laughter and music when the place was vacant and an elevator that went up and down of its own accord.

A fund-raiser for the center, Nancy Noyes, told a reporter that she wasn't afraid of "them," meaning the spirits of former town officials who worked there—or maybe a few lingering Littletonians who danced away Saturday nights; orchestra music and murmuring laughter were reported from the old ballroom. But she said if there were any ghosts around, they were really sort of "whimsical."

"I would leave my desk and come back, and everything would be moved around. I thought my co-workers were playing tricks on me," she said. A co-worker said it wasn't anyone joking around but rather "the ghosts getting feisty."

David Payne and his wife were working late in the center when the elevator started up. He looked through the building to confirm that they were indeed alone. "The security system light was still on, so no one had come in," he said. "It was disquieting. So we stopped working and left."

Strangers of Kindness

There may be vengeful wraiths prowling the meadows and crevices of the Colorado Rockies, but kinder, gentler lost souls are more common.

The little boy ghost at a Rollinsville cabin is an example. His name was Ted, so named by the children of the cabin's owner, poet/writer Jane Brakhage. She told a Rocky Mountain News reporter that the sad youngster first visited on a fine winter morning when her children were out sledding:

"Crystal got on the sled at the top of the hill. All the other kids were at the bottom . . . and she said, 'Somebody push me!' Then she felt a hand on her back and she went whoopee down the hill, got to the bottom, and there was nobody at the top. Nobody."

Jane saw the child—she thought he was about seven or so—at night, and she almost mistook him for one of her own five children. Except that he was dressed in black shaggy clothes that hung from his thin frame.

"I woke up. It was a moonlit night and I saw a child staring at me in misery, like 'I'm not comfortable. I've got the flu. I just threw up.' I said, 'What is it?' I couldn't see which kid it was. He walked across the room and stood against the banister—stood there, and he wouldn't come any closer and, finally, I reached to hold him for a while and then put him back to bed. As I reached out to grab him, he vanished, and the banister appeared in the moonlight."

Could some energetic housecleaning set loose a ghost in a house?

That question confronted a Colorado Springs art appraiser in his old Victorian home. Bernard Ewell said it seemed that whatever haunted his home had been basement-bound until the night he and his wife finished some heavy cleaning. As Ewell and his wife sat in the living room, the basement door flew open and seconds later a couple of large pinecones sitting on a shelf dropped off.

"We went upstairs," Ewell told a reporter, "and the door to the guest room was open (as was) the door to the unfinished closet. I picked up the cat and tried to toss her into the closet because she stayed in there a lot. She turned in mid-air the way cats can and hit the floor running."

Nothing much else happened for some time. Then Ewell met his elusive house-guest. The meeting came by chance when his small son was fussy late one night and wouldn't go to sleep. Ewell picked him up and cradled him in his arms as he walked around the house. He went into the dim front hall.

"I just knew there was someone coming down the stairs. I glanced up through the railings and a woman was coming down the stairs. I would guess she was probably in her mid or late 50s. Her hair was gray—about shoulder length—and she was wearing a nightgown. She leaned down and looked at me, we had direct eye contact, and she just smiled slightly. The message was, 'Oh, it's you.'"

The last he saw of her was the bottom of her nightgown disappearing around a bend in the stairs. He didn't know who she was or where she came from or why she picked that particular time to appear. He wasn't afraid. And he never saw her again.

A woman in Black Hawk, a pinpoint of a town a few miles from Central City, had the unusual experience of becoming the object of a ghost's amorous intentions.

It all happened in a Black Hawk boardinghouse—not once, but twice. The first time, the image of a man appeared in black and white with a kind of light shimmering around it. He seemed to be mouthing some words, she said. She couldn't make out what he was trying to say.

The second time it happened, the words became distinct. "His face was melted," she said. "But when his face formed it was a miner. He was all dressed up, and he said, 'I've come to court you.'"

The man—er, ghost—must have been serious. He held out a flower in his hand.

Unfortunately, the Jackson family of Pueblo didn't know if the female ghost they said inhabited their circa 1893 home was kind or gentle . . . or worse. What really worried them, however, is that their neighbors never seemed to want to tell them anything about the house. "They act like something horrible happened here but they won't tell me anything," Richard Jackson told an Associated Press reporter. "They just clam up."

Richard and his wife Bonnie said religious items would play vanishing games, as would household utensils. And then, Bonnie originally thought the house settling accounted for the noises she heard at night.

She said her husband bought a set of coasters "and by the end of the week, all but three of them were gone." She never found them.

There was at least one appearance by the ghost, Bonnie said.

"One time, my daughter had just returned from the hospital and I saw a woman watching over her crib. She told me that she was going to take care of the baby and that I didn't have to worry about it anymore. I totally freaked out," she said.

Totally reasonable.

Mr. Black's House

Daniel O'Brien didn't know what to think when he awoke that Saturday night with an intuition that someone else was in the bedroom with him. He called out but didn't get a response. He turned over and went back to sleep. A few minutes later, he was jolted awake. The door was rattling and a chair next to his bed was hip-hopping across the floor.

"You *know* me, Daniel," whispered a taunting voice. "I've come from the other world. We must speak."

He *didn't* know who it was and didn't care to find out. He flailed his arms about as if swatting away a troublesome fly and squeezed his eyes closed, shutting out as best he could the nascent voice and animated furniture. He lay unsleeping, bathed in a pool of cold perspiration as the never-ending night inched toward dawn.

Boise, Idaho, may have older ghost stories, but the strange 1892 case of Daniel O'Brien is notable not only for its age but for the prominent reporting it received in the newspapers of the day. The apprentice cigar-maker roomed with his employer, Jesse Black, owner of the Free Coinage cigar store, and his family. The short-lived haunting—all in all, it took place over just three nights—included noises, moving furniture, soft voices and, quite literally, some handwriting on the wall.

The Black house was located on Eighth Avenue between State and Washington streets in old Boise. Not much is known about the residence itself other than that it was a rental property. Apparently, it had been moved to Eighth Avenue from another part of the city sometime between 1880 and the later 1892 events involving Daniel O'Brien.

On that first night—a Saturday—Daniel thought he was suffering from simply too stunningly real nightmares. He was a skeptic, he claimed, and didn't believe in any world other than his own. Yet, he couldn't rid his consciousness, or his room, of that damned voice and the other disturbances.

Jesse Black laughed Sunday morning when he learned what had transpired the night before. Nevertheless, his boarder's guileless description of the events prompted him to invite one Albert E. Werner to spend the night in the house with Daniel as a witness to any odd events. Werner was described as a "young man well known in the city," though the basis for his prominence is absent.

The household retired early Sunday night. At about 10 P.M., Albert Werner said he awoke to find young O'Brien "paralyzed with fear" and again suffused in sweat. The door was rattling all the while.

"On the wall, don't you see it?" Daniel suddenly shouted. "There! It's a zigzag of light, like someone writing."

Werner looked intently for some time before he could pick out the streaks of light. It did indeed look as if someone was "writing with light." The words were indistinguishable.

Jesse Black came bounding into the room. He, too, saw the fiery beam across the wall.

"The spirits say my sister wishes to speak with me. The letter is there, on the wall." Daniel said in an almost hypnotic cadence. "I must be with her for these three nights. And then all will go."

But instead, Werner and Black persuaded him to leave that room and to stay with them in another part of the house. Daniel still could not sleep or escape whatever demons pursued him. He told the men that horrible faces swirled about him.

Word of the young man's awful revelations quickly spread through the neighborhood and across the city so that by Monday night more than two dozen men showed up at Jesse Black's house to solve the "mystery."

According to later accounts, "all the parties (were) perfectly reliable and included some of our leading business men, who will vouch for what (followed)."

Several men kept Daniel under observation. The witnesses said loud tapping came at intervals from the bedroom walls. "They were very audible," one man said.

All the while, Daniel only went into his former bedroom on two occasions. He had such a stricken expression that the men pleaded with him to tell them what he saw. He trembled and described a ghastly face hovering in the room. No one else saw it. He screamed in terror and fled into the hallway. It was some time before he was calmed down and even then he was visibly weak.

None of the other men could explain what Daniel had seen or the cause of the events.

"Mr. O'Brien was perfectly rational, but very weak afterwards," one observer said. "He is suffering untold agonies from what he sees."

One's immediate response is to dismiss Daniel O'Brien's claims as the product of nightmares or hallucinations. One report quaintly described him as "somewhat of a fervent worshipper at John Barleycorn's grief-bringing shrine." However, those who watched with him during the three-day haunting said he was "perfectly sober."

Jesse Black and his family were so distressed they moved out several days later.

Another Boise man, Ras Beemer, claimed that something similar had happened to a family by the name of Stapleton when they lived in the house before it was moved to Eighth Avenue.

And a source described as a "prominent man" said he had lived in the house before the Blacks but moved away when doors repeatedly opened without prompting. There was an "oppressive something about the house that made it intolerable," he claimed.

Were Daniel's visions supernatural? Were they an alcohol-induced nightmare undetected by those around him? Or were they something else?

The reasons for Daniel O'Brien's three-day trauma were apparently never explained. The mystery of the Black residence faded into obscurity.

Two of Boise's most prominent men once lived in homes that were reputedly haunted.

Bulldozers leveled the old Church House at 200 East Idaho Street on March 15, 1973. It was believed to have been built in 1895 by the grandfather of the late Sen. Frank Church, who served in the United States Senate from 1956 to 1981. The elder Church and his wife, Mary, raised five children. Their five-year-old son, Clair, died a tragic death in the house after drinking turpentine he found in the garage.

Sharon McKlusky, a young mother of three, moved into the house during 1970 and stayed for three years. She liked its spaciousness and the reasonable rent. Yet the longer she stayed the more certain she became that something was "wrong" with the house. Sometimes while standing between the door of a bedroom and the door to the attic, she felt a tingling sensation as if an electrical current had surged through her body. Shapeless forms moved across the walls, doors opened and closed by themselves, and radios clicked on and off and changed stations. She told her children nothing of her peculiar feelings.

On an otherwise ordinary day, Sharon learned that she shared the house with the ghost of a young boy. He introduced himself with a mournful cry of "I'm Eddy!" The drifting voice was not accompanied by any physical appearance, but she often felt "vibrations" in a room that she suspected little Eddy was visiting.

He might have been Elmer Edmond, a child who had either lived there or had visited—Sharon was never able to determine which.

Over the next three years, Sharon maintained that she and her children witnessed numerous anomalous events. A round ball of light floated across the living room bearing, on at least one occasion, the sweet, smiling face of a boy in its center.

A second-floor bedroom across from an attic door was used to store trunks and suitcases. One afternoon Sharon needed a sweater from one of the trunks. She stepped into the room and saw a boy in one corner and a small woman in a white dress bending over him. Sharon backed away and closed the door. Her son had earlier tried sleeping in the bedroom but said he couldn't breathe because someone was choking him. That room was relegated to storage from then on.

One of Sharon's friends claimed psychic ability. She visited the bedroom and said Eddy's ghost was there, but he was harmless. However, she said an evil, bedridden old man was still in the room.

Perhaps he was indirectly responsible for the March 1973 fire that consumed the attic and most of the second floor. Firefighters attributed it to faulty wiring, but Sharon wasn't so sure that the malevolent old man didn't resent having visitors in his spectral home.

Meanwhile, another historically prominent Boise man, Frank W. Hunt, who served a term as governor from 1900 to 1902, lived with his in-laws at 1703 Warm Springs Avenue. His daughter, Catherine Hunt, provided the first details about the ghost in that house. She lived there for the first six years of her life.

Governor Hunt married the daughter of John W. Maynard, who came to Idaho from Massachusetts in 1862. The former governor lived with his wife and the Maynards in the house John Maynard put up around an old adobe dwelling that had stood at the Warm Springs Avenue address. Some of the adobe structure was used as part of the kitchen walls in the new house.

Maynard gained fame as a farsighted frontier entrepreneur. He bought up empty land around what was then called Boise City and became a rancher and cattleman, later marrying Jane Tyler, a niece of President John Tyler. He planned to move into the city once his children were old enough to attend school. The land he found was in "lot 11 in block 6 of Boise City" in the city's original east end. He paid $100 for the acreage.

Catherine Hunt said the haunting was not especially disconcerting, but it did provide her family with hours of thrilling conversation.

"It's hard to convince three people that they didn't hear footsteps in an inaccessible part of the house. One, perhaps, but not three," Catherine said in an interview some years later. "It was always a family mystery, one the three of us shivered over for many years."

The three people she referred to were herself, her mother, and her aunt.

Catherine said she and her mother first heard the plodding pace upstairs on a night when they were waiting for her aunt to return home. They thought she'd scoff at the idea, but the footsteps continued after her arrival. They puzzled over the disturbance until Catherine's aunt decided to take the matter into her own hands. She grabbed the family's revolver, opened the doorway on the steps leading to the second floor, and blasted several shots up the stairwell. The footsteps continued for several minutes, but then abruptly stopped. At first light the next morning, the family found auntie's bullet holes in the woodwork, but no sign of a ghost or of an intruder. The mystery was never solved.

Grandfather Maynard's penchant for hiding gold added additional mystery to the old place.

"My grandfather Maynard always wanted his money where he could keep his eye on it," Catherine Hunt said. "He'd turn what cash he didn't need into gold pieces, then plop them in a lard bucket, which he hid. Naturally, this worried my mother. She kept trying to find it, hoping to persuade him to put it safely in a bank. But search as she would, the money never turned up. One day she noticed a loose floorboard in the north bedroom. She let me help pry it up. There was the lard bucket beautifully full of gold coins. Oh, such arguing there was then! My grandfather wanted to hide it again and my mother kept insisting that he bank the money. At last, mother got the whole family on her side and the pressure was too much. Grandfather banked the money. But he never got over worrying about it."

Several blocks down Warm Springs Avenue is number 916, where Dr. Carl J. Hill built a large colonial home in 1913 at a then-scandalously high expenditure of $5,000. He was on the medical staff of St. Luke's Hospital. For some undisclosed reason he moved away in 1927 and lived in two other houses before his 1930 death at the very hospital where he worked.

But though Dr. Hill left his home in body, he may not have left in spirit, at least according to some later residents. And he wasn't alone.

Stories of his occasional visits started making the rounds in the early 1930s, a few years after he died. Later, when Mary Davidson lived there, she "made a joke of it in her exuberant way," one listener said.

A 1977 restoration of the house to its 1913 stylishness brought increased live-liness from Dr. Hill, perhaps because he found the surroundings even more comfortable.

Shari Swall and her husband Roger were responsible for the remodeling. She told a newspaper reporter that she first noticed something was amiss when the attic door would swing open as often as twice a day, even after she had closed it securely. The Swalls heard shuffling feet and what sounded like boxes being moved from the same attic area.

"It doesn't alarm me. I think it's hysterical. Sometimes when we have parties we all go up to the attic to see if he's there," Shari Swall said.

When they found out the ghost might be that of old Doc Hill, they started talking to him as if he were a living person. Best of all, at least for the good doctor (who may have found himself standing around for decades), the Swalls put a rocking chair in the attic.

So he'd be more comfortable, Mrs. Swall reasoned.

What of the other ghost at 916? That one may be more myth than anything else. Charlie Davidson—his family lived there in the 1950s—was a renowned Boise history buff and raconteur. He claimed that in early Prohibition days, a young fellow rigged up a still in the attic of his grandmother's Warm Springs Avenue home. The bootlegger ran his hooch down through copper tubing and then next-door to his own home and on into the basement. It isn't known if he was ever nabbed.

Charlie Davidson claimed that the fellow's ghost lingered in the attic at 916 keeping watch over his illicit brew. He said ghosts always come back to wherever they've left a piece of their hearts.

Spirits of the Little Bighorn

When night winds blow across the grassy plains and purple shadows darken the bluffs of the Little Bighorn River, the ghosts in blue coats and in war paint walk among the living.

This is Little Big Horn Battlefield in southeast Montana. Here, on June 25, 1876, troops of the U.S. Army's Seventh Cavalry, commanded by Lieutenant Colonel George Armstrong Custer, were cut down by Sioux and Cheyenne warriors inspired by Sitting Bull, chief of the Teton Sioux. It was in popular parlance Custer's Last Stand and, ironically, the Indians' last stand. The West opened to settlement and with Sitting Bull's arrest and detention at North Dakota's Standing Rock Reservation in 1881, the Indian Wars slowly wound to an end.

Although details of that dramatic battle can never be fully known, because no white man survived and no Indian dared to speak for fear of reprisals, impressions of the battle linger. For decades, visitors and park personnel have reported seeing apparitions of both Indians and cavalrymen, and hearing frightening sounds of men as if in the throes of grisly death.

Mardell Plainfeather, a Crow Indian who was employed as a park ranger and Plains Indian historian, has never forgotten a mystifying experience she had a number of years ago.

She had her own sweat lodge near the river and had allowed an old man to use it. After he finished his rituals of religious purification, he stopped by Mardell's place to ask her to check the lodge before she went to bed to be certain that the fire was out.

Mardell drove to the lodge with her young daughter in the car with her. After pouring water over the hot stones in the lodge, she stepped outside. Something moved on the bluff above her.

"There, silhouetted against the sky, were two warriors on horseback," she said. "I knew they were warriors because I saw their feathers and shields. As I stood watching, one of them lifted himself up from his horse. They were looking down at me, sixty or seventy yards away." The moon was bright and stars stretched from horizon to horizon; there was no mistaking the men or horses. Mardell got back into her car, but said nothing to her daughter. She did admit, however, that she drove home faster than usual.

In the morning, the ranger drove back to the area to check for stray horses. That was part of her job. Indians living adjacent to the park keep horses, but they are not permitted on the battlefield.

She climbed the bluff upon which she had seen the mysterious horsemen the night before, but found nothing to indicate that horses had ever been up there nor were there any bushes or trees whose shapes might have suggested a config-uration of horse and rider at night. Then, as she gazed out past the cottonwood trees along the river and beyond over the endless plains, she got the strong feeling that the warriors she'd seen were either Sioux or Cheyenne and that they'd meant her no harm. Mardell prayed and left an offering of tobacco and sweet sage for the spirits of all the dead.

Christine Hope had a different, yet no less frightening, adventure into the world of the unexplained. During the summer she worked as a student intern at the park, Christine always enjoyed welcoming the many visitors and giving tours and talks. Her small apartment at the edge of the battleground cemetery was quite comfortable.

One night, after an exhausting day, Christine fell asleep on her living room couch. Some time after midnight she awoke with a sense of dread unlike anything she'd ever experienced. The room was deep in shadow, save for a ribbon of moon-light streaming through a curtainless window illuminating her easy chair across the room.

A man was sitting there.

Christine's mind raced. She was trapped. Alone. Strangely, the man seemed to pay her no attention. She noticed that although he was dressed in modern attire, his hair was cut differently from most men. Yet, there was something vaguely familiar about it. Then she realized his haircut closely resembled that of soldiers who'd fought in the Battle of the Little Bighorn and whose photographs she had closely studied. The silent visitor had a light beard and a handlebar mustache, and his eyes were wide and filled with terror.

Christine was too numb to move, repelled, yet oddly attracted by the fear in his eyes. Within a few seconds he was gone.

She pulled herself off the couch and turned on every light in the apartment. She cautiously approached the chair by the window. It was now just a comfortable-looking chair, one in which she had sat scores of times reading or thinking. Noth-ing about the chair or room indicated why it would be so attractive for a soldier frozen in time.

The young park intern slept fitfully for the rest of the night and was relieved when dawn finally came. Later that day she and ranger Tim Bernardis planned to explore the section of the battlefield known as Reno Crossing, deep within the Little Bighorn River valley.

At that place Major Marcus Reno and his besieged troops had been forced to retreat from the advancing warriors (Custer had already been annihilated). Pulling back into the cover of trees along the river, Reno lost control of his command. His terrified soldiers plunged into the river, striking out for the opposite shore. Few made it. The water ran red with the blood of men and horses. Their screams echoed against the bluffs. The wounded dragged their broken, bloodied bodies up the sagebrush-covered hill, only to be cut down by the Sioux and Cheyenne fighters.

As the intern and the ranger retraced the route of Reno's men late that fall afternoon, Christine stopped suddenly at a single marker by the water's edge. It was the place where Second Lieutenant Benjamin H. Hodgson had fallen. He'd been a member of Company B of the Seventh Cavalry. Christine stood silently by the memorial for a long time. Tim noticed her interest, but said nothing.

Back at the visitors' center, Tim took out a book containing the pictures and military histories of the men who had died in the Battle of Reno Crossing. He pointed to a photograph at the top of a page.

"Here's Hodgson's picture," he said to Christine, standing at his side.

She drew back. The blond beard and the flowing mustache were unmistakable. She told Tim about her experience of the previous night, and he said the ghost could certainly have been that of Hodgson; he must have died an excruciating death. In fording the river, he had taken a bullet in the leg and his horse was killed. Grabbing a stirrup thrown out by another soldier, he was dragged through the water to the opposite shore. Although bleeding profusely and barely conscious, Hodgson clawed his way up the bank. Halfway up he was shot and killed. His body rolled down to the water's edge.

As the story of the young woman's night visitor spread among park employees, few were surprised. Weird things also seem to happen, with some regularity, in buildings close to the cemetery.

An old stone house, by the burial ground, is built in the center of the site where Custer's troops fought the Indians. Constructed in 1894 as a home for the first caretaker, it has long been regarded as one of the most haunted places on the battleground. In fact, the Crow Indians called the cemetery superintendent "ghost herder." They thought his job was to keep the ghosts from ranging beyond the Monument fence. They were free to roam by night, but the raising of the American flag each morning signaled the restless spirits to return to their graves!

When park ranger Al Jacobson and his wife, Florence, moved into an apartment in the stone house, an Indian woman told Florence that something "bad" would happen to them there. The Jacobsons had heard all the ghost tales about the house and smiled indulgently. But, suddenly, they weren't so sure.

Jacobson later told reporter Mitchell Smyth, "We've been in a room when we saw the doorknob twist open—but there was no one at the door. And there have been unexplained footsteps.

"One night I was showing some home movies. The apartment upstairs was empty, but I heard someone cross the floor up there. I ran upstairs, but found no one. No one could have got out except by the stairs which I came up."

But the most peculiar incident in Jacobson's apartment had to do with a chicken. His wife, Florence, had just taken it out of the freezer when "a high-pitched whine went right through the apartment," Jacobson said. "She put the chicken down; the noise stopped. She picked it up again and the noise came back. She knew something was wrong and she threw the chicken in the garbage."

Jacobson wondered if the "ghosts" were protecting his family from eating a diseased chicken.

The experience of Ruth Massie is equally baffling. Ruth's husband, Michael Massie, served as a park interpreter during the summer of 1983 and the couple lived in one of the apartments in a fourplex near the stone house. Mardell Plainfeather, the ranger/historian, lived in one of the other apartments in the complex. Late one evening Mardell drove past the empty stone house and noticed lights burning on the second floor. Her first thought was that maintenance men had been working up there and left the lights on. She also knew the lights sometimes had a habit of turning themselves on and off and she didn't want to check the house by herself. She knocked at the Massies' door and asked Michael to go with her. He told her to go on home and he'd check the house himself. She gave him the key and went to her apartment to await his report.

Massie searched both floors. The house was empty. He snapped off the lights and left. He had just stepped outside when his wife came racing toward him, screaming his name. She'd been watching television while her husband was gone and the picture suddenly went blank and a strange voice was broadcast through the set. The voice said, "the second floor of the stone house." Ruth was terrified that something had happened to Michael.

In the morning, Mardell and the Massies tried to find a cause for the disembodied voice. There seemed to be none. Radios used occasionally on the job were all locked up in the visitors center that night, ruling out the possibility of an errant transmission.

The incident remains unexplained. Massie assumes it was a paranormal experience.

Visitors sometimes report meeting ghosts on the battlefield. In one case, a man from New Orleans disappeared for several hours and when he reappeared, in a state of shock, told rangers that he'd been transported back in time and had relived the battle!

The vaults at the Little Big Horn Battlefield Park contain uniforms, boots, rusted rifles, and various other artifacts of the massacre. And, according to those who've seen them, the vaults are eerie places indeed. When the wife of a park superintendent in the 1920s visited one of them, she said that a clammy hand reached out to seize her. She never returned.

James Thompson, a guide some years ago, was examining bloodstained clothing in one of the vaults. Suddenly, he felt dizzy and was seized by panic. He told friends later that he was convinced he was getting a "psychic echo" from a fallen soldier.

Is it possible that something reached out to Thompson from the clothing? Maybe some individuals with psychic powers can "see" into the life of a dead person merely by holding an object once owned or used by the deceased. The object gives off vibrations that the psychic can "pick up" or "feel."

Earl Murray, in his book *Ghosts of the Old West*, explains the theory as it relates to the frontier:

> . . . All living things give off electromagnetic impulses, or vibrations—psychic traces that are left behind even after death. These unseen force fields are often referred to as imprints. Such imprints are transferred, especially during a state of intense emotion, from the personality of the living being to an inanimate object. These imprints apparently remain attached to the inanimate object indefinitely.
>
> The imprints, according to psychics, reveal themselves to people who can

read them much the same as motion picture film on a screen; the psychic's mind is the screen upon which the imprints are projected. The imprints are not as clear as film, and are caught only in fragments, but they do represent a series of images that can be interpreted by the psychic's mind and conveyed through normal conversation.

Old spurs, boots, rifles, arrows, empty cartridge casings, and similar artifacts have the potential to unlock secrets from the historic past.

Psychic Howard R. Starkel unlocked some rather astonishing facts about the Battle of the Little Bighorn when he worked with historian Don G. Rickey, Jr. When given an iron spur by Dr. Rickey, with no indication of where it had come from or who had worn it, the psychic turned it slowly in his hands for a few seconds. Then, he began to relive a battle:

"I was hurt; this was found in a desolate area," he began, pointing to the spur. He said he was with other people and they were being pursued by people on horses. He was trying to get across a stream to climb the bluffs. The spur, he said, was lost on the south side just after he'd crossed the river. Its owner was killed at the top of a ridge.

Starkel described the setting in such rich detail that Dr. Rickey was astonished. He was certain he was listening to an account of the Battle of Reno Crossing. Yet, in 1876, the U.S. Army had issued brass spurs to its troops, not iron spurs such as that held by psychic Starkel. It was a museum discard that the historian had picked up to add to his own collection.

Yet the mystery of this apparent historical discrepancy between what Starkel claimed and what was known of military-issue equipment was quickly resolved. Records show that a contract surgeon named J. M. DeWolf accompanied the battalion. As a civilian, Dr. DeWolf had to outfit himself and would likely have chosen the more common iron spurs rather than the military brass ones. The surgeon had been wounded and killed after crossing the Little Bighorn. And the marker where he fell is located near the top of a ridge!

Was Howard Starkel merely building upon information he already had about the battle? He apparently knew nothing of the Battle of the Little Bighorn and, in fact, claimed no knowledge of any Indian war. And he'd never been to Montana.

Yet, that single iron spur held an unexplained form of energy that gave the psychic a direct link with a man who had died at Reno Crossing 123 years earlier.

Every year over a quarter-million visitors from all over the world make their way to the Little Big Horn Battlefield. They come to reflect upon the heroic and the tragic, the victory and the defeat, when two cultures clashed on a single summer day on the Montana plains. Most visitors probably don't imagine how close those long-dead warriors might be.

Adobe Wails

From the moment Greg Champion laid eyes on the historic St. James Hotel in Cimarron, New Mexico, he knew there was something special about the place. After more than a decade of working in various capacities for a major hotel chain, most recently in California, Champion was ready for a change of pace.

"(I wanted) an opportunity to do something for myself," the Seattle native said. "You learn so much in a structured environment like that (at a major hotel), it's logical to want to do your own thing. If you can live without a guaranteed paycheck!"

When he learned that the Wild West hotel on the historic Santa Fe Trail in northeast New Mexico was for sale, Champion decided to look it over. What he found was a genuine piece of frontier Americana.

Begun as a small saloon in 1873, the two-story hotel itself, with its two-foot-thick adobe walls, tin ceiling, and antique furnishings, has been in continuous operation since it was added to the saloon in 1880. It has sheltered some of the most legendary characters in the history of the American West—Annie Oakley, Clay Allison, Bat Masterson, Wyatt and Morgan Earp (who stopped on their way to Tombstone and the near-mythic gunfight at the OK Corral), and Doc Holliday. Zane Grey finished portions of his Western novel "Fighting Caravans" in Room 22. Buffalo Bill Cody planned his first Wild West show there. He spent several Christmases there.

The infamous Bob Ford was a guest. He was the "dirty little coward who shot Mr. Howard and laid poor Jesse in his grave." Mr. Howard was, of course, Jesse James—who actually used the name R. H. Howard when he, too, signed a St. James guest register, one of several found during a 1985 restoration.

Davy Crockett II, the son of the famed backwoodsman, stopped at the St. James, but he was nothing like his father. Davy junior and two accomplices murdered three black cavalrymen from nearby Fort Union in the hotel's saloon and took off on a six-month crime spree. He ended up in Cimarron's Boot Hill, shot and killed by the lawmen who tracked him down.

There have been twenty-six documented killings at the St. James Hotel, most of them the result of saloon gunfights, brawls, or knifings.

But Greg Champion found that he was looking at more than an historic artifact—the St. James Hotel has the reputation of being one of the most haunted places in the American Southwest. The ghosts of at least three guests still walk its worn floorboards.

"There were some jokes from the realtor about it being a haunted hotel, but I laughed," he remembered. "We have a videotape at the hotel about an Unsolved Mysteries (Lifetime TV series) episode (about the hotel). To be honest with you I never, ever looked at it until we purchased the hotel and got here. I was just in love with the hotel."

Champion first saw the hotel in February 1993. It was love at first sight, but he was savvy enough to know that buying a property as aged and as off-the-beaten-path as the St. James was first and foremost a business decision.

"I knew I really liked the hotel, but I wanted to hear someone else's perspective," Champion said. He asked a friend with a background in marketing to come along as a kind of "devil's advocate" to help him decide if the hotel could attract customers and become a paying proposition.

The hotel's owner at the time was Ed Sitzberger, a Cimarron native who had grown up across the alley from the St. James. He had bought the hotel in 1985 with his then-wife, Pat Loree, and refurbished it throughout after retiring as a mechanical engineer at Los Alamos National Laboratory.

Upon his arrival, Champion eagerly took in the Victorian Western ambiance of the crystal chandeliers, velvet curtains, brocade wallpaper, and heavy furnishings. On the walls he saw photographs and newspaper clippings about the famous guests who stayed at the St. James, once described as the most modern hotel between the Mississippi River and San Francisco.

As he went through the hotel, Champion heard all about its supernatural heritage.

"Hearing the ghost stories, and everything else that had happened here, I didn't really pay much attention to it. I never really believed," Champion insisted.

He did think it was curious that one area remained off limits to him . . . until just before he left.

"The only room I hadn't looked at was Room 18, which is always kept locked," Champion said. On the floor outside the door of that room was a vase of dead flowers. The room had not been renovated and was never rented to guests.

But that was only partially correct.

Room 18 *is* occupied. The ghost of one T. James Wright, a man who died a violent death in the hotel after supposedly winning the place in a poker game, refuses to leave his old room. He doesn't take kindly to intrusions by the living.

"Just before I left, Ed let me go in and look," Champion said. "On the credenza was a half-full bottle of Jack Daniels and an empty shot glass next to it. There were some playing cards, poker chips, and cigarettes. And some notes to T. J. Wright. I thought it was pretty neat. What a good way to keep the 'spooks' at bay!"

Champion concluded without too much hesitation that purchasing the old hotel was a good business decision—and that the stories of ghostly apparitions and mysterious events reported over the years were perhaps not mere imaginings.

"The first night we had dinner with the (Sitzbergers) and then went up to bed.

It was about nine or ten o'clock. I sat up in bed and was talking to the ghost, like some idiot!" Champion laughed. "I didn't see anything, but I said out loud, 'I really love this hotel and I'd love to buy it. If you guys have any problem with that give me a sign.' Nothing happened."

At least not right away.

Champion flew back to California. Except for his wife, no one knew about his trip to Cimarron. But if he was looking for a "sign" about his decision to buy the St. James, Champion thinks he found it in an uncanny conversation the next day with one of the employees at the hotel where he then worked in management.

"I was making the rounds through the hotel. We had maybe two hundred employees. I walked into the reservations office and one of the girls said, 'Greg, I had a dream about you last night.'"

Champion said the woman proceeded to tell him about the St. James in great detail. He was astonished.

The young woman described the dining room distinctly and correctly identified that it was a saloon back in the 1880s and 1890s. In her dream, she said, the two of them were in the room but only he knew the people present.

"Finally someone invited us to go upstairs and have a drink," Champion said she told him. "She explained in great detail going up a steep staircase from the first floor, going around a corner and then down a hallway into a room on the right. And that is exactly where Room 18 is. She and I went into the room. I talked to a gentleman who was in there but whom she didn't know. We ended up having shots of Jack Daniels. I'm not a Jack Daniels drinker and she certainly isn't."

Champion later showed her pictures he had taken of the St. James. "She turned white as a ghost," he said, only half in jest.

Champion was dumfounded that the woman had the dream on the same night he stayed at the St. James. He took it as the "sign" from the ghosts for which he had asked.

With its turbulent and colorful history, the St. James is the near-perfect repository for restless spirits not satisfied with their abrupt departure from earth.

French immigrant Henri Lambert, a cook for Gen. Ulysses S. Grant and President Lincoln's personal chef, built the hotel. Lambert came to New Mexico in 1866 to search for silver and gold but found he could make more money running a saloon. He opened one in Cimarron in 1873 and added the St. James as a hotel seven years later.

Lambert's wife, Mary, liked the hotel so much that her ghost haunts one of the rooms and periodically strolls the hallways. Her presence is detected by the sudden, strong fragrance of old-fashioned toilet water.

The great attraction New Mexico held for gunslingers and desperados was the virtually nonexistent law and order in the region. The first state-wide law enforcement agency, the New Mexico Mounted Patrol, wasn't formed until 1906. And so, into the territory rode a parade of outlaws and gunslingers who, it seemed, gravitated sooner or later to the St. James Hotel, a social center then (and now) in northeast New Mexico. Not a few of them ended up leaving the establishment feet-first.

There were badmen like the notorious, and probably psychotic, Robert Clay Allison, who once led a mob to nearby Elizabethtown where they broke into the jail and hanged an accused killer named Charles Kennedy. Allison allegedly decapitated the corpse and stuck the head on a pole that he placed prominently in the St. James saloon. Then, it is said, he danced on the bar; it isn't known if he did that to "celebrate" the beheading. He killed at least one other man in a gunfight in the saloon and left his body behind a chair, where owner Lambert discovered it the next morning. Allison got off on a plea of "self-defense."

Some twenty-two bullet holes still pockmark the circa-1903 tin ceiling of the old saloon, now used as the dining room. The original ceiling had to be replaced because hundreds of bullet holes had shredded it. Fortunately, Henri Lambert had put two layers of heavy wood above the tin so stray bullets wouldn't kill guests in the sleeping rooms above.

The violence at the hotel was a near-daily occurrence in the old days. A history of the hotel written by former co-owner Pat Loree notes that "on a typical Saturday evening, it wasn't uncommon for the bartender, as the result of gunplay, to drag out several dead bodies and replace many shattered chimneys from the kerosene lanterns that hung overhead."

But, with the outlaws came other, more easy-going, visitors. Governor Lew Wallace, author of "Ben Hur," stayed at the St. James, as did artist Frederic Remington, who occupied Room 24 when he sketched the nearby Sangre de Cristo foothills. Annie Oakley helped Buffalo Bill plan their Wild West show in the dining room. Gen. Phillip Sheridan was a guest in Room 9 in 1882 during his tour of army forts, including Fort Union, southwest of Cimarron.

Despite the St. James' popularity as a stop for tourists following the Old Santa Fe Trail, the ghosts and ghost stories of the hotel demand considerable attention from visitors and employees.

There is the ghost of Mary Lambert and the malevolent spirit in Room 18, of course, but the oddest entity there may be the "Imp," a puckish fellow who appears as a small, wizened trickster of an old man.

No one knows who he was—in life. He is the Imp because of his penchant for causing minor annoyances. Glasses in the kitchen may crack for no reason, lampshades suddenly tilt, or a pen or calculator may vanish from one location to show up in another soon after.

The Imp may also have been responsible for a bizarre episode in the hotel's kitchen. Perry Champion, Greg's brother and co-owner of the hotel, was having a discussion near a service counter with one of the cooks. A plastic bucket about six inches tall and packed with steak knives stood on a shelf above the counter a few feet away from where the men stood. Suddenly one of the steak knives sailed out of the bucket, across the counter and stuck in the floor between the men.

"My brother is not one to get very excited," Greg Champion said, "but he was like 'I'm not crazy. I saw this. There's no way that someone threw that knife. I watched it come out of the bucket and stick in the floor between the two of us.' "

It is rare for any of the ghosts to show themselves, but it happened once with the Imp.

Earlier owners had hired a youngster to come in early mornings to sweep and clean the lobby and bar. Early on the boy's first scheduled day of work, the couple were surprised to find his mother sitting close by.

The teen sheepishly explained that she was there for "protection."

From what?

Well, he allowed, when he got to work that morning, he had seen a gnome-like man sitting on a bar stool laughing at him! The boy had run home to fetch his mother so she could stay with him while he finished his first—and last—day of work at the hotel.

Mary Lambert's piquant perfume gives away her presence in the hotel's hallways. One young couple stayed in Mary's old room. When the husband found the room too stuffy for comfortable sleeping, he tried to open the window. He couldn't get it to budge. He said it was like someone was pushing down on it from the top. After several tries, however, he managed to get it partway open.

Sometime in the night he awoke to a tapping on the windowpane. He got up and looked out thinking a tree branch might be rubbing against it. He shut the window halfway and went back to bed. A few minutes later there was more beating on the window. In exasperation, he closed it completely. The couple wasn't disturbed the rest of the night. When the young husband told his story to the hotel staff the next morning, their response was that Mary probably didn't want the window open after dark.

The ghost of T. James Wright in Room 18 is more problematic. He signed the guest register three times in 1881 but little else is known about him. On his third, and last, stay at the St. James, Wright is supposed to have won the hotel in a poker game but died in a gunfight before he could stake his claim.

Guests are discouraged from renting Wright's former room, Number 18. It is kept locked, the vase of dead flowers placed conspicuously in front of the door. There is an evil associated with this spirit that is not evident in the others haunting at the St. James.

Wright does not like intruders. And he makes that sentiment known.

A visiting California physician and investigator of the paranormal said she was knocked over by "something" as she entered the room.

A hotel chef saw a hazy figure standing outside the room's door.

Former co-owner Pat Loree had a startling episode with the spirit of Room 18, as he later wrote: "In the upper left-hand corner of the room there was a spiral, swirling, milk-white something. I couldn't see the corner of the room. I stopped speaking (to a guest), and just as suddenly, this mass came sweeping down across the room at me, passed on my right side, sending me to my knees."

Another owner has been quoted as saying about Room 18: "I know he's there, and that's his room."

Greg Champion doesn't have to be convinced. He had his own encounter with the irritability of Mr. Wright.

As Champion explained it, a woman from Clayton, New Mexico, about two hours east of Cimarron, had been making frequent business trips between her home and Angel Fire, a ski resort near Taos.

"She had to drive through Cimarron a couple of times a week," Champion said. "She never knew the St. James was here because you can't see it from the highway. But every time she drove through, she was drawn to the town for some reason. She even had dreams about an old hotel and a particular room in it."

The woman finally stopped in Cimarron and located the hotel.

"She didn't know what she was looking for, she didn't know why she was here, only that she'd been drawn here by something," Champion said. "My brother and I were in the lobby (when she came in). We didn't have much to do so we took her on a tour of the hotel. We got up in the hallway where Room 18 is and walked right past it. She stopped dead in her tracks. She wanted to go in, but we said sorry, it's not renovated. We usually don't tell people that's where the ghost lives!"

Champion said the woman acted strangely from the moment she saw the room, rubbing her hands across the door while "talking to herself." He thought at one point they might have to call the police to escort her out.

But then the transom above the door popped open. "I thought she was pushing real hard on the door and somehow pushed it out," Champion recalled. His brother whispered that they would have to go in later and close it.

"She did this (rubbing the door and talking) for three or four minutes," Champion said. "There's a chandelier in the middle of the room that you can see through the transom. It started to slowly spin in a clockwise manner like somebody had put their hands on it and spun it around. The intensity never slowed."

Greg and his brother were stunned. No one was in the room, the windows were tightly shut and no amount of vibration could have caused such a distinct movement. The entire ceiling fixture was moving in about a six-inch circular arc.

"The lady decided it was time to go," Champion said. "We took her downstairs and she gave us her phone number. Perry and I walked back upstairs to look at the chandelier. It continued to spin. It went on for about forty-five minutes from start to finish before it stopped. There's nothing that would explain it. I would say that's as dramatic as it gets (here)."

Sometimes the ghosts in the St. James have turned up just beyond reach and, of course, not always at night.

Champion's wife was often the first one at the hotel in the morning and would walk past the long, antique bar gracing the dining room. Its front is mirrored. On two occasions she saw the images of a man standing behind her. One was a tall man in Western clothing and a ten-gallon cowboy hat. She turned to speak to "him" but she was quite alone. Waitresses have reported being asked a question by someone standing behind them, only to discover there's no one to whom a reply can be directed!

With the extraordinary number of killings and other documented cases of less bloody mayhem committed over the years, few observers are truly surprised that the St. James is haunted. Several psychics have said the hotel is filled with far more ghosts than have declared themselves. A psychic from Amarillo, Texas, told Champion the spirits are there reliving enjoyable experiences from their life on earth. They want to take that joy into the afterlife.

"I think that's a pretty neat way to put it," Champion agreed.

For his part, the thirty-six-year-old innkeeper came to terms with running a hostelry for the living and the formerly living, developing a sense of bemusement rather than fright.

"When it comes right down to it, I need to be convinced of things in a logical, rational manner. I still do that to this day. I think about what might have caused this or that, what physical things can I attribute it to. I used to always do that. Now I don't do that as much. Things just seem to happen for whatever reason. There are people who are freaked out every single day of their lives here. I don't know why all these things happen, but I'm not afraid . . ."

The St. James Hotel is located in the Cimarron Historic District, one mile south of the intersection of U.S. Highway 64 and New Mexico Highway 21. It is open yearround. Guests may stay in one of the thirteen rooms in the historic section, ranging from the Waite Phillips Suite—featuring a separate bedroom, sitting room, and private bath, to the Remington Room—with a double bed and shared hall bathroom. All the rooms are named after the celebrated guests who tarried a while at the St. James. A modern motel annex has twelve rooms. Reservations are recommended during the summer season.

Lost in Santa Fe

New Mexico's three-hundred-year-old capital of Santa Fe has no scarcity of haunted places. Perhaps it is the dazzling mixture of Hispanic, Native American, and Anglo cultures that has produced so many ghostly legends, or perhaps it is this way in any city that has witnessed centuries of often-violent history unfold on its dusty avenues or behind adobe walls.

Abraham Staab found his fortune supplying general merchandise to New Mexico army posts in the 1880s.

Staab was well on his way to becoming Santa Fe's richest man when he returned to his native Germany to marry Julie Schuster. She eagerly took up her new life in Santa Fe as a wealthy merchant's wife.

Abraham and Julie's elegant 1882 brick home today forms the core of La Posada de Santa Fe, 330 East Palace Avenue, one of the city's most refined hotels and itself the centerpiece of a manicured six-acre complex that also includes separate adobe cottages and lovely gardens.

The exterior of the original two-story Staab house is no longer discernible, but some inside areas remain. A visitor will be shown the house's staircase leading up to the old bedrooms. The second floor of the house has changed only marginally. Some of the rooms are used for meetings and private dining.

There is also Room 256, Julie Staab's old bedchamber. It is a guest room . . . with a difference. Mrs. Staab may still be there.

Julie Staab was, by most accounts, a gracious and popular hostess. Her home was a center of Santa Fe society and culture. Her personal life was not nearly so perfect. Although seven of her children survived childhood, it is believed that she may have had several miscarriages. One child died while still a toddler.

Julie Staab, herself, passed on at the age of 52, but nothing was said in the obituaries about her personal travails. She may have been mentally ill for several years before her death.

Her former bedroom on the second floor retains much of its original Southwestern Victorian elegance. A large chamber of some 600 square feet, Room 256 is outfitted with a king-size brass bed, antique furniture, and exquisite area rugs resting on the original hardwood floors. Even the modern color television set is hidden in a beautiful armoire.

While Julie is not a frequent visitor to her room, her fleeting figure has been glimpsed wearing a long, flowing robe with a hood covering her head. Since her room was renovated in the early 1980s, however, she hasn't been there nearly as much as she has been in other parts of the hotel.

A dining room on the second floor is one of her favorite haunts. Waitresses say a gust of wind blows through the room when there should be none, often as they set up or clear dishes for private parties. If candles remain lit after dinner guests depart, somehow they are extinguished, thin wisps of smoke curling toward the ceiling.

An employee said he had a run-in with Mrs. Staab as he cleaned the floors. He straightened up to rinse his mop when he caught her looking at him. She was translucent, but her dark, brown eyes seemed to bore right through him.

A reporter staying in Room 256 several years ago didn't see the ghost of Mrs. Staab although he stayed up all night waiting for her to appear. At about four o'clock in the morning, however, the bathroom door slammed shut for no apparent reason. The window drapes were drawn, no air was moving. The journalist couldn't explain what caused the door to close so suddenly but he wasn't ready to think a ghost had come a'calling.

Mrs. Staab may also like to browse through the hotel gift store, no doubt impressed with twentieth-century gifts and amenities, many with her name prominently displayed. Employees have reported hearing the sounds of gift books falling off shelves after the store is closed for the night. Though some attribute the noise to one of the hotel's occasional stray cats, others are not quite so sure.

In another instance, an employee heard the same sound—books being dropped—but this time it came from the lobby. When he investigated he found no one around nor any disturbance that might have accounted for it.

The main floor bar, which is near the original staircase, was the scene of another odd experience which may point to a second, male ghost. A security guard was passing by late one night when he heard a man's voice coming from the closed lounge. The four or five sentences he heard were not intelligible. A quick look inside showed him what he expected to find. Nothing.

The possibility of another ghost at La Posada is supported by the stories of a guest and an employee. A girl visiting from Denver awoke in the night to see a man dressed in a waistcoat standing at the foot of her bed. When she asked him what he was doing there, he vanished.

An employee working in an office off the lobby late at night glanced through the open office door. She saw a man lounging near the front door. She turned back to her work, but realized no one should have been out there so late. Another look told her he was gone. She said he had been wearing a long, old-fashioned coat.

There have been other incidents over the years—pots and pans rattling in the empty kitchen, a cut-glass chandelier in one of the dining rooms swinging violently back and forth. And, once in a while, dreadful sobs come from everywhere, and nowhere, in the halls of La Posada. Julie Staab is on the move.

La Posada de Santa Fe is two blocks from the historic Plaza in downtown Santa Fe and features 119 adobe accommodations, many with Kiva fireplaces. Visitors can even dine on excellent cuisine in their restaurant—The Staab House.

Another Santa Fe hotel was built in 1922 on the site of previous inns, and occasionally notorious centers of dancing, gambling, and drinking. Today, the sedate La Fonda Hotel on the Plaza, 100 East San Francisco, advertises itself as "the inn at the end of the Santa Fe Trail." From 1926 to 1968, La Fonda was owned by the Atchison, Topeka and Santa Fe Railroad, which, in turn, leased it to Fred Harvey as one of his famous Harvey Houses. Since 1968 it has been locally owned and operated.

The famous hotel's centerpiece is the La Plazuela Dining Room. Diners there might find more than an attentive wait staff hovering about them.

The story is told that in the nineteenth century the dining room was an outdoor patio with a deep well in the center. One particular gentleman lost his wealth and all his possessions at the gambling tables. In a drunken, suicidal rage over his bad luck, he dove headfirst into the well and drowned.

On occasion, guests have told staff members that in the middle of an otherwise fine meal they have seen the hazy image of a man seem to vanish into the floor. At the same time, the surroundings blur and the guests see furnishings as there might have been a century ago.

The Sisters' White

The Hopi woman, a weaver at the School of American Research, on the east side of Santa Fe, was decidedly uneasy. A late-night round of solo billiards in the game room had become an exercise in barely restrained fear. On the wall, an oil painting of one of the school's founders, Martha Root White, stared down at her. The face was smiling and pleasant, but the toga in which she was attired bespoke an eccentric personality.

The fantastic painting did not especially disturb the young weaver; what bothered her the most was nothing *inside* the room. It was the faint laughter she heard, a murmur that seemed to come from somewhere outside. Yet she was quite certain no one else was about on such a cold winter night.

One of the corners of the room was only faintly lighted. While she didn't actually "see" anything there, her attitude was akin to thinking that something awful might jump out from a darkened closet or grab one's arm after probing too far under the bed at night—an almost childish fear she could not put aside. The young artist quickly turned off the lights and left. The "presence" she sensed was so malevolent that she never again returned to that room.

The School of American Research owes its contemporary campus to two wealthy spinster sisters, Martha Root White and Amelia Elizabeth White, daughters of famed New York publisher Horace B. White. In the 1920s, they built an adobe estate they called *El Delirio*. Soon it became a popular gathering place for Santa Fe artists and writers. The sisters themselves were ardent supporters of the arts, in particular the then-neglected Indian art of the Southwest. They later opened the first New York City gallery devoted solely to Native art.

Though Martha White died in 1937, Amelia lived on at the estate until her own death at the age of 96 in 1972. She had stipulated that her famed estate and land and her other extensive Santa Fe properties be donated to the School of American Research, a center for the study of Southwest anthropology and Native American arts. The School had been established in 1907 as the School of American Archeology by anthropologists Alice Cunningham Fletcher and the colorful Edgar Lee Hewett. Both Cunningham and Hewett championed the study of American anthropology at a time when most academics focused on the ancient, classical worlds of Rome, Greece, and Egypt.

Today, the School sponsors advanced scholarship through book publishing, provides resident scholars with opportunities for reflection and writing, and organizes seminars and various other research venues in anthropology, archaeology, the humanities, and Native American arts.

Martha and Amelia White were extremely well-to-do; Amelia employed a butler to look after the house. Visiting scholars now use the room where she died. The remains of both sisters are buried under a gazebo on the property. Some twenty rare Afghan and Irish Wolfhounds raised by the sisters were buried in marked graves.

The sisters' eccentricity may account for some of the tales associated with the property, but there may be other reasons. A story not easily substantiated holds that a visiting student committed suicide. It's also thought an ancient Indian pueblo stood on the school site.

On the same night the Hopi weaver was in the billiard room, another woman stayed late to work on several written reports. Suddenly, the front doorbell chimed. Someone came in. Footsteps crossed the hallway toward her study room. She waited. A few moments later the footsteps retreated down the hallway, and the door slammed shut. She was quite positive she would have seen any visitor. The event would be repeated on several subsequent nights.

A teacher at the school often felt someone watching her near the gazebo that holds the sisters' remains. But the feeling was a contented one, as if the Whites were pleased at their legacy.

An anthropology professor, however, had a distinctly different impression in the office she used while working at the school. She had the perception of being followed around, like someone was always "reading over my shoulder."

Sometimes her office door was open in the morning, when she was quite sure she had closed it the night before. Her dog growled and bristled whenever she brought him over at night. Some items in her office seemed to have been rearranged, although nothing was ever missing. She suspected the butler did it— Amelia White's old servant hanging about to make sure the house was always tidied up.

The butler may also look after Amelia White's bedroom. A person staying there returned from vacation to find the door open. It had been locked when the person left several days before. Again, nothing had been taken.

An arroyo near the school holds additional mysteries. Laughter like that heard by the Hopi weaver comes from there. It sounds like a late-night party of stressed out scholars . . . but with no visible guests.

Sister George

Many years ago, a religious order known as the Sisters of Loretto operated a Catholic academy school in the area now occupied by the Inn of Loretto. The lovely shops in the 200 block of the Old Santa Fe Trail are believed to have been once used as the school's chicken coops!

Former shop owners say several unusual events have led them to believe that block may be haunted. And not by chickens.

A woman's light laughter and footsteps were heard in a printing shop several years ago, but that wasn't nearly as odd as what occurred to the two owners of a nearby clothing store. On their first night in business, they closed the shop and counted their receipts. Regardless of how they compared their sales slips with the money in the cash register, an extra ten dollars was always there. For the next week, they found an extra ten dollars each night. They never figured out the discrepancy.

Local folks suspect the ghostly culprit may be Sister George, a lively, caring nun known for her enormous generosity. She taught free special-education classes for poor children and gave away homemade Spanish-style suppers each night. The good nun may still give to those who toil in her old neighborhood.

The Original Love Potion Number Nine?

A strange Santa Fe legend is set in a residence popularly known as the "Oldest House," 215 East De Vargas Street, across from the Chapel of San Miguel. The story goes that two *brujas* (witches) once occupied the adobe house. They sold charms and spells and brewed a powerful love potion eagerly sought by all the young *caballeros* in the city.

One such young man came by of an evening seeking the potion so that he could win the hand of one of Santa Fe's loveliest *senoritas*. The *brujas* complied. Their anxious visitor departed with their assurances that the woman would be forever his—once she drank of the elixir. Sadly, the potion must not have been correctly mixed; she drank the potion, but married another man.

The spurned lover stormed into the Oldest House demanding the return of his money. One of the *brujas* grabbed a long butcher knife and with a single swift stroke separated his head from his shoulders.

A persistent legend insists that on the anniversary of the man's gruesome demise, his head rolls slowly down the Old Santa Fe Trail on its way to *El Palacio Real* looking for his body. And a refund.

Is the old adobe structure on East De Vargas really the "oldest house" in the next to the oldest permanent European-founded settlement in the United States? The house is now a commercial establishment selling tourist items. Owners in the past have promoted it as having been built around 1200 A.D. but that seems to be impossible as there weren't any Europeans in New Mexico for several hundred more years. Some sources claim the structure was dubbed the "oldest house" as part of the bogus 333-year centennial in 1883. (Santa Fe was founded in 1610, not 1550.) But archaeological work at the site does date the structure as early as 1740 to 1767. In 1905, archaeologist Edgar Lee Hewett wrote that fragments of the original pueblo wall were found that corresponded to the remaining walls of the pueblo of Kwapoge in northern Santa Fe and thus belonged to the city's historical period.

The property is maintained by the Christian Brothers who receive income from leasing it to retail establishments.

The Villagra Witch

Employees at the New Mexico Department of Game and Fish in the old Villagra Building in the Santa Fe capital complex may not be aware that a ghost story has made its rounds there.

What some witnesses say they have seen is an old woman in a gown from the late 1700s, bustling down a hallway with a small dog incongruously perched on her shoulder. She beckons a finger at those who see her, inviting them to follow. She vanishes before they can take her up on the offer.

One story is that the woman was hanged as a witch in seventeenth-century Santa Fe, at the same place where the Villagra Building now stands. Or, others say, there may be a cemetery somewhere beneath the structure and the spirit of one of the deceased was disturbed. Either way, it's best to look up and down the hallway when you leave there with a hunting or fishing license.

A Grieving Mother

Among the dozens of bills signed by New Mexico Gov. Gary Johnson in April 2001 was SB182, which authorized the General Services Department to buy the Public Employees Retirement Association Building, known as PERA, as part of a new office building in the West Capitol complex. The building faced the Old Santa Fe Trail, across from the capitol on *Paseo de Peralta*.

Gov. Johnson may not have known that the building and an adjacent parking lot were the subjects of a sad ghost tale about a small lady in a long black dress, a *mantilla* pulled tightly about her head. Sometimes visitors caught a glimpse of her scurrying across the parking lot. Those who saw her spoke kindly. She never acknowledged the greetings, ghosts rarely do, but she deserved sympathy.

Her son was a student at the old St. Michael's College, actually a boarding school with many youngsters from distant and isolated communities in New Mexico and beyond.

The child contracted smallpox, an always-fatal disease in the old days. He died and was buried quickly, his gravesite unmarked so that others would not panic at the thought of an epidemic sweeping the city.

The boy's mother lived in a village many miles from the nearest trail and so she was not able to be with him as he took his final breaths. No one would tell her where he had been laid to rest. She refused to go home and, in time, died of a broken heart. Her spirit is still searching for the child's earthly remains.

Mr. and Mrs. G

**MURDER/SUICIDE
ORPHANS
FIVE CHILDREN**

by
Bruce Trachtenberg
Oregonian Staff Writer

A Portland mother of five died of gunshot wounds early Sunday in an apparent murder/suicide in a north Portland home where she had sought refuge.

Her former husband turned the gun on himself after first shooting her, according to the Multnomah County Medical Examiner's Office.

Dead are Marles Hood, 36, and Billy Hood, 42. Mrs. Hood and the children had been living at the home of Mary L. Bellanger . . . where the shooting occurred.

"She came here in hopes of finding some protection," Mrs. Bellanger said. "We had known each other for about four and one-half years. We used to live next door to each other."

The Medical Examiner's Office said Mrs. Hood was beaten and killed about 2:50 A.M. Sunday after she let her former husband in the house. (Billy) Hood also died of a gunshot wound.

Arrangements for the five Hood children await action by the Multnomah County Juvenile Court and the Portland Police Bureau of Youth Division.

Mrs. Bellanger said she hopes the children can spend Christmas with her family.

"I hope the Court is good enough to let the kids stay here for Christmas. We want to try to make this the best Christmas that we can make for them. We don't want to upset them any more than possible."

The Police Youth Division said later Sunday the children would be allowed to spend Christmas at the Bellangers' home.

—*Portland Oregonian*, Dec. 24, 1973

Marles Hood didn't have a chance. She died just inside the front door, on a couch near a built-in glass-fronted cabinet. The gunshots blew the glass doors to pieces. Blood was everywhere.

The five children and the Bellanger family escaped harm. In 1973, domestic violence was an issue that most people rarely discussed even in private, let alone read about on the front page of their local newspaper. Three decades later it's impossible to determine what led this desperate man to murder his estranged wife and then turn the gun on himself, to understand what horror raced through his frenzied mind that would move him to blow away a person he must have once loved.

But that unspeakable act on the eve of Christmas Eve reverberates still in the house where two lives ended.

The ghosts of that tragic couple may still roam the Portland home in which their lives came to such a tragic end.

The three-story Victorian house looks much the same today as it did in 1973. It's in a north Portland, Oregon, neighborhood filled with turn-of-the-century homes built for managers and employees of a local meat-processing plant. They are well kept, although most are smaller than the one in which the couple died. Old sidewalks make an evening stroll inviting. Embedded in the curbs are the iron rings where suitors once tied their horses while calling on their sweethearts.

Michael and Carolyn Brown were looking for a large, older home to buy about a decade after the Hood killings and this house seemed perfect.

The Browns had first looked at the house when it was listed at $58,000 but didn't pursue the matter. When the price dropped even lower after the house sat vacant for many months, the couple became very interested.

"Michael was with his mother and sister in Europe," Carolyn remembers about the chain of events that led to their decision to make an offer on the house." My mother and I decided to go through the house. I liked it. Michael and I had seen it before the owner had moved out. When Michael called from Ireland I asked him to think about the house and when he came back we went through it again. We bought it."

The Browns offered $42,000, an amazingly low price considering the condition of the house and the generally high housing costs in the United States. Their offer was accepted.

The house was in good shape. The outside had been freshly painted, as had the interior. The beautiful fir floors had been well maintained.

The only additions the Browns had to make were the installation of new storm windows and some fresh carpeting to protect the floors. A previous owner had taken great pains to remodel the home. Even the heating system was in good shape.

Michael and Carolyn—with daughters Gennie and Cassie—moved in during November 1985. Their lives have never been the same.

Perhaps they should have paid closer attention to subtle indications that the house was somehow . . . *different.*

"For a year and a half before we came, the house was vacant," Michael recalled. "Of course, the neighborhood kind of joked about the house being haunted, just because it was an old house, and it was vacant for (so long)."

The Browns didn't know anything about the murder/suicide twelve years earlier. But then the last owner stopped by while he was visiting the city.

"He came by to see the house," Carolyn said. "As he was leaving he just said 'Oh, by the way, did you know there was a murder/suicide here?' We talked to the neighbors and they said there was a lady who had left her husband and came to this house with her kids. The husband came here real irate and killed her and ... himself."

Although Carolyn, as a little girl, always imagined it might be exciting to live in a "haunted" house, she had no way of knowing her childhood fantasy might really come true.

"What was really strange," Michael added, "is that we both had a strange feeling about the house. We didn't really discuss it between us, but we both felt that something was here."

Carolyn thought her anxiety came because of her self-described "active imagination."

"I just ignored it (feelings about the house)," she said. "I didn't mention anything to Michael, but I always had an idea, nothing specific, that there was something that we couldn't figure out about our home."

Six months later, Carolyn discovered that Michael, too, had the same wariness. And that wasn't like her husband at all. As a law enforcement officer in Portland, Michael is well trained as a fact-gatherer and observer. When the couple started comparing notes, however, they discovered a mutual inclination to believe that some things they attributed to chance or the natural creaking of an old house might be something more.

Michael confirmed the facts about the Hood murder/suicide by reading the original *Oregonian* news clipping. Perhaps, they thought, there *was* something to stories of murder victims lingering in the places where they died.

The midnight frights of a small child eventually led to the first of nearly two-dozen separate encounters the Browns had with what they believe to be the ghosts of Marles and Billy.

"Cassie was the first one to see 'them,'" Carolyn said matter-of-factly. "She was nearly three years old. She would tell me that a lady was tucking her in bed at night.

"She said she was a very nice lady, and there would be a man off to the side. The man scared her. He would never smile, just watch. He never did anything mean, just watched. Something about him just scared her. The lady would pull the blankets up and tuck her in, and she'd go back to sleep," Carolyn recalled.

"I had a habit of not tucking blankets under the mattress," she confessed. "I just pull them up so the kids can get out of bed if they need to."

When she checked on her daughter before going to bed, the blankets were often tucked under the mattress and pulled tightly up to the child's chin. She assumed Michael had done it when he kissed his daughter good-bye before going off to his overnight shift. However, the mystery deepened when they found that neither one had tucked the blankets under Cassie's mattress.

Because of her young age, Cassie had a hard time describing the night visitor. She knew, however, that the woman wasn't her mother. She said the woman had long hair. Carolyn's hair was short and usually permed.

Amazingly enough, Cassie Brown was never afraid of the lurking apparition in her bedroom. Her mother said she was just curious why the lady was tucking her in. The little girl wanted to believe that it was only a dream, yet at the same time Carolyn knew she doubted that quick explanation.

The man lingering in the background was worrisome. He stood slightly behind the woman and didn't smile.

"Cassie didn't want to concentrate on him because he made her nervous. She was scared of him, but the lady was nice," Carolyn said.

The woman didn't speak except to whisper "shhhh!" as if quieting an unsettled child. Or stopping a little girl from crying out in fright at the sight of a ghostly nanny.

To ease their daughters' fears, the Browns took to calling the couple Mr. and Mrs. G, short for Mr. and Mrs. *Ghost*.

Two years after the Browns moved in, an incident with a space heater in the girls' room mystified Carolyn:

"The girls were sleeping in Gennie's bed. Because we have a large house, heating can get expensive so we used an electric heater in the girls' room. Well, one night it was warm when we went to bed, but I woke up at about 4:30 in the morning. It was cold. I was worried about the kids so I went to their bedroom to turn on the electric heater. It was already plugged in and turned on. The room was warm."

The following morning, Carolyn asked her elder daughter, Gennie, if she had plugged it in.

"Oh no, Mom," she said, shaking her head. "I'm not allowed to do that."

"At least the kids were warm," Carolyn sighed, not wanting to linger too long on the unanswered question of just who plugged in the heater.

An event a few days later also dealt with appliances acting as if with minds of their own.

Some explanation is necessary. In the Brown's first floor living room, one particular electrical outlet has a large adapter that will hold six separate plugs. In that adapter the family plugged in a television set, two VCRs, a lamp, and a cordless telephone. The phone has a particularly heavy plug-in, so large, in fact, that if it is accidentally hit, the entire outlet adapter will fall out. If, for instance, Michael wanted to unplug the lamp, he has to hold the wall adapter in place to do so.

Early one evening, Carolyn and the girls were out of the house and Michael was sleeping until he left for his midnight shift. Before he went to bed, he had set one of the VCRs to record a program from seven to eight o'clock.

Carolyn got home at about 9 P.M. and Michael was up.

"He asked me why I unplugged the VCR. I told him I just got home. He said the VCR was unplugged, but his show was recorded. Nothing else was unplugged, just the one machine. It just couldn't have fallen out. No animals were in the house, in fact no one else was in the house and Michael was sleeping. There was no way that machine could have come unplugged at eight o'clock when no one else was home."

Michael, too, was stumped.

"That was really tangible," he said. "That was when it was really confirmed (to me). Prior to that, I thought there must be some logical explanation. But that

VCR incident couldn't be explained because there was nothing that could have done that. I couldn't believe it."

Carolyn echoed her husband's sentiment.

"We weren't sure how to react. There was a part of me that was a little excited that my childhood wish kind of came true and yet I was nervous because of the kids."

At times the family didn't even pay attention to the odd goings-on in their home.

"There was so much activity, footsteps and that sort of thing," Michael said, "that we wouldn't even go and look. I remember watching TV and we'd hear footsteps and not even bother to check."

Sometimes the incidents seemed prankish.

"One night the kids spent the night over at Michael's mother's house," Carolyn remembered. "He was at work and I was upstairs sleeping. All of a sudden I heard this man's voice downstairs. I grabbed Michael's gun and I went downstairs. The TV was on. Scared the wits out of me. I turned it off and I slept on the couch. Then the radio upstairs turned on. I stayed on the couch."

Within a few months, Carolyn seemed to arrive at an uneasy truce with what she, by then, firmly believed were the ghosts in her house—especially when they disturbed an otherwise peaceful night's sleep.

"During the summer—like that summer of 1988—when it's real hot, I let the kids sleep downstairs where it's cooler. Now one time I was sleeping on the couch, the kids were on the floor and our husky/shepherd dog was sleeping with us. Sometime around one or two in the morning, I heard walking upstairs. From my bedroom to the girls' room, back and forth among the three bedrooms. My first reaction was that Cassie was looking for me. So I yelled up to her that I was downstairs. I still heard the walking. I got up but Cassie was sleeping on the floor with Gennie.

"The next logical thing was that Fairfax, our dog, was upstairs. I called to him and his head popped up next to me. At this point I was still hearing footsteps and I thought, well, Michael's at work and all of us are down here, so . . ."

Carolyn wasn't about to let two ghosts keep her up all night.

"I went up to the landing and asked them to stop walking around because they were going to wake up the kids."

Whatever caused the disturbance stopped.

That became fairly typical behavior in the Brown household. When mysterious noises became too loud, or the aimless walking disturbed her sleep, Carolyn often asked the ghosts to quiet down. Usually it worked, although she admitted feeling foolish for carrying on conversations with invisible people.

The ghosts were particularly noisy on another late night.

Carolyn explained:

"I had just bought some furniture to go in Cassie's bedroom and there was no room for her to sleep in there, so Cassie slept with Gennie in her room. I heard knocking at maybe midnight or one o'clock in the morning. It sounded like it was at my door, but I wasn't sure. I said, 'Come in, Cassie!' But no one came in. The knocking stopped for a minute and then it came again, only louder.

"Fairfax, who was in my room, was scared. He wouldn't go to the hallway when

I opened the door. There was nobody out there. I checked on the kids; they were both asleep."

At first, Carolyn thought her girls were playing a trick on their mother, a late-night game of "let's scare mommy!" She went back to bed, leaving her door slightly ajar so that she could see down the hallway. She expected to see one or both of the girls tiptoeing toward her bedroom. Instead, Carolyn found the phantom knocking had moved to another room.

"It was coming from Cassie's room," Carolyn said, which was unoccupied that night. "I wasn't sure, but it sounded like maybe the furniture or something in the wall. It kept getting louder the more I ignored it."

Carolyn again scolded the ghosts.

"Okay, you got my attention, now knock it off! You're too loud, we're trying to get some sleep!"

That seemed to work.

The Browns' dog, Fairfax, gave some clear indications to Carolyn that he, too, was wary of all the strange noises.

"He'd do different things. He would always check on the kids in their bedrooms at night. Always. He would hardly sleep, just go back and forth between their rooms. But when things were happening, like the knocking, he wouldn't leave me, in fact he would not even leave my bedroom."

When the family left the house for some reason, Fairfax went berserk. He chewed the blinds in the front room and when they locked him in a pantry, he gnawed on the doorframe trying to get out. For a period of time Michael's sister looked after him in her home. He was fine there.

A second dog the Browns purchased, which they named Tuffy, seemed to settle Fairfax a bit. The family put both dogs in the backyard whenever they left. But Fairfax disliked the third floor and insisted on sleeping in the master bedroom each night.

The ghosts of the murdered couple, if, indeed they are what haunt the house as Carolyn and Michael Brown suspect, didn't take kindly to visitors. On several occasions, the ghosts announced their visits in most unsettling ways.

Carolyn's nephew, Jonah, got more than he bargained for when he stayed over one night.

"He heard arguing upstairs and just assumed it was Mike and I," Carolyn remembered. "Well, I was sleeping at the time and Mike hadn't even come home. Jonah didn't know that because he was sleeping on the couch. He heard the arguing and tried to ignore it and then the voices moved to the living room, around where the doorway is."

The doorway to which Carolyn was referring was the one that once led directly to the kitchen from the entryway but had been blocked off sometime earlier. It was also the exact place where Billy Hood murdered his wife and then turned the gun on himself.

Jonah had pulled the blankets up over his head, but decided to peek after a few moments.

Carolyn said he saw a woman and a man arguing. They stopped and looked at him and it scared the wits out of him. He covered his face and told them to go away.

After a few seconds of silence he looked again. They were gone. For a very long time, Jonah would not visit his aunt and uncle and after that only if there was a large family gathering.

"He's feeling better, more secure," Carolyn said. "But that was something that scared the poor guy."

A next-door neighbor, a woman named Nina, had two strange experiences in the house. She often helped Carolyn clean the three-story house. Once, when she was cleaning the third floor while the Browns were gone, she heard a scream come from somewhere below in the house. Nina knew she was alone. She quickly gathered her cleaning supplies and left for the day.

On another occasion, while dusting the second-floor landing, Nina heard the front door latch open. Someone walked across the floor downstairs. She called out that she was cleaning the staircase. She supposed Michael had come home early. There was no answer to Nina's shout. Footsteps again crossed the first floor, the front door unlatched and then closed.

"After that experience she said 'no thanks' and quit," Carolyn said.

Carolyn's brother and his girlfriend came for a brief visit. They stayed on the third floor. On a late night a few days after their arrival, the young woman was in the basement laundry room washing clothes when a voice called out:

"Hello down there!"

She ran upstairs in the belief someone had come into the house and was looking for a family member. No one was on the first floor. Carolyn and her daughters were asleep in the master bedroom.

Carolyn was told about the incident the next day.

"I said it might have been the kids yelling down the laundry chute, but I was pretty sure that the kids were sleeping since they were in my bed. She didn't completely accept my answer and she didn't do any more laundry after that."

Gennie and her little sister Cassie told their parents of numerous incidents in which they saw or heard the ghosts. One encounter even involved a classic British ghost story by author Oscar Wilde.

The girls had just seen a television adaptation of his novel "The Canterville Ghost." Cassie especially loved the ethereal title character, Sir Simon, and his attempts to scare away an intrusive American family that inherits a haunted English castle.

Carolyn Brown picked up the story from there:

"One morning, around three o'clock, I heard Cassie calling 'Sir Simon! Sir Simon! Please come back, I want to talk to you.' I leaned over and told her to go to sleep, but I kept hearing her calling to him."

When her daughter wouldn't settle down, Carolyn realized something odd was going on.

"Who are you calling, honey?" Carolyn asked.

"Well, I saw Sir Simon, mom," Cassie replied firmly.

"You saw Sir Simon what?"

"The ghost, mom, the ghost!" Cassie declared.

Carolyn asked her to explain what she meant. She was half-asleep and not fully mindful of what the little girl was trying to say.

"Well, mom," Cassie explained, "I came in here to climb into bed with you and he was standing there looking at you. Then he saw me and disappeared. But he didn't look like the guy on TV at all. He had kind of short hair like dad and he wore clothes like dad. He was kind of gray."

"That's very interesting, Cassie," Carolyn said. "But why are you calling him to come back?"

"I want to invite him to my birthday party," Cassie replied, thinking that Sir Simon would be the perfect guest.

"Honey," Carolyn said carefully, "I don't think your friends would appreciate a ghost coming to your birthday party."

Cassie and Gennie knew early on that in all probability ghosts inhabited their house. "We had to be honest with them," Carolyn said. "How else could we explain all this stuff to them?"

Cassie talked about Sir Simon for days after. Her mother patiently told her that THEIR ghosts were not the scary kinds at all. They were good ghosts who plugged in heaters when the girls were cold or tucked them in bed. She explained the nice things they did. But to the girls, living in a haunted house was quite exciting. Gennie often told the stories to her friends at school.

Carolyn cautioned them about spreading too many tales.

"I told them not to tell their friends too much because they'd be too scared to come over. You have to be careful. And I've told them that some people don't believe in ghosts, so they know that."

Nevertheless, Carolyn laughed, "They think it's funny that their mom tells the ghosts to knock off the noise."

On Christmas Eve, 1989, Gennie caught a glimpse of someone lingering around the Christmas tree. And it wasn't Santa Claus.

"She had come downstairs and saw a man looking at the tree," Carolyn noted. Gennie apparently wanted an early glimpse of the presents she would be opening later that morning. "His back was to her. She got excited because she thought that maybe it was Santa Claus or her dad. Anyway, he turned around and disappeared."

At that, the child got scared and ran back to her bedroom. She didn't tell her parents about it until much later. She later described him for her mother in ways similar to Cassie's description of her Sir Simon.

"I told her that it was Mr. G," Carolyn said. She said he was probably looking at the beautiful decorations the girls put on the Christmas tree and the fine presents spread under its festooned branches.

Suddenly appearing apparitions and disembodied voices became the norm for all the family members. Carolyn heard and saw unexplainable phenomena many times.

"We'll see a 'white thing' out of the corner of our eyes; it disappears when we turn around. Michael recently asked me if I ever saw a white apparition. I told him I thought I was the only one. I also notice a man's voice every once in a while. I'll be in the kitchen and I'll hear it from the dining room. I'd think it was Mike and I'll come out and no one is there."

She said the words were indistinct, as if someone might be talking on the telephone or carrying on a hushed conversation.

And it's not only a male voice floating through the house. At one point, Carolyn was in the living room when she heard a woman crying in the kitchen. But when she called out for the girls, thinking one of them might be in some trouble, she discovered they were upstairs and had been for quite some time.

The vivid, sudden but separate appearances of the two ghosts frightened the Browns more than anything else. Both times the ghosts decided to present themselves in the night.

For Carolyn, the encounter took place when her husband was at work, the girls were sleeping, and she was resting in bed with her door open partway. A hallway light that is always kept on provided enough illumination for her to see around the room.

"I saw a man walking toward me. My first impression was that Mike had come home early, but then I realized he was still at work. We have a ceiling light that has a pull chain. I'm looking at him and scrambling for the light, swinging my arms back and forth looking for the chain. By the time I got the light on he had gone away. The light was coming in from the hallway so I couldn't see him too clearly, but it was more than a shadow. I could see his face a bit, not plainly, but I could see him. I slept with the light on after that."

The apparition's casual stroll toward her was so natural that Carolyn was certain it was Michael home early. There was no anger or menace in his walk or demeanor, only a slow deliberate pace that ended in the brilliance of the overhead light.

A dream vividly rendered? The power of suggestion arising from living in a haunted house? A trick of light?

Carolyn doesn't think so.

The man she saw was a solid, three-dimensional figure that looked for the entire world like a human being.

Only it wasn't.

Michael Brown's encounter with the ghost of the woman he believed to be Marles Hood was so distressing that it has stayed with him to this day.

"I was on the early day shift so I had gone to bed earlier than the rest of the family," Michael detailed. "I left the door slightly ajar and the hall light was on. I had just gone to sleep when some noise woke me up. I looked up and a lady was approaching me. I thought it was my wife in some kind of a gown or negligee. I seemed to lose track of time, except I could see she was slimmer than my wife, her face was more slender and she had a straight hair style that went down to her shoulders. I actually thought it was my wife up until the time I put my arms up and the lady got really close. I realized it wasn't and that's when I let out a yell."

Carolyn came racing into the room. Her husband was sitting up in bed, the overhead light on. She asked him what had happened. He insisted everything was all right and that he just wanted to go back to sleep. It wasn't until the next day that Michael told his wife that he'd almost embraced a specter.

"That was the most tangible thing that's ever happened to me," Michael said. "That one really made a believer out of me."

Over the years Michael and Carolyn have grown accustomed to frequent reminders of their ghostly tenants. Not all are nearly as disquieting as the couple's night-time visits from Billy and Marles:

"Once Michael came downstairs," Carolyn said. "He'd been sleeping and the kids were in bed. He asked me if we'd been on the third floor. I said no. He told me there was someone walking up there. The kids were sleeping and the dog was downstairs with me. I told him he should go ask them to stop. He wouldn't. He said he would just stay downstairs with me for a while." Carolyn later performed her by-now-usual vocal exorcism and asked them to please stop the noise because they were going to bed. It stopped.

The family used the third floor for storage and as a playroom for their daughters. It's well lighted with a door that opens onto a sun deck. Sometimes it's too well lighted. Michael said: "I was across the street talking to a neighbor and I saw the lights on, which I thought was strange. I was walking back across the street to come home and the light went off." When he came in the door, Michael found his wife and children downstairs. No one had been upstairs for some time. "The third floor lights are always going on and off," Carolyn said. "I'd have to ask the kids if they'd forgotten to turn them off. It's really hard to tell when the kids forget to turn them off or when the lights are doing it by themselves." It happens often. The family goes out for a few hours in the evening, leaving the house in darkness, and when they return home lights are ablaze in various rooms. Gennie's bedroom lights were often popping on. With the exception of the bathrooms, pulling on chains that hang down from them operates all the ceiling lights on the second floor.

A window in Gennie's bedroom had a peculiar habit of opening by itself. Michael said: "I would find the inside window open. The storm was still be closed. I'd shut the window and lock it and tell Gennie please not to open it. She said she wasn't doing it. I don't know how long it went on for, but it was almost a daily occurrence. I would shut the window again, and lock it, and then I'd find it open."

Michael's paycheck stubs from work were the subjects of one peculiar episode. "We keep them in a folder in the filing cabinet," Carolyn said. "I found them out by the kitchen telephone. Of course, Michael thought I took them out and I thought he had taken them out. They stayed there for about two months before he asked if I was done with them so he could put them away. I said I didn't take them out. He said he hadn't. I asked the kids, too. That was a strange thing."

Perhaps ghosts, too, are interested in the financial affairs of the living.

Despite the puzzling episodes with lights, windows, relatives, knockings, footsteps, and even mysterious figures in the night, none seemed particularly violent. If the Browns didn't precisely "accept" the presence of ghosts in their fine old Victorian home, neither were they especially frightened by anything that happened.

The closest Carolyn Brown came to feeling that the ghost couple could cause some harm came on Christmas Eve about ten years ago. It involved, of all things, mixed nuts. The Browns had the family Christmas celebration at their house as usual because it could accommodate everyone. Carolyn's sister-in-law brought a plastic tray filled with a variety of fresh nuts.

All of their relatives had left and Carolyn was cleaning up in the kitchen. Michael had gone to bed. The children were sleeping.

"I noticed that the tray with the nuts was halfway off the table," Carolyn recalled. "I pushed it back on the table and then I started putting things away again. And then the tray just flipped backwards. It was like someone had put his hand underneath and flipped it up. The tray hit the wall and nuts scattered everywhere."

She quickly flicked off the lights and ran upstairs.

The next morning, Michael discovered the mess in the kitchen and cleaned it up. He wanted to know about the mess.

Carolyn told him what had happened. She didn't feel much like sticking around to clean up the rest of kitchen after seeing the tray fly across the room.

Early the following August, a new twist was added to the Brown family haunting.

Carolyn was making plans to paint the ceilings in several rooms. She had carefully figured out how much paint would be required. But one morning her plans were put on hold. As she looked over the living room ceiling, she noticed four brown-colored streaks extending only a few inches in one area.

"It looked like someone had taken his thumb and three fingers, rubbed them in dirt, and then dragged them across the ceiling," Carolyn said. The marks were not there the day before because she had looked at that section of the ceiling.

The high ceilings cannot be reached even with the tallest stepstool in the house. No workmen had been in the house. There seemed to be no logical explanation for how they got up there.

The mysterious smudges remained there for months afterwards.

To add to this new mystery, only a few days before the discovery of the ceiling marks one of the ghosts made an audible appearance.

Michael was working the overnight shift and therefore Carolyn wasn't surprised when she heard the bedroom door open shortly after daybreak. Dozing lightly she heard Michael walk toward her. But the footfalls quickly retreated from the room, and down the hallway. The next thing she knew the front door opened and slammed shut, causing a wind chime hanging on the doorknob to tinkle.

A bit upset by what she considered her husband's bizarre behavior, Carolyn went downstairs to investigate. She saw her husband coming in the back door. He had been taking out the garbage and had not been anywhere near their bedroom. He, too, had heard the front door slam shut and wondered who was up at such an early hour. The couple looked at each other and knew immediately that it was another piece added to their ghostly puzzle.

The family didn't seriously consider moving from their home, especially since the entities never seemed to upset the children or want to harm anyone in the family. If there had been the slightest indication that the beings were evil or malicious, Carolyn said they would have moved away. Their experience has been characterized more by a peaceful coexistence. The ghosts don't appear to dislike the Browns, just seem intent on impressing upon them their unforgettable presence.

"We've basically accepted them," Carolyn said. "We do get scared and would like it if they would go. But the kids don't want them to. The kids want them to stay. It's exciting to them."

As for why their house is haunted, Carolyn has had a lot of time to think about that:

"He (Billy) made a mistake. Is he sorry for what he did? Is he trying to make amends? I try to come up with my own interpretation. And I feel honestly that the lady likes being close to the kids, tucking them in. She misses her kids and wants to look after ours. Nothing negative has ever happened, really, I mean besides getting scared once in a while. But nothing truly threatening."

Michael and Carolyn think that the murder/suicide was an act of passion involving only them. Their ghosts don't harbor any ill will toward the living.

"I feel relieved that nothing negative has happened. We can make this whole ghostly situation a positive thing as much as possible. We can't afford to move and we don't really want to move yet. I really like the house. There's a lot we can do, especially when the kids reach their teens," Carolyn noted.

The couple has plans for remodeling the third floor into a master bedroom with a sitting room and art studio. The girls would have the second floor, while the couple's present bedroom would become the family room.

In the meantime, Michael plans to research the history of the house and find out as much as he can about the circumstances surrounding the deaths of Billy and Marles. He wants to know the personalities of the couple who linger long after death in the house where they died.

"The ghosts are pretty respectful of us," Carolyn said. "I think part of it is that we try not to react too much. I just tell them to stop what they're doing. Of course, they do give us a start now and then."

When necessary, however, Carolyn is stern with their supernatural guests.

"I told them not to show themselves in front of the kids. I will not have them scaring my children!"

Even the most pertinacious phantom is no match for a mother defending her children.

By 2001, Carolyn and Michael Brown have lived in Portland's most active haunted home for over sixteen years. They still have never considered moving away, despite the continual reminders that Billy and Marles, if they are indeed the entities that haunt the house, are still roaming about their home and the frequent interruptions to the Brown family routine by curious passersby. While Carolyn freely discusses her family's experiences, she will not let strangers in her house for impromptu tours. Nor have they considered exorcising the couple.

"Billy and Marles have become a part of the family," Carolyn Brown says emphatically. "The one thing I tell people is that if they experience anything uncomfortable with them, they should just tell them to 'go away' and they will. We've made that clear to everyone. Take a deep breath and say go away. Sometimes people just don't know how to react and fear does get the better of them. But they have become such a part of our family that more and more people are comfortable when they visit."

That doesn't mean the family isn't startled by the sudden appearance of a member of their "extended" family. Still working as a Portland area law enforcement officer, Michael has on two occasions returned home from work late at night and, as he's pulled into the drive, seen a man standing in front of the garage. Both times, he stopped short of the garage door, kept the headlights on, and pulled out his service revolver. He's been ready to yell, "Stop! Police!" as he opened the car door when the man fades away. It's then he realizes Billy has been taking a stroll around the yard.

The ghostly couple has been considerate of the Brown children through the years, Carolyn says. Cassie is now in her late teens and Gennie in her early twenties. "They never did anything to the kids."

The haunting was particularly difficult on the younger girl, Cassie. She was comforted as a toddler by her mother's use of a concoction she called a "ghost spray" to keep away ghosts.

But Carolyn thinks the ghosts somehow understood how upset the little girl was and that in turn led to a particularly dramatic incident when Cassie was still in elementary school.

"Billy and Marles went to Cassie and said she wouldn't be seeing them, that they were going away," Carolyn says. "It was at night when Marles talked to her. And then they just faded away. Cassie told us about it the next morning. Even though they were still here, neither of the girls saw them again until they were older, especially Cassie. I felt it was very respectful, very sweet of them to do that for her. I think they realized she was at the age where it was starting to disturb her."

Although the ghosts backed off their unsolicited attentiveness to the girls when they were young, once they reached their teenage years and beyond there were plenty of indications of their continued active presence.

Carolyn remembers two incidents in particular: "Gennie was in the shower and heard someone come in the bathroom. She thought it was one of us. The toilet flushed. She felt it because when the water in the toilet flushes, the water pressure changes. She put her head around the curtain but no one was there. She yelled out that it wasn't funny. This last (2000) Christmas Eve she was putting on her makeup at the mirror in the bathroom. She had the door open. Then out of the corner of her eye, she thought she saw her dad in the doorway. Well, it wasn't her dad at all but another man and he just faded away. She came downstairs complaining that all she wanted was a little privacy in the bathroom."

Cassie has also seen the couple in recent years. One night when she was asleep she felt a pressure on her arm and assumed it was one of the dogs. When she turned over, however, she saw Marles lying next to her on the bed. She's also seen Marles looking out of a second-floor window.

The ghosts are especially lively when the quiet of "their" home is disturbed.

"When we had siding put up on our house they became really active," Carolyn remembers. "They were knocking, walking around, jumping up and down, very loud. You can tell they're not happy with the noise. Recently we had the roof replaced and they were more active then, too. They just don't like loud noises."

The December 23rd anniversary of the tragic events which may have initiated the haunting also lead to more commotion. While all can be calm for months at a time, typically around late fall or the Christmas season the couple make their presence felt and seen.

"As long as we don't have company, especially kids, they'll do things," Carolyn says. "You can hear them a lot more. When we're reading or watching television, you can hear them. They want to remind us they are here. Or you see someone out of the corner of your eye. You automatically think logically and rationally that it's one of the family. That's happened to all of us. We see someone and start a conversation and then when you look directly they disappear. Or you feel them. We've become quite sensitive where we can feel when they're near even though we can't see them. It's a kind of energy. It's as if you're standing near good friends and you sometimes get energy from them. That's what it is. You just know that they're there. Sometimes you feel a little coolness, a little breeze. But sometimes it's just a feeling hard to describe."

Carolyn said Billy has becomes something of a practical joker. "They are mischievous, Billy especially. Marles is more of the caregiver. She's the one that will open the windows and close the curtains when we don't expect it. That happens in the bedroom. Or stuff is moved around or hidden. For instance, if I'm looking for something, I'll ask them to help me and then I'll find it. I've found things in the oddest places. We had a library book that had to be returned and I put it on a table. It disappeared and later we found it in a laundry basket."

Sometimes the mischief becomes too much. Carolyn got mad at them for leaving the third floor lights on. She announced one day that if they were going to keep the lights on all the time, then they could pay the electric bills. "Now they turn the lights on, but they only keep them on for about five minutes and then they turn them off again," she laughs.

The family also counts their cat and two dogs among those they've seen act strangely when they believe the ghosts are making the rounds. The cat is Jasper and the dogs are Ainsworth and Fairfax, Junior, although the latter is not a descendant of their first dog.

"The cat is interesting," Carolyn says. "He has an odd personality, anyway. You'll see him staring and he won't flinch, just stare at nothing. We used to joke that he was having a staring contest with Billy. He just refuses to move and stays there. Of course, we see nothing, but you just know he's seeing something. That happens quite a bit. When Billy or Marles are around, he'll get kind of close to us. I don't know if he's being protective or if he's jealous, but if one of us is around he'll want to be close and he's not that affectionate a cat. But all the animals do get along with the ghosts. We live in harmony."

Some of the most extraordinary experiences have occurred with friends and relatives:

Carolyn's seventeen-year-old nephew and three friends insisted upon spending a night in the Browns' house, even though Carolyn told the boys the ghosts "didn't perform on demand." The boys decided to sleep in the living room. "My nephew came into the kitchen and asked me to stop Cassie from bouncing around upstairs," Carolyn recalls. "He said it was like she was jumping off the bed and banging around. I told him Cassie, Gennie, and Mike were not home. Then he wanted to know what was making the noise." Carolyn told him.

Carolyn's sister was a "major skeptic," in her words. During one visit in particular, they both heard what sounded like someone jumping off the beds upstairs. Carolyn ignored it, as did her sister. For a while. Finally, when Carolyn assured her that everyone else was out of the house and the animals in the yard, her sister ran upstairs to look around for herself. She came back down a skeptic no longer.

A second sister came by one afternoon to drop off a package. On the porch, she heard the television playing loudly and other voices coming from inside although no one answered her insistent knocking. She was angry and couldn't understand why her sister was being so rude by not answering the door. Later, Carolyn told her no one had been home in the afternoon.

Michael's nephew, the young man who saw the ghosts of Billy and Marles late one night, only returned for family gatherings, when there was a group of people present. He has since moved from Portland. Michael's mother has no problem with extended visits. Nina, the neighbor woman who occasionally cleaned the Brown's house, returned for visits when someone was home.

Not all of the family's relatives consider the house haunted. Carolyn's grandfather, for instance, a retired doctor, does not believe in ghosts. "It's a difference of opinion and that's okay," Carolyn says of him. "But he's one who's very respectful of a difference of opinion."

Over the years, the Browns have learned more about the "personalities" of the ghosts. Marles, they've been told, is very caring, but Billy had considerable "negative energy" and stayed in the background most of the time. Carolyn hopes that is changing. "We discovered from a few psychics that the negative energy that was once here from the murder/suicide has become all positive energy because we've accepted them as family. That was nice to know, that we were able to have a positive effect."

Children seem to bring out the best in Billy and Marles. The Browns' oldest daughter, Gennie, had a baby early in 2001. Family members noticed that when she was fussy she'd often stare off into space and then calm down. Marles, they believe, was helping care for the new baby. Carolyn says they've even heard Marles's voice on a baby monitor in the nursery when the rest of the family has been downstairs.

But perhaps the oddest result of the Brown house haunting came in a most unexpected manner. Michael and Carolyn were upset with the city's valuation of their property and the subsequent taxes that were levied. Michael decided to appeal. Appearing before the appeals board, he told them that his taxes should be lowered for a reason he doubted the board had ever heard before. The board chairman said that was impossible, they'd heard every excuse in the book. Not this one, Michael insisted, and pulled out newspaper articles, a videotape of a syndicated television program, and a book to document that his house was haunted and that might harm any resale.

The appeals board agreed and promptly cut his taxes.

"The chairman admitted he'd never heard that reason before," Michael says. "And then after the meeting all the board members gathered around and wanted to hear all about the haunting!"

Billy and Marles would undoubtedly have been pleased that their nonstop residency has had another helpful impact on the kind family that has adopted them.

Lady of the Roses

Boys. What are you going to do? A mother can tell them over and over again to keep their rooms clean, to pick up after themselves, and to be sympathetic about all the work she has to do around the house. And still they'll run out of their rooms leaving a trail of toys, clothes, and bric-a-brac in their wake that mothers seem to be genetically incapable of ignoring and so they're continually waging a tidiness campaign in their sons' rooms.

Doris Sorber faced that straightforward task on a morning many years ago in Seattle, Washington, when she met the lady of the roses—she had only intended to get her son's room in order.

But for Doris, making it up to the second-floor bedroom was a time-consuming chore. Shortly after she was married in the 1940s, she contracted the polio that severely weakened her legs and eventually led to her becoming a paraplegic. She has never let that slow her down, however, especially when it came to making sure her four sons had her undivided love and attention.

"They were pretty good about keeping their rooms clean," Doris said, "but they did things like boys do." By that, she means what many mothers are reluctant to admit—that few children can pass a personal cleanliness inspection by "major mother."

So it was, on this especially warm early fall day, that Doris found herself negotiating the staircase instead of taking the nap she so desperately wanted. She had given birth just a few weeks earlier to her fourth son, Joe, who, with her two-year-old son, Kris, was napping downstairs. The two oldest boys, nine-year-old Michael and eight-year-old Daniel were in school.

"I had some clean clothes that I wanted to put in the drawer of Daniel's room," Doris said, "because I knew if I gave them to him to take up he'd just throw them all over the room. So I took them up myself."

She had to quite literally pull herself up the stairs. She sat on each step, pushed the clothesbasket up to the next step and then pulled herself up after it. In this way she negotiated the staircase and then walked with great difficulty into Daniel's small room, which was large enough for a double bed and a dresser. Along one wall was a set of locked french doors that had once led to a balcony long since vanished. A smaller door opened into an attic that ran the length of the house. Across the hall, her oldest son Michael had the second, larger upstairs bedroom.

"I sat down on the floor between the bed and the dresser, with my back to the bed," Doris remembered of that long ago day. "One leg was straight out in front of me and the other was bent under it. I don't know if it was a noise, a feeling or what it was, but I realized I wasn't alone."

Not alone.

A phrase with the power to freeze the blood of even the pluckiest of mothers if her two babies are asleep elsewhere and she is quite sure no one else *should* be in her home.

"I looked up at the doorway. A tall, dark-haired woman in a white dress stood there. She had on gardening gloves. In one hand, she had pruning shears. On her other arm she carried a wicker basket of yellow roses. I didn't say anything because I was too dumbstruck. She didn't either. She smiled at me, stepped over my outstretched leg, opened the door to the attic and went in."

The mysterious woman seemed very real, yet Doris knew intuitively there was something very, very wrong about her sudden appearance in the house.

"I managed to get to my feet and open the door to the attic. There was nothing in there, not even the dust had been disturbed," she remembered. "That made the hair raise on the back of my neck."

Still not wanting to believe the visitor had been anything but an intruder—albeit an apparently kind, well-dressed one—and puzzled as to who might have let her in, Doris struggled back downstairs to check on her newborn infant and his older brother.

On one of the steps, she found a yellow rose.

A few moments later, she looked in on her young boys sleeping undisturbed in the master bedroom.

"I said nothing to my husband or to the older boys. I wasn't even sure I had really seen anything. I decided that I was getting too tired with the new baby, the big house and all. But, then, what about the rose on the stairs?" Doris said.

The Sorber family—Doris and Andy with young sons Michael, Daniel, and Kristopher—had been living in Seattle-area apartments for several years. But with a fourth child on the way, it became clear that apartment living was not going to provide the space necessary for a family of six, certainly not one with growing, rambunctious boys. So it was that in the spring of 1953, the Sorbers launched a search for a rental house in which to move, preferably one with a big yard and on the edge of the city.

Within days, a newspaper ad caught their eye. An older house on a third acre of land in northern Seattle was for rent. The Sorbers thought the big yard would be perfect for the boys to run and romp around while the age of the house meant rent would probably be reasonable.

Once they located the place, however, Doris's heart sank. Her first impulse was to turn around and head back to the city.

"It had been an early spring and the winter accumulation of moisture had dried up and left the threat of a very dry summer," Doris remembered. "As we drove down the unpaved street we left little dust devils behind us. I was expecting another child in the fall and Kris was fussy. My two older boys were in school. Andy wasn't in a good mood either, because he never liked to shop for anything.

I was beginning to think that this was not one of my better ideas."

Along one side of the street the houses were what Doris called "respectable, street-level residences." The other side was another matter. A short distance back from the street the ground rose steeply eight to ten feet in height then leveled off again. The house they were looking for was on that side and atop a little rise.

"It was the only house on the block and confirmed what I had been thinking— that coming here was a mistake," Doris said. "It was a sorry sight, dilapidated and deserted. It had once been gray with white trim but now the white was gone from the trim and most of the gray was weather-beaten. The back of the house was level with the top of the hill, so the basement with some big picture windows held up the front, leaving the porch at least eight feet above the yard."

Steep steps led from the yard up to the porch, but several of them were missing and others were held together by only a couple of nails. The porch itself tilted at a dangerous angle and some floorboards were missing. The yard was unkempt. A large section had been garden-tilled at one time but nothing grew in it now except weeds. On the other side of the house was a "jungle" of bushes, ivy, and weeds.

"I had never seen such a forlorn, neglected place," Doris said, "but in spite of that it had a certain dignity about it, like a once-elegant lady long past her prime and down on her luck."

Much to Doris's amazement, her husband insisted on getting out to see what the inside of the house looked like.

"He climbed up the steps to the porch to look in the windows," Doris said. "How could he think we could possibly live in such a dump? Then to my amazement he came down the steps and went around the side of the house toward the back."

Doris was disappointed at the delay in getting back to town and uncomfortable because of her pregnancy. Little Kris was unhappy about having to stay in the car.

Andy was smiling as he returned from his walk around the house.

"You'd be surprised at what it looks like inside," he said enthusiastically to his wife. "It's really very nice. A few nails, a hammer, and a little paint would do wonders on the outside. Some mowing and pruning would take care of the yard. I think we should take it if the rent is right."

Doris didn't think she was hearing correctly, but she nevertheless agreed to telephone the owner as soon as they returned home. "I was so tired of apartment living that I think a tent would have looked good to me at that point."

The Sorbers signed the rental agreement. When school was dismissed for summer vacation, the Sorbers and their cocker spaniel dog "Kelly" moved into the house Doris had taken to calling "the tired old lady."

Doris was shocked at the contrast between the ramshackle exterior and the inside of the house.

"Indoors was the opposite of the outside. It was freshly painted and clean as a pin with a grandeur that the outside had hinted at," she said. She and Andy figured that previous renters had taken pains to keep the interior neat but paid no attention to how the exterior of the house or the yard looked.

The first floor consisted of a living room and a dining room separated by a tall bookcase, and a large, inviting kitchen with a door leading to the basement. A hallway extending off the dining room led to Doris and Andy's bedroom and a separate bathroom. A fireplace was situated along one wall of the living room.

Near the front door was the staircase to the two second-floor bedrooms. Because of the house's location atop the slight hill, the Sorbers were particularly enchanted with the view of Seattle out the large living room windows.

The two older Sorber boys were given the choice of which upstairs bedroom each wanted to occupy. As the oldest, Michael decided to take the larger room, which also featured big windows and a view of the city. "Whoever had been the builder had obviously enjoyed the view," Doris said. Eight-year-old Dan agreed that he would try the smaller room, the one with the locked french windows and the door to the attic.

Doris remembered an incident on their first night in the house that in some ways presaged later events.

"The morning after we moved in, Mike told me that Dan had come into his room in the middle of the night," Doris said. "Dan said he heard 'funny noises' coming from the attic, so he decided he would stay in the same room with his brother. His father also complained of hearing noises at night. I laughed at them saying that, of course they heard noises—all old houses creaked and groaned."

The next few months were taken up with cleaning the yard. Andy Sorber tilled the old garden and planted seeds. He then turned his attention to the other part of the yard and the untangling of thick brush.

"You know, whoever lived in this house sure liked roses," he told Doris one Saturday morning. "They're all over the place out there. If I can get the under-growth away from them they should be real pretty this summer."

Andy had grown up in Portland, Oregon, the city of roses. He loved roses and knew a great deal about them, Doris said.

In the early summer, the house's owner, a middle-aged woman, stopped by to check on how the Sorbers were faring. The couple learned that she had moved into the house when she married her husband and that it had belonged to his invalid mother. Her husband didn't want to leave her and so they had all lived there together. The couple eventually had two girls, but her husband became mentally ill. His mother's death worsened his condition and he was committed to an institution. When it became clear he was not going to recover, his wife filed for divorce, remarried sometime later and moved away with her daughters, but had continued to rent out the house for about the past seven years. Legally, the home still belonged to her confined ex-husband and his and her daughters.

"Her husband hadn't done much to the outside of the house," Doris remembers. "It was his mother who was the type who would garden."

The astonishing incident in her second oldest son's room occurred that early fall. But Doris still didn't know the ghostly woman's identity. That came late the next February as the weather was unusually warm and everyone was talking about an early spring. The Sorbers had begun planning their summer garden. But then came the news from their landlady that her former husband had died and his daughters had inherited the house. As their guardian, she'd decided to sell the property and put the money in a trust for the little girls.

"She had wanted to let us know that there would be buyers looking at the place and to give us time to find somewhere else to live," Doris said. "I was sorry to get the call because I had become increasingly attached to the 'tired old lady.' I thought she'd regained some of her dignity while we lived there."

The house was listed for sale but the prospective buyers were few. "I began to hope that it would not be sold," Doris said.

One day, however, the landlady arrived with a contractor interested in buying it to remodel for resale. "I could tell he wanted to buy the house, he had a lot of plans," she said.

While the contractor walked around the house and grounds, the owner talked to Doris about the years during which she lived in the house.

"She complimented me on what Andy had done to the rose garden," Doris said. "She said her mother-in-law would have been very pleased since it had been her pride and joy. She had won many prizes with her roses."

Doris immediately made the connection between the woman in white she'd seen the fall before and the landlady's former mother-in-law. "I didn't say anything to her about what I had seen, but I did get up enough courage to ask her where the old lady had died."

"Oh, she was sick a long time," she replied. "But she didn't want to die in the hospital so we brought her home. I took care of her until she died in that little bedroom upstairs."

And then she sighed.

"There are still some of her things in the attic. I didn't know what to do with them. I just left them there."

That evening the landlady telephoned confirming that she'd accepted an offer from the contractor. The Sorbers had thirty days to move out and began to look for another home.

But more mysteries were yet to come, as Doris recollected about one morning not long after the house had been sold:

"Andy was at work, the boys had gone off to school, and I was washing up the breakfast dishes in the kitchen. The baby was sleeping in his crib," Doris recalled. "I could see into the living room where Kris was playing with our little cocker spaniel. All of a sudden, the dog yelped and Kris started to cry. Both of them stopped playing and they looked toward the stairway. Kris couldn't talk well enough to tell me what he saw but he was crying. They both ran toward the kitchen, Kris looking back toward the stairway. I went to the doorway to see what had frightened them, but I couldn't see anything. I did feel a strange coldness and seconds later the front door opened and closed. I think the ghost left that day."

For the rest of the day Kris and the dog stayed by Doris's side. Never again would Kris or the dog go up the staircase.

The final connection between the former owner and the ghost Doris witnessed was made several days later. She discovered that her two oldest boys had ventured into the attic against their mother's admonitions and ransacked some of the trunks that had been left there in storage.

"I promised myself to give them 'what for' when they got home," Doris said. She found that among the belongings the boys had looked through were some snapshots. "I set about putting them in the trunks. As I picked up one, I saw it was a picture of a tall, dark-haired lady in a white dress. She had a basket of roses on her arm."

Doris had, of course, seen her before.

The Sorbers did move to another house on the south side of the city and eventually on to northern California where Doris Sorber, now a widow, lives today.

"We drove by a few months later just to see what the contractor had done,"

Doris said. "We hardly recognized the place. The rose garden looked like a lumberyard."

The house looked sturdier, she thought, but it seemed to lack the "character" it had when her family lived there. She was sad to see the changes.

The contractor never got the chance to profit from his remodeling. Authorities said it was an electrical problem, but for whatever reason the house burned to the ground.

"If there was an electrical short I'd bet it got some help from someone who did not want her house changed," she said. "I felt bad when the house was sold, not only because I was fond of it, but because she was, too. We were happy there. I think she really liked us. My husband was very good with roses and that was the reason."

Phantoms on the Trail

The Delaware Indians were prescient in having a word in their language that has evolved into Wyoming—*maugh-wau-wa-ma*—or, "large plains" or "mountains and valleys alternating." With an average of fewer than five people for each of its 97,809 square miles, Wyoming is an outdoorsman's paradise. Eight soaring mountain ranges, the storied wild rivers Bighorn, Powder, and Snake, the vast wilderness tracts of Yellowstone National Park, Medicine Bow, and Shoshone National Forests and others, and the high plains of Thunder Basin National Grassland in eastern Wyoming make the state a favorite of hikers, campers, canoeists, and hunters.

The high and wind-swept plateaus of Wyoming, however, have also given rise to stories of a mysterious pioneer scout and a jeep-driving doppelganger. They are legends as worthy of the state's folklore as the mythic exploits of Buffalo Bill Cody and Jim Bridger.

The Scout

Sam Ross* didn't expect to see a ghost on his way home to the family ranch that night. In fact, he described himself as about the most unlikely person in the universe either to believe in the supernatural or to be spooked by riding alone down the desolate trail. The story he eventually related to his friends and family, however, a tale he only told with some reluctance, nearly made a believer out of this Wyoming lad.

The setting of Sam Ross's experience is in the vicinity of Cheyenne and the time is near the turn of the twentieth century. He worked in town but lived at home on his family's ranch. Some versions of his story have him living near Guernsey, Wyoming, but that seems unlikely, as this little town of some eleven hundred people is over a hundred miles northeast of Cheyenne. Ross could not have made that distance twice a day as he did on horseback, under any circumstance.

He knew the trail well. On most days, he got back to the ranch in time for

*Name has been changed.

supper. Occasionally he found some nightlife to enjoy in town and that was the occasion on this particular night. He didn't saddle up and head for home until well after ten o'clock. A full moon had risen, illuminating the trail, while swift-moving cirrus clouds raced across the sky casting dim shadows on the prairie stretching away for miles in all directions.

Ross was in no particular hurry, although being alone at night in such desolate territory did give him a little case of the jitters, even if he would be the last to confess such a weakness. The hour was closing in on midnight when he saw another rider in the distance. The man was crouched low in the saddle, his head pressed against the side of his horse's neck, obviously spurring on the mount to all the licks he was capable of. Ross thought the man's terrific pace signaled some need for help so he, too, spurred on his horse to intersect the stranger at where he figured he would cross the trail in front of him.

Ross got to where he reckoned the rider would see him. He pulled up and waited. Surprisingly, his horse stomped the hard-packed earth and threw back its head in a nervousness that Ross had not seen before. He pulled back hard on the reins. He looked off at the dark rider bearing down on him, expecting that he'd draw up at any moment to tell him of what emergency there might be to make him gallop at breakneck speed at night over the prairie.

But the rider didn't stop or even slow down. He flew by in what Ross later described as "a rush of icy wind." Ross's own horse reared in fright. He snorted, bucked and plunged into a ditch before Ross got him under control. Both man and horse were breathing hard as he got the horse back on the trail and gave chase. The other rider had too much of a head start. Ross slowed his horse to a walk. He shook his head as he watched the horseman vanish over the dark horizon.

What little Ross noticed of the man added to his puzzlement. A wide-brimmed hat was pulled down low over his eyes, the front bill pushed up by the wind in his face. The man's clothes were rough, maybe of buckskin, offset by a big kerchief knotted around his throat. Ross couldn't make out his boots or his saddle, but he had the impression that he held a rifle in one hand and the reins in another. He saw that saddlebags were strapped tight against his horse's flanks and a bedroll rested behind the saddle.

What he noticed most, however, and what it took him the longest time to admit even to himself is that the horse and rider made no sound. Where there should have been the pounding of hooves there was silence. And that cold rush of air Ross felt against his face. It was more than you'd expect from a lone rider. His horse had reared, had nearly thrown him as the man charged across the trail. Of all that, Ross was certain. But those were about the only things. Little else on this night made any sense.

Sam Ross was a true Westerner, which means he was reluctant to tell others of his peculiar experience for fear of ridicule and some questions about his man-hood. A man of the West doesn't admit to being frightened or to seeing appa-ritions on the prairie. In time, he did tell his family and then started asking around among the old-timers in the region. He found that the honest ones among them said that they, too, had seen the phantom rider.

The story they told Ross is that the rider he saw had been a scout sent to warn settlers of an Indian uprising but he had been killed before he could issue the forewarning. The scout is condemned to ride the Wyoming prairies for all eternity and in endless repetitions of his ill-fated attempt to save the unsuspecting pio-neers.

The Driver

There are few unlikelier places to have encountered what may have been a *doppelganger* than the wilder reaches of Wyoming. This idea of a "double walker" or a person's "shadow self" is firmly embedded in European folklore but doesn't show up as often in North America. Legend has it that every person has a doppelganger, although it is invisible to the eye. They stand slightly behind us, sometimes giving advice, sometimes acting out what we have done, or will do in the future. In some cases, this ghostly twin of ourselves might have the exact opposite personality of its living counterpart—if a person is wicked, his doppelganger will be decent and vice versa.

Now what is odd about the doppelganger of lore—and what sets this Wyoming incident apart from all others—is that, according to most accounts, this "other self" will never be seen by its living double.

But that's not the situation here.

Meet a man named Gordon Barrows, a former trade magazine editor and a veteran of the Army Tank Corp during World War II. He was a Wyoming man born and bred who returned to his family ranch outside Cody, Wyoming, in 1946 after the service.

The story he told a decade later of a very special overland journey adds a uniquely American twist to the idea that a secret self accompanies us on our life's passage or, as in his case, protects us from being injured or even premature death.

His account begins following his release from the service in April 1946. He was in southern California visiting his sister when his dad back in Wyoming asked him to go to a large auction of military equipment in Oceanside where there would be a bidder preference for armed forces veterans. Barrows went down to the city just north of San Diego and ended up buying a jeep, which he shipped back to Wyoming. The idea seemed to be that it would be a handy vehicle to have around the family's sprawling ranch.

Barrows re-enrolled that fall at the University of Wyoming in Laramie, about 500 miles southeast of Cody and about as far away as he could get from his family's ranch without stumbling into Colorado or Nebraska. But he couldn't get that jeep out of his mind. Since he'd been the bidder, he considered it his own even though his dad used it for chores. All fall and through the winter he thought about how nifty it would be to have it on the sprawling campus. The first opportunity he had to act was during spring vacation and so he went home, picked up the jeep, and immediately set off to return to the Laramie campus.

"It wasn't a very sensible thing to do, if you know Wyoming weather," Barrows later wrote of the events.

The university's spring break came in March that year. Weather across the state was treacherous, with heavy snow expected at the higher elevations. The jeep was genuine army surplus—that meant not even a canvas top to protect him from the elements and a top running speed of around thirty-five miles an hour. But when you're young and brave you sometimes don't heed the advice of that little voice in the back of your head, so instead he bundled up in a wool shirt, pants, and slipped on a heavy parka.

Today, the 500-mile drive from Cody to Laramie still takes the better part of a day, even on modern roads and under the best of conditions. It is as desolate on many stretches of the roadway as it was when the first white settlers arrived. Even sixty years ago, when Barrows set out to return to the university, a winter traveler risked his life on the wretched roadways that snaked through deep canyons and across inhospitable prairie with not a farmhouse or settlement for miles around.

Barrows set off hunkered down in the four-wheel-drive jeep, not fearing his ability to get through snow so much as getting so sleepy he couldn't continue on—he wanted to make it back in time for Monday classes so he planned to drive straight through. He reached the halfway point at Casper after nine hours on the road, averaging not even thirty miles per hour.

He took the road straight out of Casper headed toward Torrington. It had begun to snow. The sun was setting. To make matters worse, the old jeep had manual windshield wipers so he had to hold the steering wheel with one hand while he worked the wipers with the other. In those days, the road south of Torrington split, one fork going left toward the capital of Cheyenne and the other toward Laramie. Going by way of Cheyenne was longer but much safer in the winter. The problem with going straight on to Laramie is that the route led up through long Telephone Canyon and from there to the seven-thousand-foot elevation of the city. Barrows knew there were virtually no farmsteads, ranches, or towns along the way.

As he neared the junction, he saw a pair of red taillights. A Greyhound bus was stopped on the side of the road. Next to it was a police car. A highway patrolman was walking toward the bus. Barrows hopped out of the jeep and walked toward them.

"Nobody's been through there," he heard the officer telling the bus driver through the open side window. "And nobody's goin' through. Road's closed through the canyon. Weather report says there's four inches of snow and more's comin'. If anybody got stuck in that canyon they might be there for a week before another car came through, and there's no ranch where you could get help."

Barrows listened and then walked a short way down the road toward the mouth of the canyon. The officer was telling the truth, nobody had been down that road. Snow lay so deep across the concrete that he couldn't even tell where the roadway began . . . or ended. The wind was pushing the snow into high drifts. He recalled that few cars tried the canyon road even in the summer. Drivers faced a road that steeply dropped hundreds of feet before climbing out again. There wasn't a rail or stone fence to stop a skidding car from sailing off the edge to the canyon floor far below.

What to do? He usually took the Telephone Canyon route, but now if he followed the bus and other cars on the safer route to Cheyenne, he'd be late and miss classes on Monday. If he waited—and it might be days before the snow cleared—he'd have to return to Casper and stay there.

He made up his mind. Making sure the jeep was in four-wheel drive, he turned around and headed back in the direction of Casper. About a quarter of a mile along the road, he stopped and flicked off his headlights. Through the swirling snow covering him and the jeep, he could just make out the taillights of the bus and the police car heading toward Cheyenne. Once their lights had disappeared, he turned on his own headlights, backed around and headed off to go through the canyon.

Barrows was near exhaustion. He'd been driving for eighteen hours straight with brief stops for lunch and to fill his gas tank. He was slapping himself on the side of his face to keep himself awake. The road into the canyon sloped steeply down. As he neared the top of the approach hill, he was startled to see a lone man walking along the left side of the roadway, away from his approaching jeep.

Barrows stopped about twenty-five feet behind the receding figure.

"I was surprised to see that he wasn't even wearing a warm parka," he said. "I knew there was no ranch, or any other place, to stop at for the thirty-five miles of the canyon—and quite a distance beyond that. The way the man was dressed, he might easily die on the road from exposure."

He wasn't worried or afraid to pick up a stranger. In the West, and especially during the winter, you offer what assistance you can to a person in distress. Barrows waited as the man turned around and started walking back toward where Barrows idled the jeep.

"When he got in range of the headlights, I saw that he was dressed in a light jacket, such as I had worn myself in the army, something called a Tank Corps jacket, with elastic cuffs and the same elastic material at the neck. And it immediately occurred to me, without any astonishment—probably because I was almost numb from the cold and lack of sleep—that he looked exactly like me."

"You look sleepy," the loner said matter-of-factly without introducing himself. "Want me to drive?"

"Thanks," Barrows replied and moved over into the passenger seat. The man got into the driver's seat.

What amazed Gordon Barrows when he thought about it later is that it all seemed to be the most perfectly ordinary of encounters. Almost as if he'd been picking up an old friend. He hadn't asked the man's name, he hadn't faltered in agreeing to let him drive; indeed, he was so worn-out that he pushed up the small metal back seat those jeeps had and lay down between the front seats with his knees on the right front seat and his head resting against the cold hard floor.

"The next thing I remember, I was waking up," Barrows would write later. "The jeep had stopped and the driver was sitting motionless behind the wheel. I sat up, brushing the parka back from my eyes."

There wasn't a sound. The engine wasn't running and the howling blizzard had passed. The sky was clear, stars twinkling across the horizon in the clear, cold Wyoming air.

He didn't know where he was until he saw a faint glow in the distance. He knew that a light in that region had to be coming from the single ranch *at the other end* of Telephone Canyon. In the time Barrows slept, his silent friend had driven the entire thirty-five mile length of the canyon.

Now before him stretched the highway straight on for an easy forty miles into Laramie.

The driver got out.

"Don't you want to go on into Laramie?" Barrows asked.

"No," the stranger said.

"Well, thanks a lot," Barrows called.

"You're welcome," the man called back as he hunched his shoulders inside the thin army-issue jacket. He turned away from Barrows and started back down the canyon road. That's the last Barrows saw of his nameless patron.

Despite the bizarre nature of the incident, Gordon Barrows said in his written memoir of the experience that he actually thought little about that trip. Not until a casual conversation with a friend some days later did he begin exploring its odder proportions.

The friend asked what way he'd come back to Laramie with the old jeep. Through Telephone Canyon? His friend inquired.

"Sure," Barrows said. "But I didn't drive all the way by myself. I picked up a hitchhiker who spelled me at the wheel through the canyon."

"You were lucky," his friend said, adding that he himself had to stay the night in Casper because the road was blocked.

Barrows grew more puzzled.

"There was something about it: That hitchhiker was walking on that stretch of road on the Casper side of the canyon, wearing nothing but a Tank Corps jacket. And he got out after we left the canyon and walked back into it."

Barrows friend snorted in disbelief.

"Into the canyon! That's impossible! He couldn't have lasted more than a couple of hours."

The more Barrows thought about it, the more he fastened his mind around that man in the jeep . . . well, the conclusion was evident.

"He looked *exactly like me*," he whispered.

Gordon Barrows got such a strange look from his pal that day that he didn't tell the story again for many years. For the rest of his life, he recalled each detail with such vivid and certain precision that he could have gone back and found the exact places on the road where he picked up the hitchhiker . . . and where he last saw his *self* walking back into snow-blocked Telephone Canyon.

CANADA

This Is What Happened Next

Noted author, ethnographer and storyteller Lawrence Millman has spent a significant amount of time in the far reaches of northern Canada and the Arctic collecting the folktales told by the Inuit and other Native peoples. In books, anthologies, and magazine articles, Millman offers vivid portraits of the culture, lifestyles, and stories of a people little known or understood by the world outside their still-isolated villages. Since he speaks four or five Inuit dialects, Millman has been able to gather the folk stories the Natives have told for centuries and include them in books such as A *Kayak Full of Ghosts, Lure of the Labrador Wild*, and *Wolverine Creates the World: Labrador Indian Tales*.

Millman, who calls himself "an inveterate collector of folktales, especially among Northern peoples," came to gather stories after living in the west of Ireland. There, he says, storytelling is a "window on culture."

A couple of personal experiences with the supernatural also led him to collect the spiritual tales of the Native Inuit peoples, and others.

"Good ghost stories address questions of life and death," Millman says. "They cut to the quick, so to speak, in the manner that another kind of legend might not. We live in a world where the religious and the spiritual are on the decline. . . . But ghost stories send us back to a preternatural past that we've lost touch with, to a past where all the elements were there, to a past where there was a certain harmony between the world and ourselves. Where, when something happened, there was an explanation other than, well, it's the gene pool, or it's a (weather) front moving in. A ghost story, at least to present-day sensibilities, is appealing because it tends to return us to a primordial element in humankind's past. Although the story itself could be violent or horrific or nasty, it cuts through all the junk of modern culture, the technology, the daily work grind, and so forth, to something truly basic in the human heart and soul."

Millman says that basic appeal has to do with elements of mortality, of the death of one's friends and loved ones, and of a place because ghosts are often associated with specific geographic locations.

"You can look at certain stories as metaphors for place," Millman notes. "They're a kind of extrapolation of what that place is all about. That's very true in some Northern stories. Many of those have to do with starvation."

A former university professor with a doctorate in English Literature, Millman distinguishes between supernatural experiences by contemporary witnesses and folktales whose origins are lost in the miasma of incalculable generations. He speaks to an example in which an acquaintance might claim his "great uncle Fred" appeared at the foot of the bed. That person might tell the story as an example of a ghost showing up in a modern setting.

However, a folktale derived from the same experience and retold over time would make "great uncle Fred's" visit mythic, according to Millman.

"It may be in the story that originally someone did see their 'great uncle Fred,' but in the telling over and over through generations, Fred disappears because no one knows who Fred is anymore. He becomes a more mythic figure. Maybe a monstrous figure. He's no longer the kind, doting, eccentric uncle who gave sweets to the children, but he may well now be a monster because retelling after retelling he takes on a different form. No one two hundred years later knows that Fred was that kind, doting uncle. So, the story has taken on a mythic quality. I think that's the origin for many of these stories. They had in fact this sort of sense of a familial anecdote, but by being told and retold they acquired a more universal importance."

In this Inuit story from Labrador, collected by Millman, one can imagine several scenarios in which the circumstances might have been based on a personal experience, although it's hard to know who might have been left to disclose what happened next:

Two hunters got caught in a bad blizzard. They took refuge in a lodge that was empty except for a bundle of furs hung from the rafters.

That night the hunters were smoking their pipes.

"I will tell you a story about two men," the elder man said. "They were caught in a bad blizzard and they hadn't brought a tent with them. . . ."

"What happened then?"

"They found a nice little lodge in the middle of the woods. . . ."

"And what happened then?"

"I'm too tired to finish. I'll tell you the rest tomorrow."

Next morning the younger man went over to his friend and shook him.

"Wake up!" he shouted.

But the man did not wake up. Nor would he ever wake up, for he had died in his sleep.

Poor fellow, thought the other: *My friend gave up his breath before he could finish his story. That means the story is somewhere in this lodge, waiting for an end. I'll have to stay here myself . . . until I find the end.*

The man looked for the end of the story all day long. Toward evening he curled up on the floor to go to sleep. He happened to glance up at the bundle of furs. Suddenly a skeleton peered out of it.

"Another person for me to strangle," the skeleton said.

Now a long bony arm reached down and grabbed at the man. He rolled away from it.

"Who . . . who are you?" he asked.

Came this reply: "I starved in this lodge long ago. Since then I've killed everyone who comes here. I killed your friend last night. Tonight I'm going to kill you."

"Isn't that rather cruel!" replied the young man.

How can I escape this murderous skeleton? the man asked himself, even as the bony arm made another lunge for his throat.

All at once he remembered his friend's unfinished story. It was still here, still in the lodge. So the man jumped into the story and that's exactly what happened next—he escaped the skeleton.

Twice Haunted

As a young boy in Moose Jaw, Saskatchewan, Regina businessman Frank Theofan could not have imagined that he would live in two houses that he steadfastly believes were haunted. And as with many old hands experienced at living with ghosts about the place, Theofan is remarkably calm as he recounts the infrequent circumstances of the mysterious sensations and sounds he can recall even now, decades later.

"There was no sense of being afraid of them," he said, referring to whatever inhabited his homes. "They weren't out to cause me any harm. It got to the point where I didn't pay attention to it."

The owner of a record shop called Bach and Beyond which specializes in classical, easy listening, light jazz, and music from the 1940s and 1950s—"I call it an adult music store," he laughs, "which is different from an adult bookstore"— Theofan does not appear to be a man who would make up lively tales of the beyond for the amusement of others. The stories he tells are of gentle hauntings by a ghost or ghosts unknown.

Theofan grew up in Moose Jaw in the 1950s and 1960s and that's where the first haunting took place, although he didn't fully understand the nature of what he was experiencing there until years later during a chance conversation with his wife and sister.

"The house I grew up in was a two-story farmhouse, or rather it *was* a farmhouse," he remembered. "My dad had the house moved on to the property from a farm outside Moose Jaw."

He has not been able to trace the house's ownership or even find out from what farm it had been moved.

Frank and his older sister had bedrooms on the second floor. His was at the top of the stairs. His sister had the room down the hall.

"It was in my sister's room that we had the odd things happen," he said.

Even odder, Frank and his sister had separate peculiar incidents in her room but neither one spoke of them to the other. "She lived in that house until she was in her 30s," he noted, "but never in 20 years did she mention anything. Never said a word."

When Frank was in high school, he would use a small dresser along one wall in his sister's room as a study desk. The doorway into the hallway was a few feet farther down the wall.

"When I sat there and did my homework I would keep glancing over at the door, you know how when someone sticks his head in the door and you see them out of the corner of your eye? You look over. Well, that's what I did but there was never anybody there."

But Frank kept that a secret for nearly two decades, until the time in the early 1970s when his sister, who was by now living in Calgary, visited Frank, his wife, and their daughter.

"My wife and my sister were talking and this thing about the bedroom at our house in Moose Jaw comes up," he said. "Now my wife had stayed in that room once before we were married but she never wanted to stay there again. After that one time she wouldn't stay the night or she'd stay over with someone else in town. But she never said anything about why."

Frank listened as the two women conversed. Then his wife revealed why she didn't like the room.

His wife said she stayed in the room only once because there was something peculiar, something creepy about the room. His sister agreed, noting that for her it was like someone was in there all the time watching you.

"I perked up," Frank said. "My sister never said anything to anybody, but for all those years she felt that way. I said that whatever it was, was over in the corner, by the door, right? She wondered how I knew that. Then my wife added that it was like someone was standing in the corner watching."

He remembered that during those years when he finished his homework in his sister's room he would continually glance toward the door. But after listening to his sister and wife compare experiences, he changed his mind about the direction from which he sensed another presence.

"I wasn't looking at the door, I was looking at the corner. As if there was someone there looking at me. It all fell together. I even took my dog up there once when we visited from Regina and the damn thing wouldn't go in that room at all. It was just weird."

Over the decades, Frank Theofan has often thought about his old house in Moose Jaw and tried to figure out what it all was that made him—and his sister and his wife—so uncomfortable in that room over the years.

"I still think that I saw something. That's why I would look. It was like someone moved over there or stuck his head through the door. But when I looked there was nothing I could see. After a while I just wrote it off. But what do you write it off to?"

Why didn't his sister move to another room or confide in her parents?

"There was no other room to move to," Frank recalled. "And you have to understand the family dynamics. My dad was Greek and quite a bit older. He would have thought she was crazy. Whether she ever confided in my mom, I don't know. She was twenty years older than me. She said it started before I was born and went on for as long as she lived in that room. And she said she never told anyone about it."

As if living in one haunted house wasn't enough, Frank Theofan says that a three-story house his family rented for a few years in Regina had some strange, albeit sporadic, activity he attributes to the supernatural.

The house was divided into three separate living quarters. Frank, his wife, and their daughter had the main floor with a living room, dining room, and kitchen, plus the two bedrooms on the second floor. They rented a third-floor suite to a friend of the family and another friend rented a small basement apartment.

"Our friend who took the basement suite came a couple of weeks after we moved in the house," Frank said. "We gave him the key and he moved in. When we got home that night he asked why, when we had been home earlier in the day, we hadn't gone downstairs to say hello. I said we hadn't been home."

Their friend was puzzled. He said someone had been there because he heard someone walking around on the first floor. After checking with the third-floor tenant and finding that he had also been gone all day, Frank thought perhaps the landlord had come over for some reason, but a quick telephone call nixed that idea.

"I thought the basement renter was just imagining things," Frank stressed.

A month or so later he came upstairs to tell Frank that the same thing had happened again earlier that day. "He knew we were at work," Frank said, "but he heard someone walking around upstairs. He thought someone had a key or some other way to get in. But we checked and couldn't find anything disturbed and the doors were all locked."

It was at about this point that the third-floor renter got into the act, Frank said.

"He came down two or three times one afternoon when we were gone. He said he heard someone walking around on the main floor, but each time he came down there was never anybody down there."

The basement renter was gone in a little over a month but it's not clear if the clattering footsteps had anything to do with the sudden vacancy. After he moved out, however, Frank discovered for himself what had up until then only been reported to him.

"I was downstairs in the basement when I heard someone start walking from the front of the house, through what was a dining room, then through the living room before they stopped at the back of the house. Then it would start at the front again!" he said.

He ran upstairs.

"It had to be something," Frank emphasized. "So I went down again and I heard it again. I could keep pace with it; I could follow it, footstep for footstep, and walk underneath them to the back. I heard the heel hit before the front of his foot came down. It was a perfect footstep."

Up until that time, Frank had put it off to the "house settling."

As before, the footsteps would suddenly recur toward the front of the house on the first floor and he'd have to run across the basement to keep pace with them. He followed the steps for a few minutes and then sneaked upstairs in hopes of grabbing the perpetrator.

"I wanted to see what the hell was going on and, of course, as soon as I got upstairs there was nothing."

The Theofans grew accustomed to the occasional wanderings by their unseen tenant. Whoever it was did not shy away from company. At an informal card party one evening with friends, the footfalls came again, crossing the two large rooms on the first floor before fading out of earshot. Frank, his wife and their guests were in the kitchen but clearly heard the creaking floorboards in the nearby rooms.

"I said, well, it must be the ghost. That was the only explanation I had."

A discussion with the landlord about the house history proved fruitless. He had bought it only three or four years before. He did know the house was built near the turn of the twentieth century after finding some newspapers of the era stuck inside the walls for additional insulation. The third floor even had some secret passages that led through the walls of some of the rooms.

The house still stands.

Frank Theofan is decidedly philosophical about his years in two haunted houses.

"I'm a bit of an agnostic," he noted. "Every once in a while I'll think that when you die, that's it, but then knowing, feeling, or believing in ghosts I think there must be something more. It has helped me think there is some kind of an afterlife. But why are there so few hauntings? There should be ghosts everywhere."

Maybe there are.

The Moose Head Inn Mystery

A cold February night was descending on the scenic Kenosee Lake region of south-eastern Saskatchewan. An occasional automobile driver passing the landmark Moose Head Inn would not have seen anything out of the ordinary. At seven o'clock on this evening, a few cars huddled in the parking lot, light spilled out of the bar windows onto the compacted snow, and snatches of a country song played on a jukebox could be heard when the front door swung open. It was well known in the neighborhood that new owner Dale Orsted was resolute in his determination to make the roadhouse the popular nightspot it had once been.

In the third-floor apartment of the inn, which doubled as an office, Dale and his girlfriend sat on a couch against one wall watching a CBC television program. The faint sounds of bar conversation and music from the floors below assured them that all was well.

That was a relief.

Over the past several weeks, as workmen replaced all the carpeting in the building and the other major renovations of the inn seemed to finally be coming to an end, the many small, unexplained annoyances and troublesome noises had frayed their nerves. Lights wouldn't stay off, doors banged open for no reason, and then there would be the footsteps, solid and distinct. The problem was there was never anybody connected to them.

Dale and his girlfriend, along with Jeff Stephen, the manager, really didn't want to think about who—or what—might be causing these vexations. Burglars or tres-passers had been discounted. There had even been those times when the trio had wondered whether they were all being subject to some sort of mass hallucination.

The young couple's serene evening of television and small talk was suddenly shattered. A loud, deep moan, the cry of someone in agony, arose from the room behind them, the one used as an office. The eerie wail lasted for a full ten seconds before it stopped as abruptly as it had begun.

When the couple gathered their wits about them and cautiously looked into the room where the sound seemed to have come from they found it as empty as they had expected it to be. They were alone in the apartment on the third floor of the three-story building. The doors going downstairs were securely locked. No other living being could have possibly gained access to their apartment.

That was just the problem. The *living* they didn't have to worry about. It seemed that it might be the *dead* with whom they were having encounters. On that night in February, the *haunting* of Moose Head Inn by an entity they came to call "Stanley" became a reality for Dale Orsted and his companions.

The history of Moose Head Inn begins early in the twentieth century when the Hungarian community near Kipling first built a church and then, a short distance away, a dance hall for the far-flung neighbors to gather on Saturday nights. That area known as Bekavar is about twenty miles northwest of Kenosee. For the next half-century, teenagers and adults enjoyed weekly parties and dances at what came to be known as Bekavar Hall. But patterns of entertainment changed and attendance dropped off. Radio, and later television, along with quicker access to the delights of metropolitan Regina and Winnipeg forced many rural community halls to close by the 1960s.

In 1966, Archebald and Ethel Grandison purchased several acres of land in the popular summer resort of Kenosee Lake, in Moose Mountain Provincial Park. Two years later the couple began construction of what they called "Grandison Hall." They bought the Bekavar dance hall and added it atop their original building; a third-floor apartment was added later.

From 1970 to 1979, it was one of the busiest and most popular nightspots in Saskatchewan because of its location in the popular provincial park. As a teen, Dale Orsted spent nearly every summer at his family's cabin in Kenosee and attended many teen dances at Grandison's hall.

Illness forced the Grandisons to sell the place in 1979 to a group of buyers, including Reg Dlouhy. He is credited with remodeling the hall into the fine nightclub that came to be known as the Moose Head Inn.

In 1989 Dale Orsted learned that his old teen hangout was for sale and acquired the business in March 1990. Within weeks the puzzling adventures Dale and others labeled a haunting started to bedevil him.

"I began some renovations in the cabaret room, on the second floor," Dale remembered. "New bars were built, the deejay booth was removed and relocated."

Then small items began to "go missing," he said, only to mysteriously reappear a few weeks later in the same place in which they had last been seen. Three people searched for a box of cash register till tape several times before it showed up right where it should have been.

"That also happened with other items in the bar," Dale said, adding that that part of the inn was not open to the public until later in 1990. Dale thought a previous employee with some sort of grievance might have been responsible, but eventually dismissed that idea.

"I had every lock in the building re-keyed or replaced and it still happened," he said.

Meanwhile, Dale and his girlfriend had moved into the third-floor apartment that also doubled as the inn's office.

"We would be awakened to a series of loud thumps in the cabaret," Dale said of a new wave of annoyances, this time in the middle of the night. "(It) would continue on and off for more than half an hour." He called the Mounted Police when it happened because of his fear that vandals had gotten inside. But the RCMP, too, could not account for the noises.

"The loudness was impossible to re-create during the daytime," Dale said. "We tried banging on doors and windows but we couldn't create the intensity or the violence of the (original)."

He installed security cameras. The banging was recorded on one camera, but instead of sounding as if someone were trying to get in, it seemed that someone was trying to get *out*—the racket clearly came from inside the inn.

"We also added motion detectors connected to an alarm in the apartment," Dale said. "On one occasion when the banging was happening, I looked up the phone number of the police and a gust of wind blew across the phone book and moved the page."

"As the police checked out the building downstairs," Dale remembered, "(My girlfriend) heard footsteps come up to the apartment. She thought I was bringing the police upstairs. However, the door leading to the stairway was locked at the time and we were on a different floor when she heard the footsteps."

She waited for Dale to call out a greeting, or stick his head in the room. He didn't, of course, because it wasn't Dale she heard. And she should have known better—distinct footfalls coming up the stairway to the locked apartment door have been heard by three other people at different times. And never does anyone knock on the door.

Other inn staff members had their own stories.

A kitchen worker said that one night the heavy door to a walk-in cooler was opened and then slammed shut.

"Before (the incident) I didn't believe in it. There's no way it could have done that. I was there," the man said later. "And now you start second-guessing a lot of stuff. It's hard to say you don't believe in ghosts."

Dale said an incident in the bar "made firm believers out of some skeptics." A dishwasher suddenly started up by itself, ran for ten seconds and then shut off. And like a saloon scene from an old Western movie when the stranger walks through the swinging doors, everyone in the room suddenly stopped talking and stared at the dishwasher, their mouths hanging open.

There were other, closer encounters:

Something brushed against co-owner Jeff Stephen's arm when he reached for a light switch in a darkened room;

Dale saw lights on one morning as he arrived for work, but by the time he got inside they were off, and no one else was there;

Doors locked one minute and unlocked the next became "routine" for the owner and manager of the inn.

For some time after the completion of Orsted's early renovations all seemed quiet at the Moose Head Inn. There were the occasional items that would go missing, or a footstep here and there in the night, but the infernal booming and banging that rattled the very walls of the inn had disappeared.

But everyone might have known it wasn't going to be all that simple. All hell broke loose when the next reconstruction phase began in February 1992.

"I removed the old carpeting from the cabaret floor," Dale explained. "That night at approximately nine P.M. extreme loud banging began to happen. We went downstairs and checked the building. No one was (there). When we went back upstairs the banging started again."

The disturbances would be repeated at about the same time every night during the renovation. Dale Orsted, his girlfriend, Jeff Stephens, and another friend all heard the unexplained noises.

"This is when we began to believe that there must be a ghost," Dale said.

The removal of the old carpeting took several weeks. All during that time, employees were subjected to nearly daily troubles attributed to the "ghost."

"Lights that were turned off, turned on," Dale said. "Doors with emergency panic hardware would bang open when people were in the cabaret. That happened at least ten different times with many different witnesses. The doors were always kept closed and needed a good push to open them."

Whatever pushed open the doors usually waited until after the crowds had gone and only a few employees were left cleaning up. Dale sometimes feared that his unseen tormentor was dangerous when small explosions, as from firecrackers, came from various parts of the inn.

The turning point came on that night when the new carpet was finally installed as Dale and his girlfriend relaxed in their apartment's small living room.

"From an adjoining room, a very eerie moaning sound lasted for about ten seconds, as if someone was in extreme pain," Dale said. That room is an office and is kept locked unless someone is using it.

There would be more trouble that night. At about four o'clock in the morning, a tremendous crash just outside their locked apartment literally knocked the couple out of bed.

"It came from the same room as the moaning did earlier," Dale recalled. "It was as loud and as violent as if you were in a head-on car crash. The impact broke dishes in our sink and water began running from the faucet. It was the first time the banging occurred upstairs where we lived. The actual crash was incredible. I can't even describe it. The panic we felt. You could feel a rush of energy."

Dale carefully crept out to check the office area.

The room was exactly as it was before; nothing was out of place. He dropped items and jumped off a steel office desk, but it wasn't until he picked up an end of the desk and dropped it that the same crash sound was created. He figured the only way the same intensity could be re-created would be to take four people and lift the desk above their heads and drop it.

The doors leading into the apartment from the lower floors were locked as usual and, as usual, the door into the office was dead-bolted. "There is no way anyone was in that room with all the locked doors," Dale insisted. That night was enough for his girlfriend. She never stayed overnight in the Moose Head Inn again.

On Monday, April 27, 1992, the Regina newspaper carried an account of the haunting at Moose Head Inn. So many people had heard about the events there, or had witnessed one or more of the episodes, that it was impossible to keep them secret.

But Dale Orsted disavows any ulterior motive. "We didn't do this as a publicity stunt," he said. "It really happened to us and the story got out."

In the article, Dale mentioned an earlier attempt to contact a Winnipeg investigator of the paranormal, Roy Bauer. While the haunting was at its peak in early February, Dale's girlfriend had called Bauer. Unfortunately, she didn't leave her telephone number and Bauer failed to write down the pertinent information about the haunting.

Bauer is an electronics engineer by training. He received a copy of the April 27th Regina newspaper article and proceeded to contact Orsted. Although the inn had been relatively "haunt-free" for several weeks, Bauer thought the case sounded interesting enough to look into. Also, the CBC-TV program "News Magazine" had earlier asked permission to accompany Bauer on one of his investigations. Bauer warned the television crew "not to expect a ghost to walk by the camera."

"I believe in what we call ghosts today, that there is something going on," Bauer said at the time. "I wouldn't necessarily say it's the spirits of people who have died (and) who have somehow remained in that location and are still roaming around in the house. . . . On the surface, that's what it seems to be and there's a very good chance that's what it is. But I'm willing to explore all possibilities."

Bauer undertook his investigation of the inn over a period of several days beginning on Sunday, May 24, 1992. After extensive interviews with Dale Orsted, his girlfriend, Jeff Stephen, and others, Bauer concluded that the cause of the disturbances was probably a ghost because the incidents had happened to too many people, including numerous visitors.

"I have classified all paranormal into three categories which are: poltergeist, haunting, and apparitions," Bauer wrote in a letter to Dale summarizing his findings. "Each of these categories has characteristics particular to that type of event." Bauer eliminated a poltergeist since the incidents had also taken place when visitors were present. He also ruled out what he termed a haunting.

What was going on was very possibly a "classic" apparition, Bauer said, adding that an apparition is similar to a haunting in that some form of "intelligence" survives after death.

"It can therefore react to events in its surroundings," Bauer said. "What most strongly indicates an intelligence is the mischievous nature of the events, seeming only to attract attention, but not repeating itself when people are waiting for things to happen."

The best example, Bauer said, was the banging that usually took place when people were asleep, but subsided when anyone got up to look around. It started up again when everyone went back to bed.

On that Sunday night, Bauer began his search for the apparition at Moose Head Inn. With the CBC cameras recording his moves, he set up sophisticated recording equipment and sensitive microphones. He hoped to catch "ghost sounds" during the early morning hours.

"(The CBC) set up two cameras in the cabaret; one was just taping and the other was taping and also being monitored upstairs in the apartment," Bauer said. He would be staying all night in the apartment Dale Orsted by now had refused to occupy. "We stayed up until three-thirty watching the monitor and listening for sounds. I had set up my tape recorder in the dining room. It was connected to a timer that would turn on for an hour at four-thirty."

It was relatively quiet all night, Bauer said. A distant echo of footsteps recorded on tape he attributed to one of the crewmembers walking around. The CBC journalist on the scene, Sasa Petricic, did report that earlier in the evening some lights that had been turned off when the cabaret was closed and locked for the night were found on about ten minutes later. No one could explain how that had happened.

By four-thirty, the CBC crew had retired to their motel rooms and Bauer had called it a night.

"The next morning I was up by eight," Bauer said. "I checked on the tape recorder to see if it had recorded anything. I started playing back the tape and noticed something unusual. I was hearing two tracks simultaneously. I had previously recorded a talk show that could still be heard, along with the recording of the dining room. I tried to duplicate this effect, but could not. It seems as though the erase head had malfunctioned and the recorder recorded on one track only. I listened to the entire tape hearing various sounds which I attributed to the machinery in the room."

The CBC crew also watched and listened to their tapes but they, too, found nothing of significance.

Despite the haunt-hunters' failure to detect any ghostly visitors, Bauer considered the Moose Head Inn a good case. "I would say yes, because of the multiple witnesses, especially since they weren't connected to each other."

Bauer has developed a grading system for the hauntings he's investigated. On the authenticity level, Bauer gives the inn a "four" rating out of a possible five. A "zero" would be a single witness, while a "five" represents many witnesses.

For severity, Bauer ranks the inn at about in the middle of his scale because there wasn't a great deal of physical disruption during the times of peak activity.

During his interviews with Dale Orsted and Jeff Stephen on Sunday, Bauer had isolated two potential causes for the apparition.

The first theory had to do with local legends surrounding the church that had owned the community hall Mr. and Mrs. Grandison had moved and re-built as their original dance hall and which has since been incorporated into the inn's cabaret.

Some residents believe the church to be haunted. Automobiles allegedly lose power when passing nearby, two people are said to have been killed within weeks of visiting the church and others claim an eerie glow emanates from the place on certain nights. Most interesting of all is the rumor that a minister committed suicide in its tower.

However, Bauer was doubtful of the church's relationship to the haunting because the community hall had never been a physical part of the church proper.

Equally doubtful is the accuracy of a minister's suicide. The son of the longest-serving minister at the church told CBC interviewers: "I'm sure there wasn't anyone who committed suicide there. Not a minister. I don't know where that story came from, but there's nothing to it. It's actually not a fact at all."

Bauer himself was not able to pinpoint any unexplained deaths connected to the church. And as for the "eerie glow," Bauer said it "seems to stem from the fact that the church is almost white, with the roof practically black. This contrast, especially when the moon is out, would reflect off the church making it visible for miles around."

The only other potential "suspect" Bauer identified was the original builder, the late Archebald Grandison. He quite literally put his entire life and fortune into the project. He suffered a heart attack shortly thereafter, never fully able to appreciate the business he built with his own hands. He died long before Orsted and Stephen bought the business.

"He did not have the opportunity to gradually give up the inn, but rather one day he was running it and the next day he wasn't," Bauer theorized. "Some portion of his consciousness and memories was drawn back to the inn. . . ."

Bauer said Archebald's ghost had been content to quietly roam the inn for years, but then became more active when Dale Orsted undertook major renovations. "Now his hard work is being changed and it is not to his liking. He becomes active to let people know he's there. . . . After the renovations are complete his anger dissipates, but he still plays pranks on people to let them know he is around and will continue (to be) so long as the inn is standing," Bauer contended.

But the case for Archebald as ghost didn't sit well with his widow, Ethel.

"My husband loved that hall and he loved the kids that came there. He really enjoyed those dances. But he wouldn't haunt it," Mrs. Grandison firmly told the CBC.

Ghost hunter Roy Bauer may be right in saying the haunting of Moose Head Inn has to do with the renovations Dale Orsted made to it, but he may have the identity of the ghost wrong. At least that's what Dale believed.

At the time of the CBC interview and Bauer's visit to the inn, Dale didn't know about Reg Dlouhy's role in transforming the inn from the Grandisons' original dance hall into the nightclub it became in the early 1980s. Dlouhy, who died in 1983, and three partners, including Eleanor Sedger (Jeff Stephen's aunt), bought "Grandison's Hall" in 1979 after Archebald became ill. Mrs. Grandison could not operate the nightspot by herself.

Reg and his brother did most of the original remodeling. The men transformed what had been a large dance hall into a unique restaurant and nightclub. New rooms were built, expensive paneling installed, an entertainment system added to the cabaret, a large bar added, and dining facilities enlarged.

Unfortunately, a dispute among the owners led to Reg Dlouhy's being bought out by his partners. According to Dale Orsted, Reg had the carpentry skills for the remodeling and worked as the on-site manager—even living in the apartment for over a year—but he had no money invested in the project.

He was "bitter over the takeover," Dale said, noting that several people who knew Reg have told him that his anger over being bought out makes it reasonable to assume he might now be haunting the inn.

"He didn't have a reason to haunt the place until changes were made" to his original design, Dale said. "I tend to believe it is more possible the 'ghost' may be Reg Dlouhy than Mr. Grandison."

Roy Bauer may have helped to pinpoint Reg as the source of the haunting even without knowing it.

In a letter to Dale and Jeff, dated June 23, 1992, Bauer recounted a telephone conversation he had with a psychic during which they discussed the case. Although Bauer still thought at that time the ghost was Archebald Grandison, the psychic's comments could be interpreted as referring to Reg Dlouhy.

"Near the end of the (telephone) conversation she started telling me things about the inn and who was haunting it," Bauer said in his letter. "She related information which I was and was not familiar with. She said she had not seen the article in the Regina *Leader-Post* nor heard the CBC interview that Dale and I did. She claimed to have fallen asleep just minutes before the News Magazine piece came on (although) she may have subconsciously remembered the show even when she was asleep." Bauer forwarded to Dale and Jeff those comments that he believed might have indicated that the psychic had "tuned in" to the haunting at the inn. The first set of comments related to the inn itself or events associated with it:

Hardwood not original. At one time all the rooms had hardwood floors.
Stairs have been changed. The stairway from the third-floor apartment to the cabaret has been altered.

Proud of the place. Reg was very satisfied with his work. The building is unique. Everyone involved in the business is proud of it.

"Ruffle" sound. There is often a noise like that of someone working in a woodshop.

Cabin-like atmosphere. The interior of the building is all wood, like that of a north woods cabin.

Female in charge/didn't like her at all. The previous owner was a female. Reg had a falling out with the owners.

Western-style buffalo. A moose head is hanging on one wall.

The psychic also noted items such as "church in the distance," "won't hurt anyone—just hanging around," "brothers," "strong-willed," "opposite of the way he liked it before," which could relate to why the ghost is making its displeasure known.

Altogether, Bauer listed twenty-five additional characteristics about the "ghost" the psychic disclosed in her telephone call. It's not possible to relate all of them to Reg Dlouhy, but several seem to point in his direction, Dale Orsted believed, especially those that deal with his stubbornness and his desire to be recognized for the original work he did at the inn.

Of the dozen or more hauntings he's investigated over the past decade, Bauer considered the events at Kenosee Lake one of his most interesting encounters.

"I would rank it as one of the most severe cases because of the banging," he said, noting that he didn't uncover anything unusual during his brief visit to the inn. "It definitely is paranormal. I don't think it can cause a lot of harm, just a lot of disruption."

Although Bauer said the Moose Head Inn haunting seemed genuine enough, his skepticism about ghostly events in general has increased over the years.

"I think many cases are like telepathic hallucinations," he said. He is quick to emphasize, however, that this doesn't imply any "mental illness" on the part of witnesses; simply that what is going on doesn't occur "in our physical space." That's especially true, he said, when only one person in a group will "see" something the others won't.

The last major "disruption" occurred after Dale installed a new center-island bar and changed the appearance of the second-floor cabaret. During the week after the work was completed, a caretaker heard chairs and tables being moved in that area after closing. He was alone in the building. Manager Jeff Stephen heard the same noises and he, too, failed to figure out its cause.

"It was like Reg was putting things back the way they were," Dale said.

The small peculiarities became almost routine for him. A heavy fire door would swing open when no one was near it, or the occasional clatter of unidentified footsteps stopped conversations in mid-sentence.

"I was ready to walk away from the place after that first week of noises nearly every night," Dale said. He was mostly concerned that there really was a human source for the mystery. "I wasn't so much scared by any entity" as he was by a burglar, he said. The inn had been broken into.

Dale Orsted was content to maintain his ownership at a distance and let the tourists and locals enjoy the ambiance and hospitality of the inn. The haunting didn't seem to have disrupted the popularity the nightspot enjoys, but Dale remained wary after hours, never quite sure what to expect when the lights went out.

Each Victoria Day, from 1997 through 2000, Dale held a psychic fair at the inn. During the first one, he and two female employees who had experienced the haunting held a séance with one of the psychics. She, in turn, identified three possible ghosts at the inn—a young man, a former cleaning lady and an old man, possibly Archebald Grandison.

Ethel Grandison died in 1999 and the inn has been relatively haunt-free since that time, but Dale was not ready to say it was all over. Dale told one interviewer that he didn't think enough time had elapsed to yet say the ghosts have moved out. He pointed out that a clairvoyant at his Victoria Day psychic fair in 2000 had said there was a very strong spirit presence.

"It's more in the not knowing what you're scared of. You know there's something there—but you don't know what it is."

Selected Bibliography

BOOKS

Allsop, Fred W. *The Folklore of Romantic Arkansas*. The Grolier Society: New York, 1931.

Brandon, Jim. *Weird America*. E. P. Dutton: New York, 1978.

Brookfield, Ada. *Brother Joshua*. Dorrance and Co.: Philadelphia, 1941.

Clark, Jerome. *Unexplained!* Visible Ink: Detroit, 1993.

Clifton, Charles S. *Ghost Tales of Cripple Creek*. n.p., 1983.

Collins, Earl. *Folk Tales of Missouri*. Christopher Publishing Co.: Boston, 1935.

Cullen, Virginia. *History of Lewes, Delaware*. NSDAR: Lewes, 1956.

Davidson, Levette J. and Blake, Forrester (eds.). *Rocky Mountain Tales*. University of Oklahoma Press: Norman, 1947.

Edwards, Frank. *Strange World*. Lyle Stuart: New York, 1964.

Eyers, Ed. *Ghost Stories of Texas*. Texian Press: Waco, Tex., 1981.

Federal Writers Project. *American Guide Series for Connecticut*. Houghton Mifflin: Boston, 1938.

Frank, Tom. *Stories and Legends of the Delaware Capes*. Miles Frederick Publishers: Dover, n.d.

Gaddis, Vincent. *Mysterious Fires and Lights*. Dell Publishing Co., Inc.: New York, 1968.

Gerrick, David J. *Ohio Ghostly Greats*. Dayton Lab: Lorain, Oh., 1975.

Graydon, Nell S. (editor). *South Carolina Ghost Tales*. Beaufort Book Shop, Inc.: Beaufort, S.C., 1969.

Hay, Peter. *Theatrical Anecdotes*, Oxford University Press: New York, 1987.

Inglis, Beth (ed.). *Current Ohio Folklore* ("The Headless Motorcyclist"), n.d.

Karolevitz, Robert F. *Paper Mountain*, n.p., n.d.

Marcatante, John and Potter, Robert R. *American Folklore and Legend*. Globe Books Co.: New York, 1967.

Merriam, Anne Van Ness (comp.). *The Ghosts of Hampton*. n.p., n.d.

Murray, Earl. *Ghosts of the Old West*. Contemporary Books: Chicago, 1988.

Norman, Michael and Scott, Beth. *Haunted Wisconsin*. Trail Books: Black Earth, Wis., 2001.

Norman, Michael and Scott, Beth. *Historic Haunted America*. Tor: New York, 1995.

Ocean Highway. The Federal Writers Project. Modern Age Books: New York, 1938.

Randolph, Vance. *Ozark Magic and Folklore*. Dover Publications: New York, 1964.

Reynolds, James. *Ghosts in American Houses*. Farrar, Straus and Cudahy: New York, 1955.

Rice, Alice Caldwell Hegan. *Flapdoodle, Trust & Obey*. (One chapter, "Mama Relates the Tale of a Conjured Chest.") Kentucky Historical Society: Louisville, 1991.

Rinehart, Mary Roberts. *My Life*. Holt and Rinehart: New York, 1931.

Saxon, Lyle. *Gumbo YaYa.* Bonanza Books: New York, 1945.

Scott, Beth and Norman, Michael. *Haunted America.* Tor: New York, 1994.

Skinner, Charles M. *Myths and Legends of Our Own Land.* J. B. Lippincott: Philadelphia, 1896.

South Carolina Folk Tales. University of South Carolina Press: Columbia, S.C., 1941.

Steiger, Brad. *True Ghost Stories.* Para Research: Rockport, Mass., 1982.

Taylor, Troy. *The Ghosts of Millikin.* Whitechapel Productions: Alton, Ill., 2001.

Walker, Danton. *I Believe in Ghosts.* Taplinger: New York, 1969.

WPA *Guide to South Carolina* The Federal Writers Project. Oxford University Press: New York, 1942.

PERIODICALS

Achenbach, Joel. "Ghosts here? It's their night." *Miami Herald,* October 31, 1985.

Anastasi, Rachel N. "Expert ties family stress to poltergeist in Horicon." *Milwaukee Sentinel,* August 22, 1988.

———. "Parapsychologist links stress, psychic events." *Milwaukee Sentinel,* February 1, 1988.

"Annie Russell: The Exclusive." *Sandspur,* Rollins College, Florida, October 15, 1986.

Austin, Ray. "Some Coloradans haunted by eerie, familiar spooks." *Rocky Mountain News,* October 31, 1984.

Bickell, Robert. "A Tragedy at the General Wayne Inn." *ExtremeChefs.com,* March 31, 2001.

Bilbo, Terry. "Forgotten souls." *Peoria Journal Star,* October 29, 2000.

"Bills Signed by the Governor." *Albuquerque Journal,* April 3, 2001.

Blakinger, Mary. "General Wayne Inn sold to developer." *Philadelphia Inquirer,* November 29, 2000.

Bowser, Andrew. "Murder, mystery at UD in 1858." *The Review,* Univ. of Delaware, October 31, 1989, pp. 9–10.

Brown, Anne Burnside. "One Headless Ghost." n.p., October 29, 1980.

Brown, Rosemary Beauchamp. "A History of the Beauchamp Family and Some Allied Lines." n.d., n.p.

Bruer, Frank. "Mobile Ghosts, Monsters Don't Confine Walks to Halloween." *Mobile (Ala.) Press Register.* October 30, 1960.

Brunsman, Barrett J. "Ghost story—Reporting on the haunted house of Horicon." *The Quill Magazine,* April 1988.

Bull, John V.R. "General Wayne Inn maintains a tradition of fine food." *Philadelphia Inquirer,* April 27, 1986.

Burrough, Bryan. "As Spooky Places Go, an Inn in the Bayous Goes a Bit Too Far." *The Wall Street Journal,* October 31, 1984.

Burrows, Ken. "Ghost In a Boise Home." *Idaho Daily Statesman,* September 23, 1973.

Cartwright, Gary. "The Marfa Lights." *Texas Monthly,* November 1984.

Carynnyk, Carol R. "A colonial inn with a penchant for surviving." *Philadelphia Inquirer,* September 16, 1984.

"Cemetery Lights May Be Electrical Says Scientist." *Vancouver Sun,* December 2, 1938.

Chalmers, Joseph J. and Horton, Tom. "Marylanders compile rich legacy of ghostly tales and legendary lore." *News American,* August 11, 1976.

"A Column of Fire Visible Every Tuesday Night." *Seward Reporter,* January 20, 1876.

"Couple shares home with ghosts of cat, governor, sentry." *Watertown (Wis.) Daily Times,* October 29, 1997.

Crawford, Byron. "Conjuring up tragedy." *Louisville Courier Journal,* April 28, 1982.

"Crowds Try to See Mysterious Light." *Daily Times,* July 11, 1952.

"A Curious Phenomenon." *The American Mercury,* N. 122, March 30, 1722.

DeShaney, Ginger, and United Press International. "Psychic 'Experts' Lend Credence to Story." *Milwaukee Sentinel,* January 29, 1988.

Dickinson, Sam. "Tales of Ghosts." *Arkansas Democrat,* May 27, 1962.

Dornfeld, Connie Polzin. "Experts: Show Compassion for Troubled Family." *Beaver Dam Daily Citizen,* February 1, 1988.

————. "Family Strives to Put Lives Back in Order." *Beaver Dam Daily Citizen*, February 26, 1988.

————. "Film crew stirs spirits in Horicon." *Beaver Dam Daily Citizen*, August 22, 1988.

————. "Haunted House in Horicon?" *Beaver Dam Daily Citizen*, January 25, 1988.

————. "Pastor Helps Silence Rumor Mill." *Beaver Dam Daily Citizen*, February 19, 1988.

Drabanski, Emily. "Haunted Casas: The Spirits of Santa Fe." *Santa Fe New Mexican*, October 31, 1992.

Dullum, Randall. "Horicon haunting recreated." *Fond du Lac Reporter*, October 27, 1988.

"Eastern Folklore—Fact or Fiction?" *Old Main Line* (Eastern Illinois University), Summer 1985.

Epstein, Pancho. " 'Oldest House in the U.S.A.' just an old come-on." *Santa Fe New Mexican*, March 30, 1992.

"FmHa Gets Horicon House." *Beaver Dam Daily Citizen*, February 19, 1988.

Fortune, Beverly. "It's a lovely haunt." *Louisville Courier Journal*, February 10, 1974.

Foster, Mary. "Big Easy ghosts find many places to hang around." *New Orleans Times Picayune*, October 28, 1989.

Franklin, Dixie. "New Light Shed on Odd Light." *The Milwaukee Journal*, August 6, 1978.

Freeborn, Frankie. "Ghost of Annie Russell lingers on." *Sandspur*, Rollins College, December 7, 1979.

Gale, Mark. "Ghost of Boyette Bridge leaves her fans cooling heels." *St. Petersburg Times*, July 14, 1980.

" 'Ghost lights' hold appeal for advertising rep." *Lake Living/Lake Travis View*, March 25, 1993.

"Ghost Sightings at Hero's Homestead." *The Mexico City News*, August 20, 1987.

"Ghosts in Newport." *Austin American Statesman*, August 27, 1995.

Glass, Ian. " 'A cloud of smoke grabbed me . . . This is it.' " *Miami News*, May 30, 1974.

Goodavage, Joseph F. "Skyquakes, earthlights and e.m. fields." *Analog Science Fiction/Science Fact*, September 1978.

Gustafson, Charles. "Reader Asks About Rendezvous With a Light." (Letter to the Editor). *Daily Times*, April 17, 1973.

"A Haunted House: An Uncanny Something in Mr. Black's Residence." *Idaho Daily Statesman*, November 15, 1892.

"The Haunted House, Its Interesting History and Strange Romance (Events in the Life of Madame Lalaurie Called to Mind)." *New Orleans Daily Picayune*, March 13, 1892.

Hayes, Paul. "Horicon calm amid a ghostly flurry." *The Milwaukee Journal*, n.d.

Hicks, John C. "The Legend of Skeleton Hollow." *Arkansas Democrat*, September 10, 1961.

Hopkins, Elaine. "Village battles safety problems at powerhouse." *Peoria Journal Star*, October 30, 1995.

Holub, Kathy. "Mystery lights return to Saratoga." *San Jose Mercury News*, October 23, 1986.

"Horicon ghosts gone?" *Madison Capital Times*, February 19, 1988.

"Horicon 'spirits' will show up on TV." *Madison Capital Times*, August 19, 1988.

"The Horicon, Wisconsin, 'Haunted House.' " *New Frontiers*, (Oregon, Wisconsin) 26 and 27 (Spring-Summer 1988).

"House has Pueblo family spooked." *Associated Press*. April 26, 1984.

Howes, Lindsey. "Ghost Stalks Mitchell Hall." *The Review*, University of Delaware, October 1979.

Jaeger, Richard W. "Horicon ghosts gone for good." *Wisconsin State Journal*, June 14, 1988.

————. "Paranormal revisited." *Wisconsin State Journal*, February 22, 1993.

Janz, William. "Who ya gonna call? Police chief of 'ghost town' haunted by havoc." *Milwaukee Sentinel*, January 30, 1988.

Johnson, William. "Ghosts and 'Hants' Play Their Parts in Folklore of Arkansas." *Arkansas Democrat*, August 9, 1931.

Kahn, Russell. "The Ultimate Fear." *Santa Fe Reporter*, October 31, 1982.

Klaus, Rob. "The Ghost of La Posada." *Impact Magazine, The Albuquerque Journal*, October 26, 1982.

Klopfenstein, Sonya. "Tunnel vision is a little scary—Bartonville sealing off tunnels under old hospital grounds." *Peoria Journal Star*, November 22, 2000.

Knapp, Karen. "Myth of Pem ghost based on live ghost." *Decatur Herald and Review*, n.d.

Lazzarino, Evie. "Ghostly tale still haunts Sigma Nu house." *Lawrence Journal World*, October 31, 1982.

Liberty, Margot. "Ghost Herder's Battlefield." *Hardin Tribune Herald*, June 22, 1961.

"Life Photographer Seeks 'Ghost Light.' " *Daily Times*, July 14, 1952.

Lilley, Valerie. "House of Spirits." *Peoria Journal Star*, November 25, 1998.

Lollar, Kevin. "Halloween spirit lurks in theater." *Sioux Falls (S.D.) Argus Leader*, October 31, 1985.

Loughran, Joe. "Old building reflects development of post." *The Huachuca (Ariz.) Scout*, October 30, 1980.

———. "Will the ghost walk at Carleton House?" *The Huachuca (Ariz.) Scout*, October 30, 1980.

McManus, Betty. "The General Wayne Inn." *Main Line Times*, October 30, 1986.

Mendt, J. Robert. "General Wayne Inn." Anthony Wayne Historical Association, Merion, Penn. (Originally printed in the *Main Line Chronicle* from a paper read before the Anthony Wayne Historical Society, n.d.)

Merrill, Debbi. "Ghost story on old post will not die." *Arizona Daily Star*, January 26, 1986.

———. "Ghost tale haunts Fort Huachuca." *Sierra Vista (Ariz.) Herald*, February 13, 1986.

Michael, William M. "I ain't afraid of no ghosts!" *Decatur Herald and Review*, n.d.

Millard, Bob. "The Haunted Tracks of Chapel Hill." *Nashville Tennessean Magazine*, February 1978.

Mingis, Ken. "Tricky ghosts are family 'friends.' " *Providence Journal Bulletin*, October 31, 1985.

Mohnacs, Joseph. "Halloween." *Woodbury (N.J.) Times*, October 26, 1986.

Moore, Robert P. "Did My Grandmother Associate With Criminals? (or Good Breeding, Bad Manners): A Genealogical Look at Jereboam Beauchamp and His Murder Case." *The Nelson County Genealogist*, Winter, 1999.

Negri, Sam. "The ghost of Fort Huachuca." *Arizona Republic*, March 23, 1986.

Nelson, James B. "Horicon couple say apparitions, noises drove them from home." *Milwaukee Sentinel*, January 30, 1988.

———. "Horicon family finds relief after beds buried." *Milwaukee Sentinel* February 19, 1988.

———. "Horicon ghosts: Rumors of eerie events draw curious crowds." *Milwaukee Sentinel*, January 27, 1988.

———. " 'Hot spots' found in Horicon home." *Milwaukee Sentinel*, February 1, 1988.

———. "Official fears Horicon may scare off film projects." *Milwaukee Sentinel*, August 25, 1988.

———. "Re-created ghost story haunts Horicon neighbors." *Milwaukee Sentinel*, August 23, 1988.

———. "Uneasy couple visit their 'ghost house.' " *Milwaukee Sentinel*, January 28, 1988.

Nolan, Jim. "Sileo gets life in slammer." *Philadelphia News*, August 2, 2001.

" 'Old Book' . . . The Tragic Story of a Demented Soul and 'The Graveyard Elm' " *Peoria Journal Star*, October 31, 1980.

O'Neill, Patty. "Was 'Mary' dorm's late-night visitor?" *Decatur Herald and Review*, n.d.

Patterson, Doris. "Are Hessian Soldiers' Ghosts Floating Around Main Line?" *Main Line Times*, October 30, 1986.

Pease, Harry S. "A Different Northern Light." *Insight Magazine, The Milwaukee Journal*, November 30, 1980.

Peiperet, James R. "Cimarron's St. James Hotel plays host to ghost." *Minneapolis Star Tribune*, October 31, 1993.

Penson, Betty. "Ghosts of Warm Springs Avenue haunt memory." *Idaho Daily Statesman*, April 27, 1980.

Persinger, Michael A. "Predicting UFO Events and Experiences." *MUFON Symposium Proceedings*, n.d.

Persinger, Michael A. "Geophysical Variables and Behavior: IX. Expected Clinical Consequences of Close Proximity to UFO-Related Luminosities." *Perceptual and Motor Skills*, 1983, 56, 259–265.

"Phantom Cemetery Light Only Glows at Bullets." *Vancouver Sun*, December 2, 1938.

"A Phantom Engineer." *Huron Erie County Reporter*, January 23, 1890.

"Police Chase Mysterious Glow." *Daily Times*, July 10, 1952.

"Professor Believes Ghost Light is Gas." *Daily Times*, July 16, 1952.

Radtke, Randy F. "Bumps in the night: Ghostly images spook locals." *Ripon (Wis.) Commonwealth Press* October 26, 2000.

Reed, Rita. "A Night in the Old West." *Minneapolis Star Tribune*, December 11, 1994.

"Restaurant owner arraigned on murder charges." *Pocono (Penn.) Record*, March 2, 2001.

Riggs, Douglas R. "Halloween tale: Getting to know the family ghost." *Providence Journal*, October 31, 1982.

Rivers, Bill. "Louisiana's Gentle Ghosts." *Morning Advocate*, September 28, 1952.

Robbins, Jim. "Assignment: Little Bighorn—113 years after Custer fell, spirits still roam grounds." *Chicago Tribune*, November 1, 1989.

Roberts, Mrs. James. "The Veil of Death." *Ozark Guide* (Eureka Springs, Ark.), Winter 1954.

Rogers, Grace. "History of Chapel Hill." n.d., n.p.

"The Ghost Light Road Still Affects People Today." *Salisbury Advertisement*, October 26, 1977.

The Royal Gazette, March 16, 1782.

Rubini, Liz. "Close Encounters of the Supernatural Kind." *Sandspur*, Rollins College, Florida October 27, 2000.

Rushing, Marie Morris. "The Kans Wilson Light, an Arkansas Legend." *Arkansas Gazette*, July 29, 1945.

———. "General Wayne Inn partner to be charged with murder, attorney says." *Philadelphia Inquirer*, August 31, 2000.

Shuttleworth, Stan. " 'Charlotte' lives on at Carleton House." *Sierra Vista Sunday News*, June 21, 1981.

Sikora, Frank. "Dead man's face marks courthouse." *The Birmingham News*, December 6, 1981.

Smith, Martha. "In Newport, chance meetings with spirits are as common as spirits themselves." *Providence Journal*, October 28, 1985.

Smyth, Michael. "Some visitors to Little Bighorn aren't ready to give up the ghost." *Chicago Tribune*, August 31, 1986.

"Some folks just can't let go, it seems." *The Milwaukee Journal*, February 25, 1987.

St. Pierre, J. L. "Is there a Ramtail ghost?" *Providence Journal*, October 26, 1975.

"State hospital records at Zeller." *Peoria Journal-Star*, November 18, 1987.

Stipp, David. "Marfa, Texas, Finds A Flickering Fame in Mystery Lights." *The Wall Street Journal*, March 21, 1984.

Sullivan, Jean. "Did They Really Have a Ghost at 1703 Warm Springs?" *Idaho Daily Statesman*, n.d.

Trachtenberg, Bruce. "Murder/Suicide Orphans Five Children." *The Oregonian*, December 24, 1973.

"True Tales of Peoria." *Peoria Herald*, September 15, 1895.

Van Doren, Trent T. "Ghosts act up in Mitchell Hall." *The Review*, Univ. of Delaware, 29 Oct. 1991, p. 3.

Ward, Joe. "Anna Beauchamp of Bloomfield: 'I must return to my good husband's arms.' " *Louisville Courier Journal*, October 29, 1978.

Watkins, Ed. "The face in the window still big draw in Carrollton." *Tuscaloosa (Ala.) News*, July 9, 1974.

Woolf, Sue. "Dead Woman's Crossing." *The Chronicles of Oklahoma*, 1985.

OTHER MATERIAL

Beard, David V. "H.M.S. DeBraak: A Treasure Debunked, a Treasure Revealed," East Carolina University, Department of History. Unpublished Thesis, 1989.

Canadian Broadcasting Corporation, "News Magazine." "The Moosehead Inn Ghost Story," n.d.

Christ, Beverly. "Ghostlore at Ripon College: School Spirit?—We've Got 'Em." Ripon College, Wisconsin. Unpublished Manuscript. 1996.

Down Home Designs. Selma, Alabama, 1983.

"The Face in the Window" or "The Ghost in the Garret." Account by the Town of Carrollton, Alaska, n.d.

Guide to Mystery and Detection (http://members.aol.com/MG4273/rineharet.html), October 5, 2001.

Heffley, Deborah Anne. "Haunting Tales of Emporia, Kansas." Written for Studies in American Folklore EN 740 C. Emporia State University, July 15, 1983.

Roadsideamerica.com (www.roadsideamerica.com/attract/ALCARface.html), July 31, 2001.

Shelby, Tom. "The Legend of the Francesville Light." Collection of the Indiana University, Folklore Archives, September 23, 1977 acquisition.

Index of Place Names

About the Authors

Michael Norman and coauthor Beth Scott are the authors of *Historic Haunted America*, *Haunted America*, and other collections of American ghost stories. Beth Scott died in 1994.